THINK AGAIN

ALAIN BADIOU AND THE FUTURE OF PHILOSOPHY

Also available from Continuum:

Theoretical Writings, Alain Badiou

Infinite Thought: Truth and the Return of Philosophy, Alain Badiou

THINK AGAIN

ALAIN BADIOU AND THE FUTURE OF PHILOSOPHY

Edited by
PETER HALLWARD

continuum
LONDON • NEW YORK

Continuum
The Tower Building   80 Maiden Lane
11 York Road   Suite 704
London SE1 7NX   New York, NY 10038

First published 2004
Reprinted 2006 (twice)

British Library Cataloguing-in-Publication Data
A catalogue record for this book is available from the British Library.

ISBN: HB: 0-8264-5906-4
      PB: 0-8264-5907-2

Typeset by YHT Ltd, London
Printed and bound in Great Britain by Biddles Ltd, King's Lynn, Norfolk

This book is dedicated to the memory of one of Badiou's most brilliant readers to date, Sam Gillespie (1970–2003).

CONTENTS

Acknowledgements   ix
Notes on Contributors   x
Abbreviations   xiii

Introduction: 'Consequences of Abstraction'   1
PETER HALLWARD

1 The History of Truth: Alain Badiou in French Philosophy   21
   ETIENNE BALIBAR
2 Philosophy Without Conditions   39
   JEAN-LUC NANCY
3 Nihil Unbound: Remarks on Subtractive Ontology and
   Thinking Capitalism   50
   RAY BRASSIER
4 Some Remarks on the Intrinsic Ontology of Alain Badiou   59
   JEAN-TOUSSAINT DESANTI
5 Badiou and Deleuze on the One and the Many   67
   TODD MAY
6 Badiou and Deleuze on the Ontology of Mathematics   77
   DANIEL W. SMITH
7 Alain Badiou and the Miracle of the Event   94
   DANIEL BENSAÏD
8 States of Grace: The Excess of the Demand in Badiou's
   Ethics of Truths   106
   PETER DEWS
9 An Ethics of Militant Engagement   120
   ERNESTO LACLAU
10 Communism as Separation   138
   ALBERTO TOSCANO
11 On the Subject of the Dialectic   150
   BRUNO BOSTEELS
12 From Purification to Subtraction: Badiou and the Real   165
   SLAVOJ ŽIŽEK
13 What if the Other is Stupid? Badiou and Lacan on 'Logical
   Time'   182
   ED PLUTH and DOMINIEK HOENS

14 The Fifth Condition   191
    ALENKA ZUPANČIČ
15 What Remains of Fidelity after Serious Thought   202
    ALEX GARCÍA DÜTTMANN
16 Badiou's Poetics   208
    JEAN-JACQUES LECERCLE
17 Aesthetics, Inaesthetics, Anti-Aesthetics   218
    JACQUES RANCIÈRE

Afterword: Some Replies to a Demanding Friend   232
ALAIN BADIOU

Notes   238
Bibliography   259
Index   267

ACKNOWLEDGEMENTS

The essays by Etienne Balibar, Jean-Luc Nancy and Jacques Rancière first appeared in *Alain Badiou: Penser le multiple*, edited by Charles Ramond (Paris: L'Harmattan, 2002); I'm grateful to Charles Ramond for his careful preparation of these texts. Daniel Bensaïd's contribution first appeared as a chapter of his book *Résistances: Essai de taupologie générale* (Paris: Fayard, 2001). Jean-Toussaint Desanti's essay was first published in *Les Temps modernes* 526 (May 1990).

NOTES ON CONTRIBUTORS

Alain Badiou teaches at the Ecole Normale Supérieure in Paris; his most important books are *Théorie du sujet* (1982), *L'Etre et l'événement* (1988) and *Logiques des mondes* (2005).

Etienne Balibar is Emeritus Professor of Moral and Political Philosophy at the University of Paris X (Nanterre) and Professor of Humanities at the University of California, Irvine (USA). His books include *Reading Capital* (with Louis Althusser, 1965), *Race, Nation, Class: Ambiguous Identities* (with Immanuel Wallerstein, 1991), *Masses, Classes, Ideas* (1994), *The Philosophy of Marx* (1995), *Spinoza and Politics* (1998) and *Politics and the Other Scene* (2002).

Daniel Bensaïd teaches at the University of Paris VIII (Saint-Denis) and is a leading member of the Ligue Communiste Révolutionnaire. His books include *Marx For Our Times* (1995) and *Résistances* (2002).

Bruno Bosteels is Assistant Professor in Romance Studies at Cornell University. His research centres on questions of literature and politics in Latin America, as well as on contemporary critical theory and philosophy. His book on Badiou and politics is forthcoming from Duke University Press, and he is finishing another manuscript entitled *After Borges: Literature and Antiphilosophy*.

Ray Brassier is Research Associate at the Centre for Research in Modern European Philosophy, Middlesex University and a member of l'Organisation Non-Philosophique Internationale (www.onphi.org). He is the translator of Badiou, *Saint Paul and the Foundation of Universalism* (2003) and co-editor, with Alberto Toscano, of Badiou's *Theoretical Writings* (2004).

Jean-Toussaint Desanti was Emeritus Professor of Philosophy at the University of Paris I; he died in January 2002. His books include *Les Idéalités mathématiques* (1968), *La Philosophie silencieuse* (1975) and *Philosophie: un rêve de flambeur* (1999).

Peter Dews is Professor of Philosophy at the University of Essex. He has held visiting positions at the University of Konstanz in Germany, and at the Graduate Faculty and Columbia University in New York, amongst others. He has published widely on issues in modern European philosophy, and is the author of *Logics of Disintegration* (1986) and *The Limits of Disenchantment* (1995). His current research concerns models of intersubjectivity in European philosophy, and the problem of evil after Kant.

Alexander García Düttmann is Professor of Visual Culture and Philosophy at Goldsmiths College, University of London. His publications include: *At Odds with Aids* (1997), *Between Cultures: Tensions in the Struggle for Recognition* (2000), *Liebeslied/My Suicides* (in collaboration with Rut Blees Luxemburg, 2000) and *The Memory of Thought: An Essay on Heidegger and Adorno* (2002).

Peter Hallward teaches at King's College London. His publications include *Absolutely Postcolonial* (2001) and *Badiou: A Subject to Truth* (2003). He translated Badiou's *Ethics: An Essay on the Understanding of Evil* (2001) and edited *The One or the Other? French Philosophy Today. Angelaki* 8:2 (August, 2003).

Dominiek Hoens is a researcher at the Jan van Eyck Academy in Maastricht, The Netherlands. He has written on psychoanalysis (affect, logical time, sinthome) and literature (Musil, Shakespeare). He is writing a Ph.D. in philosophy (University of Nijmegen) on love in Jacques Lacan's work, and is the editor of an issue of *Communication & Cognition* (Autumn 2003) on the philosophy of Alain Badiou.

Ernesto Laclau is Professor of Politics at the University of Essex and Professor of Comparative Literature at SUNY, Buffalo. His publications include: *Hegemony and Socialist Strategy* (with Chantal Mouffe, 1985); *New Reflections on the Revolution of our Time* (1990); *Emancipation(s)*, (1996), and *Contingency, Hegemony, Universality* (with Judith Butler and Slavoj Žižek, 2000).

Jean-Jacques Lecercle is professor of English at the University of Paris X (Nanterre). A specialist in Victorian literature and the philosophy of language, his books include *Interpretation as Pragmatics* (1999), *L'Emprise des signes* (with Ronald Shusterman, 2002) and *Deleuze and Language* (2002). He is currently working on a Marxist philosophy of language.

Todd May is Professor of Philosophy at Clemson University. He has written a number of books on continental philosophy, including *The Political Philosophy of Poststructuralist Anarchism* (1994) and *Reconsidering Difference* (1997). He has co-edited a Continental philosophy textbook and a book on the Israeli occupation of Palestine. He is currently finishing a book on the work of Gilles Deleuze and the manuscript for a novel.

Jean-Luc Nancy was Professor of Philosophy at the Marc Bloch University in Strasbourg until 2002. His many books include *The Sense of the World* (1993) and *Being Singular Universal* (1996).

Ed Pluth is an assistant professor of philosophy at California State University, Chico, specializing in Lacanian theory and contemporary continental philosophy. His dissertation was entitled *Towards a New Signifier: Freedom and Determination in Lacan's Theory of the Subject* (2002). He has published on Badiou and Lacan, and his current research is exploring various aspects of their theories.

Jacques Rancière is Emeritus Professor of Aesthetics and Politics at the University of Paris VIII (Saint Denis). English translations of his books include: *The Nights of Labor* (1989), *The Ignorant Schoolmaster* (1991), *The Names of History* (1994), *On the Shores of Politics* (1995), *Disagreement* (1998) and *Short Voyages to the Land of the People* (2003). His most recent works are *La Fable cinématographique* (2001) and *Le Destin des images* (2003).

Daniel Smith teaches at Purdue University, where he specializes in nineteenth- and twentieth-century continental philosophy. He has published numerous papers on topics in continental philosophy, and translated books by Deleuze, Isabelle Stengers, and Pierre Klossowski. He is currently finishing a book on Deleuze.

Alberto Toscano is lecturer in the Sociology Department at Goldsmiths College. He is the co-editor (with Nina Power) of Alain Badiou's *On Beckett* (2003). He translated Badiou's *Handbook of Inaesthetics* (2004), *The Century* (2004) and, with Ray Brassier, Badiou's *Theoretical Writings* (2004). He is the author of several articles on contemporary philosophy, political theory and aesthetics.

Slavoj Žižek is Senior Researcher at the Department of Philosophy, University of Ljubljana. His latest books are *The Puppet and the Dwarf: The Perverse Core of Christianity* (2003) and *Organs Without Bodies: Deleuze and Consequences* (2003).

Alenka Zupančič is a researcher at the Institute of Philosophy, Scientific Research Centre of the Slovene Academy of Sciences and Arts, Ljubljana. She is the author of *Ethics of the Real: Kant, Lacan* (2000), *Das Reale einer Illusion* (2001), *Esthétique du désir, éthique de la jouissance* (2002) and *The Shortest Shadow: Nietzsche's Philosophy of the Two* (2003).

ABBREVIATIONS

Note on references: Full bibliographical details for works by Badiou are provided in the bibliography at the end of the volume. Where a reference contains two page numbers separated by a forward slash, the first number refers to the original edition and the second to the translation listed below; 'tm' stands for 'translation modified'. Where there is only one page number, the reference is to the French edition. When no note accompanies a quotation, the reference is included in the next note.

CM   *Le Concept de modèle. Introduction à une épistémologie matérialiste des mathématiques* (Paris: Maspero, 1969).

TC   *Théorie de la contradiction* (Paris: Maspero, 1975).

DI   *De l'Idéologie* (Paris: Maspero, 1976).

TS   *Théorie du sujet* (Paris: Seuil, 1982).

PP   *Peut-on penser la politique?* (Paris: Seuil, 1985).

EE   *L'Etre et l'événement* (Paris: Seuil, 1988).

MP   *Manifeste pour la philosophie* (Paris: Seuil, 1989); *Manifesto for Philosophy*, trans. Norman Madarasz (Albany: SUNY University Press, 1999).

NN   *Le Nombre et les nombres* (Paris: Seuil, 1990).

DO   *D'un Désastre obscur (Droit, Etat, Politique)* (Paris: L'Aube, 1991).

C   *Conditions* (Paris: Seuil, 1992).

E   *L'Ethique: Essai sur la conscience du mal* (Paris: Hatier, 1993); *Ethics: An Essay on the Understanding of Evil*, trans. Peter Hallward (London: Verso, 2001).

D   *Gilles Deleuze: 'La clameur de l'Etre'* (Paris: Hachette, 1997); *Gilles Deleuze: The Clamor of Being*, trans. Louise Burchill (Minneapolis: University of Minnesota Press, 2000).

SP   *Saint Paul et la fondation de l'universalisme* (Paris: PUF, 1997).

CT   *Court Traité d'ontologie transitoire* (Paris: Seuil, 1998).

AM   *Abrégé de métapolitique* (Paris: Seuil, 1998).

PM   *Petit Manuel d'inesthétique* (Paris: Seuil, 1998).

LM   *Logiques des mondes* (Paris: Seuil, forthcoming 2005).

INTRODUCTION:
CONSEQUENCES OF
ABSTRACTION*

Peter Hallward

This book is a collection of critical responses to the philosophy of Alain Badiou. It is a good time for such a collection to appear – many of Badiou's own books are now available in translation, his main ideas have been already been introduced in a number of different places and formats, and Badiou himself is currently engaged in the substantial reworking of his philosophy that will soon culminate in the publication of the second volume of his major work, *Being and Event*.

Badiou's thought is nothing if not polemical, and perhaps the most suitable way to approach his philosophy is precisely through the controversies to which it immediately gives rise and the decisions by which these controversies are resolved. The essays included in this volume explore some of Badiou's most contentious decisions. These include, among others: his sharp distinction of truth and knowledge; his identification of ontology with mathematics and his consequent critique of the ontologies of Heidegger and Deleuze; his strictly axiomatic understanding of political equality and his consequent subtraction of politics from social or economic mediation; his isolation of ethical questions from both the assertion of general moral principles and the negotiation of socio-cultural differences; his distinction of subject and individual; his uncompromisingly modernist conception of art; and his idiosyncratic post-Lacanian understanding of love and sexual difference.

The introduction to this book begins with a brief overview of Badiou's general project, supplemented by equally brief explanations of three or four fundamental aspects of his ontology – those aspects which are likely to prove especially confusing for readers new to his philosophy. There follows a cursory review of the shift in emphasis under way in Badiou's current work in progress. The rest of the introduction then lists some of the critical questions that face this ongoing work. Most of these questions are addressed in one way or another by the essays collected here; Badiou responds to some of them directly in his afterword to the collection.

I

Very broadly speaking Badiou seeks to link, on the one hand, a formal, axiomatic and egalitarian conception of thought (as opposed to any close association

* I am grateful to Anindya Bhattacharyya, Bruno Bosteels, Ray Brassier, Daniel Smith and Alberto Toscano for their helpful comments on an earlier version of this chapter.

of thought with language, with the interpretation of meanings or the description of objects), with, on the other hand, a theory of militant and discontinuous innovation (as opposed to a theory of continuous change or a dialectical theory of mediation). The two principles connect, from time to time, in exceptional affirmative sequences through which an instance of pure conviction comes to acquire a universal validity. Such sequences are what Badiou calls 'truths'. Truths are affirmations to which in principle we can all *hold* true, in excess of our ability to prove that what we thereby affirm is correct or justified in any demonstrable sense. This means that his project can be introduced equally well either as a renewal of a broadly Platonic conception of philosophy – one that insists on the unequivocal, eternal validity of a truth – or as an extension of a broadly Sartrean conception of philosophy, i.e. one that coordinates an ungrounded subjective engagement with an all-inclusive responsibility. Either way, what is essential is the immediate articulation of the universal and the subjective. Badiou shares 'Plato's central concern, to declare the immanent identity, the co-belonging, of the known and the knowing mind, their essential ontological commensurability',[1] just as he agrees with Sartre, that whenever I make a genuine choice it is always a choice that 'commits not only myself but humanity as a whole'.[2]

What is essential, in other words, is the capacity of pure thought to formulate actively universal forms of affirmation. What distinguishes Badiou's position from those of both Plato and Sartre, and from those of the great majority of his own philosophical contemporaries, is the rigour with which he insists that such formulation can in each case only proceed as an abruptly inventive break with the status quo. The best examples of affirmations whose truth exceeds the resources of proof or justification are precisely ones that begin with an initially obscure but irreversible break with the established routine governing a situation – the decisions required to sustain, for instance, a political or artistic revolution, or an unexpected declaration of love. The people who adhere to the consequences of such affirmations will not easily convince sceptical onlookers of their validity, unless they are able to develop means of conviction capable of changing the prevailing logic of the situation. What Badiou calls a truth is the process that, sparked by a break with routine, persists in an affirmation whose progressive imposition transforms the very way things *appear* in the situation.

Badiou's most fundamental principle is thus simply the belief that radical change is indeed possible, that it is possible for people and the situations they inhabit to be dramatically transformed by what happens to them. He affirms this infinite capacity for transformation as the only appropriate point of departure for thought, and he affirms it in advance of any speculation about its enabling conditions or ultimate horizons. Innovation as such is independent of any cumulative dialectic, any acquired feel for the game, any tendency towards consensus or tolerance – any orientation carried by the 'way of the world'. Triggered by an exceptional *event* whose occurrence cannot be proven with the resources currently available in the situation, true change proceeds insofar as it solicits the militant conviction of certain individuals who develop the implications of this event and hold firm to its consequences: by doing so they constitute themselves as the *subjects* of its innovation. A subject is someone carried by his or her fidelity to the implications of an event – or again, what distinguishes an event from other incidents that might ordinarily take place in the situation is that these implications, themselves illuminated by the consequences of previous events, make it impossible for those who affirm them to carry on as before. And what a subject declares persists as a *truth* insofar as these implications can be upheld in rigorously universalizable terms, i.e. in terms that relate to all members of their situation without passing through the prevailing criteria of recognition, classification and domination which underlie the normal organization of that situation. The laborious, case-by-case application of these implications will eventually transform the way the situation organizes and represents itself. The most familiar of Badiou's many examples of such truth procedures are Saint Paul's militant conception of an apostolic subjectivity that exists only through proclamation of an event (the resurrection of Christ) of universal import but of no recognizable or established significance, and the Jacobin fidelity to a revolutionary event which dramatically exceeds, in its subjective power and generic scope, the particular circumstances that contributed to its occurrence.[3]

Badiou distinguishes four general fields of truth: politics, science, art and love. These are the only four fields in which a *pure* subjective commitment is possible, one indifferent to procedures of interpretation or verification. True politics is a matter of collective mobilization guided by a general will in something like Rousseau's sense, and not the business of bureaucratic administration or the socialized negotiation of interests. Within the limits of the private sphere, genuine love begins in the wake of an unpredictable encounter that escapes the conventional representation of sexual roles, continues as a fidelity to the consequences of that encounter, and is sustained through an exposure to what Lacan famously described as the impossibility of sexual relationship. True art and true science proceed in somewhat the same way, through a searching experimental commitment to a line of enquiry opened up by a new discovery or break with tradition. Mathematics is then the most 'truthful' component of science because, thanks to its strictly axiomatic foundation, it is the most firmly abstracted from any natural or objective mediation, the most removed from our habitual ways of thinking, and by the same token the most obviously indifferent to the identity of whoever comes to share in its articulation.[4]

For the same reason, Badiou explains in the difficult opening meditations of *Being and Event*, mathematics is the only discourse suited to the literal articulation of pure being *qua* being, or being considered without regard to being-this or being-that, being without reference to particular qualities or ways of being: being that simply *is*. More precisely, mathematics is the only discourse suited to the articulation of being as *pure multiplicity*, a multiplicity subtracted from any unity or unifying process. Very roughly speaking, the general stages of this argument run as follows: (i) being can be thought either in terms of the multiple or the one; (ii) the only coherent conception of being as one ultimately depends on some instance of the One either as transcendent limit (a One *beyond* being, or God) or as all-inclusive immanence (a cosmos or Nature); (iii) modernity and in particular modern science have demonstrated that God is dead, that Nature is not whole, and that the idea of a One-All is incoherent; (iv) therefore if being can be thought at all, it must be thought as multiple rather than one; (v) only modern mathematics, as founded in axiomatic set theory, is genuinely capable of such thought. Only mathematics can think multiplicity without any constituent reference to unity. Why? Because the theoretical foundations of mathematics ensure that any unification, any consideration of something as one thing, will be thought as the *result* of an operation, the operation that treats or counts something as one; by the same token, these foundations oblige us to presume that whatever was thus counted, or unified, is itself not-one (i.e. multiple).

A 'situation' as Badiou defines it is simply any instance of such a counting operation, whereby a certain set of individuals things are identified in some way as members of a coherent collection or set – think for example of the way in which citizens count and are counted in national situations, or the way employees count (or do not count) in economic situations, or how students count (or are discounted) in educational situations. Now as Sartre himself understood with particular clarity, truly radical change can in a certain sense only proceed *ex nihilo*, from something that apparently counts as nothing, from something uncountable. Every situation includes some such uncountable or empty component: its *void*. What Badiou's ontology is designed to demonstrate is the coherence of processes of radical transformation that begin via an encounter with precisely that which appears as uncountable in a situation, and that continue as the development of ways of counting or grouping the elements belonging to the situation according to no other criteria than the simple fact that they are all, equally and indistinctly, members of the situation.

II

Before going any further it may be worth pausing for a moment to address a couple of the most important concepts at work in Badiou's ontology, which play a crucial role in his project as a whole: the rivalry between subtractive and substantial conceptions of being, the difference between inconsistent and consistent forms of multiplicity, and the distinction of the void and its 'edge'. Many misunderstandings of Badiou's work stem from confusion about one of these closely interconnected distinctions.

(a) A subtractive ontology

As the name implies, a subtractive ontology is to be distinguished from a discourse which pretends to convey being as something present and substantial, something accessible to a sort of direct experience or articulation (as it is, in different ways, for the pre-Socratics, Aristotle, Leibniz or Deleuze, for instance). By subtractive ontology Badiou means a discourse which accepts that its referent is not accessible in this sense. As Badiou conceives it, being is not something that shows itself in a sort of primordial revelation; still less is it the object of some divine or quasi-divine act of creation. If being was a matter of unveiling or speech then ontology would properly be an intuitive and poetic discourse, rather than a conceptual one. Unlike the pre-Socratic effort to incant or *sing* the immediate vitality of being, the genuinely philosophical project begins, via Plato, with an indirect, diagonal procedure. The philosopher first develops a rigorous discourse designed to circumscribe the question of being – for instance, in Plato's *Republic*, the discourse of the Ideas, or for Badiou himself the axioms of set theory – in order then to show that the ground of being itself, 'the real of this discourse, is precisely that which does not submit to the discourse'.[5] The ontologist knows that the ground of being eludes direct articulation, that it is thinkable only as the non-being upon which pivots the whole discourse on being. In the *Republic*, where the generic form of being is the Idea, Plato concludes that the ultimate ground of being, the Good, is itself the Idea of that which is beyond being and beyond Idea; in mathematical set theory (the theory of consistent multiplicity) the ultimate 'stuff' presumed and manipulated by the theory is itself, as we shall see in a moment, inconsistent – it can be presented only as no-thing. In other words, ontology does not speak being or participate in its revelation; it articulates, on the basis of a conceptual framework indifferent to poetry or intuition, the precise way in which being is withdrawn or subtracted from articulation. (Whether this withdrawal refers to a transcendent and inaccessible presence beyond presence, to a One-beyond-being, or instead to a pure subtraction from every category of presence, is what distinguishes philosophy proper from the religious alternative to philosophy.)

Badiou's subtractive conception of multiplicity sets him sharply apart from many of his contemporaries, who, like Lyotard, Deleuze or Serres, generally seek in some sense to express, intuit, figure or otherwise articulate the multiple. Once ontology is identified with mathematics then being is forever isolated from the entire domain of the material, the sensual or the existential. As a result there is strictly no phenomenological dimension to Badiou's subtraction. There is no elusive point where we might perhaps 'see' being vanish into non-being, so to speak.[6]

(b) Consistent and inconsistent multiplicity

What is subtracted from ontology in this way is *inconsistent* multiplicity. The starting point of Badiou's ontology is that, if being is to be thought as multiple rather than one, then unity or oneness can only figure as the result of a uni-fication. The one *is* not, instead the one *operates* as a sort of 'law', and whatever is operated upon in this way must itself be not-one (*EE* 33). Ontology prescribes the most general rules whereby we can present as a particular thing, i.e. treat or count as *one* thing, something that, before it was thus unified or counted, was neither unified nor particular. 'Something' is already a misleading though useful way of putting it. If I can successfully count out groups of books or people then as a matter of course the things counted conform to my definition of books or people; inconsistent multiplicity is the predicate that Badiou attributes to that undefinable and purely intra-operational 'something' counted in the ontological situation, in the situation where what is counted is strictly speaking nothing other than instances of counting itself (or *numbers*). The process of unifying or counting-as-one shouldn't be understood then as an intermediary operation between consistency and inconsistency. It is rather the sole ontological operation, and it creates a horizon of inconsistency 'beyond' it as its necessary implication.

Badiou's subtractive conception of inconsistency distinguishes it from the transcendent conception defended by the founder of modern set theory, Georg Cantor (1845–1918). Cantor attributed inconsistency to quantities that cannot be collected together in a coherent set: since every coherent set can easily be manipulated (for instance by multiplication or addition) to generate a larger set, he sensibly concluded that the largest possible set, the set that might include *all* other sets, had to be inconsistent in this sense – in other words, no set at all. Cantor was happy to see in the existence of such inconsistent quantities an indication of absolute (or 'unincreasable') infinity, itself the property of a transcendent God.[7] By contrast, Badiou preserves the infinite dimension of Cantor's inconsistency, but, since he insists on the irrevocable death of God, he sees in the impossibility of any set of all sets nothing other than non-being pure and simple (*EE* 53–4). If inconsistency *is* at all, he concludes, it can only be as the banal being presumed by *any* situation or counting procedure. Furthermore, if the one is not, then multiplicity can itself 'be' in only an implicit or axiomatic sense. We know only what we are able to unify or count. We know inconsistency itself (the 'stuff' counted) must *be*, but we can know nothing about it: since nothing can be observed or presented of inconsistency we cannot even know if it is multiple (let alone infinite) in any positive sense. No less than any other properly primordial quality of being, these qualities must be decided and affirmed, pure and simple.[8]

Now while all situations are distinguished by the way that they count or treat as 'ones' the elements which belong to them, every truth procedure has inconsistent multiplicity (the something thus counted) as its only ground or criterion. Inconsistent multiplicity plays a role in Badiou's philosophy that is comparable, in certain respects, to that of practical reason in Kant's philosophy or radical freedom in Sartre's philosophy, and it evokes similarly elusive and undefinable qualities (absolute indetermination, indefinite potential, infinite excess, and so on). Like Kant's practical reason, inconsistent multiplicity is not something we can know or present as an object of perception; it is posited as something in accordance with which, exceptionally, we can *think* or *act*. Perhaps the single most important implication of Badiou's ontology is that inconsistent multiplicity can only ever be encountered via the contingent but decisive consequences of an event. An event is that moment when the ordinary rules according to which things consist in a situation are suspended, and the indistinguishable 'stuff' that is thus made consistent is for a passing instant exposed as what it is, as pure inconsistency or pure indetermination. Since inconsistency can never be presented in the normal sense of the word, no such event can endure: it is never possible to prove that an encounter with inconsistency actually took place. The impact of the encounter depends entirely on the militant conviction of those who affirm its occurrence and elaborate some means of developing its implications.

To make this point a little more concrete, imagine any ordinary situation that groups people together, for instance a family, a gathering of friends or employees, a political or professional meeting, a classroom. In each of these situations individuals count according to a large number of more or less explicit criteria, e.g. their loyalty, their vivacity, their efficiency, their intelligence, their scholastic aptitude, and so on. Of course we are free to suppose that the individuals counted in these ways are thinking or creative beings, but Badiou's presumption is that by itself no ordinary situation ever really counts its members as thinking beings, i.e. in terms that respect those undefinable or inconsistent qualities that allow them to *think*, precisely – their immeasurable potential, their affirmative intensity, their infinite capacity for inspiration, and so on. Only rarely does it happen that people act not as objects evaluated by an employer, an educator or a friend, but as participants in one of the few possible fields in which pure affirmation is possible (in the fields of politics, art, science or love). For a truth to proceed in an employment situation, for instance, the criteria normally deployed to distinguish employers from employees, and profitable employees from unprofitable ones, would somehow have to be suspended in an affirmation of generic equality. In short, the situation would have to become a political situation.

(This is why September 11th 2001, for instance, cannot qualify as an event. It is no doubt possible to think of the attack as an occasion which temporarily suspended, for those who suffered its immediate impact, the distinctions – dividing workers, managers, corporations, nationalities, etc. – that had hitherto governed the normal Twin Towers routine. The initial and immediate sympathy for the victims, expressed all over the world, was surely a response to this very suspension. As Badiou often says, however, the existence of victims is never itself enough to inspire a true subjective mobilization. The subjective mobilization inspired by 9/11 in fact proceeded, of course, to reinforce as never before the difference between American and un-American, between 'freedom' and 'terrorism', etc. In other words, 9/11 was not an event because it was not able to expose, in a consequential way, inconsistent humanity as the very being of the American or international-capitalist situation; it did not inaugurate a new way of 'indiscerning' people in terms indifferent to the status quo. Despite superficial appearances to the contrary, 9/11 did not compel its subjects to stop carrying on as before. Instead it confirmed, in the most dramatic terms, the basic principle which has long governed the global order, whereby the only lives that *count* are the lives of those who own the dominant means of exploitation and control the military resources required to preserve them.)

(c) The void and its edge

Inconsistent multiplicity is the very being of being and the sole ground of a truth. Inconsistency *per se* cannot be presented. Every situation, however, includes a link to this ontological ground, namely that which, considered according to the criteria whereby the situation counts its elements, remains uncountable. This link is whatever can be counted in the situation only as nothing rather than as *a* thing. Whereas inconsistent multiplicity, as the 'stuff' counted by any situation, is itself effectively meta-situational, this nothing or *void* is always void *for* a situation. The void is inconsistent multiplicity 'according to a situation' (*EE* 68–9). The void is the only aspect of a situation that presents nothing, very literally, which might obscure access to inconsistency. In a simple numerical situation made up of positive integers {1, 2, 3 ...}, for instance, the number zero is obviously its void; zero is what cannot be counted as a 'one', zero is what doesn't count. In situations which count only property, wealth or consumption, human capacities which cannot be counted in such terms will remain empty or indiscernible as far as the situation is concerned; so too, within the ordinary routine of situation of parliamentary democracies, will popular political capacities whose expression is indifferent to the business of electoral representation. Marx conceives of the proletariat, to take the most obvious case, as the void of the developing capitalist situation.

Every situation, in other words, has its ways of authorizing and qualifying its members as legitimate members of the situation: the void of such a situation includes whatever can only be presented, in the situation, as utterly unqualified or unauthorized. It is precisely these unqualified or indiscernible capacities that make up the very being of the situation. The indiscernible being counted by a situation, the void as such remains for the same reason forever uncountable, forever devoid of any discernible place in the situation. What qualifies as void is scattered indifferently throughout every part of the situation – proletarian qualities can in principle be attributed to *every* member of the capitalist situation, for instance, just as in a certain sense zero is included in every other number.

By contrast, what *can* come to be counted, and what does have a well-defined place in the situation, is whatever falls within what Badiou calls 'the edge of the void' (or 'eventalsite', for it is this edge which defines the place in which something decisive can happen in a situation, in which an event can take place; it is this place which thus 'concentrates the historicity of a situation' [*EE* 199–200]).

It is essential to avoid confusing the void and the edge or border of the void. The void itself is uncountable, it cannot be presented as an element or treated as unity of any kind. The *edge* of the void is occupied by that foundational element which, as far as the situation is concerned, contains nothing other than the void. (In our crude version of the numerical situation, this is simply the number 1 itself – the number which 'contains' nothing other than 0.[9]) The edge is itself discernible as a minimal unity of sorts, but as one that has no members or units of its own, or rather no members that other members of the situation can individuate in a meaningful way. In Marx's capitalist situation, for instance, the working class occupies the edge of the (proletarian) void: the situation certainly counts this class as one of its elements, but has no significant ways of counting *individual* workers as thinking or creative people, as opposed to more or less diligent and deferential employees, or as consumers, or as patriots . . . In today's French and British situations, a similar logic applies to immigrant workers and asylum seekers, just as it does to Jews or Arabs in anti-Semitic situations or gays in homophobic situations: Jews or immigrants are 'in' these situations but only as instances of the label which defines them, and not as individuals in their own right. People who inhabit the edge of a situation's void are people who have nothing which entitles them to belong in the situation, they do not themselves count for anything in it. Having nothing, they occupy the place from which the void as such might be exposed, via an event. (Strictly speaking then, only in the wake of an event can it ever be meaningfully admitted that there were previously uncounted members of the situation who now demand to be counted equally with other members of the situation.)

What Badiou further calls the *state* of a situation is designed to foreclose this possibility. The state includes all the various ways in which a situation organizes and arranges itself to make sure that its uncountable or unqualified aspects are not only never presented in the situation but also never re-presented in it. This is an all-important distinction: an element is *presented* in a situation if it belongs to it, if it counts as one of the members of that situation; an element, or group of elements, is also *represented* in a situation if it is included as a discernible part (or 'subset') of the situation, i.e. if it falls under one or several of the ways in which a situation can distinguish and classify its elements – think for instance of the ways in which any social situation groups its members according to residence, occupation, wealth, status, etc. By lending a certain stability to the way these infinitely varied groupings are themselves grouped, the state provides the basis for whatever passes as order in the situation. The state is what arranges a situation in such a way as to ensure the power of its dominant group (or ruling class).

Now a truth is nothing other than the process that exposes and represents the void of a situation – or, for it amounts to the same thing, that suspends the state of a situation. This exposure begins with an event, the occurring of which is located at the edge of whatever passes as uncountable in the situation. A truth *proceeds* when, in the wake of the event, those elements that affirm its implications assemble a group which, as a group, appears inconsistent or unrecognizable (hence 'inexistent') in the situation. Such is the case when, for instance, a popular uprising triggers the composition of a proletarian political capacity or subject, a capacity whose very possibility is denied by the capitalist situation. Other obvious political examples include the uprisings in South Africa and Palestine, the American civil rights movement, the rural mobilizations in Chiapas and Brazil. In other words, a truth process makes it possible to group the elements of a situation so that they *all* count in the same way, so that their simple belonging to or presentation in the situation determines the way they are represented in it. A truth is a grouping or representing of elements that has no other order or norm than presentation itself. Along the way, such a 'generic' grouping will develop the new forms of knowledge required both to individ-uate the originally indistinguishable inhabitants of the evental site and to discern hitherto unauthorized or unimaginable combinations of elements. (Remember that since it can never belong to a situation, since it can never be presented in or counted as an element of the situation, the precise threat posed by an exposure of the void is that it might come to be actively *represented* or included in the situation. The threat is that some ordinarily non-unifiable or inconsistent combination of elements might 'lend a figure' to the void as an anarchic *part* or sub-set of the situation [*EE* 112–13]. An event is thus the occasion for a process whereby inconsistency, though never presentable as such, might come to be represented in an 'illegal' or 'revolutionary' way, one that challenges the normal representation or state of a situation.)

III

All three of these major distinctions turn, clearly, on the pre-eminent role played by the void in Badiou's ontology. The new work in which Badiou has been engaged since the early 1990s maintains this pre-eminence but approaches it in a somewhat different way. The key point of reference remains the anarchic disorder of inconsistent multiplicity, but Badiou has recently been paying more careful attention to the way situations are always experienced as 'solid, related [*lié*], consistent', to the ways in which any situation is itself situated, localized, caught up in relations with other situations. What he calls 'onto-logy' is concerned with just how pure inconsistent being is made 'captive to being-there', made subject to the logical constraints of a particular localization or place (*CT* 193). The elements of a situation not only are, they are *there*, they are alongside other elements, they exist or *appear* in the situation more or less intensely than other elements. 'Logic' is the name Badiou now gives to the rules which order the way things appear in a situation, or 'world'. An element whose every aspect is apparent in the situation exists at the highest or maximum level of intensity in that situation. Other elements will have aspects that are only dimly apparent, and an element whose every aspect is effectively invisible in the situation is minimally existent or apparent in the situation. Every situation has at least one 'inexistent' element, and as you might expect, minimal existence characterizes those who inhabit the edge of the void (or evental site) of a situation.

Take today's American situation, for instance. We know, abstractly, that its every member is, in his or her pure being, nothing other than an uncountable or indiscernible inconsistency; these members count in the American situation according to all the myriad criteria (linguistic, historical, sociological, economic ...) which collectively structure this situation as 'American'. Certain things appear as more distinctively American than others, and the logic of the situation ensures a broadly stable set of rules for distinguishing the maximally American elements (cowboys, the Pentagon, baseball, etc.) from minimally American elements ('communists', 'Arab terrorists', cricket, etc.). Much of the ordinary business of being American involves discussion about just how these various elements should appear – the degree to which the country should be explicitly Christian, the extent to which organized labour may participate in politics, the ways in which women and 'minorities' should enjoy equal rights, the degree to which same-sex or inter-racial partnerships should remain hidden, etc. The mobilization of a truth, by contrast, imposes *revolutionary* change upon a situation's logic. When in the wake of an event 'being seems to displace its configuration under our eyes, it is always at the expense of appearing, through the local collapse of its consistency, and so in the provisional cancellation of all logic. Because what comes then to the surface, displacing or revoking the logic of the place, is being itself, in its fearsome and creative inconsistency, or in its void, which is the without-place of every place' (*CT* 200). Going back to our example: although its actual course will be doubly unpredictable (on account of its eventual occasion and haphazard progression), any truth in the American situation will have to proceed in such a way as to dissolve the logic which distinguishes American from un-American. For what it's worth we can day-dream, today, about a process that might undermine American corporate power or the military-industrial complex, that might oblige US tolerance of economic independence in the third world, etc. Needless to say, no such development is possible without a radical transformation of the very logic of the American situation, and no such possibility will amount to anything in the absence of a mobilization capable of inventing, step by step, both the means of such indistinction and the discipline required to sustain it.

There is little to be gained by speculation about future truths and equally little to be gained by the simple commemoration of past truths. The question of truth is indifferent to memory, indeed is indifferent to time itself, at least in the normal sense; truth is concentrated in the present. Truth's time is the consequential present, the present of eventual consequences.

As a final example, consider Badiou's recent analysis of the Paris Commune (March–May 1871) in these terms.[10] In the situation of Paris at the end of the Franco-Prussian war what *appears* in the sphere of consecrated political power is a Prussian occupying force, a fragile Republican regime willing to accommodate the invaders, a national assembly dominated by rural and reactionary interests, and a regular army determined to squash the potential threat to its monopoly of violence posed by the mainly working-class National Guard. On the other hand, what appears outside this sphere includes a chaotic mix of proletarian organizations determined to resist the Prussian advance at all costs – trade unions, loosely organized militia groups, the Central Committee of the National Guard, and so on. What both sides of this divided situation accept, on the eve of the Commune's declaration, is the proletariat's own *political* insignificance or incapacity. The proletariat is certainly visible in the situation, but either as a purely social phenomenon or as the incarnation of unrest and disorder. If Adolphe Thiers' government is the most dominant, most apparent or 'maximally existent' term of the situation, the political capacity of the workers is its minimally existent term.

An event figures here as the beginning of a process whereby that which had been minimally existent in the situation comes, through the invention of new forms of discipline and organization, to exist absolutely. The subjective political capacity of the workers, inexistent before the Commune, comes in the wake of its inaugural declarations to exist in its own right, independently of any incorporation within the existing institutions of the state. Unlike Marx and Lenin, who applaud the Commune as a break with the old state of things while deploring its failure to secure new versions of state powers (a failure that was to be corrected, in what became the 'official' Leninist conception of things, via the development of a more durable Communist *Party*), Badiou sees in this failure its true significance: the Commune is affirmative proof of a 'structural gap between true political invention and the state'.[11] If the 'Left' is the general name we might give to that recurring process whereby a popular political mobilization is captured, pacified and 'betrayed' by representatives of the state (in France, the process punctuated by the sequences dated 1830, 1848, 1870, 1945, 1968, 1995 . . .), then the Commune begins as a radical break with the entire *logic* of the Left. And the Commune remains true, today, insofar as it continues to inspire the renewal of such a break.

IV

In what remains of this Introduction I'd like to draw up a rough list of what seem to me, at this stage in its reception and development, to be the main questions and objections facing Badiou's project. The most obvious and probably most far-reaching of these concern his generally non-relational if not anti-dialectical orientation.[12] Many of these questions have been raised, one way or another, by the various contributors to this book; I hope they will forgive me if for the sake of economy I omit specific attributions here.

Now the great strength of Badiou's project is that, in keeping with a tradition that goes back to Kant, if not to Saint Paul (a tradition whose recent members include, in different ways, Sartre, Fanon and Lacan), he insists on the difference between what people are and what people can do. It can always happen, if inspired by a truth, that 'what you do comes to be worth more than you'.[13] Badiou's enterprise is built on this distinction, and without some version of it there is surely no significant place, in the grand scheme of things, for either philosophy or thought. But Badiou's version of the difference is an especially intransigent one: for him there is effectively *no* relation between being and acting, and the result is a notably abstract conception of acting. An event, in its *happening*, is precisely something 'other than being' (*EE* 193, 205), and a true act has inconsistency as its only criterion and ground. There is no clear sense in which we might conceive of a relation *with* inconsistency, and in the absence of such a relation, every subject is 'sustained only by his own prescription', every truth 'says itself only of itself'[14] and 'needs nothing other than itself'.[15]

INTRODUCTION   **13**

The implications of this non-relational orientation are considerable. Badiou rejects any constituent relation between truths and historical or social 'development', along with any detailed notion of interaction between various levels of socio-historical causation – geographic, demographic, economic, technological, etc. He refuses any constituent mediation between subjects and the individuals they transform, between evental sites and the situations to which they belong, between the occurring of events and the sites that they occupy,[16] between what things are and the identifiable qualities that they present – more, he refuses any relation between pure or inconsistent being and actual or material beings *tout court* (whose actuality or materiality is effectively relegated to the domain of mere contingency). To be sure, Badiou is careful to insist that ontology is one situation of thought among others; historical or social situations are obviously not reducible to their mathematical profile. Nevertheless he implies that the only true way to *think* such situations is 'in the spirit' of mathematics, i.e. axiomatically, immediately, decisively, by finding some way of evacuating whatever passes for 'reality' in the situation, some means of penetrating its specifically social or substantial opacity.

Both Badiou's ontology and his conception of truth are thus abstract in a peculiarly strong sense of the word: as far as their situations are concerned, both are grounded very literally on *nothing*. The crux of the matter clearly turns on the status of the void (or 'inexistence') as the conceptual core of Badiou's notion of truths. Badiou's work makes little sense if we forget that 'between thought and the real there is a hole, an abyss, a void; the truth is first of all the effect of a separation, a loss, or a voiding'.[17] Remember that the void is what, with the resources available in the situation, cannot be discerned as *any* sort of individual or one. The void is indifferent or undifferentiated: 'one void cannot differ from another, since it contains no element (no local point), which might indicate this difference'.[18] The void, in short, is that to which it is impossible to relate.

1. My first and most elaborate question is then: does the brutal alternative between 'one' and 'nothing' suffice as an *elementary* principle of distinction? That certain elements of a situation count for less than others is uncontroversial, as is the fact that a situation might include virtually indiscernible elements – 'somethings' or 'someones', you might say, rather than easily identifiable persons, qualities or things. Badiou's ontology says, in brief, that nothing is all that can be presented of such a someone or something. It is this initial presumption which in turn prepares the ground for Badiou's reassertion, in each sphere of truth, of Marx's most radical but also most problematic idea: the conversion of 'nothing' into a kind of 'everything', the process whereby those who have nothing are led to assert the universal truth of their situation. Every truth operates in this non-dialectical conjunction of all and nothing. The Commune, for instance, is itself the process whereby 'that which was worth nothing comes to be worth everything'.[19]

Those someones who appeared as nothing will come to say everything – such is the basic logic of Badiou's conception of truth. That he shares versions of this logic with other conceptions of singular or self-constituent power is one issue. The more important question concerns the price that must be paid for so dramatic a simplification of real situations, for this refusal to allow for differentiation of the void. The dangers involved in thinking of the proletariat in this way, for instance, are well known. But already at this elementary ontological level, don't we need at least one other term in addition to inconsistency and consistency, namely the relation between the two? In the mathematical schema this relation, the means whereby what figures as nothing is counted as one (the way zero is made to belong to one) is nothing other than the one itself: one *is* the operation that counts nothing as one. Set theory has no need to acknowledge a relation between nothing and one (or between inconsistency and consistency), since there can obviously be no relation *with* nothing. But by the same token, however, if there is certainly nothing to block the extension of set theory to situations grounded on something rather than nothing, there is also no clear reason why set theory should have something rather than nothing to say about such situations. For in every situation other than the mathematical situation, what is identified or counted as one is not nothing but something, precisely, and the relation between something and one is surely irreducible. In every situation other than the mathematical one, in other words, there *is* a fundamental relation between the being of the situation and the ways this being comes to consist. It is this relation that drops out of Badiou's articulation of everything and nothing (just as it drops out of Kant's disjunction of phenomena and things in themselves, or Sartre's distinction of being for-itself and being in-itself). By the same token, a version of this relation seems to return in an abrupt and problematic form as soon as it is a matter of 'representing' or 'lending a figure to' the void, i.e. as soon as it is a matter of truth.[20]

 (It is no accident that Badiou is especially careful to circumscribe the most obvious link between what we are and how we are presented, namely language. If fundamentally we *are* speaking beings, and if language is advanced as the most general medium of our presentation, then the rigid demarcation of consistency from inconsistency collapses in advance; it is exactly this consequence that Badiou's steadfast refusal of the linguistic turn is designed to forestall.)[21]

 Badiou's ontology describes only that which can be rigorously abstracted from a situation. His presumption is that such abstraction, or subtraction, isolates all that can be said about the pure being of any being. It achieves this, however, at the cost of rendering absolute the ancient distinction between what a being *is* and the qualities that it *has*. Analysis of the latter effectively becomes a matter of contingency pure and simple. Is this a price that those committed to the analysis of biological, psychological or historical situations, for instance, should be willing to pay? (Or again, for it is the same question: is mathematics really the only discourse authorized to pronounce scientific *truths*? Do the more empirical sciences really proceed without thought?)[22]

2. Nowhere are the non-relational implications of Badiou's ontology more far-reaching than as regards his sharp distinction between presentation and representation, between a situation and the state of a situation. All relations

between elements are relegated to the domain of representation, knowledge and the state; the most basic axioms of Badiou's ontology presume that the elements of a situation can be adequately individuated and presented without reference to inter-elemental relations of any kind. Consequently, suspension of the state or the interruption of representation is supposed to allow these elements simply to be presented as what they *are*. A truth, itself purged of any contamination with knowledge, is supposed to assemble an unrelated set of pure if not isolated singularities, a collection of 'extreme particularity', an infinite mass of individuals freed from every form of bond, *liaison* or rapport. A truth assembles a collection whose only criterion is the fact that all its members *belong* to the situation.[23] But again: doesn't this strict separation of presentation from representation remain essentially abstract? Is it possible to account for complex forms of individuation on the basis of this distinction? And if not, can Badiou sustain his claim that each truth remains the truth *of* its particular situation?

3. The question about ontology's relation to social or historical contingency twists round when we enquire about the justification of two of Badiou's most insistent ontological principles – that 'the One is not' and that 'every situation is infinite'. The primary basis for these principles is not so much ontological as historico-political, precisely: they are twin consequences of the assertion, inspired by modern scientific atheism, that God is dead, and thus that if infinity exists at all it is a characteristic of every situation rather than the exceptional attribute of a divine transcendence. Ontology alone does not establish either principle: the axiom of infinity certainly does not imply that *all* sets or situations are infinite, and, as Cantor's own piety suggests, the fact that there can be no all-inclusive set of all sets does not by itself disprove the existence of a properly transcendent limit to the very concept of set (a limit to the distinction of 'one' and 'not-one'). When pressed on this point, Badiou justifies his principles in terms of their strategic political utility, rather than their strict ontological integrity.[24] A similar question arises with respect to the derivation of that most basic quality of all contemporary truths, namely their generic equality: is it possible to isolate, in a non-dialectical way, the extent to which this quality has emerged from purely subtractive or subjective procedures, rather than as part of the multidimensional historico-political tendencies at work in the development of capitalism and modernity?

4. One implication of this last point is easily generalized. Badiou insists on the rare and unpredictable character of every truth. On the other hand, we know that every truth, as it composes a generic or egalitarian sampling of the situation, will proceed in such a way as to suspend the normal grip of the state of its situation by eroding the distinctions used to classify and order parts of the situation. Is this then a criterion that subjects must presume in advance or one that they come to discover in each case? If not the former, if truth is entirely a matter of post-evental implication or consequence, then there can be no clear way of distinguishing, before it is too late, a genuine event (which relates only to the void of the situation, i.e. to the way inconsistency might appear within a

situation) from a false event (one that, like September 11th or the triumph of National Socialism, reinforces the basic distinctions governing the situation). But if there is always an initial hunch which guides the composition of a generic set, a sort of preliminary or 'prophetic' commitment to the generic – just as there is, incidentally, in Cohen's own account of generic sets, insofar as this account seeks to demonstrate a possibility implicit in the ordinary extensional definition of set[25] – then it seems difficult to sustain a fully post-evental conception of truth. In short: is the initial decision to affirm an event unequivocally *free*, a matter of consequence alone? Or is it tacitly guided by the criteria of the generic at every step, and thereby susceptible to a kind of anticipation?

5. Applied now to the category of the event itself this question concerns, unsurprisingly, its radically exceptional character. In each case, 'it is not from the world, in however ideal a manner, that the event holds its inexhaustible reserve, its silent (or indiscernible) excess, but from its being unattached to it, its being separate, lacunary'.[26] This detached and undecidable status of the event is itself largely a consequence of the 'total disjunction' between the evental site and the rest of the situation. 'Having no element in common', their 'non-relation' is one of 'absolute heterogeneity' or alterity (*EE* 207). Since it takes place within a site that, as far as the situation is concerned, contains nothing at all, the reality of the event depends entirely upon a decision to affirm its existence; from the perspective of those who take this decision, an event ' "mobilizes" the elements of its site and adds to it its own presentation'. To be sure, once affirmed, an event (considered as a multiplicity or as a being) certainly gathers together the elements of its site. My question here concerns the apparently abrupt quality of this 'addition' at work in its *self*-presentation, in the way an event manages, without reference to any intelligible process of mediation, to 'interpose itself between the void and itself' (*EE* 203; cf. 219). The question concerns the way an event, as an *occurring*, is precisely something altogether 'other' than being, something that apparently comes out of nowhere, something founded literally on nothing, something that indicates and belongs to itself, an 'interval' occasioned by pure chance and experienced as a moment of 'grace'.

Badiou offers, admittedly, an account of inter-evental temporality (whereby 'an intervention presents an event for the advent of another event') that goes some way towards answering this question. It is the consequential and inter-evental quality of an intervention, he claims, that allows him to distinguish his account from the excesses of 'speculative leftism', which mistakenly 'imagines that the intervention is authorized only by itself'.[27] It would be equally mistaken, however, to confuse this inter-evental aspect with a conventionally causal or dialectical dimension. 'I don't think', Badiou insists, that 'events are linked in a global system. That would deny their essentially random character, which I absolutely maintain.'[28] But is this dismissal of causality worth its high strategic price? By what criteria can we isolate the element of pure contingency from cumulative structural contradictions or varying levels of solidarity and organization operative among the elements of the evental site? What is the status of eagerly anticipated or laboriously prepared events? To what extent is an event the result of preliminary acts of resistance?[29] Isn't it more accurate to say that events are *relatively* unpredictable, that some are more unexpected than others, since what is unprecedented for some members of the site may be experienced (if not opposed) by others as part of a larger and longer trajectory?

Just how useful is it, moreover, to describe in terms of '*total* disjunction' the actual relations – of exploitation, oppression, marginalization, etc. – at issue between a situation and the members of its evental site?

6. In a related sense, is it enough to explain the process of subjectivation, the transformation of an ordinary individual into the militant subject of a universalizable cause, or truth, mainly through analogies with the process of conversion? It is certainly essential to maintain (after Saint Paul) that anyone can become the militant of a truth, that truth is not primarily a matter of background or disposition. If it exists at all, truth must be equally indifferent to both nature and nurture, and it is surely one of the great virtues of Badiou's account of the subject that it, like Žižek's or Lacan's, remains irreducible to all the forces (historical, social, cultural, genetic ...) that shape the individual or ego in the ordinary sense. On the other hand, the lack of any substantial explanation of subjective empowerment, of the process that enables or inspires an individual to become a subject, again serves only to make the account of subjectivation unhelpfully abrupt and abstract. Isn't there a danger that by disregarding issues of motivation and resolve at play in any subjective decision, the militants of a truth will preach only to the converted? Doesn't the real problem of any political organization begin where Badiou's analyses tend to leave off, i.e. with the task of finding ways whereby a truth will begin to ring true for those initially indifferent or hostile to its implications?

It is not so much a matter here of repeating Merleau-Ponty's familiar objections to Sartre's initially absolute or disembodied conception of freedom as of wondering why Badiou has no developed alternative to the early Sartre's own notion of a fundamental *project* at work in an individual's situation, a guiding and cumulative sense of direction which, though it may always be altered by a genuine decision, nevertheless conditions the situation of any such decision. Still less does Badiou conceive of truth in the more dialectical terms developed by the later Sartre, in line with the basic idea that 'we can always make something of what we are made to be'.[30] Least of all does he articulate truth together with those technical forms – language, writing, tools, technologies and so forth – which, understood broadly along Bernard Stiegler's lines, both shape this making *and* simultaneously open that temporal horizon, the prospect of an unpredictable future, in which something like a decision is possible in the first place.[31] A truth in Badiou's sense is not something that transforms an individual already equipped with a certain subjective direction and momentum: instead a truth rouses its subjects pure and simple, as if *ex nihilo*. 'The subject is absolutely non-existent in the situation "before" the event. We might say that the process of truth *induces* a subject.'[32]

Coming back then to my previous question: is it possible to defend both a haphazard conception of truth, where any subjectivation proceeds in the wake of a chance inspiration, together with a notion of truth conceived (after the great French *résistants* Albert Lautman and Jean Cavaillès) as 'logical revolt', as a matter of long-standing or automatic principle which precisely does *not* depend on whatever takes place?[33] To take just one typical though accidentally celebrated case: when Otto Frank (the father of Anne Frank) asks his employee Miep Gies to help protect his family from the Nazis she immediately replies, like many thousands of *résistants* in similar situations: 'yes of course [...]. I simply couldn't do anything else'.[34] No doubt Gies' life as a resistant begins with this decision, but what is gained by suggesting that this new life bears little or no relation to her previous life and her previous decisions? How can we think this conjunction of the automatic and exceptional without some sort of continuity across both individual and subject? If nothing else, how are we then to understand the fact that so many more people chose differently from Gies?

7. Again somewhat along the same lines, just how far can we push the isolation (or 'purity') of a truth from other aspects of a situation? To what extent is every artistic truth, for example, oriented towards the subtraction of whatever qualifies as 'non-art' – culture, society, lived experience, etc.? For Badiou, true art (exemplified above all by Mallarmé's poetry) performs the evacuation of all mimesis or representation and absolves itself of any accommodation with 'reality', always on the assumption that reality itself is never anything more than compromise or alienation. As Pierre Macherey notes, such a subtractive conception of art misses the various ways in which any representation not only evokes a familiar presence but also accomplishes a certain 'de-presentation of what it represents', its projection into a mimetic distance which *may* also become a critical distance (such that its 'reality effect' is not necessarily alienating).[35] Isn't art more fruitfully thought in terms of the ways that it explores the relation *between* art and non-art?

Most obviously, to what extent can we abstract an exclusively political truth from matters relating to society, history and the state? Take those most familiar topics of 'cultural politics': gender, sexuality and race. No doubt the greater part of the still incomplete transformation here is due to militant subjective mobilizations that include the anticolonial wars of liberation, the civil rights movement, the feminist movements, Stonewall, and so on. But has cumulative, institutional change played no role in the slow movement towards racial or sexual *indistinction*, precisely? More importantly: since under the current state of things political authority is firmly vested in the hands of those with economic power, can a political prescription have any enduring effect if it manages only to distance or suspend the operation of such power? If a contemporary political sequence is to last (if at least it is to avoid the usual consequences of capital flight and economic sabotage) must it not also directly entail a genuine transformation of the economy itself, i.e. enable popular participation in economic decisions, community or workers' control over resources and production, and so on?[36] In today's circumstances, if a political prescription is to have any widespread *consequence*, isn't it essential that it find some way of bridging the gap between the political and the economic? Even Badiou's own privileged example indicates the uncertain purity of politics. The declaration of 18 March 1871 (which he quotes as the inaugural affirmation of a proletarian political capacity) commits the Communards to 'taking in hand the running of public affairs',[37] and throughout its short existence the Commune busies itself as much with matters of education, employment and administration as with issues of equality and power. Is a sharp distinction between politics and the state helpful in such circumstances? Do forms of discipline subtracted from the state, from the party, apply in fact to anything other than the *beginning* of relatively limited political sequences? Does the abstract ethical imperative, 'continue!', coupled with a classical appeal to moderation and restraint,[38] suffice to safeguard the long-term persistence of political sequences from the altogether necessary return of state-like functions (military, bureaucratic, institutional . . .)? To what extent, in short, does Badiou's position, which he presents in anticipation of an as yet obscure step beyond the more state-centred conceptions of Lenin and Mao, rather return him instead to the familiar objections levelled at earlier theories of anarchism?

8. My last questions concern Badiou's remarkable new work on appearing and being-there. At least three issues are worth raising.[39]

First, what is the precise relation between ontology and the 'onto-logy' of appearing? In what sense is there being and then *also* (if not afterwards) appearing? What sort of separation – temporal, causal, phenomenal – is implied in this 'then' or 'also'? This remains a little obscure since, though Badiou generally insists that the pure being of a being puts no constraints on its being-there, on how it appears in the situation, nevertheless both at what he calls the 'atomic' level of an object (the level that includes the irreducibly characteristic elements of an object) and within the circumstances of a 'site' (defined now as an element which itself comes to determine the way it appears in the situation), a being *does* prescribe the immediate nature of its being-there. So does the logic of appearing have anything more than a derivative force? Is this force really strong enough to account for the issue that, by Badiou's own admission, was left more or less unexplained in *Being and Event*, namely the way in which a situation is *structured* (since the concept of set is itself more or less structure-free)? On the other hand, coming back now to question 2, above: can any such account succeed without undermining Badiou's hitherto sharp distinction between structure and meta-structure, i.e. between presentation and representation or between situation and state (*EE* 109–11), and with it the very distinction between knowledge and truth?

Second, to what extent can the general category of relation be adequately subsumed within the simple mathematical relation of *order* (meaning relations of greater than or lesser than)? How far does relation itself here remain a derivative matter of the measurable difference between independent degrees of 'self-identity'?[40]

And third, to what extent then does this mathematics of the transcendental provide only a *description* rather than an explanation of that which appears? Relational individuating concepts like power, struggle, hegemony, and so on, still play no clear role in the theory. As a result, can Badiou's account of appearing do anything more than depict the ways things already are in the situation, i.e. spell out the rules according to which the situation now simply is the way that it is?

Versions of these questions have conditioned my reading of Badiou's work ever since I first encountered it, with no small amount of enthusiasm, some ten years ago. If I might conclude on a personal note, I should confess that over time and under the force of argument much of their importance has steadily eroded away: they strike me now more as matters of tactics and emphasis, rather than principle. It was not always so. I suspect, and I hope, that many of Badiou's readers will share a comparably complex mix of responses to his work.

1

THE HISTORY OF TRUTH: ALAIN BADIOU IN FRENCH PHILOSOPHY*

Etienne Balibar

The twenty-first meditation in Alain Badiou's *Being and Event*, which is devoted to Pascal, opens with the following quotation from the *Pensées*: 'The history of the Church should properly be called the history of truth.'[1] The *pensée* in question is numbered 858 by Brunschvicg, and 776 by Lafuma. Although it is not my intention here to discuss Badiou's proposed interpretation of Pascal for its own sake, or to discuss all the problems raised by this provocative formula, I must begin with a few comments on both points.

Reduced to a sentence, this *pensée* of Pascal's has a very strange status: although it is not impossible to relate it to others in such a way as to outline a possible Pascalian doctrine of history or of truth, of even of their reciprocity, it has yet to find its rightful place in any of the various arrangements of the *Pensées* that have been proposed. In his very interesting attempt to reconstruct the continuity of the several Pascalian 'discourses' that may have existed prior to the posthumous fragmentation of the *Pensées*, Emmanuel Martineau is unable to find any satisfactory place for it, which suggests *a contrario* that it marks a discontinuity, a singular utterance, and that it is in some way in excess of the theoretical economy and the writing regime of the *Pensées*.[2] We might add that it has very rarely been commented upon as such in the enormous literature devoted to Pascal, which means, amongst other things, that its genealogy remains obscure, despite the undeniable family resemblance to major theological formulations of medieval origin and, going further back, of Augustinian origin, such as that of the *traditio veritatis*, which designates the function of the Church within the history of salvation. For my own part, I am tempted to think that Pascal was the first person to formulate the phrase *histoire de la vérité* in French, and I will come back in a moment to the enigma of its posterity.

Turning to the few discussions of this fragment that do exist, we find that in the conclusion to his *Blaise Pascal: Commentaires* (1971), Henri Gouhier sees it as the slogan for a militant struggle designed to provide a topical inscription for

* This chapter, translated by David Macey, was first published as ' "Histoire de la vérité": Alain Badiou dans la philosophie française', in *Alain Badiou: Penser le multiple*, ed. Charles Ramond (Paris: L'Harmattan, 2002), pp. 497–523.

the truth of the Church Fathers, the tradition of which is preserved by the Church. This means that it is always possible for it to correct its errors by going back to its origins.[3] For his part, Jean Mesnard extends its meaning to the sequence of the Old and New Testaments, and makes it the basis for a whole theory of 'figures', or of the twofold movement of the veiling and unveiling of the truth that has been going on since the world began, and whose overall meaning is supplied by the sequence of prophecies and miracles.[4]

To the extent that Badiou himself elucidates the formula – and he does so only indirectly, as the phrase is used as the epigraph to a chapter in which, although it is not formally discussed, it does find an interpretation – his reading is midway between Gouhier's pragmatism and Mesnard's grand narrative: the Church is not so much a pre-existing institution established by divine right, as a retroactive effect of an 'interventionist logic' or of the decision to choose in which that logic is concentrated. That decision's sole referent in reality (i.e. in history) is the absolutely anti-natural and undecidable event of the miracle, indeed the most miraculous of all miracles, namely the coming of the Saviour, which contradicts all rules ('the symbol of a suspension of the law' [EE, 239]) and therefore demonstrates the inadequacy of rules. It should also be noted that this chapter in Badiou's book is one of those – there are not many of them, but they are all significant – which include professions of atheism on the part of an author who speaks in the first person. Such professions are always found together with references to militant faith or to fidelity as correlates of the eventual (événementielle):

> Even though I can scarcely be suspected of Christian zeal, I have never enjoyed this self-seeking nostalgia for a scientific and moralizing Pascal, I know full well that the real target of those who denounce Pascal's com-mitment to Christianity is in fact his militant conception of truth [...]. What I admire above all else in Pascal, on the contrary, is precisely the attempt, in difficult circumstances, to swim *against the current*, not in the reactive sense of the word, but in order to discover modern forms for an old conviction (EE 245).

I find it very interesting that Badiou should not only place a meditation on Pascal at the heart of his study of ontology, but that he should also choose to cite this excessive and enigmatic formula. It would be interesting immediately to ask Badiou what – in a transposition that is certainly devoid of any Christian zeal – becomes of the term *Church*, which is tautologically placed by Pascal in a complete equivalence ('should properly be called') with 'truth', as defined, at least, by the modality of history: is it a meaningless remainder, a hidden key, or a relative condition? But that is not how I wish to begin, as I do not believe that any theologico-political principle is immediately at work in the theorization of truth elaborated by Badiou, or that its importance can be marked in that way. I am convinced, on the other hand, that Badiou has intervened in an original manner, or a 'strong' way, in a philosophical conjuncture marked by a char-acteristic debate about the question and even the phrase 'history of truth', not in

order to offer a different conception, but to disagree with most of his contemporaries by swimming against the current. What he has done, not only by
using the expression but also by signalling its Pascalian usage, is of the greatest
interest, both for the reason he gives and for another reason on which I will now
dwell for a moment by outlining the most schematic points of reference for
what might, in other circumstances, form a chapter in a history of French
philosophy in the second half of the twentieth century.

I DERRIDA, CANGUILHEM, FOUCAULT

The expression *histoire de la vérité* is not, whatever what we might think, a very
common expression. And nor is it an expression that can be easily translated,
not in the sense of finding a literal equivalent (there is nothing to prevent
anyone saying 'History of the Truth' in English, *Geschichte der Warheit* or even
Warheitsgeschichte in German, or *Historia de la verdad* in Spanish – in the sense
that Borges wrote a *Historia de la eternidad*), but in the sense of establishing its
acceptability within the philosophical idiom. And yet it is one of the main
themes of the logico-phenomenological, and logico-epistemological, debate
which, from the end of the 1950s to the beginning of the 1980s, helped –
perhaps for the last time – to confer upon French-language philosophy a relative
autonomy with respect to its international environment. To demonstrate that
this is the case, one has only to study the way in which an expression that is, I
repeat, both unusual and restrictive circulates in the writings of a constellation
of authors. At the same time, it signals the differences between them: it constitutes, in other words, the index of a point of heresy that both unites and
divides them, or brings them together in a 'disjunctive synthesis' around their
differend. Let me simply give three essential points of reference: Derrida,
Canguilhem, Foucault.

I will begin with Derrida and Canguilhem, who both use the expression in a
hypothetical and, ultimately, critical way. Derrida does so in certain key passages in his *Edmund Husserl's Origin of Geometry: An Introduction*, which dates
from 1962:

The culture and tradition of truth are marked by a paradoxical historicity.
In one sense, they can be divorced from all history, as they are not
intrinsically affected by the empirical content of real history [. . .]. For
both those who confine themselves to historical facticity and those who
lock themselves into the ideality of value, the historical originality of the
story of truth can only be that of myth. But in another sense, which is in
keeping with Husserl's intention, the tradition of truth is history at its
most profound and most pure [. . .]. Once phenomenology escapes both
conventional Platonism and historicist empiricism, the moment of truth
it wishes to describe is indeed that of a concrete and specific history whose
foundations are the act of a temporal and creative subjectivity [. . .]. Only
a communitarian subjectivity can produce and fully vouch for the historical system of truth [. . .]. In any case, if a history of truth does exist, it

can only be this concrete implication and reciprocal encirclement of totalities and absolutes. Which is possible only because we are dealing with ideal and spiritual implications [. . .]. Husserl therefore provisionally refrained from discussing the historical content of the *Erstmaligkeit* only in order first to raise the question of its objectivation, or in other words its being launched into history and its historicity. For a meaning [*sens*] enters history only when it has become an absolute object, that is to say an ideal object which must, paradoxically, have broken all the moorings that tied it to the empirical ground of history. The preconditions for objectivity are therefore the preconditions for historicity itself.[5]

I cite these formulations at some length because their object is obviously very close to the object we will be dealing with in *Being and Event*. In a sense, it is still the same debate. Here, Derrida 'reads' the problematic of the history of truth in the Husserlian text he is translating, but elsewhere – in a series that began with *Of Grammatology* and that still continues in recent texts such as *Spectres of Marx* – he absorbs it into his own critical discourse at the cost of a decisive torsion: the history of truth becomes a fable, a delusion or trap [*leurre*], but that delusion is as essential as a transcendental appearance:

This experience of the effacement of the signifier in the voice is not an illusion like any other – as it is the precondition for the very idea of truth – but we will demonstrate elsewhere how it deludes itself [*se leurre*]. That delusion is the history of truth. . .[6]

The history of the ghost remains a history of phantomalization, and the latter will indeed be a history of truth, a history of the becoming-true of a fable, unless it be the reverse, a fabulation of truth, in any case a history of ghosts, or ghost story [*histoire de fantômes*].[7]

We in fact know that, for Derrida, the temporalization of idealities is always already caught up in the movement of the dissemination of their meaning because their status as writing or, more accurately, as *archi-écriture* has inscribed in their origins the gap of a difference that escapes all appropriation or mastery.

I will immediately contrast these formulations of Derrida's with others from Canguilhem. They are contained in a single but essential text: the 1969 essay 'What is a Scientific Ideology?':

A history of the sciences that describes a science in its history as an articulated succession of *facts of* truth [faits de *vérité*] does not have to concern itself with ideologies [. . .]. A history of the sciences that describes a science in its history as a gradual purification of *norms* of verification cannot but concern itself with scientific ideologies. What Gaston Bachelard described as, respectively, the obsolete history of the sciences and the sanctioned history of the sciences must be both separated out and interlaced. The sanction of truth or objectivity in itself implies a condemnation of the obsolete. But whilst what must later become obsolete does not at first initially expose itself to sanctions, verification itself cannot make truth appear [...]. By insisting on writing the history of mere truth, we write an illusory history. M. Suchodolski is right on this point: the history of mere truth is a contradictory notion.[8]

I have demonstrated elsewhere that this formulation is related, on the one hand, to the famous expression borrowed from Koyré to resolve the long posthumous debate, which actually founds modern epistemology, about the status of Galilean science with respect to hypotheses and proofs: 'Galileo did not always speak the truth, but he was in the true.'[9] Which is to say that he worked by establishing 'the true' within the unfinished process of the verification of a mathematical theory of physico-cosmological invariants or 'laws of nature'. On the other hand, it is also related to the reworking of the analysis of 'episte-mological obstacles' in terms of scientific ideologies, which demonstrates not only that error is characteristic of scientific objectivity but also that it relates to the conflict that constitutes its practical relationship with the imaginary and with life. That is why, as it happens, Canguilhem describes error as the 'mark of thought'. As we can see, Canguilhem adopts the idea of a history of truth only in a hypothetical sense, and does so in order to transform it into its opposite or, rather, to make it contain its opposite and thus give it a constituent meaning.

In order to complete and specify these two formulations we would have to inscribe them within their own genealogy. Where Derrida is concerned, we would have to look in particular at Merleau-Ponty's phenomenological analyses (which he in a sense takes up where – as we are now in a better position to know – Merleau-Ponty left off)[10] of 'rationality in contingency' and the sensible preconditions for the intersubjectivity that 'step by step links us to history in its entirety', on the basis of the last writings of Husserl.[11] Where Canguilhem is concerned, we would have to look at Bachelard's attempts to theorize an 'epistemological history of the sciences' in which the actuality and efficacy of science, and the division it establishes, determine, through recurrence and rectification, the meaning or direction (sens) of progress in the order of expla-nation. In a sense, Derrida is attempting to invert Merleau-Ponty by exploding his representation of meaning, just as Canguilhem attempts to correct Bache-lard and to ground his idea of the normativity of knowledge in a critical anthropology. It is very striking to discover (and it would take only a short while to demonstrate the point) the extent to which both attempts are, whether they admit it or not, informed by a meditation on – or by the after-effect of – Cavaillès' formulations in Sur la Logique et la théorie de la science,[12] whose enigmatic evocation of a dialectic of the concept, as opposed to the activity of consciousness, provides a constant stimulus to the search for a viable philoso-phical formula, irreducible to both historicism and essentialism, for the equating of truth with historicity. We would also have to recall in some detail how these formulations (starting with Cavaillès himself, as he cites Husserl's Crisis) form a counterpoint to the gradual reception of Husserl's work on historicality (Geschichtlichkeit) and the Heideggerian theme of history of Being

(*Seinsgeschichte*), on which any position with respect to the problem of 'the essence of truth' must obviously be based. *Histoire de la vérité* is in a sense the French equivalent of *Geschichtlichkeit* or of the *Seinsgeschichte-Unverborgenheit*, but the profoundly idiomatic use made of it by both Derrida and Canguilhem also reveals an irreducible discrepancy, which probably relates to a very different idea of 'culture'. This takes us to the heart of the great debate, which is both epistemological and metaphysical (or post-metaphysical), characteristic of the French philosophical moment of the second half of the twentieth century.

But we now have to introduce a third character, who was by no means averse to playing the role of spoilsport: Michel Foucault. 'The history of truth' figures in remarkable fashion in several of his texts, most of them later than the ones I have just evoked, rather as though he were attempting to summarize the debate whilst at the same time decisively displacing it. The *histoire de la vérité* becomes a 'political history of truth' (which is not to be confused with a history of political truth, always assuming that there can be such a thing). At first sight, this seems to mean the 'subjective' sense of the *historia rerum gestarum*, or in other words that, when we are dealing with any enunciation of the truth, even in the form of scientific disciplines and their logical norm, we must reconstruct the system of the relations of power and the institutional divisions that govern its discursive being or its discursive materiality. But, ultimately, it also has the 'objective' sense of *res gestae*, or in other words the 'politicity' intrinsic in the 'truth-telling' of the 'discourse of truth' that constitutes the *active* moment in the relations of power, which is the prime issue at stake in the differential between domination and resistance, at least in certain historical societies. More specifically, this reworking of the concept, which means that the history of truth 'should properly be called' a *political* history of truth, must be inscribed within an uninterrupted series.

I will look only at the most obvious points of reference by taking us all back to our not too distant readings. First, *L'Ordre du discours*, where – at the cost of a break with Canguilhem's epistemology that still pays tribute to it – we find the final, rationalist and even *aufklärerisch* version of Foucault's Nietzscheanism: 'It is as though, from the great Platonist divide onwards, the will to truth had its own history, and it is not the history of constrictive truths ...'[13] Next, *La Volonté de savoir*, where the question of the history of truth intersects with that of politics and that of modes of subjectivation:

> Western man has become a confessing animal [...:] confession frees, but power reduces one to silence; truth does not belong to the order of power, but shares an original affinity with freedom: traditional themes in philosophy which a 'political history of truth' would have to overturn by showing that truth is not by nature free – nor error servile – but that its production is thoroughly imbued with relations of power.[14]

And finally *L'Usage des plaisirs*, together with a series of texts – now readily accessible – contemporary with the turn executed by Foucault in his projected history of sexuality, in which he establishes an equivalence between the notion of the history of truth and the history of thought, which are indissociable from certain truth games (reluctantly, I will not comment here on that expression's Wittgensteinian connotations):

> What I have tried to maintain for many years is the effort to isolate some of the elements that might be useful for a history of truth. Not a history that would be concerned with what might be true in the fields of learning, but an analysis of the 'games of truth', the games of truth and error through which being is historically constituted as experience, that is, as something that can and must be thought.[15]

Foucault thus brings about a total inversion of the entire problematic of the 'principle', no matter whether it is thought logically, in terms of criteria, or transcendentally, in terms of conditions of possibility, and also of any philosophical investigation into the realization or non-realization of the principle in history or, conversely, into the historicity or historiality of the principle's constitution (including its antinomic constitution or impossible constitution). He replaces it with a problematic of *necessary truth-effects* and of the recognition of discourse as a discourse of truth, no matter what the contingency of its causes. He reinscribes the question of 'true thinking' in a pragmatics of 'true speaking', but that pragmatics is a genealogy of relations of power, and a construct and critique of history. Make no mistake about it: at the heart of this history, which is 'our' history, it is not a mere logic of the instrumentation of the will to truth and true speaking that is being deployed by figures of power and the norm, but an *agôn* that makes it an issue or the political issue *par excellence* – as we can see from, among other things, Foucault's final research into the question of *parrhèsia*.

Let me make two comments. First, the position gradually elaborated by Foucault represents, as we know or as we can see quite clearly, precisely what Badiou calls a *sophistics* in which the subordination of the question of truth, not to the question of meaning (as with the phenomenologists) but to that of expression and its language games, results in a prioritization of effect and efficacy: not the effects and efficacy of *the* or *a* truth, but truth as effect, i.e. as phenomenon, and as efficacy, or in other words as a power-differential induced by knowledge (including self-knowledge). Foucault's position is still comparable with that not only of Nietzsche, Wittgenstein or Heidegger, but also of Pascal. I find proof of this in the echo that we hear in passing of certain formulations in the *Provinciales* (XII) about relations between truth and power, and especially in the way that we find the same short-circuiting of the question of truth and the question of the *statist* (in the broad sense of the term) political institution. We might metonymically describe as a 'Church' any order of discourse in which the question of truth is posed as a question that brings into play the being of the subject. Foucault may well be a heretical Pascalian, or an anti-Pascal Pascalian, but he remains a Pascalian.

Second, and to go back for one last time to questions about words and the destiny of words, just where do Derrida, Canguilhem or Foucault find the simple and paradoxical expression *history of truth* – which designates both the point where their preoccupations converge (and we can clearly see that what is at stake is nothing less than the status of philosophy and its relationship with knowledge) and the heretical point that crystallizes all their differends, their dispersal to opposite points of the political compass – where do they find it, if not in Pascal? Being a philologist and having become a Talmudist, I want to follow the chain of utterances and texts. *Who*, before the Derrida/Merleau-Ponty differend of the year 1960, before questions about the historicity proper to science circulated between Bachelard, Canguilhem and Koyré in the late 1950s and early 1960s (and they were already being echoed, in 1961, by an aston-ishing 'review' published by Michel Foucault in *La Nouvelle Revue Française*),[16] who could have used, or even coined, this expression – along with all the problems that it raises – in *French*? For the moment, I can find no one but Pascal, and specifically this one utterance. We have to admit that it is tempting to assume that Pascal is the forgotten cause of the configuration taken, so long after the event, by the French philosophical debate, or, to adopt a different representation, that he signals a *latency period* that is coextensive with the whole of modernity, and that lasts until the metaphysical question on which it feeds can finally be named.

You can now see why I was so struck by Badiou's use of Pascal's formula, even though he does not resolve all its enigmas, at a central point in *Being and Event* and in connection with an author who is regularly invoked (together with, from this point onwards, Saint Paul and a few others) as the archetypical 'militant of truth', as the exemplary representative of this 'intervention' or 'decision about the undecidable' without which truth, in the strict sense of the word, does not exist. (Only knowledge exists, and knowledge has no effect upon the constitution of the subject.) Once it became clear that this is no mere coincidence, and that it indeed provides a way of characterizing both Badiou's solution to the difficulties involved in the contemporary encounter between metaphysics, logic or epistemology, and politics or history, and also his inscription of this solution in a tradition to which he is, as he himself puts it, trying to 'give modern forms', then I had to take it completely seriously and even make it the main theme of this chapter.

My hypothesis will therefore be as follows: Badiou is trying, or at least has tried, to develop a conception of the history of truth (or more specifically, to construct a concept of truth which is at the same time, and in an original manner, the concept of its history) so as to occupy, within the configuration I have outlined, a position *other* than those we can identify thanks to the names Derrida, Canguilhem and Foucault. In doing so he is attempting to prove the hitherto unsuspected existence of that position. This would allow him to turn a triangle into a quadrilateral, weaving together the questions of the relationship between truth and meaning, between the being of discourse and its effects, between the continuity and discontinuity of knowledge, between the univocity and the equivocity of the true, in a way that relates neither to the idea of a transcendental appearance, nor to the idea of an intellectual dialectic, nor to the idea of self-knowledge, and which would thus oblige us to rework our understanding of this philosophical conjuncture, and to recognize that it is not complete. It would no doubt be possible to take these remarks as the starting point for a formal discussion of the relative symmetries and distances between the protagonists, as with any system of oppositions, but I would prefer, in a necessarily schematic way, to concentrate upon Badiou's project and to try to identify at least some of the questions it raises (for me).

I will do so in two stages: first, I will attempt to demonstrate, by recalling some well-known texts, that Badiou's 'meta-mathematics' (which is my term for the 'matheme of the indiscernible' that Badiou extracts from set theory) in itself constitutes an intrinsic way of historicizing the relationship between truth and its conditions; second, by hijacking the Sartrean expression 'the legend of truth' [*légende de la vérité*], I will attempt to demonstrate how the concepts of truth and universality are articulated, or how the doctrine of the pure multiple or 'the multiple without "one"', which implies that truths are radically singular (and which, strictly speaking, makes the common noun 'truth' meaningless), is complemented after the event by a doctrine of subjective universality which forces us to conclude that the multiple is in its turn, if not subsumed, at least correlated with a qualitative unity that is not numerical or no longer numerical, and which becomes immanent within it.

The point of articulation between these two movements, or the point where what is in excess of the order of knowledge is converted into a principle of fidelity, is of course a radical conception of 'choice' or decision-making, not within the order of action or of pure practice (as appears to be the case with a German philosophical tradition going from Kant to Fichte, and from Fichte to Carl Schmitt or even Heidegger), but within the order of thought (as is the case for certain French philosophers, assuming that the adjective has a univocal meaning: Pascal, of course, but also Descartes – the Descartes of the 'creation of eternal truths' – Mallarmé, and perhaps a certain Sartre). The particular difficulty raised by this articulation (which it is tempting to liken, in a neo-Platonic context, to a conversion followed by a procession [*une conversion suivé d'une procession*]) is whether or not, and how, the 'genericity' that constitutes the hallmark of 'truth procedures' continues to exist on both sides of the divide. It is possible that this genericity, which concerns subjective universality (or 'universalism', as Badiou finally puts it in more political terms, or the 'Universal church' or, if I may be so bold as to say so, 'Catholicity', as Pascal and Saint Paul would have it), is in reality the object of a second postulate or a peremptory declaration. In any case, it has to do with the question of *the name*, and the use of *names*. We should therefore ask ourselves what retroactive effect its transformation into the foundations of universalism has upon the construction of the historicity of truths, or the way we understand it. I am not, however, able to discuss that question fully and will therefore have to be content with a few hypotheses about it.

II BADIOU'S META-MATHEMATICS

To take the first point. I have spoken of meta-mathematics, but I am not going to spend too long justifying that indicative term. My point is that Badiou is no doubt the first person in France since Cavaillès to have taken seriously not only the need to discuss the question of truth in terms of an essential relationship with mathematics, which is immanent in the construction of axioms, but also the question of whether or not that relationship can, whilst still being articulated with the question of principles of demonstrative procedures, be extricated from all subordination to the logical concept of a rule and from syntactico-semantic correspondence.[17] Cavaillès restricted himself – or was restricted by his early death – to juxtaposing a critique of various philosophies of axiomatics and their intra-scientific effects, with an epistemological history of the emergence of set theory, and a philosophical aporia relating to the idea of a dialectic without a consciousness. Badiou is attempting *to use meta-mathematical means* – that is, mathematics applied to mathematics itself – *actually to construct a definition, theory or concept of truth*. To be more accurate, he is attempting to demonstrate that that concept is 'already there', even though it has not been there for long, and that we have only to recognize it or give it its name: 'an indiscernible generic extension of a situation'.

On this ground, he immediately encounters not a rival, but a predecessor with whom he is on polemical terms: not simply the logical empiricist notion of 'verifiability' in general but, much more specifically, Tarski's schema of the 'concept of truth in formalized languages'. Remember that Tarski's schema has nothing to do with the question of verification criteria, that it merely, if we can put it this way, postulates that such criteria do exist, or in other words that they are implemented practically, and that they can be subsumed with the general – and supposedly intuitive – notion of a 'correspondence' between an utterance and a state of things or a situation. That, then, is not his problem, but his starting point. His object is to give a mathematical definition of correspondence and to demonstrate that, on certain conditions or within certain limits, mathematical proof can be 'founded' as a truth procedure. What Tarski is trying to mathematicize – in the sense of equating it with a mathematical construct (even and especially if it is a matter of the mathematicization of logic) – is not the criterion of truth, but the very concept of truth. Hence his polemic against philosophers. Its weak point is the denunciation, in banal neo-positivist style, of the obscurities and absurdities of their language, but its strong point is the assertion that their essentialist ambition no longer has any object.[18] I think that Badiou wanted to occupy this ground and completely reverse the situation by taking as his ally and supporter the most recent of the great theorems to have emerged from research into 'the limitation of formalisms', namely Cohen's theorem.[19] I recall (and not simply to evoke a youthful comradeship) that Badiou began by taking a lively interest in the 'theory of models' and in the various uses – 'scientific' or 'ideological', as we used to say at the time – that could be made of the concept of a model, to which he devoted a little book in 1969 (it originated in the *Cours de philosophie pour scientifiques* of 1967–68).[20]

It seems to me that Badiou's position is as follows: first, paradoxically, Tarski's schema makes only an *instrumental* and weak use, rather than an intrinsic use, of set theory, which is in keeping with his watering down of ontology into logical semantics, whereas it is possible to make an *intrinsic* and strong use of it.

Second, Tarski's schema relies, as he himself makes perfectly clear, upon the reduction of the concept of truth to a supposedly more general, and therefore more basic, concept: that of satisfying a propositional function within a determinate domain (set) of objects. The problem of truth is therefore transformed (1) into the problem of the conditions under which the properties of the axioms of a formal system can be satisfied by any choice of constants or by any interpretation within a domain of objects or what, like Badiou, we might term a situation, and in which being 'always true' extends to the whole class of expressions constructed on the basis of those axioms by applying rules of proof (theorems), and (2) into the problem of the limits of the validity of this correspondence or modelling. Badiou remarks that the idea of 'satisfaction' is merely a concept from set theory, and therefore requires it not to serve as an instrument for moving from the satisfaction of propositional functions to the truth of theories, but to *define* what constitutes a principle or condition of possibility for the 'well-founded' use of the name 'truth', as applied to those constructs.

Third, and finally, Tarksi's schema is inscribed within a general account of theorems of limitation or finitude, and can be interpreted – as Tarski himself interprets it – as meaning that there are both extrinsic and intrinsic limitations to the very notion of truth. Extrinsic limitations, because the proposed schema is meaningful only when applied to formalized languages, or even to a certain class of formalized languages. This leaves wide open the question of ordinary language, which constantly comes back to haunt its philosophical applications, as we can see for example in Davidson (can 'ordinary' language in theory be formalized? Or is it *de la langue* which, by its very essence, resists all formalization and therefore invalidates the claim of logical semantics to be dealing with the question of truth in general?) Intrinsic limitations, because the main result of Tarski's schema is a rigorous demonstration that there is, even though it is empirically non-assignable, an irreducible gap between syntactic provability and semantic verification, or, if we wish, between the mathematizable versions of concept and intuition.

Badiou's response consists, first, in demonstrating that the problem of extrinsic limits is meaningless, given that the objective of a theory or definition of truth is not to determine the frontiers of the mathematical or the mathematizable, and to ignore the non-mathematical, but to construct or exhibit in the mode of mathematical certainty the paradoxical 'being' of truths. This brings us close to the philosophical interpretation of their concept, provided only that those truths are derived from a 'knowledge' in accordance with a proof procedure or, more generally, a process of rational enquiry that gives an effective meaning to the notion of an encyclopaedia, or in other words a classification of the properties of objects belonging to a certain infinite domain. Second, the problem of intrinsic limits has precisely the opposite meaning of that assigned it, once we accept Cohen's findings and establish a continuity between them and the series of *decisional acts* or decisions made in *a situation of undecidability* that makes classical set theory possible: from 'the choice of the axiom of choice' to Cohen's 'forcing', which, if I have understood it correctly, means that, being a 'generic part' of a situation, the nameable indiscernible *also* has all the properties of the situation under consideration, albeit it in an undecidable manner and in defiance of all procedures for the application of a law (cf. *EE* 361ff.). At this point, the idea of limitation turns into its opposite: it does not mean finitude in the sense of a *non plus ultra* injunction or a frontier between the knowable and the unknowable, but it does mean that an absolute does indeed lie at the heart of any knowledge that is retroactively constituted as a site of truth, as a domain for the production of a truth that is both in excess of and excessive with respect to that knowledge (a truth in the sense that it neither contains nor prescribes, but is still the truth *of that situation* or, more accurately, *for* that situation, to which it gives generic expression). This means that every knowledge contains an absolute to the extent that infinity does exist and that the infinite is indissociable from the indiscernible and the aleatory, defined in the radical, ontological sense of the term. We have here in a sense a repetition, an extension, of Cantor's conversion of the famous 'paradoxes of infinity', which embarrassed classical philosophers and seemed to defy reason, into a *definition* of infinite sets – which are the real objects of set theory – and into the principle behind their systematic ordering (the 'aleph' series).

Badiou also says that this form of the absolute, which he calls the 'wandering [*errance*] of excess', and which is synonymous with the fact that the event is necessary to being, not in the sense that it is reducible to being, but insofar as the event exceeds being in determinate or 'situational' fashion, introduces the agency of the subject into knowledges, or perhaps obliges us to give the name 'subject' to the operator of the forcing that reduces truth (*vérité*) to veridicity, or event to knowledge.[21] Such a subject must obviously be totally impersonal, and, *a fortiori*, one that is quite foreign to the question of consciousness, and therefore to the whole empirico-transcendental doublet, as well as the conscious/unconscious alternative. And yet this subject does possess certain qualities. Its generic name is, if you like, itself indissociable from certain 'qualities' that describe the modalities of its operation. Here we begin to approach the question of the effects of nomination in Badiou's philosophical discourse, and that is a difficult question because it is at once totally disqualified and practically unavoidable. Its prime quality, and perhaps the only one that counts, is 'fidelity' – fidelity to the event constituted by the emergence of an indiscernible which is itself in excess of knowledges that faithfully follow investigative or cognitive procedures. 'Fidelity' could also be called a link, or a link without a cause, a random link instituted by a dependency that has no conditions of dependency. The subject is not dependent upon conditions, or is another name for the unconditional character of truth or, to be more accurate, of every truth, of every truth-event. It is probable that this represents another way of thinking the 'non-being' of decision-making or, rather, as Badiou puts it, of the intervention. It would be worth exploring the link with a certain philosophical tradition. I am thinking in particular of the Cartesian God who 'creates eternal truths': Badiou's subject is, perhaps, such a God, but a God both multiplied to an infinity that is itself recreated by random situations, and reduced to anonymity. I will not venture so far as to invoke here the interpretation of Mallarmé's throw of the dice, as that is beyond my competence.

Before reaching any conclusions about this first point, I would like to make two comments. The first is telegraphic. I have described Badiou as the anti-Tarski. This means that his construct has a potentially devastating power that could destroy the defences of so-called analytic philosophy, to the extent that it can still recognize itself in Tarski's semantics: it is difficult to see how it could put up any resistance, if it took the trouble to look at it carefully. Following Tarski's own suggestions, we have become accustomed to thinking that there is an Aristotelian basis to semantics, to the extent that the 'T schema' is grounded in the inversion of the liar's paradox and in a certain interpretation of the principle of non-contradiction. This may seem quite in keeping with the fact that, for his part, Badiou constantly claims to be a Platonist, even if it means effecting a subversion or inner reversal in which the Multiple replaces the One. For my own part, I am tempted, rather, to relate Tarski's 'realism' and the conditions of its generalized reception to an old Thomist tradition in that the distinction between object-language and metalanguage reintroduces an objective transcendental that divides the agencies of truth between an adequation of the intellect to things, or demonstrable truths, and a more basic adequation of things to the intellect, or a system of rules of correspondence or semantic limitation itself.[22] This means that Tarski's schema has profoundly hierarchical implications. And this highlights the powerful *egalitarianism* of Badiou's conception of multiple truths, which are themselves related to an indefinite number of infinite multiplicities that are at once similar in terms of their emergence procedure, and absolutely independent of one another. Although I can do no more than raise the question here, this would add further interest to a closer comparison, which Badiou has not to my knowledge undertaken (even in his 1994 lecture on the *Tractatus*),[23] with other radically egalitarian semantics and quasi-ontologies, such as those of Frege and Wittgenstein, which do not in my view imply even the least degree of ontological reduplication or any transcendental guarantee, even though they may be either antinomic or unsatisfactory.

My second comment is this: if Tarski is not so much an Aristotelian as a neo-Aristotelian, or in other words a Thomist, is Badiou a Platonist and if so, in what sense? I do not think there is anything simple about this question, and not only because of the paradox inherent in replacing Plato's Idea with the intervention of a 'multiple with no "one"'. As has already been said, it is not certain that Plato himself was a 'Platonist' in the sense of giving the One a unilateral primacy over the Multiple, as Aristotle constantly accused him of doing. I am tempted, rather, to see Badiou as a neo-Platonist for whom the 'Ultra-One' of the event lies beyond knowledge and therefore essence, or 'in the vicinity of nothingness', in the sense that Badiou describes the impersonal subject, or the operator of the forcing of truth in the situations whose truth they represent, as lying 'on the edge of the void'. But that is still too crude a formulation, and I prefer to leave the question in suspense at the point where the two themes – or perhaps they are one and the same – of the principle and historicity intersect, as the philosophical interpretation of the metamathematical clearly depends upon them.

Badiou is evidently not one of those who disparage principles. To be more accurate, he is not one of those who disparage the anhypothetical. On the contrary, it seems that his post-Platonist project consists in reinterpreting the idea of the anhypothetical in the strict sense of an absence of conditions or, more specifically, as the dissolution of the conditional link with its set of conditions and as a retroactive effect of this dissolution on that link. In other words, not only does Badiou quite naturally not want the anhypothetical itself to be dependent upon conditions; he does not want it to be the *condition for conditions*. He does not want, we might say, conditions to derive, emanate or proceed from it in any causal sense. The anhypothetical is truth for conditions insofar as it is absent from the efficacy or the power to determine the conditions that it names. Perhaps it is this that makes one think of neo-Platonism.[24] The absolute causes nothing: it is neither caused nor causal. This also means – and this is the precondition for an abolition of hierarchical schemata – that the anhypothetical is nowhere, neither above nor below. It is not a Foundation or base. It is not an intelligible Sun. Is it a Good? Let us wait and see. This means, finally, that the absolute is an example of a radically detotalized totalization. That is at least one way of understanding the 'generic' property of the indiscernible: it contains within it, without any control, all the predicates of the determinate and discernible elements of the situation or, if we like, all that can be named within a given infinite universe.

But are these characteristics of the anhypothetical or the absolute really anything other than Badiou's way of thinking – at this level – the history of truth? I suggest that they are not. In the chapter (meditation 35) of *Being and Event* devoted to the 'theory of the subject', Badiou once more takes up Pascal's question and advances a new formulation: 'the hazardous historicity of truth' (*EE* 445). What does this historicity consist in? Or, to be more specific, in what sense does it merit the name *historicity*, which takes us back to the heretical point in contemporary philosophy to which I made allusion at the beginning, and which therefore cannot be used in an absolutely arbitrary fashion? I suggest that this historicity lies in the juxtaposition of the following moments, which are like so many stages in an abstract or typical narration, and which are therefore subtly out of step with the 'dialectical' prototype of Plato's cave but also, and whether we like it or not, with the movement of a 'negation of a negation' (the difference being that the representations of a journey, movement, transition, totalization, and so on, have to be radically evacuated). First, the deployment, within a given situation, of 'generic procedures', and therefore the constitution of the infinite language of that situation and the knowledge specific to it. Second, an event constituting a truth that 'makes a hole in knowledge', and whose concept can be constructed on the edge of ontology, as the existence of a generic indiscernible. Third, the 'subjective' forcing of the truth from the event within that very situation, which does not constitute a reorganization of the state of that knowledge, and which therefore leaves it unchanged in a sense, but which establishes after the event the veridicity of its procedures, whilst at the same time manifesting its infinity, and the infinite openness of their field of application. Historicity is basically the same thing as the concept of a principle that is neither conditioned nor conditioning; it is the heterogeneous association of a determinate knowledge and a name for the truth, which demonstrates precisely the infinite or radical incompletion of that knowledge.

This historicity is, as we can see, intrinsic. It is not something that *happens to* truth, and nor is it something that truth *generates*; if truth were of the order of being, it would, rather, be what true 'is'. Let us say that it connotes truth's negative, or subtractive, relationship with being: its *pros ti*.

III THE LEGEND OF TRUTH

I will now outline, in no more than allusive terms, what I announced as a second movement or a reflexive presentation – I hope it is not too inaccurate, though I can see its limitations – of what I see as the meaning of Badiou's propositions about the relationship between the question of truth and that of universality. I have borrowed the expression 'the legend of truth' from a text, much of which has been lost, by the young Sartre because I wanted a change of terminology, and also to draw attention to something new: *something does happen to truth* now. (Even if, in its total impersonality, we can assume that the truth remains indifferent to this development, the same is presumably not the case for its subject; or perhaps we have to assume that the subject is also present in the truth–subject doublet, or must be distinguished by name if the relationship with truth is not to be one of indifference. We are, after all, talking about militancy, and the idea of an indifferent militancy really would be a difficult paradox to sustain.) What happens to truth is that it comes to be a support for a foundation, or perhaps we should say that what happens to multiple truths is that they are the support, the non-existent and purely subjective basis for a multiplicity of foundations. And that is not exactly a minor adventure.

If we have to choose our references or textual supports here, I think we should refer not to the texts collected and collated first in *Conditions*, and then more recently in the *Court Traité* or the *Abridged Metapolitics*, but to *Being and Event*, together with *Saint Paul*, the little book *Ethics* and, in some respects, the *Deleuze* too. What I have to say consists of questions rather than assertions. These questions do not, ultimately, relate to the problem of the univocity of the universal. To the great scandal of many Deleuzians – which may or may not be justified – Badiou sees fit to attribute to Deleuze a 'metaphysics of the One', and contends that the thought of differences is not its opposite, but on the contrary its realization, in the form of a schema for the infinite differentiation of intelligibles. He even sees fit to describe the *univocity of Being* as a point of agreement or disagreement around which their respective 'Platonisms' cluster:

the Platonism of differential ideas and the virtual, and the Platonism of the Multiple and the possible. I conclude that, strictly speaking, the category of univocity is not, for Badiou, applicable to the universal but to being, and that it is thanks only to the meanders of an ill-advised polemic that he appears (because he is reacting to the formula 'an equivocity of the universal') to be defending completely the opposite thesis. For Badiou, the universal is basically a category of subjectivity that escapes ontology, whereas the idea of univocity is, it seems to me, basically 'ontological'. If there is a problem here, it lies, rather, in the powerful dualism of Badiou's philosophy. In negative terms, we can, however, say that the universal or universals are necessarily *non-equivocal*, which is another way of saying that they essentially derive from a 'fidelity' to the unique event (but not the one event) that founds them.

If they have nothing to do with univocity, what are my questions about? Essentially, at this stage in my work, two points: first, the meaning acquired by the notion of 'fidelity' in the light of a transition from the question of truth to that of the universal, or what I call 'legend'; and, second, the strange reduplication that makes the true/false opposition connote the universal itself – we have a 'true universal' and a 'false universal', or if we prefer to use the terminology of the book on *Ethics*, we have Good and Simulacrum (*du Bien et du Simulacre*).

To conclude, let us examine each of these points. The question of fidelity becomes clearer, which is to say that its difficulty becomes more apparent, if we suggest that the difference between a 'hazardous historicity of truth' and the legend of truth, or the adventure of its transformation into a universal or its 'universalization', is a new movement of extension – a movement that I am tempted to characterize, following Canguilhem, as a presumptuous transcendence of the relationship between knowledge and truth that provided our starting point. This movement is one of extrapolation, because we have to take into consideration the fact that the subjective movement which is inseparable from the truth, since it results from the fact that truth exists only as the choice and forcing of the indiscernible, in fact begins before the truth and takes us beyond it, and that between this 'before' and this 'beyond', we have, if not a dialectic, perhaps a negative correspondence, which it is tempting to call a correspondence 'on the edge of the void', to use an expression dear to Badiou's heart. To be very schematic, this means that being, or the being of the existent, is essentially the 'void', or in other words, and contrary to the teachings of the metaphysical tradition, that the notions of being and property are originally incompatible. Being consists of nothing other, to begin with, than belonging or membership (or indeed, originally, nothing other than the degree zero or neutral figure of belonging: non-belonging). All properties are derivatives. Similarly, at the opposite extreme, universalism as such is, for Badiou, anti-communitarianism, or in other words an in-common without a community or a membership without membership that creates no property links, no ontological or anthropological difference, but only fidelity to an Event. It is perhaps no accident that we find here formulae similar to certain of Derrida's negative expressions, which are themselves derived from Blanchot.[25] That is why, even though it means displacing the notion's point of application, Badiou thought he could recognize himself in Saint Paul — the theologian of the Christian kenosis, and the very inventor of that category.

The fact remains that the transference of the operator of fidelity from one side of the event to the other, from the register of retroactive intervention into the field of knowledge to the register of militant anticipation within the field of history, presupposes at least — though this 'at least' is very likely to become an 'at most' — the presence of *name*, or a change in the function of nomination. In one of the articles in the 'Dictionary' appended to *Being and Event*, Badiou writes of *unicity*: 'The empty set is unique [. . .] any unique multiple can be given a proper name, such as Allah, Yahweh, Ø or Omega.' I am therefore tempted, with Stanislas Breton's fine article on the 'violence of tautological propositions' in mind,[26] to add that tautology is the privileged mode of the enunciation of any name specific to unicity: the empty set is empty, God is God, the Law is the Law (or the General Will is the general will, and not particular wills, as Rousseau might have said, and Badiou does evoke Rousseau in connection with the idea of a generic part), the Revolution is the Revolution, the Worker is the Worker, and so on.

My question is therefore: at what moment, to what extent, and in accordance with what subjective modality, does generic fidelity, which has become the operator that founds the universal (or that constitutes a multiplicity-to-come that is not virtual but situationally possible, as an action — being militant — rather than an act, and which *annuls differences*, or which regards them as indifferent), come to be dependent on a proper name?

A second and final question: what is the meaning of the return of the true/false opposition in the theorization of the universal, *after* the concept of truth has been disintricated from that of veridicity (which is, apparently, the only thing to stand in a relationship of opposition to the false or the *pseudos*)? And what relationship exists between this return — if it does occur — and the introduction of the category of the Good into the critical discussion of the problem of ethics, or in other words into the defence of an ethics of truths against an ethics of the Other or of Justice? This is not a simple question, and we must be wary of simplifying it. It arises because Badiou is trying here to trace a double line of demarcation on two edges, and using two quite different evaluative criteria.

On the one hand, we have a demarcation between the true or veritable universal, typified by Christian or Communist militancy (or what Badiou and Balmès once called the insistence of 'communist invariants'),[27] and the false universal typified by the laws of exchange and the market, the capitalist universal, or money.[28] One might think that this a pure *petitio principi*: where is the criterion that allows us to make this distinction? But Badiou's allusions to the problem allow us to suggest that, in his view, we are dealing with what logicians would call an analytic proposition: the universal of the market is false because — or at least this would appear to be what experience teaches us — its condition of existence is not the elimination of communitarian differences but, on the contrary, their multiplication and their systematic exploitation. Fair enough.

On the other hand, we have a more subtle demarcation between two forms of veritable universalism, and it appears when Badiou explains that Saint Paul's fidelity to Christ's revelation is indiscernible from fidelity to an evental truth in the order of knowledge, even though we are dealing, on the one hand, with – and I quote – a 'fable' or 'fiction' in which *we* can no longer believe (who is this 'we'? presumably the 'we' of atheists, assuming that the term does not connote a particularity), and, on the other hand, with an 'effective truth' related to investigative procedures, and not a revelation.[29] It seems, then, that this difference is what had to be *neutralized* in some way in order to bring out the generic characteristics of the subjective universalization of a singularity, of the relationship between fidelity and event, as opposed to the existing opposition between the true universal and the false universal. The universal must also be based on the false, or at least the non-true or fiction, if we are to be able to understand the radical difference between it and its simulacrum or even its extreme simulacrum, that being – if I may be so bold as to say so – the 'forcing' of difference as the name of truth. I suspect or at least I wonder whether we do not have here one of the profound reasons which, conjunctural requisitions and polemics aside, lead Badiou to go one step further in his fidelity to Platonism, by reintroducing the mutual convertibility of the True and the Good into the principle of his ethics.

2

PHILOSOPHY WITHOUT CONDITIONS*

Jean-Luc Nancy

What follows is the combination of two sets of remarks. The first is addressed to Alain Badiou – an address I was supposed to deliver at a colloquium devoted to his work, but which circumstances prevented me from attending. The other is a response to a question raised by another accidental occasion, that of the university curriculum: what are we to say about metaphysics today? For me, the link between these two occasions for discourse is perfectly straightforward: when I was asked to talk about Badiou, or talk to him, I immediately said to myself: 'philosophy without conditions'. These words came to me spontaneously, to signal something which is not so much an opposition as a heterology. Although Alain Badiou and I are close to one another on more than one point, and although we could have a philosophical exchange on more than one point, we inhabit utterly different sites of thought. And what is more, this very fact, which is to say, the possibility of sharing this common space in which such heterotopias are possible, in which they are even necessary (the possibility, in other words, of sharing the same philosophical space in the marked disparity of its sites) – this very fact is the source of the resistance or at least the reservation which Badiou's localization, if I may put it that way, elicits from me. For this common space is necessarily given as a philosophical space in which, as a matter of principle, more than one definition of philosophy is allowed. The definition of philosophy must allow for its own multiplication. For me, this necessary allowance defines philosophical possibility in general, and this possibility is articulated, on the one hand, with regard to its own condition, in a specific historical situation – that of the West – while on the other hand, with regard to its most general structure, it is articulated in a quest for the unconditioned. There is a historical condition that defines an undefinable quest for the unconditioned. This double character constitutes what is known as metaphysics, considered in its umbilical link to what is known as technics [*la technique*]. This is the theme I would briefly like to consider here.

Through his watchword *conditions*, which, taken in its absolute sense and as index of a concept, he only ever writes in the plural (as in the title of an

---

* This chapter, translated by Ray Brassier, was first published as 'Philosophie sans conditions', in *Alain Badiou: Penser le multiple*, ed. Charles Ramond (Paris: L'Harmattan, 2002), pp. 65–79.

important work from 1992), Alain Badiou submits philosophy to the prescription of certain conditions. Science, politics, art and love form the four
'truth procedures' which together make up four 'conditions', themselves in a
historically variable relation to the philosophy which they prescribe and condition; the function of the latter consists in 'exhibiting' each of these conditions
insofar as it constitutes a 'truth procedure'.[1]

Each of these procedures is prescriptive because a truth procedure or process
is played out in each of them in a specific way, and each of them is conditioning
because the business of philosophy always consists in drawing out this or that
species of truth. Thus, what could be called the operation of 'verification', in the
precise sense provided by the present context (that of making or bringing forth
a truth, rather than guaranteeing a conformity), sees the respective emphasis of
its conditions shift according to the variable inflections of the course of history.
In spite of this, however, philosophy is not itself historical. It is rather an
invariant for the varied movements that affect the conditions, both among
themselves and in relation to philosophy. Or at least it has been this invariant
since it has existed as philosophy, obviously. Which, for Badiou, basically
means: since Plato. Philosophy as posited 'from' itself, and only from itself: as
we shall see, this is the point at which my resistance begins. Nevertheless,
Badiou is not the only one to posit philosophy thus, and no doubt more or less
all of philosophy has proceeded in this way with regard to itself. This does not
make it any less problematic, and perhaps Badiou's vigorous and very determined intervention among us allows the question to be raised with greater
urgency than ever before: what shall philosophy say about its own provenance?

Badiou's thesis concerning conditions has considerable advantages, in particular
that of preventing philosophy from being understood or understanding itself as
the subsumption of the diversity of experiences beneath a truth which would
determine a single ultimate stake for them. In this regard, Badiou takes up in a
very decisive way what could be called the youngest tradition of philosophy: that
of a deconstruction (I use this word in a provisional way) of its own enthronement
as 'queen of the sciences', a deconstruction involving nothing less than a fundamental re-evaluation of the nature and stakes of the previously mentioned
'sciences' as well as of the supposed sovereignty of a discourse of 'truth'.

According to Badiou, philosophy carries out its veritative function by laying
out around the void, or 'against the backdrop of the void', a certain set of
'compossible truths' (C 80) – which, in their very compossibility, remain
incommensurable among themselves. The plurality of truths and the void of
their communal 'verification' belongs, factually, to the necessity of a thought
that has passed through the event called 'the death of God', and thus through
Nietzsche, and through the process whereby being has been released from a
certain forgetting, or from a forgetting of its withdrawal (or, more precisely, a
forgetting of its forgetting, as Heidegger also puts it), a forgetting henceforth
characterized as the 'metaphysics of presence' (an expression that best summarizes, no doubt, the case conducted by this young tradition against the
notion of a truth that might be non-empty, and thus full and finalizing,
whether this truth be of the sciences, history, or man). A radical incommen-

surability then opens up, or at least it comes to light, having doubtless been in effect ever since the philosophical beginning itself: an incommensurability opened simultaneously within the void (this is its 'emptiness'), within the essence of being (this is its infinite singularity or finitude), as well as between experiences, languages, subjects – and also between the subject and his or her self – and finally between beings in general (as the correlative distension of 'nature', 'technology' and 'history'). Hence an incommensurability opened up within philosophy itself, which we might call, mixing lexical registers, 'a metaphysics in internal subtraction'.

By putting things in this way I recognize that I am forcing Badiou, against his will, into a tradition which he does not acknowledge as such, indeed one which he seeks to challenge and keep at a distance, albeit while marking the complex nature of his relation to that tradition – a relation which the semi-citational, semi-parodic character of the title *Being and Event* openly and explicitly acknowledges. (A title which is in fact citational twice over, with respect to Heidegger and to Sartre: it would be an interesting exercise to compare the three formulations, to which I would willingly add a fourth: *Être étant* [*To Be Being*, or *Being Being*] or the indistinction of being and existence, which is one aspect of my own position here.)

Be that as it may, let me immediately acknowledge that while Badiou takes his point of departure from Heidegger (and thanks to this point of departure) he has nevertheless gone to considerable lengths to turn his back on him, if only so as to avoid, at least, the traps inherent in the possible substantialization or (and) personalization of 'being' (or at the very least, inherent in its instantiation and identification). Because of this, Badiou's relation to 'fundamental ontology' is not dissimilar to that developed by Levinas, albeit in a diametrically opposed fashion (a void opening up for the one, the face opening up for the other).

I can only be in agreement with every ontology that no longer seeks to be the depository [*dépositaire*] of being, but that instead aims to depose or deposition being. Such ontologies seem to me to have their primary *impetus* not in Being but in 'being' understood by Heidegger as a verb, i.e. as a transitive verb, deposing or depositioning itself through its act (thereby differing from itself, in accordance with the vein developed by Derrida in this same young tradition of ours). And I can only admire the force with which Badiou carries out what could be called his own difference (both with and without an *a*) or his counting-out [*décompte*] of being. Force is, in every regard, his defining characteristic and tone: both in terms of his physique and his metaphysics [*métaphysique*]. And this is more than mere wordplay: this strapping fellow, I maintain, is a body invested by its own metaphysics. We would have to scrutinize the language of this body, the grain of its idiom and its voice, something which I cannot do here, so that I will have to confine myself to citing fragments of sentences wherein some of the fierce, beautiful and truthful accents resonating through this fabric of thought can be heard: 'There is a breach of being, a subtraction from the indifferent ingratitude of the grey-black [. . .] There is a not-allness, both in the self-coincidence which speech exhausts itself in situating and in the ingratitude of the earth' (C 347).

Nevertheless, we have a serious disagreement on one point – and it is the seriousness of this *differend* which motivates me here, taking this word in the sense given to it by Lyotard, our mutual friend, which is to say, the sense in which the differend cannot simply be resolved one day, or overcome; the sense whereby it is its preservation, rather than its liquidation, that maintains the 'not-allness' of *philosophy* itself.

This point is the point of history, or at least it can be situated on the basis of the question of history. And the latter, for Heidegger, cannot be separated from the question of being. Badiou writes:

> The dominant idea [in the Heideggerian tradition] is that metaphysics has reached a point of historical exhaustion, but that what lies beyond this exhaustion has not yet been given to us [. . .]. Philosophy is then caught between the exhaustion of its historical possibility and the non-conceptual arrival of a salutary overturning. Contemporary philosophy combines the deconstruction of its past with the empty expectation of its future. My entire goal is to break with this diagnosis [. . .] Philosophy must break with historicism from within itself (C 58).

I see here the effect of a double misunderstanding.

First of all, the exhaustion of metaphysics is *historical* only insofar as it is the exhaustion of historical possibility as such (or of the meaning of history), in the sense whereby such exhaustion has been acknowledged at least since Nietzsche, but perhaps also, in a more convoluted fashion, since Hegel himself. (In the Heideggerian conception of history, no doubt, this exhaustion is combined with the renewal and, if I may be allowed to put it this way, the recharging of a destinal motif which I too do not accept. But at the very least this combination leaves behind certain traces that cannot be ignored on 'destinality' itself: traces which render the latter discontinuous or at least out of synch with 'History'.)

Historical possibility proper, understood in the sense which philosophy (or metaphysics: the possibility of a metaphysical history and of a metaphysics of history) ended up engendering through the course of its history, is the possibility that a process might carry through to its end the realization of a rationality and a *Grund*. In other words, it is the possibility that the historical process might function like a natural process – this is a point worth noting, in anticipation of what will follow. Metaphysical history is history conceived as *physics*, i.e. as a 'natural history', to take up once more an ancient expression in which 'history' did not yet mean a process, but rather a 'collection'. The truth of this history was that once completed, it would deny itself as history by (re)becoming nature.

What is exhausted in this conception is the notion of *carrying through to an end* [*la menée à terme*]. Whether the end [*le terme*] be called presence, subject, supreme being or total humanity, it is the capacity for having and absorbing a *terminus ad quem* which is exhausted. It is thus, very precisely, the very idea of exhaustion in a final term, or *teleology*, which is exhausted. For it is this exhaustion (fulfilment, maturity) which philosophy, having remodelled the anamnesic movement of Platonic u-topia or ec-topia in conformity with the Christian notion of salvation, had constituted as History. Thus, what has been exhausted is the presence of a terminal present of history, a presence which would no longer be a *praes-entia*, or a being whose mode of being is being-ahead-of-itself, but only a being equal to itself, indifferent in itself.

That exhaustion is exhausted – that natural history is broken and *denatured* – this is what is attested to by the break which philosophy carries out with respect to itself or on itself. This break is a historical rupture with its own history, which Heidegger calls 'the end of philosophy' in order to indicate the depth and gravity of that which, in history, thereby happens to History (and that in virtue of which a 'history of being' or a 'destinality' of its 'sendings' can only be *denatured* at the very least). In this regard, the break with history which Badiou encourages us to carry out (a break with a *historical (meta)physics* of philosophy) is itself merely a continuation of a break to which, I repeat, Hegel himself was no stranger, if it is true (and the point would be worth demonstrating) that Absolute Knowledge knows itself to be genuinely and absolutely inexhaustible, to the point that its knowing is only such through its own interminability. (But this is not to say that what I call 'continuation' reabsorbs Badiou, or Heidegger or others into Hegel, as though into the seed from which they sprang. It is as much on the basis of Badiou, Heidegger or others that this relative continuity can be demonstrated, which is to say, that a new question of history, of the philosophy of history and the history of philosophy, can emerge.)

Consequently (and this is my second point), even if it is, as Badiou puts it, 'without a concept', the expectation of the future is nonetheless, as in the case of Kantian aesthetic judgment, the postulation of a truth (and/or a universal) as a truth that is not given [*donnée*]. Not given, neither as seed nor as final term, truth as such is primarily open and open to itself: it is the structure and substance of an encounter with itself, the awaiting of and/or fidelity toward itself. In this sense, truth is 'empty', to use Badiou's term. Which means, in his terminology, that it is devoid of meaning: or, in my terminology, 'devoid of signification', i.e. devoid of fulfilled meaning, of germinal and terminal meaning. Which it seems to me means for the both of us (and for several others also): devoid of the exhaustion of which I spoke, devoid or rather emptied of 'fullness', of the plethora or saturation of an achievement or a coming to an end, emptied of the plethora and thereby open in itself and on to itself.

This is precisely the point at which it is necessary to dissipate the ambiguity or haziness that envelops the notion of 'deconstruction' in the lines by Badiou quoted above. (He himself is not really responsible for this haziness, which has already been in effect for some time, as so often happens to many notions, and which might in the end necessitate a change of name.) From Heidegger's *Abbau* (perhaps even from Husserl's[2]) to Derrida's 'deconstruction' there is at least a guiding thread [*fil conducteur*], both in the sense of a continuity and in the sense of a conductor of energy, the formula for which could be stated as follows: the exhaustion or evacuation of the fullness of history (of its sense, its reason or its salvation) opens possibilities, requirements and potentialities which are not so much initial (in the sense of a reopening or reinscription of Plato, Paul or Augustine) as anterior to the beginnings themselves, buried beneath them, and in that sense still latent. 'To deconstruct' means to disassemble that which has been erected over the beginnings so as to allow what has been hollowed out beneath them to arrive. Thus, it is at once to undermine (rather than destroy) the edifice of philosophical (or metaphysical) tradition and the historical auto-positioning of that tradition. What has been erected, on the basis of which beginnings, and how did these beginnings come to characterize themselves as such? Or again, and perhaps (as I hope to show) above all, what provenance can we ascribe to these beginnings? In the final analysis (and although neither Heidegger nor Derrida ever explicitly say so), perhaps 'deconstruction' simply means this: from now on, philosophy cannot be absolved from the question of its own historicity. And this applies not only to the sense of its internal his-toricity, but also to that of its external provenance. (This is why it can only be a matter of edges, extremities, ends or bounds of philosophy, obviously without this amounting either to an accomplishment or a cessation.)

Beginnings of philosophy: the word has to be written in the plural, since one cannot designate just one, although neither can one not designate any at all. Philosophy as such did in fact begin, and announced that it had begun: doubtless, it can never announce itself without also announcing that it has begun (Plato, Descartes, Kant, etc.). This is how it has provided itself with the representation of its own necessary beginning, at least through the instituting of its name as *philosophia* and the concept or concepts that it connotes, concepts that we can only determine, both in the end and in order to begin again, by beginning to philosophize. In this way, philosophy always institutes itself through a mixture of decision and indecision with regard to itself, and 'deconstruction' is ultimately born with and alongside philosophy since it constructs itself on the basis of the consideration that it has to be anterior both to its construction and even to its own plan [*plan*].

This mixture of decision and indecision – or the decision to posit itself without a clearly established decision about itself, or as the immediately infinite mobilization of this decision – can be more precisely analysed in terms of the following characteristics: as it began, philosophy prescribed itself to itself, as its own most proper law, both an impossible anamnesis (in the immemorial) of its own origin, and a blind perspective on the truth that it awaits and toward which it tends or to which it lays claim. On the one hand, philosophy presents itself as without beginning or as beginning by itself (who comes to free a prisoner from the cave?), while on the other hand, truth absents itself in the darkness or dazzlement of that which has to come precisely insofar as, to speak like Badiou, it must come to pass without ever arriving [*évenir sans jamais advenir*], like the last step, never taken, never secured, that crosses beyond the dialectical ascension.

This double postulation of a step back into the immemorial and a step forward into unarrival [*l'inadvenir*] is characteristic of what we call 'meta-physics', and when we say that metaphysics has 'ended' we only say that it exhausts whatever would presume to complete its retrospection as well as its prospection. The former and the latter must be unachievable, they must be the unachievable as such, in conformity with the essence of philosophy, which thereby also proves to be indissociable from its history: its immobility stretched in the absencing of its provenance and its end.

It follows from these premises that two propositions must be asserted together: metaphysics has neither beginning nor end, and metaphysics begins and ends. Perhaps it never stops beginning and ending the 'without-beginning-or-end'. This is the sense in which it is *finite* in the structural rather than diachronic sense: it is finite in that it articulates an *un-givenness* of meaning or direction (an 'un-givenness' which probably constitutes the 'void' of its truth: in this regard Badiou and Heidegger seem to me to have more in common than is usually supposed – ontological finitude is that which opens onto the void, but which, in so doing, opens being). Structural finitude deconstructs historical completions (for example, this or that figure of rationalism, empiricism or criticism, and even the figure of onto-theology as such, or the figural figure that Lacoue-Labarthe has christened 'onto-typology'). Similarly, enjoying a limitless reach, metaphysics itself always begins, has begun, and begins again as *Abbau* of that which is *gebaut* (and which always has something of the temple and the palace, of the abode and the monument, and also of empire or enterprise).

From the outset – or else in advance of itself, between the twelfth and ninth centuries BCE – philosophy was deconstruction of the structures of a crumbling world: the mythico-religious world of given meaning and of truth as full and present. In this world, in which a certain number of determinate techniques had just been elaborated (iron, writing, commercial compatibility – we will come back to this), tragedy opens as forming at once the last manifestation of ritual and sacrifice and the first evidence of a flight of meaning and an abyss of truth: in fact, it is at this moment that the terms or concepts or questions of meaning and truth are engendered.

The four conditions that Badiou distributes, and whose names and notions are also engendered at this moment – politics, science, art and love – make up a quadruple multiplication of this flight and this opening. I will not stop to analyse the four dispositions of what could be called the West's inaugural *breakout* [*échappée*]: it is easy to see how each of them is structured by this breakout into the *ab-sense* [*absens*] (to take up a word of Blanchot's). Politics, science, art and love are four structures of impossibility. By the same token, what constitutes the community of the four is yet another dimension of the breakout, one that is transversal to them: it is the mutual incommensurability among the four conditions (an incommensurability that is unknown or immediately diminished in a mythico-religious world). Philosophy is the shared site of this incommensurability: it articulates the breakout or *ab-sense* as general regime of the incommensurable. Thus, what will later be called metaphysics is engendered as the articulation of this incommensurability: that of being within itself, of being insofar as it *ek-sists* to itself, or that of anarchic and a-telic principles and ends.

That there has been an arrival of metaphysics is something that is not only a factual given (de facto, it arrives at a particular moment in the history of peoples in the Mediterranean space – although not without an Eastern *analogon* in the shape of Buddhism or Confucianism: in this sense it is the *factum rationis* of philosophy), but it is moreover this very fact, this arrival, that constitutes metaphysics. For metaphysics arrives, it is engendered, as a breaking-out, a departure: namely, the departure of the gods (a departure whose initial name in the West is monotheism, already pregnant with 'the death of God' – and one could add: what is Platonism if not the weaving together of tragedy and monotheism?). This departure is not merely a disappearance, a leave-taking, or a suppression. It is first and foremost a marking: a mark of absence (and Plato's line could be called such a mark), a subtraction, to speak like Badiou, or a withdrawal, to speak like Heidegger and Derrida.

If metaphysics is born as the science of principles and ends, it is because principles and ends are *crossed out* [*barrés*], if I may be allowed to use the amphibology which the slang makes possible: they have been erased, they have departed (the slang also suggests *incised* [*taillés*]), or even, more elaborately, divided from themselves and in themselves. And in any case, it is only on the basis of the moment in which they are *crossed out* that they appear as such, as 'principles' and as 'ends': subtracted from their very authority (at the founding and ending of temples, empires, lineages).

But this subtraction arrives from somewhere (it arrives somewhere, in the contingency of a site and an era, in any case) or through some force or other (of which even the unexpected occurrence is contingent: nothing establishes any necessity in what takes place, even though it potentially takes place at the level of humanity and the world). This force, in all respects, is that of *technics* [*la technique*]. Behind that which, in a very precise sense that we will have to clarify, will become *techno-logy*, there exists a set of techniques like those of iron, those of commerce (in terms of accounting as much as in terms of navigation), those of writing, or those of town planning. At this moment in the history of technology, something like a phase transition occurs. A movement that is contemporaneous with man (quite simply, technics as homonidity, *homo faber* as producer or conceptualizer of *homo sapiens*, technician of itself), a movement that, from the outset, proceeds by way of subtraction or evacuation, assumes a different character: instead of ensuring subsistence, it produces new conditions for it, or produces a strange 'subsistence' within nature or outside it. The production of the means of subsistence already defined the Neolithic stage. Subsequently – which is to say, between the tenth and seventh centuries BCE, on the crest of Asia Minor – it could be said that a production of ends begins to take shape.

This movement (hominidity) appears to itself as its own principle and its own end. In other words, it appears to itself as strictly without principle and without end, since it proceeds from an initial unmooring which could be called 'the human condition' and whose permanence consists in the extreme instability and mutability of what has thereby been unmoored. Thus, contingency shapes the necessity of this 'history'. Let us call it – as though feigning belief in some putatively originary, whole and stable 'nature' – *denaturation*. Accordingly, it could be said that 'humanity' is the indexical name for the indeterminate and infinite end of hominid denaturation.

It is through denaturation that something like the representation of a 'nature' or an autotelic and thereby non-technical order can be produced – a representation which thereby creates for itself the extremely difficult problem of conceiving how denaturation can have arisen out of nature and within nature (how does the deficient animal, the animal without fixed conditions, arise?). Thus, it is also at this juncture that there simultaneously arises, on the one hand, a specific technique of interrogation *peri phuseôs* or *de natura rerum*, and on the other, an attempt to think the non-natural provenance of nature under the auspices of a 'creation *ex nihilo*'. These are the various ways in which metaphysics shapes from the outset the interrogation of denaturation as such; or in other words, the interrogation of the emergence or breakout of principles and ends; or alternately, of being as distinct from all beings.

That there is something like a nature, *phusys* or *natura* – and here one should be suspicious of the gap Heidegger claims to be able to measure between these two names, as though he were measuring the recession of a more natural 'nature', one which would not have harboured the possibility of human technics – this is only possible so long as one opposes this 'nature' to a non-nature. In other words, the very theme of 'nature' is itself denaturing. The 'physics' of the pre-Socratic Ionians is the technique for manipulating this object 'nature' arising at the moment when the mythico-religious order falls apart: this physics is a technique of crossed out [*barrés*] ends and means.

Thus, ultimately, the name *metaphysics*, which subsequently arises as though by accident, is not really accidental at all. It has already been prepared through the complex of techniques that has produced 'nature' as the object of a manipulation that is at once theoretical and practical. Yet at the same time, it turns 'technics' into something whose principle and end reside explicitly within itself – which is what occurs in commerce, in writing, *or* in the very production of principles and ends. It is necessary that this movement be a *becoming* precisely because it consists of that which is not given and because technics in general is the know-how [*savoir faire*] that applies to what is not yet made. Thus, with technics, history comes to be opposed to 'nature'. But it is just as necessary that this becoming does not form a *sense or orientation* [*sens*], whether progressive or regressive (*this is the sense* [*sens*] in I which I agree with Badiou as to the opposition between 'sense' or 'meaning' and 'truth'). The anxiety about meaning, which will nonetheless have governed an entire era of metaphysics, is merely the recurring effect of a mythico-religious 'physics' seeking to regain control of itself in spite of metaphysics or through it. This is why metaphysics continuously occupies the radical ambivalence of a breakout and a closure, or the difficult topology that allows closure to occur through a breakout and a breakout to occur through a closure.

Thus, there is a precondition that renders what Badiou calls conditions possible. This is a precondition which is at once and indissociably historical, technical and transcendental: by which I mean that it is necessary insofar as it is the reason for philosophy as metaphysics, and yet contingent because there is no sufficient reason for this reason – unless it be that of this general and congenital (connatural . . .) denaturation of nature which harbours the possibility of man as technician. (It seems to me that Rousseau is the best – hence also the most problematic – thinker of this infinitely convoluted denaturing inscription within nature as such, which is also the inscription of the flight of the gods.) Politics, science, art and love (which is a very Rousseauist quadrangle, when one comes to think of it) all answer, within a mutual incommensurability, to the technical condition in the state of its metaphysical autonomization: each of them is structured by the unassignable character of its own principle and end, each of them is a technique or a technical configuration, or rather, each of them opens out onto an indefinite chain of technical transformations. Which is why this quadrangle is as much conditioned as it is conditioning with respect to philosophy.

(One could also articulate the four terms relative to each other by demonstrating not only how each of them serves as end for the three others, so that the structure is always kept open and untotalizable, but also how each position as 'end' is incommensurable with the others while simultaneously forming their *telos* and boundary.)

But this is also or primarily why philosophy as such *begins* (and is in no way the mere continuation of the mythico-religious), and why it begins as *technics* of sense and/or truth. When meaning or sense is denatured – or de-mythified – truth emerges as such. It emerges as a question of constructing sense (the principle and end of being as such) or as a punctuation of the *absense*, and finally always as the two entwined together in every metaphysical construction and deconstruction worthy of the name. There is nothing surprising in the fact that, at a given moment, sophistry becomes the correlate and counterpoise of a technical complex (once again, commerce, law, town planning, the city – in the Asia Minor of the pre-Socratics). For it is more that just a technique of the *logos*, invented and taking shape alongside other techniques. With the concept of *logos* as such, which stretches from the order of discourse to that of verifying autonomy, a technique takes charge of the production of sense itself, rather than merely of subsistence or even 'super-sistence' [*sursistance*]. This is the sense in which I am here characterizing metaphysics as a *techno-logy*: the sense of a breakout into a verifying autonomy of technics, or of 'denaturation'.

It would then be necessary to ask oneself – although I will simply signal it as a possibility here – whether this might not be the reason why, with Socrates, philosophy from the outset presents itself in terms of a dialogue with techniques, or through their meta-technical interpellation: first with sophistry, then by exemplifying itself through mathematics, or various crafts such as that of the cobbler, the carpenter or the general. Similarly, it ought to be remembered that Aristotle thinks philosophy could only arise once all the requirements of subsistence[3] had been satisfied: as though philosophy itself consisted in putting into practice another kind of satisfaction, but one in continuity or analogy with the technicist posture. (Moreover, one could also ask whether the wonder which, in the same passage, Aristotle [following Plato] designates as the source of philosophy does not in fact designate the technique appropriate for a non-knowing; which is to say, neither the ignorance that awaits a teacher, nor the inexperience awaiting initiation – both of these being modalities of the mythico-religious world – but the knowing which begins by articulating itself on the basis of its own abyss.)

One could also envisage – and again, I cannot develop this further here – the possibility, which is to say, the necessity of determining the history of technics to date in its fundamental contingency without granting it any sense other than that of the indefinite relation which technics has with itself and with the breakout of its denaturation. In this respect, one could examine the succession of techniques for the immediate supplementation of the human body (tools, weapons, clothes), for the production of subsistence (agriculture, livestock farming), exchange (money, writing); then, going even further, the production of sense and truth (sophistry, philosophy), of richness as such, of production as such (capital, labour), of society (democracy), and finally, of nature itself or of its complete denaturation, whether this be through mutation or wholesale destruction (biological engineering, ecological engineering, ethological engineering . . .). But what would simultaneously kick-start this entire series and set the tone for it, functioning as its principle and end – albeit one which is without principle or end – would be an archi-technics: the pro-duction of the pro-ducer or the ex-position of the ex-posed; the 'nature' of man as denaturation within him of the whole of 'nature', or what we now call 'the symbolic'. In other words, the opening of an empty space in which the infinite 'creation' of the world is (re)played – unless this turns out to be the space within which the symbolic as such, and humanity along with it, might be crossed out and drowned out.

Thus, the movement of technics would have a sense in a sense that is neither directional nor signifying. The sense in which, for example, one says that someone has 'business sense' and according to which, generally speaking, one 'has a sense' of this or that technique, would be the sense of principles and ends (of being as such, or of existence) precisely where neither principles, nor ends, nor being, are given, and where, lacking sense, existence exposes itself, making of this lack its truth as such. Metaphysics is the name of this sense: know-how combined with the denaturation, or infinitization, of ends. What this implies above all is not a knowing but an *ethos*: the *logos* itself as *ethos*; in other words, the technique or art of composure [*tenue*] and of the sojourn in the breakout of the *absense*. This is the art of holding to that which, in general, allows us to keep going with composure [*de tenir et d'avoir de la tenue*]: 'To hold fast to this point! Philosophy has no other goal! Let each find this point and hold to it! The point from which arises within you the capacity for thought and for joy!' – thus speaks Ahmed the philosopher.[4]

3

NIHIL UNBOUND: REMARKS ON SUBTRACTIVE ONTOLOGY AND THINKING CAPITALISM

Ray Brassier

As far as 'nihilism' is concerned, we recognize that our era pays witness to it insofar as nihilism is understood as the rupture of the traditional figure of the bond [*lien*], unbinding [*dé-liaison*] as the form of being of everything that assumes the aspect of the bond [. . .] [E]verything that is bound [*relié*] testifies that it is unbound in its being, that the reign of the multiple is the groundless ground of what is presented, without exception . . . (*MP* 37).

Two basic yet apparently irreconcilable fidelities orientate Badiou's thought. On the one hand, a fidelity to the Parmenidean axiom: 'It is the same thing to think and to be.' On the other, a fidelity to materialism.[1]

Against the phenomenological privileging of intentional *Sinngebung* (sense-bestowal) and the concomitant denigration of the mathematical axiomatic as a sense-less combinatorial incapable of attaining to the dignity of ontological thought, Badiou invokes Parmenides to explain his decision to identify set theory with the science of being qua being: 'In mathematics, being, thought, and consistency are one and the same thing.'[2] Against the Deleuzian virtualization (and hence idealization) of multiplicity, Badiou reasserts the necessity of the materialist commitment to the unequivocal 'univocity of the actual as pure multiple'.[3]

Yet there seems to be a conflict of fidelities here. For the Parmenidean identity of thinking and being, which underlies Badiou's decision in favour of the set-theoretical identification of being as void, seems to assert the sovereignty of thought (a sovereignty underlined by Badiou's endorsement of Mao's 'We shall know everything we did not know before' [cf. *TS* 217]). How can this be reconciled with Badiou's materialism, which would seem to require denying the ontological sovereignty of thought?

The answer is deceptively simple. It is the identification of being as void through axiomatic set theory that purges materialism of the methodological idealism whereby matter is reinscribed in a concept. By embracing a subtractive ontology, materialism requires only one name for being: that of the void or null-set, Ø. Being and thinking are 'the same' to the extent Badiou tends to define both of them subtractively – as void and truth respectively. Being is void as subtracted from presentation, while thought is truth as subtracted from knowledge.[4] Thus, Badiou severs being from phenomenological plenitude in the same gesture whereby he dissociates thinking from the cognitive capacities of the human animal. But what are the conditions for this gesture? By what right does Badiou simultaneously subtract being from the element of phenomenological presencing and thought from the arena of intentional consciousness?

Badiou's materialism requires philosophical thought to be placed under extra-philosophical condition, that it be heteronomous rather than autonomous or *causa sui*, as it is for the idealist or phenomenologist. Thus, he maintains, a truly contemporary philosophy must operate under the condition of the disparate truths generated by post-Cantorian mathematics, poetry from Hölderlin to Celan, inventive politics from the Cultural Revolution to the contemporary struggles of illegal immigrant workers, and the Lacanian reconceptualization of the unconscious.[5] But pre-eminent among these conditions is post-Cantorian set theory. Bearing in mind Badiou's fundamental distinction between the order of knowledge (normative, verifiable) and that of truth (anomalous, unverifiable) – between legitimation and decision – it becomes apparent that the identification of axiomatic set theory with the long sought for 'science of being qua being' constitutes a decision, and hence an unverifiable subtraction from the order of knowledge. It affirms a fidelity to the Cantor-event.

Thus, the evental condition for philosophy's abdication from its ontological pretension is also that whereby it decides that being is nothing. Where ontology, in the shape of axiomatic set theory, sutures itself directly to the void of being,[6] philosophy re-appropriates its rigorous systematicity by abjuring the claim to the kind of auto-positional self-sufficiency pursued in the systems of German Idealism (specifically those of Fichte, Schelling and Hegel). Philosophy becomes capable of re-assuming systematic consistency only insofar as it supervenes on the historial contingency of its evental conditions. It assumes its own groundlessness by deciding that it is another thought – Cantor's – that has succeeded in suturing itself to the void of being, maintaining its independence from the norms of objective knowledge through the very gesture whereby it separates itself from the thinking of being qua being. In doing so, philosophy creates a space for the compossibilization of truths which have been subtracted from the realm of ontological consistency and the domain of objective verification.

Badiou reconfigures philosophy's claim to rational consistency by unbinding it from the myths of enlightenment and the superstition of teleological meta-narratives.[7] For if, as Badiou insists, 'History' does not exist,[8] then neither does 'the History of Being' as crypto-transcendental condition for thought. It is precisely by acknowledging the aleatory contingency of its historicity, its eventual conditioning, that philosophy frees itself from the myth of its uncircumventable historial destination, whether the latter be construed in terms of an ineluctable progress according to 'the History of Spirit', or that of an irrecusable decline according to 'the History of Metaphysics'. Rare, fragmentary and discontinuous, historicity is constituted through those eventual contingencies in which philosophy finds its occasioning conditions.

Yet it is precisely on account of its constitutive historicity that the decision to identify being as nothing remains philosophical rather than mathematical. It is utterly foreign to Cantor's mathematical heirs – just as it is foreign to the poetic practices, political procedures and psychoanalytical discourses that delineate the space of possibility within which this decision functions as coordinating vertex. But if it is underdetermined by its conditions, from where does this decision derive its imperative character? Badiou hints at an answer of sorts:

> This is obviously the only thing that can and must be saluted in capital: it exposes the pure multiple as the ground of presentation, it denounces every effect of Oneness as a merely precarious configuration, it deposes those symbolic representations in which the bond found a semblance of being. That this deposition operates according to the most complete barbarism should not distract us from its genuinely ontological virtue. To what do we owe our deliverance from the myths of Presence, from the guarantee it provided for the substantiality of bonds and the perenniality of essential relations, if not to the errant automation of capital? (*MP* 37).

My contention here is that the condition whereby philosophy embraces the necessity of a subtractive ontology (and simultaneously abjures its ontological pretension) is provided by a quasi-condition that is transversal to the four regimes of truth acknowledged by Badiou: capitalism as 'over-event' of universal unbinding. There is something like a 'quasi-truth' of Capital as condition for conditions, rendering the philosophical identification of being as void not merely possible but imperative.

II CAPITALISM, UNIVERSAL UNBINDING AND THE VOID

For Marx, as for us, desacralization is in no way nihilist if by nihilism one means that which declares that access to being and truth is impossible. On the contrary, desacralization is a necessary condition in order for the latter to become accessible to thought [...] The] residues of the empire of the One, because they obstruct truth procedures and designate the recurrent obstacle to the subtractive ontology for which capitalism is the historical medium, constitute an anti-'nihilist' nihilism...[9]

Capital, the 'historical medium' for subtractive ontology, unbinds nihil from the fetters of Presence, pulverizing the domain of phenomenological sensefulness and exposing the insignificant neutrality of the multiple as ground of presentation.[10]

The most powerful recent philosophical characterization of that unbinding is provided in Deleuze and Guattari's *Capitalism and Schizophrenia*:

> As far as capitalism is concerned, we maintain at once that it has no external limit and that it has one: it has one in the shape of schizophrenia, which is to say, the absolute decoding of flows, but it operates only by pushing back and warding off that limit. It also has and doesn't have internal limits: it has them in the specific conditions of capitalist production and circulation, which is to say, in capital as such, but it operates only by reproducing and widening those limits at an ever larger scale. The power of capitalism resides in the fact that its axiomatic is never saturated, that it is always capable of adding a new axiom to the preceding ones.[11]

Integrated global capitalism is a machine – and a machine is nothing other than an automated axiomatic system – but an astonishingly supple and adaptive one, singularized by its fluidity, its metamorphic plasticity. Whenever confronted by a limit or anomaly, capitalism has the wherewithal – the intelligence? – to invent a new axiom in order to incorporate the unexpected, constantly reconfiguring its parameters by adding a supplementary axiom through which it can continue expanding its own frontiers. Far from being stymied by its incompleteness, the capitalist axiomatic lives off it. Far from being threatened by its 'contradictions', capitalism thrives on them. It is an open system, an aleatory axiomatic, continually redefining its own structural boundaries, perpetually living off its own impossible limit.

Let us, for the sake of argument, risk a hazardous analogy between the role played by cosmic schizophrenia as locus of absolute unbinding (or deterritorialization) for Deleuze and Guattari and that played by the excess of the void for Badiou.[12] According to Deleuze and Guattari, what renders the capitalist socius unique and unprecedented among all other social formations is the fact that it reveals the common ontological source of social and desiring production even as it perpetuates itself by continuously warding off the threat of their convergence. Similarly, for Badiou, the void, the 'material' from which every consistent presentation is woven, is included in every multiple presentation, while the threat posed by its errant inconsistency is foreclosed to presentation through the re-presentation that neutralizes and configures its excess.[13] If capitalism is the name for that curiously pathological social formation in which 'everything that is bound [*relié*] testifies that it is unbound in its being, that the reign of the multiple is the groundless ground of what is presented, without exception', it is because it liquidates everything substantial through the law of universal exchangeability, simultaneously exposing and staving off the inconsistent void underlying every consistent presentation through apparatuses of 'statist' [*étatique*] regularization. 'Capital' names what Deleuze and Guattari call the monstrous 'Thing', the cancerous, anti-social anomaly, the catastrophic over-event through which the inconsistent void underlying every consistent presentation becomes unbound and the ontological fabric from which every social bond is woven is exposed as constitutively empty.

Thus, although capitalism invests the operations of the state, it seems to me that contrary to what Badiou generally suggests, its effects cannot be summarily reduced to those of the state. The errant automation of Capital will not be explained by referring it to the excess of the state. Although the political truth procedure assigns a fixed measure to the excess of the state, the extent to which it thereby measures the unlocalizable excess of Capital is questionable.[14]

In fact, I would like to suggest that the void's excessive or undecidable inconsistency finds objective determination in the errant automation of Capital as well as subjective measure in the political truth procedure. In order to do this, let us first examine what Badiou means by 'truth procedure'.

Badiou distinguishes between the infinite but indeterminate cardinality of the state and the infinite but determinate cardinality whereby the political truth procedure measures the excess of the state (cf. *AM* 162). That measure or determination of an indeterminate infinity is effected through forcing, a procedure that 'constrains the correctness of statements according to a condition that anticipates the composition of an infinite generic subset'.[15] Forcing describes the process whereby a truth procedure hazards assertions on the basis of the supposition that, although unverifiable within the situation as it stands, they will prove verifiable according to an extension of this situation that can and will exist even though it does not exist as yet. Through forcing, the knowledge that constrains the possibilities of thought within an actual situation is supplemented and those possibilities reconfigured by the situation's generic extension, which is brought about by statements made according to a condition anticipating the existence of the elements that will legitimate them. Thus, while the elements of a generic sub-set cannot be named – since the latter is incomplete on account of its infinity and indiscernible because its components cannot be enumerated by means of predicative definition – the generic extension can be brought into being according to a process whereby statements are made about these indiscernible elements according to the hypothesis that *if* this or that element existed in the putatively complete generic sub-set, *then* this or that statement about this or that element *would be* correct.

Every truth procedure supported by a subject has two crucial characteristics according to Badiou:

1. It is random or aleatory. Chance provides the aleatory substance of subjectivation because the subject of the truth procedure forces the generic extension through a series of entirely random choices; distinguishing x from y without recourse to a principle or concept by which to differentiate x from y.[16]
2. It is interminable because the generic sub-set is infinite. But since the subject proceeds via a series of finite discriminatory steps (a or b, c or d, etc.), it is an infinity woven from finite series of discrete sequences. This interminability delineates the generic infinite's composition out of the finite, and hence its immanence to finite situations.[17] Thus, Badiou writes

of truth that 'between the finitude of its [subjective] act and the infinity of its [generic] being, there is no measure' (C 192).

Now, as far as the first point is concerned, it seems to me that Badiou is curiously reliant on a suspiciously commonsense or intuitive notion of 'chance' or 'randomness'. This suspicion is compounded by the eagerness with which Badiou wishes to dissociate the deductive fidelity concomitant with truth procedures from any 'merely' mechanical process of calculation.[18] Yet it is precisely this venerable distinction between thinking and calculating – often a cipher for the familiar philosophical opposition between subjective freedom and objective necessity – which Alan Turing subverted from within mathematics itself. Turing showed how any deductive procedure could be defined in terms of recursive functions, algorithmically generated, and therefore automated as a computable function.[19] And this automation of computable functions is entirely compatible with the straightforwardly intuitive characterization of 'chance' Badiou seems to invoke in his account of the deductive process that constitutes truth. For algorithms excel at unprincipled distinctions wherein nothing intrinsic to the terms themselves plays a role in effecting the discrimination. One merely has to specify a condition, *any* condition: if the sky is green, then rabbits are bigger than elephants. To believe that a discriminatory procedure, no matter how 'arbitrary', is truly 'spontaneous' and non-mechanical in anything but the most superficial of senses, is to relapse into the superstitions of phenomenological voluntarism.

Turing demonstrated the identity of proof and computation,[20] circumscribing the realm of proof through that of computable functions. Now, it is obvious that there is supposed to be a fundamental distinction between the deductive process involved in proof and that involved in what Badiou calls truth. But Turing did more than merely demonstrate the possibility of automating proof procedures. He used a technique similar to Gödel's to delimit a realm of *non-computable functions*, and thereby a realm of non-provable mathematical statements. He constructed a function that could be given a finite description but that could not be computed by finite means in order to show how even a 'universal computing machine' capable of duplicating the operations of any possible computer could not compute in advance whether or not a given program would carry out its task within a finite length of time or carry on indefinitely. This non-computable function is known as the 'halting function': given the number of a computing machine and the number of an input tape, this function returns either the value 0 or the value 1 depending on whether the computation will ever come to a halt. Through the halting function, Turing showed that there exists no finite proof procedure whereby one can prove whether or not a given mathematical statement is provable.

Thus, in order to show that the distinctions fuelling the truth procedure are aleatory and unverifiable in a sense that does not depend on some pre-theoretical notion of spontaneity, and in order to sustain his distinction between thought and calculation – as well as his even more fundamental distinction between truth and knowledge – Badiou needs to show that truth procedures effectuate non-computable functions.

Moreover, as far as the second point is concerned, if forcing delineates the cusp between the finitude of truth's subjective act and the infinity of its generic being, it does not necessarily follow from this either that it must index some putatively unquantifiable upsurge of subjective freedom or that this cusp must be 'without measure'. And as it happens, following in the footsteps of Gödel and Turing, Gregory Chaitin[21] has recently elaborated an extremely interesting metamathematical characterization of randomness in a way which – at least in my admittedly non-expert opinion – seems both to undermine the distinction between the subjective measure of excess and its objective calculation, and to determine the abyss between the finitude of truth's subjective act and the infinity of its generic being.

III CHAITIN: ALGORITHMIC RANDOMNESS

What follows is no more than a clumsy philosophical sketch of Chaitin's work. The latter finds its initial impetus at the intersection of Gödel's incompleteness theorem and Turing's 'halting function'. In a move that clearly exhibits the latent affinity between these metamathematical concerns and those of trans-cendental epistemology, Chaitin provides a metacomputational specification of the uncomputable by determining the *halting probability* for a universal Turing machine as a real number lying somewhere between 0 and 1. And just as there can be no computable function determining whether or not a program will halt, there can be no computable function determining the digits of this halting probability, which Chaitin, with admirable dramatic flair, names Ω. Unlike π, which can be compressed as a ratio and whose digits can be generated through a program shorter than the bit string it generates, Ω is strictly uncomputable. This means that its shortest program-length description[22] is as long as Ω itself, which is infinitely long and consists of a random, i.e. *incompressible* string of 0s and 1s exhibiting no pattern or structure whatsoever: each digit is as unrelated to its predecessor as one toss of a coin is from the next.

Not satisfied with having demonstrated Ω's theoretical possibility in the abstract realm of universal Turing machines, Chaitin set about proving Ω's actuality in the very concrete domain of elementary number theory, the cornerstone of pure mathematics. Other mathematicians[23] had already shown how to translate the operations of Turing's universal computer into a Dio-phantine equation – an equation involving only the addition, multiplication and exponentiation of whole numbers – thereby establishing a correlation between the interminability of a given program and the insolubility of a given algebraic equation. Following their lead, Chaitin saw how he could construct a link between the halting probability and number theory by encoding Ω's bits in such an equation. But rather than trying to determine specific whole number solutions for his equation, Chaitin set about determining whether or not there was a finite or infinite number of them as a function of Ω's first N digits.[24] Chaitin's equation is 200 pages long, with 20,000 variables, X_1 to X_{20000}, and a single parameter, N.[25] It has finitely or infinitely many natural number solutions depending on whether the Nth bit of Ω is respectively a 0 or a 1. Since the number of solutions to the equation jumps from finite to infinite in a completely arbitrary fashion as a function of N, Chaitin argues that 'determining whether this equation has finitely or infinitely many solutions is just as difficult as determining the bits of Omega'.[26]

Moreover, each of Ω's bits, each number of solutions, constitutes an irreducible, separate mathematical fact; one that cannot be deduced unless it is added as an axiom – it takes N bits of axiom to prove N bits of Ω. Since a formal axiomatic system amounts to a computation in the limits of infinite time, Ω's algorithmic incompressibility shows that although the set of theorems implied by an axiomatic system can be algorithmically generated (in some arbitrary order), no algorithm can determine whether or not a given theorem belongs to that set. Thus, Chaitin concludes, incompleteness is far more than a marginal, metamathematical anomaly. It is a central, possibly even ubiquitous mathematical predicament. There are non-deducible, un-provable mathematical truths everywhere, quasi-empirical 'facts' that are gratuitously or *randomly* true and that can only be integrated by being converted into supplementary axioms.

Isn't there a case then for maintaining that Ω indexes the 'not-all-ness' (*pastout*), the constitutive incompleteness whereby the Real punctures the consistency of the symbolic order, at least as much as the excess of the void does for Badiou? But that it does so as a mercilessly unpredictable burst of objective randomness – undecipherable noise – rather than as a 'grace accorded to us', a liberating upsurge of subjective freedom?[27] Doesn't the eventual excess which, for Badiou, indexes the inconsistency of the Real and necessitates the uncomputable freedom of axiomatic decision,[28] find embodiment in Ω's objective randomness at least as legitimately as in subjective intervention?

Moreover, doesn't the pathological peculiarity of the capitalist machine consist in its ability to do just this: convert random empirical facts into new axioms? Integrated global capitalism is constitutively dysfunctional: it works by breaking down. It is fuelled by the random undecidabilities, excessive inconsistencies, aleatory interruptions, which it continuously reappropriates, axiomatizing empirical contingency. It turns catastrophe into a resource, ruin into opportunity, harnessing the uncomputable.

IV THE REAL AS AUTOMATED RANDOMNESS OR THINKING CAPITAL

There cannot be two or more unnameables for a singular truth. The Lacanian maxim 'there is Oneness' is tied here to the irreducibility of the real, to what could be called the 'grain of real' jamming the machinery of truth, which in its power is the machinery of forcings, and hence the machinery for producing finite veridicalities at the point of a truth that cannot be accomplished. Here, the jamming effected by the One-real is opposed to the path opened up by veridicality (C 209).

Here is my conjecture: Ω's incompressible algorithmic randomness indexes the uncomputability of the real, which Capital's errant automation at once exposes and wards off, unleashes and regularizes. But if Capital functions as the real condition through which philosophy simultaneously identifies the void of being, abjures its ontological pretensions, and becomes the harbinger of truths, might its automated randomness not also function as that unnameable Thing which Badiou's philosophy cannot acknowledge: the unthinkable determinant for its own identification of being as void?

Might Ω – the real as inconsistent randomness – not also provide an entirely *objective* determination of the excess of the void as embodied in the errant automation of Capital? What if the void's undecidable excess found embodiment in the objective randomness of Capital's non-computable dysfunctions, as opposed to the subjective 'freedom' of evental decision? What if Ω furnished a real, objective measure of what Badiou describes as the 'abyss' between the finitude of truth's subjective forcing and the infinitude of its generic being? Perhaps the condition for Badiou's subtractive ontology is a thought of Capital, or more precisely, an acknowledgment that capitalism – blind, monstrous, acephalic polymorph – thinks. What if it were precisely the thought that this Thing thinks that was still unthinkable for this philosophy?

4

SOME REMARKS ON THE INTRINSIC ONTOLOGY OF ALAIN BADIOU*

Jean-Toussaint Desanti

Aristotle's oft-repeated definition of what we call 'ontology' at the beginning of *Metaphysics* 3 ('the science that establishes itself speculatively [*theôrei*] in the realm of being as being') contains many perplexing terms. 'Science' [*epistemè*] is one of them. But the most perplexing is the little word 'as' [*on ê on*]. One sees in it an invitation to think 'being' intrinsically, i.e. in such a way as to determine nothing in its concept other than what properly and exclusively pertains to it. But 'intrinsically' (the famous '*kath'auto*') can be understood in two ways: maximally or minimally. Those who choose the maximal interpretation will try to render being equal to its concept: they will try to think under the name 'being' the deployment of this very concept in the richness and inter-connectedness of its moments. Those who choose the minimal interpretation will ask themselves the following question: what is *the least* that must be thought in order to define the status of the proposition '*there are* beings'?

In each case, the intrinsic theoretical requirements indicated by the word '*ê*' ['as'] will have to be rigorously respected. By reiterating Aristotle's phrase in *Being and Event*, Alain Badiou evidently chooses the minimal interpretation. Perhaps he thinks it alone allows one explicitly to safeguard the intrinsic character of the ontology he seeks to elaborate. But this choice in no way entails that ontology itself should be minimal. On the contrary, it is obliged to be maximal in at least this sense: so as to be sufficient for defining and circum-scribing the regulated realm of that which presents itself as 'being' [*étant*] and as happening to being or coming into being [*advenant à l'étant*]. That it be sufficient simply expresses the intrinsic character whose necessity we have already established. What presents itself as minimal must then posit itself, in essence, as the basis for the maximal domain of all determinations locatable in the realm of beings. Consequently, the fundamental 'ontological' problem consists in providing a precise definition of this maximality, while bearing in mind the fact that 'maximal' as it is used here cannot be synonymous with 'unextendable' or 'fixed' (lest we lose the intrinsic character of the envisaged

* This chapter, translated by Ray Brassier, was first published as 'Quelques Remarques à propos de l'ontologie intrinsèque d'Alain Badiou', *Les Temps modernes* 526 (May 1990): 61–71.

ontology). Which means that 'Being [*L'Etant*] as a whole' cannot be 'plunged' into any sort of 'space' other than its own. Its immediate position is not that of a compact substance but that of the multiple presented, which only ever applies to its own multiples (or, if you prefer, operates only on them).

But 'operating' is a dangerous word, at least when we are obliged to confront the criteria of the intrinsic, as indicated by the expression '*on ê on*' – an obligation which Badiou takes entirely seriously. Thus for example, while discussing Leibniz's proposition ('that which is not *a* being is not a *being*'), in which he sees both ontology's essential moment and its impasse, Badiou, in order to avoid this dead-end, is driven to write: 'we must conclude that the one, which is not, exists only as an *operation*. In other words: there is no one, there is only the counting-as-one' (*EE* 32). It seems clear to me that the project of a pure ontology (an intrinsic theory of being as being) would stumble here with its very first step, were one to ask oneself this 'preliminary' question: what is it to operate? Who operates here and in what realm? In this case, clarification of the object–act correlation would at least have to be the (transcendental) propaedeutic required for any meaningful ontology, if we are to avoid postponing indefinitely a pure theory of 'being as being', or even annulling its object.

As a result, the project for such a theory must rest upon a 'reform of philosophical understanding' capable of eliminating such preliminary questions and of rigorously preserving the intrinsic character of the '*on ê on*'. In the case which concerns us here (in which the use of the word operation is problematic), this means purifying the concept of operation in such a way as to *entitle* us to respond to the question 'who operates and in what realm?' with the answer 'no one and nowhere', i.e. with an answer that eliminates the question, and with it many other questions too, in particular this one: how are we to access the modes of presence of what seems to give itself as present? All this to say that an intrinsic ontology does not admit of half-measures; it is fundamentally abrupt, leaving no room wherein to delineate some means of working toward the question of the 'meaning' of being. More than a few readers may find this abruptness, which is very marked in Badiou's text (in its very idiom), disconcerting. But so long as these readers share the speculative passion for the intrinsic they must be willing to pay the price for it. This is a price Badiou is immediately willing to pay, and one he pays upfront. From the outset he installs his discourse in a version of set theory and decides to submit to its norms. There are many possible versions of it. Badiou chooses the one he considers to be the surest: the Zermelo-Fraenkel (ZF) system, expressed in first-order notation. This is a choice that seems to be justified by the preliminary concern for the intrinsic, since the 'basic ontology' of ZF is minimal and in it the tradition-laden concepts of 'relation', 'function' and 'operation' are unburdened of their usual accompanying modes of representation and reduced to their simplest expression (intrinsically defined in terms of ZF itself without extraneous additions).

The 'reform of philosophical understanding' and the presentation of the science of the *on ê on* can now both be undertaken at the same time. The latter will be the 'science of multiples as such', i.e. set theory, while the reform will consist, *at least*, in acceptance of the formal norms of rationality peculiar to the elaboration of the ZF version of such a theory. I am careful to say 'at least', since this is not the only condition required to put the theory to work. Be that as it may, whoever pursues this path will take care never to abandon the initial terrain and never to admit anything that, once stated, would be inconsistent with those initially verified norms. Thus, the passion for the intrinsic deploys itself and perseveres in itself as a passion for the formal, in its mathematical (or better, set-theoretical) version.

Is this surprising? Not at all, at least not in my eyes. Once we accept that a reform of philosophical understanding is necessary, all we can do is try to establish ourselves within a realm of rationality (whilst continuing to revise it if necessary) that is *given* in an explicit and relatively canonical form. In the present context, 'establishing ourselves' means 'taking part in the production of the required discourse'. Hence the abruptness of true thought, in which the moment of 'passage' is annulled. *'Habemus enim ideam veram'*, as Spinoza used to say. We only ever enter into that place where we already were. The one thing that is violent here, and brutally so, is the given norm of truth. In the present case, the ZF axiomatic enters into the realm of traditional questions concerning Being with such violence that it seems to put an end to the questioning as such. From the outset, it presents itself as the given matrix for all ontology. Such is the price to be paid for the stubborn preoccupation with the intrinsic, indicated by the use of the words 'as such'. What might be seen as a baroque extravagance (some sort of mathematician's folly on Badiou's part) instead presents itself as the necessary deployment of a requirement internal to the initially problematic concept of the *on ê on*. In my eyes, this is enough to guarantee the philosophical seriousness of the project. Nevertheless, certain problems remain.

There is first of all the question of the 'margin', which we said intrinsic ontology excludes by definition. Yet there is always some sort of thought at the margins of whatever, in and of itself, demands to be deployed as 'thought' [*le penser*]. This is a speculative situation that the venerable Parmenides had already noted by calling mortals – those to whom the inaugural injunction 'never shall you force non-being to be' is addressed – *'dikranoia'* (two-headed people). That this injunction is addressed to them also means that it drags them along or abandons them, mesmerized, on the edge of the path which it forges – 'at the margins', precisely. Although it is not entirely accurate to put it this way, I would say that so long as they are mortal (which is invariably the case), whoever devotes themselves to philosophy is a two-headed being: they are always accompanied by whatever occupies the margins of the thought they seek to elaborate. Hegel himself did not escape this, nor did Spinoza. Their fundamental, logically consecutive discourse occasionally stops and starts as though justifying itself before the noise that populates the margin. Badiou, a mortal philosopher, must also be *dikranos* – 'two-headed' – to some degree or other, and hence must be obliged to deal with the margin, which is the source whence much noise comes.

To my mind this is indicated by the tradition-laden word ('meditation') which Badiou uses to designate his chapters. Three closely related requirements can be discerned in this word: the fidelity to an initial decision (the choice in favour of the intrinsic); the deployment of a movement of thought orienting itself within its own discourse; and the 'exhibition' of the conceptual connections which render that discourse consistent. That these requirements are closely related means, at the very least, that the initial decision will always be taken up again, reproduced, its validity ceaselessly renewed in the coordinated unfolding of the discourse itself. The decision taken from the margin, formulated as an injunction fixing the fate of ontology, is thus re-thought in the very deployment of ontology as such. Its 'marginal' origin is thereby cancelled. But the movement of discourse still and always entails a necessary settling of scores with its margin (what was said; what was thought; what we would need to re-think; what we should try to do in order to live, etc.); without it this discourse would be the discourse of nothing. 'Meditation' is indeed the most suitable word when it comes to designating the unity of this certainty and these doubts.

We are thereby led to expect that, understood in this sense, a 'meditation' will have to be deployed as a multi-layered discourse, with layers that are at once horizontally distinct and vertically interconnected. This requirement results from the state of tension in which the 'margins' are held together with the essential ontological framework, whose matrix is provided by ZF. In order to illuminate this point I will phrase things in terms that are inaccurate but convenient. Let us say the margin is never silent, and that it inscribes itself upon itself (marks itself), organizing itself into a series of 'writings'. I use the word 'writing' in a very general sense here. I call writing anything which, as it is produced, leaves a trace: falling rain; a drifting leaf; an utterance; a natural catastrophe; an assassination; theft by a pickpocket; an encounter; a thunderbolt; a firedamp explosion; the glimpse of a face; a sitting rabbit; an uprising; a phrase; the sound of a voice, etc. This is a baroque list, which I could continue indefinitely, one whose only purpose is to allow us to perceive the nature of what I mean by 'margin': the 'writing' of an *excess* which is not necessarily coordinated, although it is susceptible to a localized coordination in the fragile wakes left by some of its assemblages. But the same is not true of the fundamental ontological framework. It is of course also a writing. But contrary to what happens in the case of those writings at the margins, which escape altogether, the excess engendered in and through ontological writing must always be amenable either to recuperation – at the price, if need be, of a fundamental reconfiguration in the basic theory – or on the contrary, to formal exclusion from the theory (cf. Cantor's 'inconsistent multiplicities'). As a result, meditative thought is caught in the tension that binds these two writings together. Its task consists in trying to rewrite what is written in the margin and in capturing its excesses – a task that entails the putting back into motion of ontological writing itself (the *set-theoretical foundation*). And the state of tension results from the fact that the margin, which is essentially other, can neither be abolished nor excluded, unless it be at the price of total silence. Consequently, the margin must be 'redrafted', the way one redrafts a poor sketch. By now you will have guessed that in this instance 'ontology' provides nothing that we can know. It is not a realm of the intrinsic populated by 'objects in themselves'. It provides the system of necessary formal procedures, of rule-bound notations, which allow the excesses of the margin to be 'rewritten' – and hence of 'redoing' what has always been known as 'life', 'history', 'actions', etc.

The *dikrania* (two-headedness) proper to mortals must be fully assumed. The task of thought consists in connecting the two heads, which in the present instance means connecting two kinds of discursiveness. The whole problem consists in defining *precisely* the strict procedures that would allow this connection. But precision comes at a price. And to the extent that in this instance it is Cantor's legacy – which achieves exactitude in the ZF formalization – that provides the theoretical basis for the entire enterprise, we must begin by putting that legacy to the test. This means making it function in conformity with its own intrinsic requirements in a context other than the one in which it originated. But how can we put this Cantorian legacy to work without reworking it from within? Thus, I believe it is a mistake to say Badiou has 'applied' set-theoretical concepts, or even deduced something or other from ZF. Rather, it seems to me that he has put set theory back on track with a view to rewriting the writing of the margins of ontology, which 'in itself' is abrupt and brutally explicit. This was something that had to be done in any case. No ontology (however minimal it might be) can be reduced to a purely instrumental function. Within ZF, then, it is essential that we unearth the roots of the conceptual deployment required by a movement of meditation that aims to capture the writings of the margin.

What follows is a typical example (to which I will confine myself): the way in which Badiou believes he has been able to mobilize for his own philosophical purposes Paul Cohen's 'forcing' procedure, elaborated in order to establish the independence of the continuum hypothesis and the axiom of choice.

Let us agree to set technicalities aside, not least because Badiou's book is entirely self-sufficient in this regard. Anyone willing to make the effort will find in it, admirably set out, all the mathematical instructions required in order to follow its argument. I propose instead to ask the following question: how is it that Badiou seems to have had no option other than to accept completely the 'procedure' of forcing, and more specifically, the version of it put forward by Cohen himself? Why has he embraced it so seriously and wholeheartedly as to discern in it a 'revolution in thought' – one which, moreover, he claims has gone 'unthought' by mathematicians themselves? It is always possible to evade such questions by claiming, in a manner at once lazy and malicious, that 'Badiou has used Cohen for his own purposes. He has contrived a "gadget", which he has exported into another realm where it has been put to work to serve his own theoretical interests.' Only a careless reader, oblivious to the internal logic of Badiou's text, could make such a claim. But then a careless reader would be wholly incapable of reading Badiou: whoever enters into this text either abandons it or else grasps its movement and perseveres with it. As I see it, the fact that Badiou takes up forcing is the price he has to pay for his decision to install himself from the outset within an intrinsic ontology. The fact that he sees in forcing a 'revolution in thought' is a consequence of the way in which he conceives of and engages in thought's work: the attempt to rewrite and capture that which is ceaselessly and tirelessly marked as excess in the margins of ontology. As a result, the task of generalized rewriting, in which consists the work of thought (insofar as it has its basis in an intrinsic ontology), seems to inscribe itself in the 'repetition' of a highly localized situation, internal to ZF *written in first-order notation*, once the problem of obtaining a proof for the independence of the axiom of choice and the continuum hypothesis has been explicitly formulated. This is well and truly a case of *dikrania*.

In order to avoid turgid technical pedantry, allow me to invoke a fiction. Imagine that there are people obliged to move about in a territory whose border they cannot cross because this border is so contrived as to push them back, however close they come, each and every time they approach it. They would soon begin to suspect that this effect had its source on the far side of the border. They would in fact have no choice but to believe this, for since there are no clues within their own territory allowing them to point to the source of this effect, the latter is all the evidence they have for the existence of the border. It would be as though their border was 'infinitely' distant for them: they would be incapable either of reaching or crossing it. Nevertheless, this border would still comprise a 'beyond' because its effect would not be produced from within the bounds of their territory. In order to designate their situation as one of *subjection*, of assignation to this strange territory, we will simply call these people (they could be 'human', but this is of no importance here) 'subjects'. But since 'being subjected to the territory' also means here 'being subjected to what lies beyond it', these particular people would end up trying to contrive some way of designating, or marking, what might be going on in this beyond, all the more so because they would come to attribute an infinity of effects, which they would undergo as 'subjects', to the effect of the border itself. As subject to these effects, however, they would be unable to mark or designate their points of origin within their own territory. The *dikrania* or two-headedness of a subject consists then (at least in the fiction I am proposing here) in the fact that such a subject must express the connection between an 'internal infinite' and an 'externalized infinite' – an 'indiscernible real' but one which, again as subject, it has to 'mark'.

What could such subjects possibly do to get themselves out of this predicament, i.e. to carry out their function as *markers of a real* to which they are bound but which they cannot ever visit for themselves? Answer: invent a certain kind of 'mathematics', whose procedures would initially allow them to grasp their internal infinite with the maximal degree of precision compatible with their constitution and the information available to them. But as their principal concern would remain the externalized infinite (since in their eyes it would harbour the secret of their subjection), they would have to contrive this internal mathematics in such a way as to enable them, with its sole resources, to formulate meaningful if not consistent propositions about this infinite. And they would possess no information with which to do this other than that provided by the site they inhabit, which means no information other than that furnished by their grasp of the internal infinite.

The point of this fable is simply to allow us to understand the speculative motive that encourages a philosopher to find in forcing an ontological significance which at first sight it did not seem to possess in the original realm within which Cohen defined it. Originally, this realm was that of a well-grasped 'internal infinite': a *model* of the formal theory (ZF) in first-order notation, one that is denumerable, transitive and constructible (in Gödel's sense), and in which the axiom of choice (AC) and the continuum hypothesis (CH) are both *valid*. Let us call this model M_0. The problem consists in using M_0 as the basis from which to obtain an extension of the model (call it M_1) that would still be a model of ZF but in which neither AC nor CH would be valid. One might think that in order to obtain the required extension it would be enough to append some new sets onto those of M_0 and to possess enough 'symbols' with which to name them. But by proceeding in this way (i.e. arbitrarily) we risk inviting awkward consequences. For it could be that among the appended sets some fail to conform to the codes of information governing the sets of M_0. For example there is no guarantee that the information encoded in the writing of the relation of belonging in M_0 is enough to ensure that axioms which are indispensable in ZF (for instance the axiom of substitution or the axiom of foundation) will remain meaningful in M_1. One of the aims of the method of forcing is to eliminate this disastrous possibility. Since we have no information other than that provided by M_0, it is important we define within M_0 'sets of conditions' that are such as to allow us to recognize in the desired extension (i.e. the 'new' sets) those that indeed belong to a model of the formal system ZF, and to retain only these. Cohen called such sets of conditions 'generic', by which he meant that they allow us to 'engender' new sets which belong to a model of ZF by definition. The whole problem consists in discovering a way of obtaining such sets of conditions and finding a suitable (and still first-order) formal notation by which to define them with all the stringency required in order to eliminate 'undesirable sets' in a sure and precise fashion.

The only purpose of this crude account is to allow us to grasp the situation in which mathematicians deprived of such a procedure would find themselves: they would be disarmed before the excess of the infinite as such, which in the present instance has the function and import of the real. All this turns, of course, on the problem formulated above: how are we to obtain a model of ZF that confirms neither AC nor CH? This is a local requirement which seems to provide Badiou with a 'mathematized concentrate' of the situation of the subject at the heart of the excess of the real. In our present instance the 'real' is the Cantorian universe as engendered through the infinite iteration of the operation of the power-set axiom, i.e. the operation that, for every given set E, produces P(E), the set of its parts. The result is an actual, genuinely untamed infinity, within which one must learn to distinguish distinct, normalized regions (at least relative to the legitimate operations carried out on well-defined basic sets). In the case of this universe (which is definitely not a set), an axiom such as AC and a conjecture such as CH bear the mark of the subject assigned to the deductive consequences of the theory and immersed in this universe which has been named but which remains indiscernible on its own terms. Here, the agency of the subject appears as the necessary manifestation of a point of normative decision which must bring determination to the very heart of that which opens up only in excess; the *subject* of this excess, moreover, is obliged to admit that he himself is immersed in it.

In Cohen, this instance of decision is discernible at the end of his book *Set Theory and the Continuum Hypothesis*. Having established the existence of a model of ZF in which CH is false, as well as the existence of a model of ZF in which it is true, Cohen concludes by stating that in his eyes CH is 'obviously false'. The continuum, he claims, is 'so incredibly rich' there is no reason why it should simply be equivalent to M_1. For Cohen, the procedure that consists in iteratively forming the set of parts is incomparably more powerful than that which consists in numbering the alephs.[1] At this juncture, one is tempted to say that the mathematician is like Spinoza's God, who 'never lacks material for producing anything, from the lowest to the highest degree of perfection'.[2] Forcing brings some kind of legitimate determination to this 'material'. The subject assigned to the realm in which the procedures of forcing are carried out always remains on the near side of this realm's border. But this subject owes it to himself to transgress this border without ever being able to go beyond it. This is characteristic of the speculative situation which I named *dikrania* above, and which as far as I can tell Badiou has decided to accept.

Nevertheless, it seems to me that because of his choice of a set-theoretical matrix (ZF), Badiou's intrinsic ontology is too impoverished to accomplish what he expects of it. Must an intrinsic ontology deploy itself within a set-theoretical universe? Do contemporary mathematics offer possibilities that would allow for another basic ontology? For my part, I believe they do, though I doubt such an ontology could still satisfy the criteria of the intrinsic as indicated so long ago by the little word '$\hat{e}$'. But this problem would require a new analysis.

5

BADIOU AND DELEUZE ON THE ONE AND THE MANY

Todd May

Many philosophers seem to think of Deleuze's work as concerned primarily with multiplicity and difference. Like Foucault, Nancy, Derrida, and others of his generation, Deleuze's thought is taken to be an attempt to articulate difference over and against identity, multiplicity over and against unity. What makes Badiou's treatment of Deleuze so provocative in his book *Deleuze: The Clamor of Being* is his argument that Deleuze's philosophy, although a thought of difference and multiplicity in a certain sense, is primarily a thought of the One. Contrary to popular belief, it is the One rather than the Many that drives Deleuze's work. In a corpus which draws upon the works of Nietzsche, Hume and Proust as well as Spinoza and Bergson, it is the latter, according to Badiou, that constitute the real foundation for Deleuze's philosophical views.

What I would like to attempt in these few pages is a reconstitution and a consideration of Badiou's claim. His argument that Deleuze's philosophy as a thought of the One rather than the Many is trenchant and challenging. Ultimately, I think Badiou overstates the case, and will try to show how Deleuze can respond to Badiou's critique. In doing so, however, I will not try to return Deleuze to the camp of the Many. Rather, I believe, as I have argued elsewhere,[1] that Deleuze is a thinker of the One *and* the Many, of unity *and* difference. Ultimately, Badiou's contribution is one of allowing us to see how the One plays a neglected role in Deleuze's thought, and removes him from the grip of those, including sometimes Deleuze himself, who would see his work as a privileging of multiplicity and difference at the expense of unity and coherence. However, in cleaving to the other pole, privileging the One as Badiou does, he misses what seems to me an essential element of Deleuze's thought. Deleuze's claims about the univocity of Being are made in support of a resistance to any transcendence, and if we see that resistance properly, the difficulties Badiou discovers in Deleuze's thought are not as urgent as he seems to claim.

Badiou's position is stated at the outset of the Deleuze book. 'Deleuze's fundamental problem', he writes, 'is most certainly not to liberate the multiple but to submit thinking to a renewed concept of the One.'[2] This, Badiou thinks, is the driving force behind the entirety of Deleuze's philosophical and critical corpus. Although he treats a variety of figures, Deleuze's work is essentially '*monotonous*, composing a very particular regime of emphasis or almost infinite repetition of a limited repertoire of concepts, as well as a virtuosic variation of names, under which what is thought remains essentially identical' (D 26–27/ 15). Look at any book or essay by Deleuze; what lies beneath it, if not on the surface, is a thought of the One, a return of philosophy to the univocity of Being. 'The thesis of the univocity of Being guides Deleuze's entire relation to the history of philosophy' (D 39/24).

How can it be that Deleuze, this thinker of multiplicity, the philosopher who writes that 'difference is behind everything, but behind difference there is nothing',[3] be a thinker of the One, of the univocity of Being? In part, the evidence is in Deleuze's own work. In *Difference and Repetition*, the work from which the preceding quote is drawn, Deleuze traces a history of the univocity of Being from Duns Scotus through Spinoza to Nietzsche, in whom the univocity of Being finds its proper articulation. In *Expressionism in Philosophy: Spinoza*, Deleuze writes approvingly that Spinoza's 'philosophy of immanence appears from all viewpoints as the theory of a unitary Being, equal Being, common and univocal Being'.[4] In his book on Bergson, Deleuze credits Bergson with the discovery of a single, unitary temporality beneath the disparate, spatialized time that we commonly conceive.

However, in considering the puzzle of how a thinker of difference can at the same time be a thinker of the One and of the univocity of Being, we need to bear in mind that, in Deleuze's view, there is no contradiction between the two. 'Being is said in a single and same sense of everything of which it is said, but that of which it is said differs: it is said of difference itself.'[5] Deleuze, the thinker of difference, is also Deleuze, the thinker of the univocity of Being, the thinker, as Badiou would have it, of the One. Badiou recognizes this, and sees it as one of the two key theses of Deleuze's concept of the univocity of Being. '[U]nivocity', he writes, 'does not signify that being is numerically one, which is an empty assertion. The One is not here the one of identity or of number, and thought has already abdicated if it supposes that there is a single and same Being. The power of the One is much rather that "beings are multiple and different, they are always produced by a disjunctive synthesis, and they themselves are disjointed and divergent, *membra disjoncta*".'[6]

Having granted this, however, Badiou points out that in order for the multiplicity of beings to remain compatible with the univocity of Being, that multiplicity must be *formal* rather than *real*. In other words, there are no real divisions within Being, which is One. There are only formal distinctions that are carried over into the beings themselves, no ontological ones. In the terms Deleuze uses in *Expressionism in Philosophy*, substance *expresses* itself in various attributes and modes, but that which is expressed is not ontologically distinct from the expressing substance. 'What is expressed has no existence outside its expressions; each expression is, as it were, the existence of what is expressed.'[7]

This leads to the second thesis that Badiou sees characterizing Deleuze's concept of the univocity of Being. 'Thesis 2: In each form of Being, there are to be found "individuating differences" that may well be named beings. But these differences, these beings, never have the fixedness or the power of distribution that may be attributed, for example, to species or generalities [...]. For

Deleuze, beings are local degrees of intensity or inflections of a power that are in constant movement and entirely singular' (D 40/25). Here Badiou interprets Deleuze's concepts of singularity and intensity in terms of beings. Beings are the intensities and singularities expressed by Being. They are intensities and singularities that can be 'named beings', which is to say that they are phenomenologically accessible. However, they are not themselves ontologically salient. What *is* ontologically salient is Being itself, which lies behind these beings and within which these beings constitute formal but not real distinctions among themselves.

Badiou sees a difficulty here in Deleuze's thought. It is not yet the deep difficulty we will discuss later, the difficulty that will raise questions about the coherence of Deleuze's entire project. But still, it is, as Badiou puts it, a philosophical cost of embracing the One. 'The price to be paid', he writes, 'for inflexibly maintaining the thesis of univocity is clear: given that the multiple (of beings, of significations) is arrayed in the universe by way of numerical difference that is purely formal as regards the form of being to which it refers (thought, extension, time, etc.) and purely modal as regards its individuation, it follows that, ultimately, this multiple can only be of the order of simulacra [...]. But, in this case, what meaning is to be given to the Nietzschean program that Deleuze constantly validates: the overturning of Platonism?' (D 41–42/26).

In other words, if we maintain the thesis of the univocity of Being and hold that beings are themselves only formally distinct, then beings themselves are merely simulacra whose ontological reality lies only in their participation in the Oneness of being that expresses them. On this Spinozist reading of Deleuze (the passage cited above casts Deleuze's thought in terms of Spinoza's tripartite distinction between substance, attributes and modes), Deleuze returns to the very Platonism he was trying to jettison. The real is the One, and beings are only real inasmuch as they are expressions of, and therefore participate in, that One.

Here, I believe, Badiou misreads Deleuze's project of overturning Platonism. If one must jettison Spinoza in order to overturn Platonism then Badiou is surely right, since the embrace of Spinoza runs deep in Deleuze's thought. But what exactly does the 'overturning of Platonism' consist in? In his article 'Plato and the Simulacrum', Deleuze addresses that question directly. The goal of overturning Platonism is not to deny the simulacrum, but rather to deny the distinction between simulacrum and copy. The copy is the faithful representation of the original One from which it derives. The simulacrum is the degraded or false representation. To maintain a distinction between copy and simulacrum, then, requires the possibility that beings can *resemble* (in at least some sense of that term) the One or the Being from which they derive or which they express. And *that* is something Deleuze expressly denies, as we will see in detail below in the discussion of the virtual and the real. Thus, for Deleuze, 'to reverse Platonism' means to make the simulacra rise and affirm their rights among icons and copies [...]. The simulacrum is not a degraded copy. It harbours a positive power which denies *the original and the copy, the model and the reproduction*.'[8] Nothing in the Spinozist approach is incompatible with that project, as long as Deleuze maintains, as he does, that *expression* does not require *resemblance.*

Let me note, in anticipation of my later argument, that the motivation for overturning Platonism in the specific sense in which Deleuze attempts it has to do with Deleuze's larger project of jettisoning any form of transcendence. The Platonic distinction between the copy and the simulacrum is founded on the distinction between copy and the original, which requires that there be a transcendent original of which the copy is a lesser imitation. Deleuze's Nietzscheanism lies in rejecting transcendence in any form; thus what bothers him about the Platonic distinction between original and copy, and by extension copy and simulacrum, is that such a form of thought requires transcendence. Deleuze's thesis of the univocity of Being is designed expressly to counter any form of ontological transcendence.

However, it is transcendence that Badiou thinks haunts Deleuze's thought. Transcendence is the deeper problem I mentioned above. It is the problem that threatens the entirety of Deleuze's philosophical approach. To see how transcendence might find its way into Deleuze's thought, we need to return to the thread of Badiou's argument. For Badiou, if Deleuze is to maintain the thesis of the univocity of Being, he needs to be able to conceive his ontology of two sides: from the side of Being and from the side of the beings that Being expresses. '[A] single name [for Being] is never sufficient [. . .]. Being needs to be said in a single sense both from the viewpoint of the unity of its power and from the viewpoint of the multiplicity of the divergent simulacra that this power actualizes in itself' (D 45/28). In other words, to maintain the univocity of Being, Deleuze must be able to articulate Being both from the standpoint of Being and from the standpoint of beings, and do so in a single and same sense.

According to Badiou, Deleuze articulates this single and same sense from the standpoint of both Being and beings in a series of conceptual doublets over the course of his work: the virtual and the actual, time and truth, chance and the eternal return, and the fold and the outside. I will focus on the first doublet, the virtual and the actual, both because it is the doublet that appears most consistently across Deleuze's corpus and because it crystallizes the deep difficulty that Badiou discovers in Deleuze's thesis of the univocity of Being. In countering that difficulty, I will return to Deleuze's concept of time, although not, as Badiou would have it, in relation to truth and falsity.

' "Virtual" ', writes Badiou, 'is without doubt the principal name of Being in Deleuze's work. Or rather the nominal pair virtual/actual exhausts the deployment of univocal Being' (D 65/43). What, then, are the virtual and the actual? It is probably best to approach them by way of contrasting them with the possible and the real. For Deleuze, the possible would be an image of the real; it is the real minus its character of actually existing. The possible can be conceived as what might be real but is not real. As such, it resembles the real, because it is what the real would be if indeed it realized that particular possibility. The virtual is in contrast to the possible in two ways. First, it is real; it exists, or, as Deleuze sometimes says, subsists or insists. As he notes in *Difference and Repetition*, '*The virtual is real in so far as it is virtual.*'[9] Second, the virtual does not resemble the actual as the possible resembles the real. If the actual actualizes the virtual, then that which is actualized is not a possibility brought into existence that existed merely as image before; rather it is something that, although expressed by the virtual, does not resemble it.

For Deleuze, the virtual is difference in itself, pure difference. 'The reality of the virtual consists of the differential elements and relations along with the singular points which correspond to them.'[10] We might think of the virtual as the reservoir of difference out of which the specific differences that are phenomenologically accessible to us are actualized. In *Difference and Repetition*, Deleuze marks the distinction between the virtual and the actual by invoking two terms, differen*t*iation and differen*c*iation. 'We call the determination of the virtual content of an Idea differen*t*iation; we call the actualization of that virtuality into species and distinguished parts differen*c*iation. It is always in relation to a differen*t*iated problem or to the differen*t*iated conditions of a problem that a differen*c*iation of species and parts is carried out, as though it corresponded to the cases of solution of a problem.'[11]

In getting a grasp on the virtual/actual distinction, Constantin Boundas once suggested to me a helpful analogy (one that also recurs briefly in *Difference and Repetition*): the relationship between genes and the living beings that result. If we think of genes as differen*t*iated structure or code or as Deleuze puts it, 'Idea', then the specific living being is what actualizes the virtual of that structure, code, Idea. The living being is not the real of which the genes are the possible: the genetic material is as real as the living being. Moreover, the living being hardly resembles the genes. We might think of the living being, at least loosely, as a particular 'solution' to the 'problem' that is differen*t*iated in the genes. (The analogy, of course, has its limits. For instance, genes carry a relatively fixed code, whereas the differen*t*iation of the virtual is characterized precisely by its lack of fixture.)

We can see, then, that the distinction between the virtual and the actual corresponds to the earlier distinction between Being and beings. To say that the actual actualizes the virtual is the same thing as saying, with Spinoza, that attributes and modes express substance or the One. As Badiou puts the point, 'The virtual is the very Being of beings, or we can even say that it is beings qua Being, for beings are but modalities of the One, and the One *is* the living production of its modes' (D 72/48).

Before turning to the difficulty that Badiou sees with the virtual and the actual, let me note in passing that we can now see why Badiou thinks of Deleuze's philosophical approach as 'monotonous'. For Badiou, the structure of the One and its modes keeps returning in Deleuze's thought, no matter whom he discusses. It is always a submission of the Many to the One that concerns Deleuze; the terms may differ, but the approach remains the same.

Given this approach, however, what is the difficulty Badiou cites? It lies in the attempt to maintain a distinction between the virtual and the actual without falling from the One into the Two, and thus into transcendence. As Badiou notes, in order for Deleuze to maintain the primacy of the One, '[a]s the ground of the object, the virtual must not be thought apart from the object itself' (D 77/51). Why not? Because if the virtual is ontologically distinct from the object, then there is no longer a One that expresses itself, but a transcendent Being that gives rise to beings: the One becomes a Two, or a Many.

The question is, then, how can we think of an object as both virtual and actual? For Badiou, there is no way to do so without losing the distinction between the virtual and the actual. Deleuze, in order to solve this problem, 'undertakes an analytic of the indistinguishable'.[12] In the object, both the virtual and the actual exist, but the virtual is indiscernible from the actual. 'Deleuze ends up by posing that the two parts of the object, the virtual and the actual, cannot in fact be thought of as separate' (D 80/53). But that, precisely, is the problem. In Badiou's eyes, Deleuze here faces a dilemma, and either the virtual or the actual must give way. If the virtual is indistinguishable from the actual, then that can only mean either that the virtual has taken on the 'simulacrul' (if I may be permitted that unwieldy adjective) character of the actual, in which case it is no longer a ground for the actual; or, alternatively, if the virtual remains the ground of the actual, then the object must be thought purely in terms of the virtual, and the actual becomes merely epiphenomenal, a wisp of image over-laying the virtual and not actually existing. 'The more Deleuze attempts to wrest the virtual from irreality, indetermination, and non-objectivity, the more irreal, indetermined, and finally nonobjective the actual (or beings) becomes [...]. In this circuit of thought, it is the Two and not the One that is instated' (D 81/53).

To sum up the difficulty, Deleuze cannot think specific objects, beings, as at once virtual and actual without collapsing the distinction between the two. Something must give way. And according to Badiou, what needs to give way is the One: 'the One is not, there are only actual multiplicities, and the ground is void' (D 81/53).

This difficulty is a particularly troubling one for Deleuze. It goes to the heart of his philosophical project, because if the One, in being thought, collapses into the Two, then what is reintroduced is the transcendence Deleuze dedicated his philosophical approach to avoiding. Badiou believes that transcendence can only be overcome by abandoning the One. If he is right, then Deleuze's project is doomed from the start. Immanence is incompatible with the One. 'Deleuze's virtual ground remains for me a transcendence' (D 69/46).

Can one save Deleuze from Badiou's critique? Is it possible to retain the One without sacrificing the immanence Deleuze holds dear? Before attempting to articulate a defence of Deleuze, let me state for the record that I have some sympathy for Badiou's wariness about the virtual, which I have expressed elsewhere.[13] My worry there, similar to that of Badiou's, is how to conceive the ontological status of the virtual, what to make of Deleuze's claim that the virtual is as real as the actual, but that it has some sort of distinct ontological status by virtue of the fact that he says it 'insists' or 'subsists' rather than 'exists'.[14] I believe that the two concerns are complementary. Although Badiou approaches his critique from the point of view of the object, whereas my concern starts from the point of view of the virtual itself, we both arrive at the worry that the virtual is empty of content, either by resistance to inferential clarification (me) or by having either to collapse into the actual or go transcendent (Badiou). What I would like to attempt, then, albeit briefly, may well serve as an answer to my concern as well as Badiou's (although I will focus on Badiou's critique rather than my own).

In order to respond to Badiou's critique, it is best, I believe, to return to what I take to be the heart of Deleuze's philosophical motivation: the resistance to transcendence. In this resistance, Deleuze is at his most purely Nietzschean. Nietzsche's rejection of transcendence is rooted in his rejection of the condemnation of life by means of values exterior to it. Christianity, of course, provides the most telling example. In Christianity, values are projected out onto a transcendent being (God) that, in turn, judges (and finds wanting) the very life that projected those values in the first place. Life is condemned by the recourse to a transcendence that judges it. What is required, in order to counter this transcendence, is a philosophy of immanence. Not a philosophy that just says Yes to everything in life (Nietzsche's donkey), but a philosophy that allows for creativity and development but does so without recourse to a transcendent that would dominate them.

Deleuze fashions his immanence in order to meet these Nietzschean requirements. And in thinking about his concept of the One, of Being, we need to keep in mind that his concept of the One is supposed to support a thought of immanence, of anti-transcendence. In this sense, I want to break from Badiou in what at first may seem a small way. For Badiou, it is the One that is primary to Deleuze's philosophy; immanence falls out from that. For me, it is immanence, the necessity of abandoning any form of transcendence, that is the fundamental requirement of Deleuze's philosophy. The One must be conceived in terms of immanence, not the other way around.

What difference might this inversion make? My suggestion here is that we think of Deleuze's One, be it Being as difference or Spinoza's substance or the desire of *Anti-Oedipus* or (as we shall see in more detail below) Bergson's ontological memory as *whatever it is that supports immanence*. In other words, in any given philosophical work of Deleuze's, the One does not have an independent standing about which we might ask whether it is immanent or transcendent. (This is in direct contrast to Badiou's approach, which asked after the One and found it to be either transcendent or reducible to the actual.) Rather, the idea of the One *means* that whatever ontological concepts are in play must be conceived in such a way as to conform to immanence. If, therefore, we are conceiving a Deleuzian ontological concept as implying transcendence, then we must see whether there is another way to conceive it so as to interpret it immanently instead.

Such a requirement does not, by itself, get us very far. It does not tell us, for instance, whether Deleuze's ontological concepts in fact *can* always be interpreted immanently. It might well be that although Deleuze himself would prefer an immanent interpretation of all of his ontological concepts, the structure of his own thought militates against that preference. And, in fact, we may take that to be exactly what Badiou is arguing: the invocation of the One requires an embrace of the very transcendence Deleuze seeks to overcome. In order to answer that argument, we need to revisit the concepts of the virtual and the actual. But in doing so, what I would like to bear in mind is that this revisiting should be seen as addressing the question of whether we can conceive the virtual and the actual immanently rather than transcendently, instead of in terms of the One. From the answer to that question, the issue of the One will sort itself out in accordance with what I take to be the more fundamental movement of Deleuze's thought.

What might be the role of the concepts of the virtual and the actual in a thought of immanence? In approaching that question, we need to ensure that the immanence they constitute is not a static one, but instead dynamic and evolutionary (if we understand that latter term, with Darwin, as not implying a goal). This is in keeping with Deleuze's Nietzschean motivation. He wants to articulate an ontology that allows for creativity, for the novel and the unexpected. In *What is Philosophy?*, co-authored with Felix Guattari, he writes, 'Philosophy does not consist in knowing and is not inspired by truth. Rather, it is categories like Interesting, Remarkable, or Important that determine success or failure.'[15] If he is to articulate such an ontology, he needs it to be dynamic rather than static.

We can gather a hint of the proper approach by returning to Boundas' suggestion of the analogy between the virtual/actual distinction and genetics. The gene, as virtual, unfolds into specific living beings. The gene is both real (rather than imaginary) and does not resemble the living being which emerges from it. And yet, it does set (many of the) conditions under which a specific living being arises. It is the problem to which the living being is the solution. Deleuze's own ontology is, of course, not merely biological; it is far more ambitious and encompassing. But if we follow the hint the analogy provides, we can, I believe, see our way to a proper conception of the virtual and the actual. This hint lies in temporality, in the temporal unfolding of the virtual into the actual. The gene unfolds into a living being (which itself unfolds without losing its genetic inheritance) *over time*.

If we follow this hint, it is Bergson more than Spinoza who provides the necessary guidance in conceiving the relation of the virtual to the actual. In *Deleuze*, Badiou separates his discussion of time from his discussion of the virtual and the actual. This, I believe, is a mistake, since it is primarily from the viewpoint of time that the virtual and the actual should be considered. For Bergson, the past does not follow the present; nor is the present separate from the past. They are of a piece. This is the famous concept of 'duration' in Bergson. Without the past, there can be no actual present; the present would be only an ideal vanishing point. Conversely, without the present the past would have no source. The two, although in some sense ontologically distinct, are also ontologically bound to each other. For Bergson, the present proceeds from the past, and the past, at all points, is the entirety of the past, not a specific set of discrete moments (which would be too spatialized a conception of the past). As Deleuze puts the point, 'The past and the present do not denote two successive moments, but two elements which coexist [...]. The past does not follow the present, but on the contrary, is presupposed by it as the pure condition without which it would not pass.'[16]

For Deleuze, moreover, there is, in accordance with Bergson's thought, only a single past. There may be many psychological pasts, corresponding to specific personal histories. But those psychological pasts participate in a single onto-logical past from which each present arises. 'Bergson concludes that there is one Time and one Time only, as much on the level of the actual parts as on the level of the virtual Whole.'[17]

The question then is, if the past and present are a single time and yet are not collapsed into each other, what is their relationship? As Deleuze reads him, Bergson sees the relationship as one of the virtual to the actual. Both the past and present exist, both are real, but the past exists virtually and the present is actualized from the virtuality of the past. The past is pure multiplicity, dif-ference in its pure form. The present, by contrast, is a specific actualized multiplicity, a specific difference, or, as Deleuze sometimes terms it, a quan-titative difference. To see this idea in its full implications would require a much longer treatment than I can offer here, but Deleuze sums the point up suc-cinctly in the following passage, distinguishing

> two types of multiplicity. One is represented by space [...]. It is a multiplicity of exteriority, of simultaneity, of juxtaposition, of order, of quantitative differentiation, of *difference in degree*; it is a numerical mul-tiplicity, *discontinuous and actual*. The other type of multiplicity appears in pure duration: it is an internal multiplicity [...] of heterogeneity, of qualitative discrimination, or *difference in kind*; it is a *virtual and continuous* multiplicity that cannot be reduced to numbers.[18]

The relation of the present to the past, then, is the unfolding relationship of *expression* as it was found in Spinoza: a single past expresses itself in unfolding presents that are at the same time inextricably woven together with the past and yet distinct from it in being spatial and phenomenologically accessible.

Seeing things this way brings Deleuze several advantages. First, although this is of less concern to Deleuze, the idea of the present unfolding from the past and within the context of conditions set by the past is one that has some intuitive appeal. We recognize that, in many senses, the past does in fact set the conditions and parameters for the shape of any given present moment. Second, and more to the point, to see the present as unfolding from a pure multiplicity allows for an ontology that is dynamic: that allows for the Interesting, the Remarkable, or the Important to appear. If difference in itself is the source for every particular present, this allows the widest possible latitude for the types of presents that might appear.

Finally, and this is the crucial point, this conception of time allows Deleuze to conceive difference in both its virtual and actual aspects without resort to any sort of transcendence. The past coexists with the present in a single time; it is not ontologically transcendent to it. This coexistence is in some sense ontolo-gically One (there is one time) and in some sense *not* ontologically One (the past is, by virtue of being a virtual difference in kind, ontologically distinct from the present, which is difference in degree). Thus, by asking after transcendence first and the One only afterwards, we can capture Deleuze's project and see the particular sense in which he embraces the One, without requiring him also to embrace transcendence in order to preserve the One.

We can also see here how Deleuze's thought is not a thought of pure difference, if by pure difference we mean difference without unity or without the One. To think difference and immanence together requires some sort of unity, some sort of One. And this is why, contrary to common interpretation, his thought is no more a thought of pure difference than it is a thought of pure unity or Oneness; it is a thought of difference *and* unity, the Many *and* the One.

Seen temporally, as opposed to spatially, the relationship of the virtual and the actual seems not to be as problematic as Badiou thinks. It is true, as Badiou cites, that Deleuze sometimes talks of the virtual and the actual as though they were parts of objects, for example when Deleuze says in *Difference and Repetition* that 'the virtual must be as strictly a part of the real object – as though the object had one part of itself in the virtual into which it plunged as though into an objective dimension'.[19] But such thinking is too spatial; it betrays the role that Bergson's concept of duration plays in Deleuze's thought. Better is Deleuze's clarification a few pages later: 'Beneath the actual qualities and extensities, species and parts, there are spatio-temporal dynamisms.'[20] It is this latter thinking that captures the spirit of Deleuze's philosophical approach, his attempt to bind dynamism to immanence, Bergson to Spinoza (under the guiding intuition of Nietzsche).

By shifting the discussion from spatial to temporal terms, then, we are able to preserve the distinction between the virtual and the actual without falling into the dilemma Badiou poses to Deleuze. The idea of a single time that has both virtual and actual aspects does not require us to choose between a collapse of the virtual into the actual (or vice versa) and the reintroduction of transcendence. In fact, it is precisely the turn to Bergson that helps avoid this. Temporal thinking, unlike spatial thinking, does not require us to think in terms of parts of objects; instead, it turns thought toward aspects of temporal unfolding.

If this shift in conception of the virtual is right, then Deleuze's thought can meet the challenge of coherence Badiou raises against it. This is not to say that Deleuze's ontology is in general better or more adequate than Badiou's. Whether, in the end, ontology should be conceived by means of an immanence with deep roots in the One (and again, not the other way around) or instead by means of a multiplicity without the One is another question. Whether we ought to choose the ontological proliferation that Deleuze's thought proposes or instead embrace the more austere ontology of Badiou cannot be decided on the basis of these considerations. Although in his *Deleuze* Badiou often generously counterposes his thought to Deleuze's as though it were a matter of ontological preference, what is really at stake in that little book is the coherence of Deleuze's entire approach. What I have tried to offer here is a defence of that coherence, not a justification for the larger preference. Such a justification will have to await a more sustained treatment of the divergent ontologies of these provocative and alluring thinkers.

6

BADIOU AND DELEUZE ON THE ONTOLOGY OF MATHEMATICS*

Daniel W. Smith

Deleuze once wrote that 'encounters between independent thinkers always occur in a blind zone', and this is certainly true of the encounter between Alain Badiou and Gilles Deleuze.[1] In 1988, Badiou published *Being and Event*, which attempted to develop an 'ontology of the multiple' derived from the mathematical model of axiomatic set theory. Soon afterward, he tells us, he realized – no doubt correctly – that his primary philosophical rival in this regard was Deleuze, who similarly held that philosophy is a theory of multiplicities, but whose own concept of multiplicities was derived from different mathematical sources and entailed a different conception of ontology itself. In 1997, Badiou published a study of Deleuze entitled *Deleuze: The Clamor of Being*, in which he confronted his rival directly and attempted to set forth their fundamental differences. The study, Badiou tells us in the introduction, was occasioned by an exchange of letters he had with Deleuze between 1992 and 1994, which focused directly on the concept of multiplicity and the specific problem of an *immanent* conceptualization of the multiple. On the opening page of the book, Badiou notes that 'Deleuze's preferences were for differential calculus and Riemannian manifolds [. . . whereas] I preferred algebra and sets' (*D* 8/1) – leading the reader to expect, in what follows, a comparison of Deleuze's and Badiou's notions of multiplicity based in part, at least, on these differing mathematical sources. Yet as one reads the remainder of *Deleuze: The Clamor of Being*, one quickly discovers that Badiou in fact adopted a quite different strategy in approaching Deleuze. Despite the announced intention, the book does not contain a single discussion of Deleuze's theory of multiplicities; it avoids the topic entirely. Instead, Badiou immediately displaces his focus to the claim that Deleuze is not a philosopher of multiplicity at all, but rather a philosopher of the 'One'. Nor does Badiou ever discuss the mathematical sources of Deleuze's theory of multiplicity. Instead, he puts forth a secondary claim that, insofar as Deleuze *does* have a theory of

* A shorter version of this chapter was presented at the conference 'Ethics and Politics: The Work of Alain Badiou', which was held at the Centre for Critical and Cultural Theory at the University of Cardiff on 25–26 May 2002, and organized by Jean-Jacques Lecercle and Neil Badmington. My understanding of Badiou's work is strongly indebted to Peter Hallward's book *Badiou: A Subject to Truth* (Minneapolis: University of Minnesota Press, 2003), which presents a helpful overview and critical analysis of Badiou's philosophy. I would like to thank Peter Hallward for providing me with a copy of the manuscript of his book, and for the insights and clarifications he provided on both Badiou and Deleuze during several e-mail correspondences.

multiplicity, it is not derived from a mathematical model at all, as is Badiou's own, but rather from a model that Badiou terms variously as 'organic', 'natural', 'animal' or 'vitalistic'.[2]

Critics have rightly ascertained the obvious aim of this double strategy of avoidance and displacement: since Badiou presents himself as an ontologist of the multiple, and claims that his ontology is purely mathematical, he wants to distance Deleuze as far as possible from both these concerns. I would like to argue that, in order to get at what is interesting in the Badiou–Deleuze encounter, these all-too-obvious strategies of avoidance and displacement need to be set aside, since the real terms of the confrontation clearly lie elsewhere. Badiou's general philosophical (or meta-ontological) position turns on the equation that 'ontology = axiomatic set theory', since mathematics alone thinks being, and it is only in axiomatic set theory that mathematics adequately thinks itself and constitutes a condition of philosophy. The Badiou–Deleuze confrontation must consequently be staged on each of these fronts – axiomatics, set theory, and their corresponding ontology – since it is only here that their differences can be exposed in a direct and intrinsic manner.

From this viewpoint, the two crucial differences between Badiou and Deleuze immediately come to light. First, for Deleuze, the ontology of mathematics is *not* reducible to axiomatics, but must be understood much more broadly in terms of the complex tension between axiomatics and what he calls 'problematics'. Deleuze assimilates axiomatics to 'major' or 'royal' science, which is linked to the social axiomatic of capitalism (and the State), and which constantly attempts to effect a reduction or repression of the problematic pole of mathematics, itself wedded to a 'minor' or 'nomadic' conception of science. For this reason, second, the concept of multiplicity, even within mathematics itself, cannot simply be identified with the concept of a set, whether consistent or inconsistent; rather, mathematics is marked by a tension between extensive multiplicities or sets (the axiomatic pole) and virtual or differential multiplicities (the problematic pole), and the incessant translation of the latter into the former. Reformulated in this manner, the Badiou–Deleuze confrontation can be posed and explored in a way that is *internal* to both mathematics (problematics versus axiomatics) and the theory of multiplicities (differential versus extensive multiplicities).

These two criteria will allow us to assess the differences between Badiou and Deleuze in a way that avoids the red herrings of the 'One' and 'vitalism'. Although Badiou claims that 'the Deleuzian didactic of multiplicities is, from start to finish, a polemic against sets',[3] in fact Deleuze nowhere litigates against sets, and indeed argues that the translation (or reduction) of differential multiplicities to extensive sets is not only inevitable ontologically but also *necessary* scientifically. For Deleuze, problematics and axiomatics (minor and major science) together constitute a single ontological field of interaction, with axiomatics perpetually effecting a repression – or more accurately, an arithmetic conversion – of problematics. Badiou, by contrast, grants an ontological status to axiomatics alone, and in doing so, he explicitly adopts the ontological viewpoint of 'major' science, along with its repudiation and condemnation of 'minor' science. As a result, not only does Badiou insist that Deleuze's concept of a virtual multiplicity 'remains inferior to the concept of the Multiple that can be found in the contemporary history of sets', but he goes so far as to claim 'the virtual does not exist', in effect denying the entire 'problematic' pole of mathematics.[4] Interestingly, this contrast between Badiou and Deleuze finds a precise expression in a famous poetic formula. Badiou at times places his entire project under the sign of Lautréamont's poetic paean to 'severe mathematics', which Deleuze, for his part, cites critically: 'In contrast to Lautréamont's song that rises up around the paranoiac-Oedipal-narcissistic pole [of mathematics] – "O severe mathematics ... Arithmetic! Algebra! Geometry! Imposing Trinity! Luminous triangle!" – there is another song: O schizophrenic mathematics, uncontrollable and mad ...'[5]

It is this *other* mathematics – problematics, as opposed to the 'specifically scientific Oedipus' of axiomatics – that Deleuze attempts to uncover and formalize in his work. The obstacles to such a project, however, are evident. The theory of extensional multiplicities (Cantor's set theory) and its rigorous axiomatization (Zermelo-Frankel et al.) is one of the great achievements of modern mathematics, and in *Being and Event* Badiou was able to appropriate this work for his philosophical purposes. For Deleuze, the task was quite different, since he himself had to construct a hitherto non-existent (philosophical) formalization of differential or virtual multiplicities which are, by his own account, selected against by 'royal' mathematics itself. Since Badiou has largely neglected Deleuze's writings on mathematics, in what follows I would first like to outline the nature of the general contrast Deleuze establishes between problematics and axiomatics, and then make some brief remarks about the 'problematic' status of Deleuze's theory of multiplicities. With these resources in hand, we can then return to Badiou's specific critiques of Deleuze, partly to show their limitations, but also to specify the more relevant points of contrast between Badiou and Deleuze.

I

Let me turn first, then, to the problematic-axiomatic distinction. Although Deleuze formulates this distinction in his own manner, it in fact reflects a fairly familiar tension within the history of mathematics, which we must be content to illustrate hastily by means of three historical examples. The first example comes from the Greeks. Proclus, in his *Commentary of the First Book of Euclid's Elements*, had already formulated a distinction, within Greek geometry, between problems and theorems.[6] Theorems concerned the demonstration, from axioms or postulates, of the inherent properties belonging to a figure, whereas problems concerned the construction of figures using a straightedge and compass. In turn, theorematics and problematics each involve two different conceptions of 'deduction': in theorematics, a deduction moves from axioms to the theorems that are derived from it, whereas in problematics a deduction moves from the problem to the ideal accidents and *events* that condition the problem and form the cases that resolve it. 'The event by itself', writes Deleuze, 'is problematic and problematizing.'[7] In Greece, problematics found its classical expression in Archimedean geometry (especially the Archimedes of 'On the Method'), an 'operative' geometry in which the line was defined less as an essence than as a continuous process of 'alignment', the circle as a continuous process of 'rounding', the square as the process of 'quadrature', and so on. Proclus, how-ever, had already pointed to (and defended) the relative triumph, in Greek geometry, of the theorematic over the problematic. The reason: to the Greeks, 'problems concern only events and affects which show evidence of a *deterioration* or a projection of essences in the imagination', and theorematics thus could present itself as a necessary 'rectification' of thought – a 'rectification' that must be understood, in a literal sense, as a triumph of the rectilinear over the cur-vilinear.[8] In the 'minor' geometry of problematics, figures are inseparable from their inherent variations, affections and events; the aim of 'major' theorematics, by contrast, is 'to uproot variables from their state of continuous variation in order to extract from them fixed points and constant relations', and thereby to set geometry on the 'royal' road of theorematic deduction and proof.[9] Badiou, for his part, explicitly aligns his ontology with the position of theorematics: 'the pure multiple, the generic form of being, *never* welcomes the event in itself as its component' (*CT* 71–2).

By the seventeenth century, the tension between problems and theorems, which was internal to geometry, had shifted to a more general tension between geometry itself, on the one hand, and algebra and arithmetic on the other. Desargues' *projective geometry*, for instance, which was a qualitative and 'minor' geometry centred on problems–events, had been quickly opposed in favour of the *analytic geometry* of Fermat and Descartes – a quantitative and 'major' geometry that translated geometric relations into arithmetic relations that could be expressed in algebraic equations (Cartesian coordinates). 'Royal' sci-ence, in other words, now entailed an arithmetization of geometry itself, a conversion of geometry into algebra. Projective geometry would be revived two centuries later in the work of Monge, the inventor of descriptive geometry, and Poncelet, who formulated the topological 'principle of continuity', though it maintained its 'minor' status because of its concern with problems–events. In topology, figures that are theorematically distinct in Euclidean geometry, such as a triangle, a square and a circle, are seen as one and the same 'homeomorphic' figure, since they are capable of being continuously transformed into one another, like a rubber band being stretched. This entailed an extension of geometric 'intuitions' beyond the limits of empirical or sensible perception. 'With Monge, and especially Poncelet,' writes Deleuze, commenting on Léon Brunschvicg's work, 'the limits of sensible, or even spatial, representation (striated space) are indeed surpassed, but less in the direction of a symbolic power of abstraction [i.e., theorematics] than toward a trans-spatial imagina-tion, or a trans-intuition (continuity).'[10] In the twentieth century, computers have extended the reach of this 'trans-intuition' even further, allowing math-ematicians to 'see' hitherto unimagined objects such as the Mandelbrot set and the Lorenz attractor, which have become the poster children of the new sciences of chaos and complexity. 'Seeing, seeing what happens, has always had an essential importance, even in pure mathematics', continues Deleuze, noting that 'many mathematicians nowadays think that a computer is more precious than an axiomatic.'[11] But already in the early nineteenth century, there was a renewed attempt to turn projective geometry into a mere practical dependency on analysis, or so-called higher geometry (the debate between Poncelet and Cauchy). The development of the theory of functions, for instance, would eventually eliminate the appeal to the principle of continuity, substituting for the 'minor' geometrical idea of smoothness of variation the 'major' arithmetic idea of mapping or a one-to-one correspondence of points (point-set topology).

It was in the late nineteenth and early twentieth centuries that this double movement of major science toward 'theorematization' and 'arithmetization' would reach its full flowering, primarily in response to the problems posed by the invention of the calculus. In its origins, the calculus was tied to problematics in a double sense. The first refers to the ontological problems that the calculus confronted: the differential calculus addressed the problematic of *tangents* (how to determine the tangent lines to a given curve), while the integral calculus addressed the problematic of *quadrature* (how to determine the area within a given curve). The greatness of Leibniz and Newton was to have recognized the intimate connection between these two problematics (the problem of finding areas is the inverse of determining tangents to curves), and to have developed a symbolism to link them together and resolve them. Yet for two centuries, the calculus, not unlike Archimedean geometry, itself maintained a problematic status in a second sense: it was allotted a para-scientific status, labelled a 'barbaric' or 'Gothic' hypothesis, or at best a convenient convention or well-grounded fiction. In its early formulations, the calculus was shot through with dynamic notions such as infinitesimals, fluxions and fluents, thresholds, passages to the limit, continuous variation – all of which presumed a *geometrical* conception of the continuum, in other words, the idea of a process. For most mathematicians, these were considered to be 'metaphysical' ideas that lay beyond the realm of mathematical definition. Berkeley famously ridiculed infinitesimals as 'the ghosts of departed quantities'; D'Alembert famously responded by telling his students, *Allez en avant, et la foi vous viendra* ('Go forward, and faith will come to you').[12]

For a long period of time, the enormous success of the calculus in solving physical problems delayed research into its logical foundations. It was not until the end of the nineteenth century that the calculus would receive a rigorous foundation through the development of the limit-concept. 'Rigour' meant that the calculus had to be separated from its problematic origins in geometrical conceptions or 'intuitions', and reconceptualized in purely arithmetic terms (the loaded term 'intuition' here having little to do with 'empirical' perception, but rather the ideal geometrical notion of continuous movement and space). This programme of 'arithmetization' – or more precisely 'discretization' – was achieved by Karl Weierstrass, in the wake of work done by Cauchy (leading Giulio Giorello to dub Weierstrass and his followers the 'ghostbusters').[13] Geometrical notions were reconceptualized in terms of sets of discrete points, which in turn were conceptualized in terms of number. As a result, Weierstrass was able to give the concept of the variable a purely *static* interpretation. Early interpreters had tended to appeal to the geometrical intuition of continuous motion when they said that a variable *x* 'approaches' a limit; Weierstrass' innovation was to reinterpret this variable *x* arithmetically as simply desig-nating any one of a collection of numerical values (the theory of functions). Weierstrass' limit-concept (the epsilon-delta method) thereby eliminated any dynamism or 'continuous variation' from the notion of continuity, and any interpretation of the operation of differentiation as a process. Dedekind took this arithmetization a step further by rigorously defining the continuity of the real numbers in terms of a 'cut'. Cantor's set theory, finally, gave a discrete interpretation of the notion of infinity itself, treating infinite sets like finite sets (the power set axiom) – or rather, treating all sets, whether finite or infinite, as mathematical objects (the axiom of infinity).[14]

Weierstrass, Dedekind and Cantor thus form the great triumvirate in the development of the 'arithmetic' continuum. In their wake, the basic concepts of the calculus – function, continuity, limit, convergence, infinity, and so on – were progressively 'clarified' and 'refined', and ultimately given a set-theoretical foundation. The assumptions of Weierstrass' discretization problem – that only arithmetic is rigorous, and that geometric notions are unsuitable for secure foundations – are now largely identified with the orthodox or 'major' view of the history of mathematics as a progression toward ever more 'well-founded' positions.[15] The programme would pass through two further developments. The contradictions generated by set theory brought on a sense of a 'crisis' in the foundations, which Hilbert's formalist (or formalization) programme tried to repair through *axiomatization*: he attempted to show that set theory could be derived from a finite set of axioms, which were later codified by Zermelo-Frankel et al. Gödel and Cohen, finally, in their famous theorems, would eventually expose the internal limits of axiomatization (incompleteness, undecidability), demonstrating, in Badiou's language, that there is a variety of mathematical forms in 'infinite excess' over our ability to formalize them consistently. By the mid-twentieth century, the historical efforts of major science in the direction of theorematics (the Greeks) and arithmetization (the seventeenth century) had been transformed into the dual programme of *discretization* and *axiomatization*.

II

This historical sketch, though brief, can help us clarify the differences between the respective projects of Badiou and Deleuze. In identifying ontology exclu-sively with axiomatic set theory, Badiou is explicitly choosing to align his ontology with the position of 'major' mathematics, which has often been characterized as an 'ontological reductionism'. In this view, as Penelope Maddy describes it, 'mathematical objects and structures are identified with or instantiated by set-theorematic surrogates [discretization], and the classical theorems about them proved from the axioms of set theory [axiomatization].'[16] Badiou tells us that he made a similar appeal to Deleuze, insisting that 'every figure of the type "fold", "interval", "enlacement", "serration", "fractal", or even "chaos" has a corresponding schema in a certain family of sets' (D 72/47). Deleuze, for his part, fully recognizes this orthodox position, with its introduction of 'rigour' and its search for adequate 'foundations': 'Modern mathematics is regarded as based upon the theory of groups or set theory rather than on the differential calculus.'[17] Deleuze nonetheless insists, however, on the ontological irreducibility of problematics, noting that the recognition of the irreducibility of problems and their genetic role has become 'one of the most original characteristics of modern epistemology'.[18] Badiou's ontology presumes a double reduction: of physics to mathematics, and of mathematics to axiomatic set theory. The reasons Deleuze rejects this reductionism, even within mathematics, can be encapsulated in a few summary points.

First, according to Deleuze, mathematics is constantly producing notions that have an objectively problematic status; the role of axiomatics (or its precursors) is to codify and solidify these problematic notions, providing them with a theorematic ground or rigorous foundation. Axiomaticians, one might say, are the 'law and order' types in mathematics: 'Hilbert and de Broglie were as much politicians as scientists: they re-established order.'[19] In this sense, as Jean Dieudonné suggests, axiomatics is a foundational but secondary enterprise in mathematics, dependent for its very existence on problematics:

> In periods of expansion, when new notions are introduced, it is often very difficult to exactly delimit the conditions of their deployment, and one must admit that one can only reasonably do so once one has acquired a rather long practice in these notions, which necessitates a more or less extended period of cultivation [*défrichement*], during which uncertainty and controversy dominates. Once the heroic age of pioneers passes, the following generation can then codify their work, getting rid of the superfluous, solidifying the bases – in short, putting the house in order. At this moment, the axiomatic method reigns anew, until the next overturning [*bouleversement*] that brings a new idea.[20]

Nicolas Bourbaki puts the point even more strongly, noting that 'the axiomatic method is nothing but the "Taylor System" – the "scientific management" – of mathematics'.[21] The push toward axiomatics at the end of the nineteenth century arose at the same time that Taylorism arose in capitalism: axiomatics does for mathematics what Taylorism does for 'work'.[22]

Second, problematic concepts often (though not always) have their source in what Deleuze terms the 'ambulatory' sciences, which includes metallurgy, surveying, stonecutting and perspective. (One need only think of the mathematical problems encountered by Archimedes in his work on military installations, Desargues on the techniques of perspective, Monge on the transportation of earth, and so on.) The nature of such domains, however, is that they do not allow science to assume an autonomous power. The reason, according to Deleuze, is that the ambulatory sciences subordinate all their operations to the sensible conditions of intuition and construction – *following* the flow of matter, *drawing and linking up* smooth space. Everything is situated in the objective zone of fluctuation that is coextensive with reality itself. However refined or rigorous, 'approximate knowledge' is still dependent upon sensitive and sensible evaluations that pose more problems than they solve: problematics is still its only mode.

Such sciences are linked to notions – such as heterogeneity, dynamism, continuous variation, flows, etc. – that are 'barred' or banned from the requirements of axiomatics, and consequently they tend to appear in history as that which was superseded or left behind. By contrast, what is proper to royal science, to its theorematic or axiomatic power, is 'to isolate all operations from the conditions of intuition, making them true intrinsic concepts, or "categories" [...]. Without this categorical, apodictic apparatus, the differential operations would be constrained to follow the evolution of a phenomenon.' In the ontological field of interaction between minor and major science, in other words,

> the ambulant sciences confine themselves to *inventing problems* whose solution is tied to a whole set of collective, non-scientific activities but whose *scientific solution* depends, on the contrary, on royal science and the way it has transformed the problem by introducing it into its theorematic apparatus and its organization of work. This is somewhat like intuition and intelligence in Bergson, where only intelligence has the scientific means to solve formally the problems posed by intuition.[23]

This is why Deleuze suggests that, despite its ontological irreducibility, problematics is by its very nature 'a kind of science, or treatment of science, that is very difficult to classify, whose history is even difficult to follow'.[24]

Third, what is crucial in the interaction between the two poles is thus the processes of *translation* that take place between them – for instance, in Descartes and Fermat, an algebraic translation of the geometrical; in Weierstrass, a static translation of the dynamic; in Dedekind, a discrete translation of the continuous. The 'richness and necessity of translations', writes Deleuze, 'include as many opportunities for openings as risks of closure or stoppage'.[25] In general, Deleuze's work in mathematical 'epistemology' tends to focus on the reduction of the problematic to the axiomatic, the intensive to the extensive, the continuous to the discrete, the non-metric to the metric, the non-denumerable to the denumerable, the rhizomatic to the arborescent, the smooth to the striated. Not all these reductions, to be sure, are equivalent, and Deleuze analyses each on its own account. Even today, there are notions with mathematics that remain outside the grasp of the discretization programme – most notably the geometric continuum itself, the non-discrete 'continuous continuum', which still maintains its problematic status. At times, Deleuze suggests, axiomatics can possess a deliberate will to halt problematics. 'State science retains of nomad science only what it can appropriate; it turns the rest into a set of strictly limited formulas without any real scientific status, or else simply represses and bans it.'[26] But despite its best efforts, axiomatics can never have done with problematics, which maintains its own ontological status and rigour. 'Minor science is continually enriching major science, communicating its intuitions to it, its way of proceeding, its itinerancy, its sense of and taste for matter, singularity, variation, intuitionist geometry and the numbering number [. . .]. Major science has a perpetual need for the inspiration of the minor; but the minor would be nothing if it did not confront and conform to the highest scientific requirements.'[27] In Deleuzian terms, one might say that while 'progress' can be made at the level of theorematics and axiomatics, all 'becoming' occurs at the level of problematics.

A recent example can help serve to illustrate this ongoing tension. Even after Weierstrass' work, mathematicians using the calculus continued to obtain accurate results and make new discoveries by using infinitesimals in their reasoning, their mathematical conscience assuaged by the (often unchecked) supposition that infinitesimals could be replaced by Weierstrassian methods. Despite its supposed elimination, in other words, the 'non-rigorous' notion of infinitesimals continued to play a positive role in mathematics *as* a problematic concept, reliably producing correct solutions. In response to this situation, Abraham Robinson developed his *Non-Standard Analysis* (1966), which proposed an axiomatization of infinitesimals themselves, at last granting mathematicians the 'right' to use them in proofs.[28] Using the theory of formal languages, he added to the ordinary theory of numbers a new symbol (which we can call i for infinitesimal), and posited axioms saying that i was smaller than any finite number $1/n$ and yet not zero; he then showed that this enriched theory of numbers is consistent, assuming the consistency of the ordinary theory of numbers. The resulting mathematical model is described as 'non-standard' in that it contains, in addition to the 'standard' finite and transfinite numbers, non-standard numbers such as hyperreals and infinitesimals. Transfinites and infinitesimals are two types of infinite number, which characterize degrees of infinity in different fashions. In effect, this means that contemporary mathematics has two distinct rigorous formulations of the calculus: that of Weierstrass and Cantor, who eliminated infinitesimals, and that of Robinson, who rehabilitated and legitimized them. Both these endeavours, however, had their genesis in the imposition of the notion of infinitesimals *as* a problematic concept, which gave rise to differing but related axiomatizations. For Deleuze, the ontology of axiomatics is itself poorly understood if it does not take into account the ontological specificity and irreducibility of problematics.

Fourth, this means that axiomatics, no less than problematics, is itself an inventive and creative activity. One might be tempted to follow Poincaré in identifying problematics as a 'method of discovery' (Riemann) and axiomatics as a 'method of demonstration' (Weierstrass).[29] But just as problematics has its own modes of formalization and deduction, so axiomatics has its own modes of intuition and discovery (axioms, for instance, are not chosen arbitrarily, but in accordance with 'intuitive' notions of a line or set).

In science an axiomatic is not at all a transcendent, autonomous, and decision-making power opposed to experimentation and intuition. On the one hand, it has its own gropings in the dark, experimentations, modes of intuition. Axioms being independent of each other, can they be added, and up to what point (a saturated system)? Can they be withdrawn (a 'weakened' system)? On the other hand, it is of the nature of axiomatics to come up against so-called *undecidable propositions*, to confront *necessarily higher powers* that it cannot master. Finally, axiomatics does not constitute the cutting edge of science; it is much more a stopping point, a reordering that prevents decoded flows in physics and mathematics [i.e. problematics] from escaping in all directions. The great axiomaticians are the men of State within science, who seal off the lines of flight that are so frequent in mathematics, who would impose a new *nexum*, if only a temporary one, and who lay down the official policies of science. They are the heirs of the theorematic conception of geometry.[30]

III

Let me turn now to the theory of multiplicities. For Deleuze, the distinction between problematics and axiomatics is reflected in the distinction between two different conceptions of the multiple: differential or continuous multiplicities (problematics) and extensional or discrete sets (axiomatics). As we have seen, royal or 'major' mathematics is defined by the perpetual translation or conversion of the latter into the former. But it would be erroneous to characterize differential multiplicities as 'merely' intuitive and operative, and extensional sets as conceptual and formalizable. 'The fact is', writes Deleuze, 'that the two kinds of science have *different modes of formalization* [. . .]. What we have are two formally different conceptions of science, and ontologically, *a single field of interaction* in which royal science [axiomatics] continually appropriates the contents of vague or nomad science [problematics], while nomad science continually cuts the contents of royal science loose.'[31] One of Badiou's most insistent claims is that Deleuze's theory of multiplicities is drawn from a 'vitalist' paradigm, and not a mathematical one. But in fact, Deleuze's theory of multiplicities is drawn *exclusively* from mathematics — but from its problematic pole. Badiou implicitly admits this when he complains that Deleuze's 'experimental construction of multiplicities is anachronistic because it is *pre-Cantorian*'.[32] More accurately, however, one should say that Deleuze's theory of multiplicities is *non*-Cantorian. Cantor's set theory represents the crowning moment of the tendency toward 'discretization' in mathematics; Deleuze's project, by contrast, is to formalize the conception of 'continuous' multiplicities that corresponds to the problematic pole of mathematics. Problematics, no less than axiomatics, is the object of pure mathematics: just as Weierstrass, Dedekind and Cantor are the great names in the discretization programme, and Hilbert, Zermelo, Frankel, Gödel and Cohen the great names in the movement toward formalization and axiomatization, it is Abel, Galois, Riemann and Poincaré who appear among the great names in the history of problematics.

Deleuze, to be sure, is fully aware of the apparent anachronism involved in delving into the pre-Weierstrassian theories of the calculus (Maimon, Bordas-Demoulin, Wronski, Lagrange, Carnot . . .). 'A great deal of truly philosophical naiveté is needed to take the symbol *dx* seriously', he admits, while still maintaining that 'there is a treasure buried in the old so-called barbaric or pre-scientific interpretations of the differential calculus, which must be separated from its infinitesimal matrix.'[33] But the reason that Deleuze focuses on the role of the differential (*dx*), however, is clear: in the calculus, the differential is by nature problematic, it constitutes 'the internal character of the problem as such', which is precisely why it must *disappear* in the result or solution.[34] Deleuze will thus make a strong distinction between differential relations and axiomatic relations. Even in *Difference and Repetition*, however, the calculus is only one of several mathematical domains that Deleuze utilizes in formulating his theory of multiplicities: 'We cannot suppose that differential calculus is the only mathematical expression of problems as such [. . .]. More recently, other procedures have fulfilled this role better.'[35] What is at issue, in other words, is neither the empirical or 'vital' origin of mathematical problems (e.g., in the ambulatory sciences) nor the historical moment of their mathematical formalization (pre- or post-Cantorian). 'While it is true that the [continuous] continuum must be related to Ideas and to their problematic use', Deleuze writes, 'this is on condition that it no longer be defined by characteristics borrowed from sensible or even geometrical intuition.'[36] What Deleuze finds in pure mathematics is a rigorous conception of the constitution of problems *as such*, divorced not only from the conditions of intuition, but also from the conditions of their solvability. It is on the basis of this formalization that Deleuze, in turn, will be able to assign a precise status to mathematical notions such as continuous variation and becoming – which can only be comprehended under the mode of problematics.

Space precludes a detailed analysis of the mathematical origins of Deleuze's theory of multiplicities, which relies on work done in group theory (Abel, Galois), the theory of differential equations (Poincaré), and differential geometry (Riemann).[37] We can, however, present the formalized conditions of such multiplicities that Deleuze presents in *Difference and Repetition*. (1) The elements of the multiplicity are merely 'determinable', their nature is not determined in advance by either a defining property or an axiom (e.g. extensionality). Rather, they are pure virtualities that have neither identity, nor sensible form, nor conceptual signification, nor assignable function (principle of determinability). (2) They are nonetheless determined reciprocally as singularities in the differential relation, a 'non-localizable ideal connection' that provides a purely intrinsic definition of the multiplicity as 'problematic'; the differential relation is not only *external* to its terms, but *constitutive* of its terms (principle of reciprocal determination). (3) The values of these relations define the complete determination of the problem, that is, 'the existence, the number, and the distribution of the determinant points that precisely provide its conditions' *as* a problem (principle of complete determination). These three aspects of sufficient reason, finally, find their unity in the temporal principle of progressive determination, through which, as we have seen in the work of Abel and Galois, the problem is resolved (adjunction, etc.).[38] The strength of Deleuze's project, with regard to problematics, is that, in a certain sense, it parallels the movement toward 'rigour' that was made in axiomatics: just as axiomatics presents a formalized theory of extensional sets, Deleuze attempts a formalized theory of differential multiplicities, freed from the conditions of geometric intuition and solvability. In undertaking this project, he had few philosophical precursors (Lautman, Vuillemin), and the degree to which he succeeded in the effort no doubt remains an open question.[39] Nonetheless, it is enough to establish the point that the *differend* between Badiou and Deleuze concerns, not the distinction between the One and the Multiple, as Badiou argues, but rather the more profound distinction between two types of multiplicity, which correspond to the distinction between axiomatics and problematics (or 'major' and 'minor' science).

IV

Equipped now with a more adequate understanding of Deleuze's conception of problematics, we can now return to Badiou's critique and see why neither of his two main theses concerning Deleuze articulates the real nature of their fundamental differences. Badiou's thesis that Deleuze is a philosopher of the One is the least persuasive, for several reasons.

First, Badiou derives this thesis from Deleuze's concept of univocity, proposing the equation 'univocity = the One'. But already in Scotus, the doctrine of the 'univocity of Being' was strictly incompatible with (and in part directed against) a neo-Platonic 'philosophy of the One'. Moreover, Deleuze's explicit (and repeated) thesis in *Difference and Repetition* is that the only condition under which the term 'Being' can be said in a single and univocal sense is if Being is said univocally of *difference as such*. To argue, as Badiou does, that Deleuze's work operates 'on the basis of an ontological precomprehension of Being as One' is in effect to argue that Deleuze *rejects* the doctrine of univocity.[40] In other words, 'Being is univocal' and 'Being is One' are strictly incompatible theses, and Badiou's conflation of the two, as has been noted by others, betrays a fundamental misunderstanding of the theory of univocity.[41]

Second, while it is nonetheless true that Deleuze proposed a concept of the One compatible with univocity (e.g. the 'One-All' of the plane of immanence as a secant plane cut out of chaos),[42] Badiou seems unable to articulate it in part because of the inconsistency of his own conception of the One, which is variously assimilated to the Neo-Platonic One, the Christian God, Spinoza's Substance, Leibniz's Continuity, Kant's unconditioned Whole, Nietzsche's Eternal Return, Bergson's *élan vital*, a generalized conception of Unity, and Deleuze's Virtual, to name a few. The reason for this conceptual fluidity seems clear: since the task of modern philosophy, for Badiou, is 'the renunciation of the One', and only a set theoretical ontology is capable of fulfilling this task, the concept of the 'One' effectively becomes little more than a marker in Badiou's writings for *any* non-set-theoretical ontology. But the fact that Augustine – to use a famous example – became a Christian (believer in God) by renouncing his Neo-Platonism (adherence to the One) is enough to show that these terms are not easily interchangeable, and that renouncing the One does not even entail a renunciation of God. Moreover, Kant had already shown that the idea of the 'World' is a transcendent illusion: one can only speak of the 'whole' of Being ('the totality of what is') from the viewpoint of transcendence; it is precisely the 'immanence' of the concept of Being (univocity) that *prevents* any conception of Being as a totality.

Third, and most important, the notion of the One simply does not articulate the difference between Badiou and Deleuze on the question of 'an immanent conception of the multiple'. Extensive multiplicities (sets) and differential multiplicities (e.g. Riemannian manifolds) are *both* defined in a purely intrinsic or immanent manner, without *any* recourse to the One or the Whole or a Unity. The real *differend* must be located in the difference between axiomatics and problematics, major and minor science.

Badiou's thesis concerning Deleuze's 'vitalism', by contrast, comes closer to articulating a real difference. (Badiou recognizes, to be sure, that Deleuze uses this biological term in a somewhat provocative manner, divorced from its traditional reference to a semi-mystical life-force.) Although Deleuze's formal theory of multiplicities is drawn from mathematical models, it is true that he appeals to numerous non-mathematical domains (biology, physics, geology) in describing the intensive processes of *individuation* through which multiplicities are actualized. 'Vitalism' enters the picture, in other words, at the level of individuation – hence the distinction, in *Difference and Repetition*, between the fourth chapter on 'The Ideal Synthesis of Difference' (the theory of multiplicities, which appeals to mathematics) and the fifth chapter on 'The Asymmetrical Synthesis of the Sensible' (the theory of individuation, which appeals to biology). But this distinction is neither exclusive nor disciplinary: even in mathematics, the movement from a problem to its solutions constitutes a process of actualization: though formally distinct, there is no ontological separation between these two instances (the complex Deleuzian notion of 'differen*t*/*c*iation).[43] Badiou's resistance to this 'vitalism' can no doubt be accounted for by his restricted conception of ontology. For Badiou, the term ontology refers uniquely to the discourse of 'Being-as-being' (axiomatic set theory), which is indifferent to the question of existence. For Deleuze, by contrast, ontology (using Heideggerian language) encompasses Being, beings, *and* their ontological difference, and the determinations of 'Being-as-such' must therefore be immediately related to beings in their existence. This is why the calculus functions as a useful test case in comparing Deleuze and Badiou. The movement toward rigour in mathematics, by 'royal' science, was motivated by the attempt to establish a foundation for the concepts of the calculus internal to mathematics itself. Badiou situates his work exclusively on this path, characterizing axiomatic set theory as 'rational ontology itself'.[44] Deleuze, by contrast, while fully admitting the foundational necessity of axiomatics, equally emphasizes the role of the calculus in the comprehension of existence itself. 'Differential calculus', he writes, 'is a kind of union of mathematics and the existent – specifically, it is the symbolic of the existent. It is because it is a well-founded fiction in relation to mathematical truth that it is consequently *a basic and real means of exploration of the reality of existence*.'[45] In physics, a law of nature, as Hermann Weyl notes, is necessarily expressed as a differential equation, and it is the calculus that establishes this link between mathematics and existence (Einstein's general relativity, for instance, made use of the tensor calculus). While axiomatics established the foundations of the calculus *within* mathematics, it is in the calculus itself that one must seek out the relation of mathematics itself with *existence* (problematics). This is a fundamental difference between Badiou and Deleuze: Badiou eliminates existence entirely from his ontology (there is no 'being' of matter, life, sensibility . . .), whereas in Deleuze existence is fully a dimension of ontology as such: 'force' is a determination of the being of matter (Leibniz); 'vitalism' is a determination of the being of living things (Bergson); 'intensity' is a determination of the being of the sensible (Kant); and so on. It is this genetic and problematic aspect of mathematics that remains inaccessible to set theoretical axiomatics.

Badiou's neglect of the 'problematic' dimension of Deleuze's thought results in numerous infelicities in his reading of Deleuze. In *Deleuze: The Clamor of Being*, Badiou's approach is guided by the presumption that 'the starting point required by Deleuze's method is always a concrete *case*' (D 25/14). But this is a false presumption: for Deleuze, the starting point is always the *problem*, and 'cases' are themselves derived from problems. The fundamental question is to determine which problems are interesting and remarkable, or to determine what is interesting or remarkable within the problem as such (group theory). If one starts with the case, it is in order to determine the problem to which it corresponds ('the creation of a concept always occurs as the function of a problem').[46] Nor can one say that Deleuze simply falls back on the 'concrete' (ignoring 'the real rights of the abstract') with the aim of producing phenomenological descriptions of the 'figural' (resulting in 'a metaphorizing phenomenology of pure change' (D 144–6/98–9). Not only does this imply a simplified view of the concrete (as Deleuze notes, 'the true opposite of the concrete is not the abstract, it is the *discrete* [. . .]. Lived experience is an absolutely abstract thing'),[47] it entirely ignores the distinction between axiomatics and problematics, and the fully 'abstract' character of the latter. This avoidance, in turn, leads Badiou to make several misguided interpretive claims. In his book *Bergsonism*, for instance, Deleuze explicitly defines Bergsonian 'intuition' as an elaborated method that consists in 'the stating and creating of *problems*'.[48] Badiou, to support his own theses, instead reinterprets intuition bizarrely as a method that thinks beings as 'merely local intensities of the One'.[49] Similarly, Deleuze has suggested that 'the intuitionist school (Brouwer, Heyting, Griss, Bouligand, etc.) is of great importance in mathematics [. . .] because it developed a conception of *problems*, and of a *calculus of problems* that intrinsically rivals axiomatics and proceeds by other rules (notably with regard to the excluded middle)'.[50] Badiou, for his part, strangely describes the intuitionist school as having pursued a purely 'descriptive' task that starts from the sensible intuition of 'already complex concretions' (CT 45).

Badiou's emphasis on axiomatics also affects his readings of Deleuze's work in the history of philosophy. Badiou, for instance, complains that 'Deleuze neglects the function of mathematics in Spinoza', for whom 'mathematics alone thinks being' (*CT* 72). But this is not correct either: Deleuze explicitly criticizes Spinoza for allowing his mathematics to assume a purely axiomatic form. 'In Spinoza', he writes, *'the use of the geometric method involves no "problems" at all.'*[51] This is why, in his readings of Spinoza, Deleuze emphasizes the role of the scholia (which are the only elements of the *Ethics* that fall outside the axiomatic deductions, and develop the theme of 'affections') and the fifth book (which introduces problematic hiatuses and contractions into the deductive exposition itself).[52] No doubt it is this emphasis on the problematic aspects of the *Ethics* that rendered Deleuze's Spinoza 'unrecognizable' to Badiou, who focuses on the theorematic and axiomatic apparatus.[53] Indeed, with regard to problematics, Deleuze suggests that Descartes actually went further than Spinoza, and that Descartes the geometer went further than Descartes the philosopher: the 'Cartesian method' (the search for the clear and distinct) is a method for solving problems, whereas the analytic procedure presented in Descartes' *Geometry* is focused on the constitution of problems as such ('Cartesian coordinates' appear nowhere in the *Geometry*).[54] In all these characterizations, one at times senses in Badiou the semi-patronizing attitude of the 'royal' scientist, who sees Deleuze's thought mired in problematics and its inferior concepts, and lacking the robustness required for work in 'severe mathematics' and its 'delicate axiomatics'.

But perhaps the most striking omission in Badiou is his neglect of Deleuze's political philosophy, since the latter is derived directly from these mathematical models. The central thesis of *Capitalism and Schizophrenia* (whose very title reflects the axiomatics–problematics distinction) is that capitalism itself functions on the basis of an axiomatic – not metaphorically, but literally.[55] This is because capital as such is a problematic multiplicity: it can be converted into *discrete* quantities in our pay cheques and loose change, but in itself the monetary mass is a *continuous* or intensive quantity that increases and decreases without any agency controlling it. Like the continuum, capital is not masterable by an axiom; or rather, it constantly requires the creation of new axioms (it is 'like a power of the continuum, tied to the axiomatic but exceeding it').[56] In turn, capital produces other flows that follow these circuits of capital: flows of commodities, flows of population, flows of labour, flows of traffic, flows of knowledge, and so on – all of which have a necessarily 'problematic' status from the viewpoint of the capitalist regime. The fundamental operation of the capitalist State, in Deleuze's reading, is to attempt to control these 'deterritorialized' flows by axiomatizing them – but this axiomatization can never be complete, not only because of the inherent limits of any axiomatic, but because new problematics are constantly being created that resist any axiomatic or discrete reduction. 'The true axiomatic', Deleuze says, 'is social and not scientific'.[57] To take one well-known example: for Deleuze 'minorities' are, in themselves, non-denumerable multiplicities; they can be brought into the capitalist axiomatic by being denumerated, counted, given their identity cards, made a part of the majority (which is a denumerable multiplicity, i.e. a multiplicity of discrete numerical elements); but there is also a power to minorities that comes from *not* entering into the axiomatic, a power that does not reduce minorities to a mere 'tear' or 'rupture' in the axiomatic, but assigns to them an objective and determinable ontological positivity of their own *as* problematic.

From a Deleuzian viewpoint, then, the fundamental limitation of Badiou's ontology lies in its complete elimination of problematics from ontology, and this limitation consequently appears in two forms. On the one hand, for Badiou, Being is presented in purely *discrete* terms: what is 'subtracted' from the 'count-as-one' rule that constitutes consistent sets (knowledge) is an inconsistent or 'generic' multiplicity, the pure multiple of Being, which in itself remains indiscernible, unpresented, and unnameable as such (the void). An event – that which is not 'Being-as-Being' – if one occurs, intervenes 'on the edge' of this void, and constitutes the condition of a truth procedure. But this entire characterization revolves in the domain of the discrete: what is truly 'unnamed' within it is the entire domain of problematics and its 'repressed' notions, such as becoming and continuous variation. Such is the substance of the critique Deleuze addresses to Badiou in *What is Philosophy?*. 'The theory of multiplicities', he writes, 'does not support the hypothesis of any multiplicity whatever', that is, a purely discrete or 'generic' multiplicity.[58] The discretization programme found its point of 'genesis' in problematics, and in any adequate mathematical ontology there must therefore be 'at least two multiplicities, two types, from the outset' – namely the continuous *and* the discrete, the non-metric *and* the metric, and so on. 'This is not because dualism is better than unity', continues Deleuze, 'but because the multiplicity is precisely what happens between the two', that is, in the movement of conversion that translates the continuous into the discrete, the non-metric into the metric, etc. It is precisely this movement of translation, and Deleuze's own formalization of problematic multiplicities, that we have attempted to sketch out above.

On the other hand, for Badiou, the 'truth' of Being is presented in a purely *axiomatic* form. As a result, the articulation or 'thinking' of an inconsistent multiplicity – the operation of a 'truth procedure' – can only be *subjective*, and not ontological, since it is only by means of a purely subjective 'decision' that an event can be affirmed, and the hitherto indistinguishable discrete elements of the multiplicity can be named, thereby altering the 'situation' through the declaration of an axiom (for instance, in politics, in the axiom that 'all men are equal'; in love, the axiom 'I love you'; and so on). Badiou necessarily dissociates this process of subjectivation from ontology itself, since it is only the subject's 'fidelity' to the event that allows the elements of the altered situation to achieve consistency. Hence the duality Badiou posits between 'Being' and 'Event', and the separation of the articulation of Being from the path of the subject or truth. In this sense, Badiou's philosophy of the event is, at its core, a philosophy of the 'activist subject'. For Deleuze, by contrast, the genesis of truth (and the genesis of axiomatics itself) must always be found in *problematics*: Being necessarily presents itself under a problematic form, and problems and their ideal events are always ontological, not subjective. The generation of truth, in other words, is derived from the constitution of problems, and a problem always has the truth it 'deserves' insofar as it is completely constituted *as* a problem. The greatness of the calculus in mathematics is that it provided a precise symbolism with which it could express problems that, before its invention, could not even have been posed, much less solved. If Badiou is forced to define truth in purely subjective terms, it is because he wrongly limits his ontology to axiomatics, and denies himself the real ontological ground of the category of truth.

The path followed by Badiou in *Being and Event* is almost the exact inverse of that followed by Deleuze in *Difference and Repetition*, and these two paths, finally, can be seen to exemplify Deleuze's own distinction between an immanent and a transcendent ontology. For Deleuze, a purely immanent ontology is one in which there is nothing 'outside' Being or 'otherwise' than Being, and thus for him problematics and axiomatics must both belong fully to ontology. Since Badiou limits his ontology to axiomatics, he is forced – in order to account for everything Deleuze ascribes to the order of problematics – to reintroduce an element of transcendence, which appears in the form of the *event*. For Badiou, there can be no ontology of the event, since the event itself produces an 'interruption' in being, a 'tear' in its fabric: the event is 'supplemental' to ontology, 'supernumerary'. But this is exactly how Deleuze has defined the 'modern' way of saving transcendence: 'it is now from *within* immanence that a breach is expected [... and] something transcendent is re-established on the horizon, in the regions of non-belonging', or as Badiou would say, from the 'edge of the void'.[59] Whereas an immanent ontology 'never has a supplementary dimension to that which transpires upon it', an ontology of transcendence 'always has an additional dimension'.[60] Though Badiou is determined to expel God and the One from his philosophy, he winds up reassigning to the event, as if through the back door, the very characteristics of transcendence that were formerly assigned to the divine (as Badiou declares triumphantly, 'I conceptualize absolute beginnings').[61] In this sense, Badiou's is indeed an analogical and reflexive ontology that requires a mechanism of transcendence to 'save' the event. Deleuze often insisted on the irreducibility of 'taste' in philosophy, and seemed willing to characterize his *differend* with Badiou as a difference in philosophical taste. If the preceding analyses are correct, it would seem that it was precisely Badiou's 'taste' for discretization and axiomatization in mathematics that entailed an inevitable appeal to transcendence: the eruption, within Being itself, of a supplemental event that is *not* Being-as-being.

7

ALAIN BADIOU AND THE MIRACLE OF THE EVENT*

Daniel Bensaïd

Marx had the temerity to declare that philosophy would eventually wither away through the accomplishment of its own strategic development: it was now no longer merely a matter of interpreting the world, but of changing it. Today, by way of contrast, Alain Badiou proposes to reiterate the philosophical gesture *par excellence*; a 'Platonic gesture' in opposition to the tyranny of opinion and the renunciations of anti-philosophy. In this way, he sees himself as raising philosophy up once more after its abasement in the face of those 'fascinating forms of thought' that had captivated it. 'Scientific thought gave rise to the variants of positivism, political thought engendered the figure of a philosophy of the state, while art, lastly, has exercised an exceptional attraction since the nineteenth century. Fascinated, captivated, and even subjugated by art, politics, and the sciences, philosophy has been driven to the point of declaring itself inferior to its own predilections.'[1]

In the wake of the 'Galilean event', philosophy in the Classical age fell under the domination of its scientific condition. In the aftermath of the French Revolution, it came under the sway of its political condition. Lastly, with Nietzsche and Heidegger it withdrew in favour of the poem. Whence Badiou's diagnosis of a philosophy that has become 'captured by a network of sutures to its conditions, especially its scientific and political conditions', a philosophy sadly resigned to the idea that it is henceforth impossible for it to express itself in 'systematic form'. The principal effect of this submission apparently consists in the renunciation, pure and simple, of any 'desire for a figure of eternity' that might be non-religious, 'internal to time as such' and 'whose name is truth'. By losing sight of its own constitutive aim, philosophy has become estranged from itself. No longer knowing whether it possesses a place of its own, it has become reduced to its own history. As it turns into 'its own museum' it 'combines the deconstruction of its past with the empty wait for its future' (C 57–8).

The aim of the programme delineated by Badiou seeks to liberate philosophy from this threefold grip of science, history and the poem, to withdraw it from the twin anti-philosophical discourses of dogmatic positivism and Romantic

---

* This chapter, translated by Ray Brassier, was first published as 'Alain Badiou et le miracle de l'événement', in Bensaïd, *Résistances: Essai de taupologie générale* (Paris: Fayard, 2001), pp. 143–70.

speculation, to dispense with 'every kind of religion'. For 'we cannot lay claim to atheism so long as the theme of finitude continues to dominate our think- ing'. Only by espousing once more 'the solid secular eternity of the sciences' will we attain atheism; only by reducing the infinite to its 'neutral banality' as a 'mere number' can we hope to tear ourselves free from a 'disgusting veneer of sacralization' and re-inaugurate a 'radical desacralization' (C 163–4).

Along the path of this renewed philosophical conquest, Badiou's discourse is coordinated around the concepts of truth, event and subject: a truth is sparked by an event and spreads like a flame fanned by the breath of a subjective effort that remains forever incomplete. For truth is not a matter of theory but is a 'practical question' first and foremost: it is something that occurs, a point of excess, an evental exception, 'a process from which something new emerges',[2] as opposed to an adequation between knowledge and its object. This is why 'each truth is at once singular and universal'.

This truth in process is opposed to the worldly principle of interest. Initially, Badiou's thought remained subordinated to the movement of history. But truth has become more fragmentary and discontinuous under the brunt of historical disasters, as though history no longer constituted its basic framework but merely its occasional condition. Truth is no longer a subterranean path mani- festing itself in the irruption of the event. Instead, it becomes a post-evental consequence. As 'wholly subjective' and a matter of 'pure conviction', truth henceforth pertains to the realm of declarations that have neither precedents nor consequences.[3] Although similar to revelation, it still remains a process but one which is entirely contained in the absolute beginning of the event which it faithfully continues.

This is why, contrary to Kant, for whom the truth and universal relevance of the French Revolution was to be found in the enthusiastic and disinterested gaze of its onlookers, for Badiou, the truth of the event is that of its partici- pants: it should be sought for or listened to in the living words uttered by Robespierre or Saint-Just, rather than in the detached commentaries produced by Furet and the Thermidorian historians; in the tragic decisions made by Lenin (and Trotsky), rather than the judgments made out of harm's way by Hélène Carrère d'Encausse and Stéphane Courtois.

This is an idea of truth that exceeds what can be proved or demonstrated. It posits conditions far more demanding than those that merely require the consistency of discourse, the correspondence between words and things, or the reassuring verification of ordinary logics. In this sense, it is an entirely mate- rialist concept: for Badiou, there can be no transcendental truth, only truths in situation and in relation, situations and relations of truth, oriented toward an atemporal eternity.

These are truths that cannot be deduced from any premise. They are axio- matic and foundational. Thus, all true novelty arises 'in obscurity and confu- sion'. It is up to philosophy to recognize and declare its existence. By the same token, it is only retrospectively that the event is acknowledged as such, by way of an 'interpretative intervention'. The petrification or substantialization – bureaucratic, statist [*étatique*], academic – of these evental and processural truths is equivalent to their negation. It takes the form of that recurrent disaster whose proper name is Thermidor.

For Badiou, the distinction between truth and knowledge is crucial (cf. *EE* 269; *C* 201). Truths take place. Each of them surges forth as an 'immediately universalizable singularity', which is characteristic of the event through which it comes to be. This logic of universalization is decisive, for once we have renounced the universal, it is always at the risk of 'universal horror' (*TS* 197). Vengeful and subordinate particularisms that demand recognition of their rights remain impotent in the face of capital's false and despotic universalism, to which must be opposed another universality. Philosophy appears here as a 'wager endowed with a universal bearing', at each step coming up against either 'a specialized and fragmentary world' in the catastrophic form of religious, communitarian or national passion – claims according to which only a woman can understand a woman, only a homosexual can understand a homosexual, only a Jew can understand a Jew, and so on. If every universal first subsists in a singularity, and if every singularity has its origin in an event then 'universality is an exceptional result originating in a single point, it is the consequence of a decision, a way of being rather than knowing'.[4]

Thus, the possibility of philosophy orbits around truth as a category that cannot be conflated with either common sense or scientific knowledge. Science, politics and aesthetics each have their own truth. It would be tempting to conclude from this that philosophy harbours the Truth of truths. But Badiou resists this temptation: 'The relation between Truth and truths is not one of domination, subsumption, foundation or guarantee. It is a relation of sampling: philosophy is a tasting of truths.' Hence, philosophy consists in a thinking that extracts, one that is 'essentially subtractive', one that punctures. As the poet Mandelstam said, it is the hole at the centre of the ring that matters because that is what remains after the bread is eaten. Similarly, Badiou enjoins us to admit that philosophy's central category is empty and must remain so in order to welcome the event.

Is philosophy then a question of listening rather than saying? Of listening to or echoing that which resonates within an empty space? Such listening would allow us to resist the philosophical discourses of postmodernity, which constitute the contemporary form of anti-philosophy. Through their pretension to 'cure us of truth' or to 'compromise the very idea of truth' by way of a general debunking of meta-narratives, these discourses become self-refuting because they capitulate to the confused free-for-all of public opinion. What is being played out in this business is the duel between philosopher and sophist, 'for what the sophist, whether ancient or modern, presumes to impose is the claim that there is no truth, that the concept of truth is useless or doubtful since there are only conventions' (*C* 62). This sardonic challenge, which puts truth to the test of opinion, constantly tempts the philosopher to declare the existence of a unique site of Truth, whereas all that is really required is the riposte that 'by the operation of Truth as an empty category, there are truths'. Any reply (whether positivistic, statist or poetic) claiming to shore up this void would in fact be 'excessive, overstretched, disastrous' (C 72)

The fact that the site from which truths might be grasped must remain empty has the notable consequence that the struggle between philosopher and sophist can never end. It is, in effect, a struggle between the philosopher and his own shadow, his other, who is also his double. The ethics of philosophy consists in keeping this dispute alive. The annihilation of one or other of the disputants – by decreeing that 'the sophist has no right to exist', for instance – would be properly disastrous. For 'the dialectic includes the utterances of the sophist' and the authoritarian temptation to silence the latter 'exposes thought to disaster' (C 74–5).

This disaster is not merely hypothetical. It is, alas, something that has already happened. Because he installs thought in this contradictory relation between the philosopher and the sophist, between truth and opinion, it would seem that Badiou is obliged to address, both in general and for himself, the question of democracy – but it is precisely this question that he continuously represses. A new danger threatens: that of a philosophy haunted by the sacralization of the evental miracle.

Truth, following in the wake of 'that which happens', is a matter of 'pure conviction', it is 'wholly subjective', and is a 'pure fidelity to the opening brought about by the event'. Apart from the event, there are only current affairs and the common run of opinion. The event is Christ's resurrection, it is the storming of the Bastille, it is the October Revolution, just as it is illegal immigrant workers taking to the streets in order to become agents in their own right, in order to break out of their status as clandestine victims; it is the unemployed stepping out from the ranks of statistics to become subjects of resistance, or the sick refusing to resign themselves to being mere patients and attempting to think and act their own illnesses.

In keeping with a similar logic, Pascal refused to provide argumentative proof for the existence of God, preferring instead to invoke the evental experience of faith. Pascalian grace or Mallarméan chance thereby present themselves as versions of the call of a 'militant vocation', as the emblematic form of the pure, truth-engendering event.

For Badiou, the relation between this event and the ontology of the multiple constitutes the central problem for contemporary philosophy. What exactly is an event? Aleatory by nature, the event cannot be predicted outside a singular situation, nor even deduced from that situation without some unpredictable chance operation. In this way the Mallarméan dice-throw illustrates the 'pure thought of the event', which bears no relation to leaden structural determination. This event is characterized by the unpredictability of what might just as well not have occurred. This is what lends it an aura of 'secularized grace' (SP 89). It comes about retroactively through the sovereign naming of its existence and the fidelity to the truth which comes to light in it. Thus, according to Péguy, the uncountable zero of the French Revolution's 'nought anniversary' merely pays witness to what can be done in its name through the imperious duty to carry on its legacy.

Accordingly, the genuine event remains irreducible to all instrumental reckoning. It is of the order of an encounter that is amorous (love at first sight), political (revolution), or scientific (the eureka). Its proper name suspends the situational routine insofar as it consists in 'forcing chance once the moment is ripe for intervention' (*TS* 187). Yet this propitious ripeness of the opportune moment unexpectedly refers us back to the historicity that determines and conditions the latter. Inadvertently, it seems to contradict the oft-repeated claim that the event is entirely eruptive and cannot be deduced from the situation.

In what does this ripeness of circumstances consist? How is it to be gauged? Badiou remains silent on this score. By refusing to venture into the dense thickets of real history, into the social and historical determination of events, Badiou's notion of the political tips over into a wholly imaginary dimension: this is politics made tantamount to an act of levitation, reduced to a series of unconditioned events and 'sequences' whose exhaustion or end remain forever mysterious. As a result, history and the event become miraculous in Spinoza's sense – a miracle is 'an event the cause of which cannot be explained'.[5] Politics can only flirt with a theology or aesthetics of the event. Religious revelation, according to Slavoj Žižek, constitutes its 'unavowed paradigm'.[6]

Yet the storming of the Bastille can be understood only in the context of the *Ancien Régime*; the confrontation of June 1848 can be understood only in the context of urbanization and industrialization; the insurrection of the Paris Commune can be understood only in the context of the commotion of European nationalities and the collapse of the Second Empire; the October Revolution can be understood only in the particular context of 'capitalist development in Russia' and the convulsive outcome of the Great War.

The question of the subject, which functions as the third term in Badiou's discourse, tends to confirm our suspicions: in the wake of Althusser's 'process without a subject', Badiou presents us with a subject without history. Or maybe this is just another version of the same effort to hunt down historicism.

'The subject is rare', says Badiou.[7] Rare like the event, rare like truth, and as intermittent as politics, which, according to Rancière, is always 'a provisional accident of the forms of domination' and always 'precarious', always 'punctual', its manifestation only ever allowing for a 'subject in eclipse'.[8] Yet this vanishing subject is that through which a truth becomes effective: I struggle, therefore I am. I am, because I struggle. Truth is thereby defined as a *process of subjectivation*. It is not the working class that struggles. The latter, as a category of sociological discourse, would be a subordinate, functional component of the structure (of the relentless reproduction of capital). What struggles is the proletariat as subjectivized mode of a class determining and proclaiming itself through struggle.

Similarly, for Pascal, the world does not necessarily lead to God without the rigorously aleatory decision of the gambler who brings it into existence (*PP* 87).

Similarly, for Lukács, the political subject is not the class, which remains imprisoned within the vicious cycle of reification, but the party that subverts the structure and breaks the cycle. The party sustains the proletariat as subject striving to dissolve those class relations by which the latter is held captive. The class only becomes subject through its party.

We must wager! Badiou appropriates Pascal's injunction: we must 'wager on a communist politics' because 'we will never be able to deduce it from capital'. By virtue of its uncertain relation to the empty site of truth, a site modelled on Pascal's hidden God, the wager provides the philosophical figure for every engagement, in stark contrast to the dogmatic certainty of positive knowledge and cynical, worldly, senile scepticism. It pertains to a type of thinking that is irreducible to the dogmatic certainties of positive science as well as to the fickle whims of public opinion: 'Pascal's wager cannot concern the sceptic, for whom the limited values of the world are enough, nor the dogmatist, who thinks the world provides him with values that are authentic and sufficient, since they obviously exclude the need to wager. Which is why, insofar as both are in possession of certainties or truths that are enough for them to live on, it is possible to see them as equivalent.'[9] He who glimpses truth in the throw of the dice is not necessarily a believer looking to God to provide the basis for his unshakeable confidence. On the contrary, he alone can wager for whom God has withdrawn, leaving behind a gaping hole from whence the dialectical (rather than romantic) representation of modern tragedy can spring forth.

This wager has little to do with doubt. It is a sign of confidence in a practical certainty, albeit one liable to disappointment, one that is paradoxical, continuously threatened by a contrary possibility. To wager is to commit oneself. It is to gamble the whole on a single part. It is 'to bet on the assertion, which is always unprovable, that there exists a possible relation between meaning and that which is given through the senses, between God and the empirical reality behind which he hides; a relation which cannot be proved yet to which one must commit one's entire existence'. Thus, labour on behalf of the uncertain 'is never absolute certainty, but rather action, and thereby necessarily a wager'. In this sense, Lucien Goldmann already saw how Marxism 'continued the Pascalian legacy'.[10]

Yet in Badiou, the intermittence of event and subject renders the very idea of politics problematic. According to him, politics defines itself via fidelity to the event whereby the victims of oppression declare themselves. His determination to prise politics free from the state in order to subjectivize it, to 'deliver it from history in order to hand it over to the event', is part of a tentative search for an autonomous politics of the oppressed. The alternative effort, to subordinate politics to some putative 'meaning of history', which has ominous echoes in recent history, is he suggests to incorporate it within the process of general technicization and to reduce it to the 'management of state affairs'. One must have 'the courage to declare that, from the point of view of politics, history as meaning or direction does not exist: all that exists is the periodic occurrence of the a priori conditions of chance'. However, this divorce between event and history (between the event and its historically determined conditions) tends to render politics if not unthinkable then at least impracticable (*PP* 18).

Badiou's philosophical trajectory appears, indeed, like a long march towards 'a politics without a party', the consummation of a subjectivation that is at once necessary and impossible. Isn't a politics without a party actually a politics without politics? In Badiou's account it is Rousseau who founded the modern concept of politics insofar as politics begins with the event of the contract rather than with the assembling of a structure: the subject is primarily its own legislator. Consequently, there is no truth more active than that of a politics which erupts like a pure instance of free decision when the order of things breaks down and when, refusing the apparent necessity of that order, we boldly venture forth into a hitherto unsuspected realm of possibility.

Politics as such comes about, then, on the basis of its separation from the state, which is the very opposite and negation of the event, the petrified form of anti-politics; politics proceeds via a 'brutal distancing of the state'. Nothing in the domain of the state can be against the state, just as nothing in the domain of economics can be against economics. So long as the economy and the state maintain their grip on the situation, politics is only a matter of controlled protests, captive resistances, reactions subordinated to the tutelary fetishes they pretend to defy. The only possible politics in such circumstances is, to use Gramsci's terminology, a subaltern politics. For Badiou, the separation between politics and the state lies at the very root of politics. More precisely: it lies at the root of a politics of the oppressed, which is the only conceivable form in which politics can endure once it has vanished under the pressure of totalitarianism or the market.

Systematically elaborated during the course of the 1980s and 90s, Badiou's philosophical discourse must be understood in the context of the reactionary liberal restoration. It is opposed to market determinism, to communicational consensus, to the rhetoric of fairness, to the despotism of public opinion, to postmodern resignation and to the anti-totalitarian vulgate. It tries to combine an injunction to resistance and an art of the event.

Taking the lover's fidelity to the first encounter as its example, militant engagement consists in a political fidelity to an initial event, a fidelity experienced as resistance to the mood of the times: 'What I admire above all in Pascal is the effort, undertaken in difficult circumstances, to go against the current, not in a reactive sense, but in order to invent the contemporary form of an ancient conviction, as opposed to simply following the course of things and adopting the facile cynicism which all transitional periods inculcate in the weak-minded, the better to claim that the pace of history is incompatible with the quiet will to change the world and universalize its form' (*EE* 245). Pascal is indeed indispensable when it comes to confronting an era of resignation and consensus. This Pascalian counter-current finds an exact echo in what Walter Benjamin sees as the obligation to 'go against the grain of history'. Both lay claim to a dialectics of fidelity, one capable of preventing conviction from collapsing into disillusionment and of safeguarding tradition from the con-formism into which it constantly threatens to lapse.

If the future of a truth 'is decided by those who carry on' and who hold to this faithful decision to carry on, the militant summoned by the 'rare' if not exceptional idea of politics seems to be haunted by the Pauline ideal of saint-liness, which constantly threatens to turn into a bureaucratic priesthood of Church, State or Party. The absolute incompatibility between truth and opi-nion, between philosopher and sophist, between event and history, leads to a practical impasse. The refusal to work within the equivocal contradiction and tension which bind them together ultimately leads to a pure voluntarism, which oscillates between a broadly leftist form of politics and its philosophical circumvention. In either case, the combination of theoretical elitism and practical moralism can indicate a haughty withdrawal from the public domain, sandwiched between the philosopher's evental truth and the masses' subaltern resistance to the world's misery. On this particular point, there exists an affinity between Badiou's philosophical radicality and Bourdieu's sociological radi-cality. Haunted by the 'epistemological cut' that forever separates the scientist from the sophist and science from ideology, both Badiou and Bourdieu declare a discourse of mastery. Whereas a politics that acts in order to change the world establishes itself precisely in the wound left by this cut, in the site and moment in which the people declare themselves.

Detached from its historical conditions, pure diamond of truth, the event, just like the notion of the absolutely aleatory encounter in the late Althusser, is akin to a miracle. By the same token, a politics without politics is akin to a negative theology. The preoccupation with purity reduces politics to a grand refusal and prevents it from producing lasting effects. Its rarity prevents us from thinking its expansion as the genuinely achieved form of the withering away of the State. Slavoj Žižek and Stathis Kouvélakis have rightly pointed out that the antinomies of order and event, of police and politics, render radical politici-zation impossible and indicate a move away from the Leninist 'passage a l'acte'.[11] Unlike 'the liberal irresponsibility of leftism', a revolutionary politics 'assumes full responsibility for the consequences of its choices'. Carried away by his fervour, Žižek even goes so far as to affirm the necessity of those consequences 'no matter how unpleasant they may be'. But in light of this century's history, one cannot take responsibility for them without specifying the extent to which they are unavoidable and the extent to which they contradict the initial act whose logical outcome they claim to be. Thus, what must be re-examined is the whole problem of the relation between revolution and counter-revolution, between October and the Stalinist Thermidor.

Since 1977, Badiou's thought has developed by gradually distancing itself, albeit without any explicit break, from the Maoism of the 1960s. In a situation dominated by the twin political liberalisms of the centre-right and the left-left, one in which vague feelings of resistance can assume the bigoted form of reactive nationalism or religious fundamentalism, Badiou's politics of the event signal an explicit stand against the complementary phenomena of imperial globalization and identitarian panic. Consensus, as Badiou himself proudly proclaims, is not his strong point. He strives, against the contemporary current, to save the Maoist event and the proper name of Mao from the petrifying grip of history. And he gallantly claims never to have stopped being a militant, from May 68 to NATO's war in the Balkans.

Throughout this long march, May 68 is equivalent to the encounter on the road to Damascus. It revealed that history, 'including the history of knowledge', is made by the masses. Henceforth, fidelity to the event will mean a stubborn refusal to surrender, the intractable refusal of reconciliation and repentance. After Mao's death, the year 1977 marks a new turning point, signalled in France by the electoral gains made by the *Union de la gauche*, and in the intellectual realm by the appearance of the *'nouvelle philosophie'*. In the United Kingdom and the United States, Thatcher and Reagan prepare to take power. The liberal reaction is proclaimed. The 'obscure disaster' is underway.

Badiou will subsequently strive to 'think politics' as a resistance to 'the linguistic turn', to analytical philosophy, to any relativist hermeneutics. Against wordplay, against the apologia for 'weak thought', against the capitulation of universal reason before the kaleidoscope of differences, against all the pretences of a triumphant sophism, Badiou wants to hold fast to truth. He mobilizes the systematicity of the 'Platonic gesture' against the fragmentation of philosophy and philosophical fragments, in which there is no room for truth, in which cultural populism replaces art, in which technology supplants science, in which management wins out over politics and sexuality triumphs over love. Sooner or later, these distortions would lead to the policing of thought and the capitulation already anticipated, in the 1970s, by the little gurus of desire.

For Badiou by contrast, as for Sartre, man only attains genuine humanity, albeit an ephemeral one, through the event of his revolt. Whence the still unresolved difficulty of holding together event and history, act and process, instant and duration. As a result, by way of a novel, ironic ruse of history, the politics of historically indetermined singular situations becomes akin to the very postmodern fragmentation it sought to resist: 'what I call politics is something that can be discerned only in a few, fairly brief sequences, often quickly overturned, crushed or diluted by the return of business as usual'.[12]

The 'early Badiou' had been tempted to subordinate philosophy to the sovereign course of history. Henceforth, it is the event that interrupts historical development. Thus, as Slavoj Žižek remarks, Badiou can be seen as a thinker of revelation, 'the last great author in the French tradition of Catholic dogmatists'. Yet the claim to found a politics on the pure imperative of fidelity, one that challenges every project inscribed within the continuity of historical perspective, seems perilous.

'God preserve us from socio-political programs!' exclaims Badiou, in a horrified gesture of refusal before temptation or sin.[13] Carried by a pure maxim of equality, a politics without parties or programmes seems to have no goal to strive toward. It is entirely concentrated in the present of its declaration: 'The only political question is: what is it possible to achieve in the name of this principle [of equality] through our militant fidelity to this declaration?'[14] Such a politics is supposed to be a matter of 'prescription' rather than programme, prescriptions illustrated by unconditional commands such as 'every individual counts as one'; 'the sick must receive the best care without conditions'; 'one child equals one pupil'; 'anyone who lives here belongs here'. These maxims, which have the dogmatic form of religious commandments, provide principles of orientation that counter the unprincipled accommodations of *Realpolitik* or naked opportunism. But by refusing to confront reality and the prosaic experience of practice, they allow one to keep one's hands clean in a manner akin to Kantian morality.

Nevertheless, the realities of relations of force, from which it is not so easy to escape into the pristine realm of theological prescription, catch up with this conception of politics as pure will. Following an evolution that is again parallel in some ways to that of Pierre Bourdieu, *La Distance politique* praised the strikes during the winter of 1995 for their salutary resistance to a liberal 'decentralization' carried out exclusively for the benefit of capital and the market.[15] It even went so far as to declare that, up to a point, the state is the guarantor of 'the public domain and the general interest'. The public domain and the general interest? Well! Is there not a faint whiff of sophistry here?

Yet this sudden reversal is not so surprising. Holy purification is never more than a short step away from voluptuous sin. If, as Badiou was already claiming in 1996, 'the era of revolutions is over', the only available options are either to withdraw into the haughty solitude of the anchorite or learn to get used to the contemptible state of current affairs.[16] For how, in effect, does one imagine a State as 'guarantor of the public domain and the general interest' without parties or debates, without mediations or representations? When *L'Organisation politique* ventures onto the terrain of practical constitutional proposals, it comes as no surprise that all it has to offer are banal reforms, such as abolishing the office of President of the Republic (however indispensable this may be), demanding the election of a single Assembly, requiring that the Prime Minister be leader of the principal parliamentary party, or recommending an electoral system that guarantees the formation of parliamentary majorities – in other words, as Hallward dryly remarks, 'something remarkably similar to the British Constitution'.[17]

This sudden conversion to realism is the profane converse of the heroic thirst for purity. Rather than a 'warrior outside the walls of the state', Badiou defines the militant as a 'lookout for the void, guided by the event'. But by staring so continuously out into this desert of Tartars, from where the enemy who is to turn him into a hero will come, the lookout ends up dozing off before mirages of the void.

As we hinted earlier, all these contradictions and aporias can be traced back to the refusal of history and to the unsettled score with Stalinism. For Badiou, the bankruptcy of the Marxist-Leninist paradigm goes back to 1967. Why 1967? Is it because of the turning point in the Chinese Cultural Revolution and the crushing of the Shanghai commune? Why not earlier? To avoid having to examine Maoism's historical record and its relations with Stalinism in greater depth? Françoise Proust has rightly noted that what is at stake here is a desperate attempt to get out of Maoism by 'taking leave of history'. But the price of this great historical silence is exorbitant. It ends up rendering democracy unthinkable and impracticable, as absent from Badiou's thought as it was from Althusser's.[18]

Françoise Proust emphasizes that by itself the imperative of 'fidelity to fidelity' only leads to a sterile formalism in the face of 'a world that offers us nothing but the temptation to give in'. Fidelity to the revolutionary event is indeed continuously threatened by Thermidor and by the Thermidorians of yesterday and today. The same holds for Thermidorians in love, which is to say those who have fallen out of love, as for Thermidorians in politics. There are so many occasions for giving up! So many temptations to bow one's head and submit to expediency! So many pretexts for resigning oneself, for becoming reconciled, through lassitude, through wisdom, for reasonable reasons, whether good or bad, so as not to pursue the politics of the worst available option, by choosing the lesser evil (which will turn out to be a shortcut to the worst option), to cut one's losses, or simply to present oneself as 'responsible'. But how, on what timescale, does one measure the responsibility of a politics?

This failure to clarify his relation to the legacies of Stalinism and Maoism lies at the root of Badiou's inability to clarify his relation to Marx. He remains content to state – the very least he could do – that Marxism as a singular term does not exist, even though its crisis conceals far more than any anti-Marxist could ever imagine. By the same token, he refuses the infidelity implied in the label 'post-Marxist'. But despite the vague invocation of a dogmatic Marxism, there is an extent to which he legitimates the accusation of positivism: 'Marx and his successors, who in this regard showed themselves to be dependent on the dominant suture of the time [i.e. of philosophy to science], always claimed to be elevating revolutionary politics to the rank of science' (*MP* 43). How much of this pretension is attributable to Marx, however, and how much to his epigones and the orthodoxy codified in Stalin's immortal booklet *Historical Materialism and Dialectical Materialism*? Are they both talking about the same kind of science? How does Marx think? And how can 'the Platonic gesture' account for this dialectical thinking?

Badiou, who is generally a meticulous and penetrating reader, suddenly gives the impression of not quite knowing what to do with a Marx who cannot be shoehorned into the straightforward dichotomy between philosopher and sophist, between science and non-science: 'Marx is anything but a sophist, although this does not mean that he is a philosopher.'[19]

'Anything but ...'? With Badiou, this reinforced negation has the character of a compliment. But what is this 'anything'? Neither philosopher nor sophist? In the case of Marx, Plato's foundational dichotomy ceases to be valid. Can one be a philosopher incidentally, slightly, extremely, passionately; in other words, can one have an incidental and occasional relationship to truth? And if Marx is only a philosopher 'secondarily', yet in no way a sophist, then what is he 'principally'? What is this disconcerting mode of thinking and acting whereby Marx circumvents the binary alternative between sophist and philosopher?

Instead of confronting these questions, which follow logically from his own assessment, Badiou evades them by pulling out his trump card: that of the double aspect. Following the example of Marx the man, who was both scientist and militant, it seems that Marx's work has a double aspect: on one hand, 'a theory of history, of the economy and of the State, conforming to the ideal of science'; on the other, 'the founding of a historical mode of politics', the 'classist' model, whose charter is provided by *The Communist Manifesto*. Between the two, philosophy occupies a 'position by induction'. And this is all we are told.[20]

It would seem that, despite his declaration that henceforth it would no longer be enough merely to interpret the world, despite everything and even despite himself, Marx basically remained a philosopher by default and by remission. Badiou does not examine this way of doing science, one so at odds with the 'dominant positivist suture' of the time, that Marx stubbornly persists in calling 'critique'. The latter strives to think in a manner worthy of its object, which is to say, in a manner worthy of capital. Yet something new takes shape here, in the way in which thought, without submitting to the vicissitudes of politics, bears a relation of conflictual indivisibility to politics while continuously interrogating its practice.

What then of Marx? Is he everything other than a sophist? Certainly, when one sees him ridiculing the mirages of public opinion in the name of 'German science'. Or everything, including a sophist? Certainly, when one sees him excoriating Proudhon's 'scientific excommunications' and doctrinaire utopias. For like Freudian *Witz*, critique is mocking and ironic. It opposes its great burst of irreverent red laughter to the yellow laughter of the priest.

In Badiou, fidelity to an event without a history and a politics without content has a tendency to turn into an axiomatics of resistance. Rimbaud's logical revolt, the logical resistance of Cavaillès or Lautman, figure here as instances of a commitment that evades all calculation and that is supposed to provide a paradoxical resolution for the absence of relation between truth and knowledge. For the axiom is more absolute than any definition. Beyond every proof or refutation, the axiom, in sovereign fashion, engenders its own objects as pure effects.

Emerging out of nothing, the sovereign subject, like evental truth, provides its own norm. It is represented only by itself. Whence the worrying refusal of relations and alliances, of confrontations and contradictions. Badiou invariably prefers an absolute configuration over one that is relative: the absolute sovereignty of truth and the subject, which begins, in desolate solitude, where the turmoil of public opinion ends. Hallward rightly sees in this philosophy of politics an 'absolutist logic' that leaves little space for multiple subjectivities, shuns the democratic experience, and condemns the sophist to a sort of exile.[21] Badiou's quasi-absolutist orientation preserves the ghost of a subject without object. This is a return to a philosophy of majestic sovereignty, whose decision seems to be founded upon a nothing that commands the whole.

8

STATES OF GRACE: THE EXCESS OF THE DEMAND IN BADIOU'S ETHICS OF TRUTHS*

Peter Dews

I

What could it mean to propose an ethics today? Of course, we all grow up with a sense of our obligations in the sphere of personal interaction. But we also have an increasing sense that this is not where the burning issues lie. We live in a world of conflict and suffering, governed by economic and social forces whose global reach, overwhelming power and unmappable complexity seem to render the improving efforts of the individual derisory. What is more, even if we succeed in overcoming our initial sense of impotence and dismay, in opting for some kind of *engagement*, we have no guarantee that the result of our commitment will ultimately turn out for the good; nor can we entirely escape the suspicion that our primary achievement may be to have salved our own consciences, rather than make a genuine contribution to the betterment of the world. Yet at the same time, conscience is not dead. On the contrary, it is precisely the universal scope of modern morality which leads to our distress at the dreadful injustice of the world, an injustice which the process of globalization increasingly highlights, while at the same time making it appear ever more irremediable. We are condemned, it seems, to a state of 'unhappy consciousness', in the precise Hegelian sense of that term – to being haunted by an ideal which we experience as both inescapable and unattainable.

With his habitual powers of insight and anticipation, Theodor Adorno expressed an acute sense of the inner conflicts generated by this situation in his lecture course on *Problems of Moral Philosophy*, delivered at the University of Frankfurt in 1963.[1] Centring his discussion on Kant's ethical thought, Adorno presents the proponent of the categorical imperative, with all his contradictions, as the greatest explorer of our modern moral condition. On the one hand, Adorno defends the stringency of Kant's moral theory against Hegel's notorious criticism of its abstraction and formalism. Hegel's 'seemingly more human and appealing account of ethics', Adorno argues, implies reconciliation with the

* A few passages of this chapter appeared in an earlier form in a review article, 'Uncategorical Imperatives: Adorno, Badiou and the Ethical Turn', *Radical Philosophy* 111, January–February 2002.

disastrous 'way of the world', whereas Kant's principle of universality 'elevates his ethics above every determinate configuration of the world that confronts it, above society and existing conditions, and it also makes him more critical of limited and finite moral categories'.[2] Yet on the other hand Adorno also claims that the antagonistic relation between particular and universal, the social dislocation which Kant's philosophy seems better equipped to confront, has reached such a pitch in the contemporary world that the implicit image of human interaction which underpins Kant's ethics no longer applies. 'It is only where our universe is limited', Adorno argues,

> that something like Kant's celebrated freedom can survive. In the immeasurably expanded world of experience and the infinitely numerous ramifications of the processes of socialization that this world of experience imposes on us, the possibility of freedom has sunk to such a minimal level that we can or must ask ourselves very seriously whether any scope is left for our moral categories.[3]

It is perhaps not surprising that, confronted with this situation, attitudes towards the value of ethics as a distinct domain of enquiry should oscillate unstably. Indeed, it can be argued that this is a feature of the post-Kantian relation to ethics in general.[4] The recent history of cultural theory in the Anglophone world offers a salient example. If one recalls the take-off of post-modern theory, back in the 1970s, there was an unmistakable sense of exhilaration in the air. The decentring of subjectivity, the unleashing of the forces of textuality, corporeality and desire, the jettisoning of the critic's role as guardian of values, were experienced as a liberation. Fashionable thinkers were thrilled to lose themselves in a maze of proliferating rhizomes, to ride the rollercoaster of the will-to-power. They eagerly nodded assent when Foucault declared that 'experience [. . .] has the task of "tearing" the subject from itself in such a way that it is no longer the subject as such, or that it is completely "other" than itself so that it may arrive at its annihilation, its dissociation'.[5] The mood of the moment was '*jouissance* now, pay later'. Yet a decade or so later, questions of conscience and obligation, of recognition and respect, of justice and the law, once dismissed as the residue of an outdated humanism, have returned to occupy, if not centre stage, then something pretty close to it. The so-called 'ethical turn' in deconstruction, the popularity of Emmanuel Levinas's thought, the surge of interest amongst Lacanian theorists in such matters as 'radical evil', Pauline *agapē* and Kierkegaardian faith, are only the most obvious manifestations of this trend.

But, compared with earlier shifts of theoretical emphasis, there is something rather reluctant, even shamefaced about this 'turn to ethics'. In the introduction to a recent set of essays collected under that title, the editors try to make the best of it: 'Ethics is back in literary studies, as it is in philosophy and political theory, and indeed the very critiques of universal man and the autonomous human subject that had initially produced resistance to ethics have now generated a crossover among these various disciplines that sees and does ethics "otherwise". The decentering of the subject has brought about a recentering of the ethical.'[6] But many of the essays thus introduced betray a distinct unease or confusion about the scope and validity of ethical discourse, even while registering an obscure sense of its necessity. As Judith Butler frankly admits, at the start of her Nietzschean response to Levinas: 'I do not have much to say about why there is a return to ethics, if there is one, in recent years, except to say that I have for the most part resisted this return, and that what I have to offer is something like a map of this resistance and its partial overcoming.'[7] Chantal Mouffe states her misgivings even more bluntly, as she complains about 'the triumph of a sort of moralizing liberalism that is increasingly filling the void left by the collapse of any project of real political transformation'.[8] It is clear that all the new talk of responsibility and justice has not just followed on smoothly from poststructuralist contextualism, from the critique of what the editors of *The Turn to Ethics* quaintly persist in believing was once the pervasive notion of an 'ideal, autonomous and sovereign subject'. It is not so easy to do ethics 'otherwise'.

II

In this context, Alain Badiou's little treatise, *Ethics: an Essay on the Understanding of Evil* (1993) holds a particular interest. For Badiou's thought still vigorously nurtures the anti-humanist impulses of the French philosophy of the 1960s and 1970s. Once part of the theoretical circle around the mandarin journal of post-Althusserian 'anti-humanism', *Cahiers pour l'analyse*, and, throughout most of the seventies, a Maoist militant, Badiou is not about to be fobbed off with any naïve restoration of the moral subject. He begins his book with a vigorous defence of the honour of Foucault and Althusser, which leads into a vehement denunciation of the contemporary resurgence of ethical discourse, in particular the 'pious' discourse of human rights. Yet, at the same time Badiou also proposes a new positive account of ethics, what he terms an 'ethics of truths', and even develops an account of what influential thinkers would no doubt, until recently, have dismissed as an outdated metaphysical category – Evil [*le Mal*].

In brief, to behave ethically, for Badiou, is to remain faithful to a moment of inspiration or insight and to pursue whatever line of thought and action is required to sustain this fidelity. Such disclosures of truth can occur, on his account, in four fundamental domains – politics, science, art and love. They do not transform and dynamize a pre-existent knowing and acting subject. Rather, it is the irruption of an always singular truth through the tissue of everyday 'opinion' which first brings a subject – individual or collective – into being. Hence, for Badiou, there is no universal human subject. There is a plurality of subjects, called on to sustain the particular irruptions of truth through which they are constituted, to cleave faithfully to them against the insistent tug of the merely animal side of human existence. From this perspective, evil is not regarded merely as a lapse or privation, an effect of the inertial drag of our nature. Rather, following a tradition that ultimately derives from Kant, it consists in a perversion whose possibility is intrinsic to the ethical realm. Or, as Badiou states, 'Evil, if it exists, is an unruly effect of the power of truth' (E 55/ 61).

It is not hard to see how this conception provides a platform for Badiou's attack on the universalism of the contemporary discourse of human rights. In his view, it is not simply that such discourse offers no more than well-meaning asseverations, powerless to alter the actual state of the world. Rather, its function is unambiguously ideological. In the opening sections of *Ethics* Badiou expatiates vehemently on his conviction that the language of human rights, multiculturalism and respect for the alterity of the other are merely the means by which the white, affluent West seeks to assure its own good conscience, whilst continuing to ravage and exploit the rest of the world. The discourse of human rights, Badiou asserts, not only debases human beings, treating them primarily as subjects of corporeal need. It splits the supposedly 'universal Subject of rights' between 'the haggard animal exposed on our television screens', on the one hand, and the 'sordid self-satisfaction' of 'the good-Man', the 'white-Man' on the other (E 14/13).

Badiou is not mistaken, of course, in suggesting that the discourse of human rights has come to provide a crucial ideological cover for economic and cultural imperialism, not to mention outright military intervention. No one doubts the murderous hypocrisy with which the Western powers, led by the US, have invoked the language of human rights in recent years. But 'human rights' have also been a rallying call for many activists around the globe. In the form of the Helsinki Accords, they were a major focus for the East European opposition in the years leading up to 1989. They were equally important tactically for Latin America's struggle against the dictatorships, and continue to provide a vital *political* point of leverage for many indigenous populations, not to mention the Tibetans, the Burmese, the Palestinians. The United States, as is well known, continues to refuse recognition to the recently established International Criminal Court, fearful, no doubt, that members of its own armed forces, and perhaps of former administrations, could be amongst those arraigned before it.

Now, in one sense this criticism could be regarded as unfair, since Badiou is far from being an out-and-out anti-universalist. On the contrary, his whole philosophical effort, in both *Ethics* and in numerous other writings, has been directed towards the thinking a new kind of universalism – one which would no longer be vulnerable to charges of abstraction and formalism, but would rather express the scope of an experience of truth which cannot be detached from a singular situation. To this extent, a defence of human rights discourse primarily in terms of its *political* utility might be seen as playing into Badiou's hands, since it implies that the practical impact of the discourse derives not from its demonstrable universality, even if this were to be conceded, but rather from the kind of impact which a universalist claim can make in a specific socio-political situation. This suggests, then, that it is time to look more closely at Badiou's own proposal for an 'ethics of truths', given that one central aim of this ethics is to move beyond the tension between the particular contexts of emergence of ethical claims and their purportedly universal range.

I have already suggested that, for Badiou, ethical commitment begins with the experience of singular truth that erupts through the tissue of established knowledge or opinion. 'At the start, in a given situation, there is no truth, unless it is supplemented by an event. There is only what I term veridicality. Cutting obliquely through all the veridical statements, there is a chance that a truth may emerge, from the moment that an event has encountered its supernumerary name' (*MP* 17/37tm). So a truth-event is not simply an occurrence in the pre-given field of experience. Rather it is that which inter-pellates the subject, we could say, calling him or her into being as the subject defined by faithfulness to the specific truth-disclosure. As Badiou writes, 'I call "subject" the bearer of a fidelity, the one who bears a process of truth. The subject, therefore, in no way pre-exists the process. He is absolutely non-existent in the situation "before" the event. We might say that the process of truth *induces* a subject' (*E* 39/43). Yet at the same time Badiou also stresses that, once a truth has emerged, through our fidelity to this singular process, its claim is universal: 'Only a truth is, as such, *indifferent to differences*. This is something we have always known, even if sophists of every age have always attempted to obscure its certainty: a truth is *the same for all*' (*E* 27/27).

Perhaps the most vivid of Badiou's concrete explorations of this process occurs in his book on Saint Paul, published a few years after *Ethics*. Analysing Paul's extraordinary conversion, and his militant commitment to the truth of the risen Christ, Badiou emphasizes that the universal scope of truths does not depend on any general features of human subjectivity, or on any ontological foundation. It is the 'paradoxical connection between a subject without identity and a law without support which grounds the possibility in history of a uni-versal preaching' (*SP* 6). The encounter with truth has a universalizing impact, in the sense that it detaches human individuals from their embeddedness in the particularity of life within a community. It radically transforms them, con-stitutes them as the subjects of the truth that they now bear. One consequence of this conception, of course, is that there can be no external assessment of the validity of truths, no rational tribunal superior to the individual truth-event itself. And Badiou is perfectly frank about this: 'There is no authority before which the result of a truth process can be made to appear. A truth never derives from Critique. It is supported only by itself, and is the correlative of a new type of subject. Neither transcendental nor substantial, entirely defined as a militant of the truth in question' (*SP* 117).

III

Viewed from a sceptical perspective, it might seem that Badiou's thought, and the conception of ethics to which it gives rise, embodies an uneasy compromise between the antinomian impulses typical of postmodernism, on the one hand, and the mainstream philosophical tradition. Badiou is tough on postmodern conceptions of the 'end of philosophy' (cf. *MP* 7–26/27–45), yet his own position seems to continue the valorization of the singularity and unpredict-ability of the disruptive event – typical of poststructuralism and postmodernism – while seeking to endow this event with all the prestige of a more classical notion of truth. As we have seen, whilst Badiou asserts that the destiny of truths is universal, he makes clear the status of such universality is not amenable to any form of discursive investigation or assessment. He openly states: 'What arises from a truth-process [...] cannot be communicated. Communication is only suited to opinions [...]. In all that concerns truths there must be an *encounter*. The Immortal that I am capable of being cannot be spurred in me by the effects of communicative sociality, it must be *directly* seized by fidelity' (*E* 47/51). Of course, this claim inevitably raises the question of how we distinguish authentic from inauthentic truth-events, how we determine the genuineness of the disclosure to which subjects are called to be faithful. And, to his credit, Badiou acknowledges that this is a crucial problem for his position. The constant emphasis on the singular, incommunicable character of the event of truth on the one hand, combined with its extension into a universal ethical claim, raises all too clearly the possibility of a false, coercive universality. And it is precisely this possibility which, for Badiou, lies at the heart of evil.

An important test for Badiou's position, then, must surely be whether he can establish – through an account of *false* universality – a viable distinction between an orientation towards the Good, and one towards Evil. However, in line with his rejection of general rules or procedures for the determination of truth, Badiou also opposes what he calls 'the idea of a consensual or a priori recognition of evil' (*E* 55/61). In contemporary thought, he suggests, the Nazi extermination of the European Jews has been set up as the paradigm of transgression of the moral law, as the very embodiment of 'radical evil'. But this focus on one historical event, however monstrous, has contradictory effects. On the one hand, the particular crime of the Final Solution, undergoes a *'mise en transcendence'*, it becomes the 'measure without measure', entirely comparable to the notion of the 'Altogether-Other' in Levinas' theologically oriented phenomenology: 'What the God of Levinas is to the evaluation of alterity (the Altogether-Other as incommensurable measure of the Other), the extermination is to the evaluation of historical situations (the Altogether-Evil as incommensurable measure of Evil)' (*E* 56/63, 56/62). But, on the other hand, while claimed as unique, the Final Solution also becomes the standard against which all other evil is measured: 'As the supreme negative example, this crime is inimitable, but every crime is an imitation of it' (*E* 57/63).

For Badiou, then, evil must not be transformed into a transcendent power. Rather, we can identify three dimensions of evil, each of which derives, in some way, from a disturbance in the event of truth. Firstly, evil can consist in the *terror* produced by commitment to what he calls a 'simulacrum' of truth. Such terror occurs when the supposed breakthrough of truth is related to the 'closed particularity of an abstract set' rather than to the unspecifiable void which it reveals at the heart of a specific situation. Thus the breakthrough of the National Socialist 'revolution' was addressed to the German *Volk*, it did not raise a claim to broader significance by negating the particularity of the situation from which it emerged. Secondly, evil can consist in the *betrayal* of a truth, a lack of the nerve and commitment required to pursue its implications as far as they will go. Finally evil occurs in the form of *disaster* when the power of a truth is made absolute; in other words, when there is a failure to acknowledge the fact that the situation in which a truth has emerged can never be rendered fully transparent, that a truth-process cannot entirely appropriate, through nomination, its own contingent context.[9]

What criteria for distinguishing between good and evil are supplied by this account? It is clear that in Badiou's definition of his first form of evil, *terror*, there is a gesture towards universality. Terror arises when a proclamation of truth is addressed to a determinate audience, rather than being addressed 'to all' (*E* 68/76). Thus he writes: 'Every invocation of blood and soil, of race, of custom, of community, works directly against truths; and it is this very collection [*ensemble*] that is named as the enemy in the ethic of truths.' Yet Badiou's third form of evil seems to consist precisely in the universalizing of a truth, made possible by its detachment from its original context through an appropriative act of naming. As Badiou writes: 'The Good is Good only to the extent that it does not aspire to render the world good. Its sole being lies in the situated advent of a singular truth. So it must be that the power of a truth is also a kind of powerlessness' (*E* 75–6/85). And he continues: 'That truth does not have total power means, in the last analysis, that the subject-language, the production of a truth-process, does not have the power to name all the elements of the situation.' Hence, 'every attempt to impose the total power of a truth ruins that truth's very foundation' (*E* 75/84).

Leaving aside Badiou's second category of evil, *betrayal*, which arguably reverts to a more traditional conception of evil as failure or lack, I want to concentrate on the apparent conflict between his descriptions of terror and disaster. This conflict arises, it seems, because Badiou offers no third alternative between the address of a (simulacrum) of truth to a determinate group and the *forcible* imposition of a conception of the good on others, a coercive 'universalization'. Hence his strange claim that 'The Good is only Good to the extent that it does not aspire to render the world good' (*E* 75/85). This is surely incoherent: what genuine vision of the good could be content to leave the world lying in evil? Badiou, it seems, does not consider the possibility that the spread of a truth – which necessarily first emerges in a singular situation – and hence of an orientation towards the human good, could be mediated by the communication and dialogical exploration of an original insight, since this would presuppose a 'universal' human subjectivity of the kind he denies. But is this position sustainable? Seeking to define what is objectionable about the violent exclusivism of simulacra of truth he writes: 'however hostile to a truth he might be, in the ethic of truths every "some-one" is always represented as capable of becoming the Immortal that he is. So we may fight against the judgements and opinions he exchanges with others for the purpose of corrupting every fidelity, but not against his *person* – which, under the circumstances, is insignificant, and to which, in any case, every truth is ultimately addressed' (*E* 68/76). So even Badiou it seems, despite his opposition to 'Kant and the notion of a general morality' (*E* 28/28), has to acknowledge a meta-ethical rule concerning the inviolability of the person, one which determines the legitimate scope of the means by which truths can be propagated. Indeed, despite his declaration that 'there is no ethics in general [...] because there is no abstract Subject, who would adopt it as his shield' (*E* 37/40), Badiou concludes his *Saint Paul* by asserting the inviolability of the basic ethical principle 'love the other as yourself', and arguing that the task of the 'universalizing subject' is to dissolve its own otherness in the universal (*SP* 118).

IV

At this point it seems obvious to ask: *why* is Badiou so committed – at least in his theory of subjectivity – to an anti-universalist emphasis, to the claim that 'there is not in fact one single Subject, but as many subjects as there are truths' (*SP* 28), given that it generates these inconsistencies? One answer would be that, in many respects, Badiou seeks to be a thinker of radical immanence. He repeatedly directs his fire against that 'pathos of finitude' which has been such a prominent strand in twentieth-century European philosophy, most strikingly in the thought of Heidegger and his successors. In his view the thematics of finitude is no more than an inversion of religious consciousness, lingering on in an era when God is unequivocally dead. 'As far as philosophy is concerned, the task is to finish with the motif of finitude and its hermeneutic accompaniments. The key point is undoubtedly to disconnect the infinite from its age-old collusion with the One, and to restore it to the banality of being-multiple, as mathematics invites us to do since Cantor' (*CT* 21). From Badiou's point of view, even Deleuze's philosophy of immanence is subverted by its adherence to the thought of the 'One', the reflexive totalization of immanence, as it were. He insists that we must 'sacrifice the Whole, sacrifice Life, sacrifice the great cosmic animal whose surface Deleuze enchants' (*CT* 72). But although this commitment to immanence may explain the basic orientation of Badiou's thinking, if anything, it exacerbates its inconsistencies. For Badiou's ethics is hardly an ethics of immanence, in the sense of affirming the untrammelled unfolding of being. On the contrary, his ethics appears radically dualistic. For on the one hand, we have the human being portrayed as a 'mortal and predatory animal', caught up in the 'varied and rapacious flux of life' (*E* 45/49, 14/12), on the other the human capacity to become what Badiou audaciously calls 'an Immortal', through participation in the irruption of a truth. Or, as he puts it:

> The 'some-one' thus caught up in what attests that he belongs to the truth-process as one of its foundation-points is simultaneously *himself*, nothing other than himself, a multiple singularity recognizable among all others, and *in excess of himself*, because the uncertain course of fidelity *passes through him*, transfixes his singular body and inscribes in an instant of eternity (*E* 41/45).

In fact, the structure of Badiou's thought seems remarkably similar, in some respects, to that of Levinas, despite his attack on Levinas's grounding of ethics in 'a principle of alterity which transcends mere finite experience' (*E* 23/22). For both thinkers set up an exaggerated contrast between the conatus of the human being as a natural being, and the irruption of an event which breaks the cycle of self-preservation, constituting the subject of a process which, as Badiou says, 'has nothing to do with the "interests" of the animal' and 'has eternity for its destiny'.[10] Although it is not the face of the Other, and the trace of the divine which this discloses, but the event of truth as a 'rare and incalculable supplementation' (*CT* 72), which breaks through the oppression of the totality in Badiou, nonetheless a contrast emerges between the immanence of the domain of natural life and its transcendent interruption. But Levinas merely offers one contemporary parallel, of course. In general, Badiou's ethical thought can be placed squarely within the tradition that understands the ethical demand as exceeding, almost by definition, our finite human capacities to satisfy it. Resolutely opposed to any form of hedonism ('every definition of Man based on happiness is nihilist' [*E* 35/37]), Badiou poses the question: how do we escape from the 'animal's desire to grab its socialized chance' and find our way towards the 'Good as the superhumanity of humanity?' (*E* 30/32).

v

It will already be clear that, despite his militant proclamation of atheism ('There is no God' [*E* 25/25]), Badiou's thought is shot through with quasi-religious metaphor. But even this realization may not prepare us for his use of an explicitly religious concept to bridge the gap between human capacities and the claim of the truth-event on our fidelity – namely, the concept of 'grace'. The problem is stated quite clearly in *Ethics*:

> I am altogether present there, linking my component elements via that *excess beyond myself* induced by the passing through me of a truth. But, as a result, I am also suspended, broken, annulled; dis-interested. For I cannot, within the fidelity to fidelity which defines ethical consistency, take an interest in myself, and thus pursue my own interests [. . .]. There is always only one question in the ethic of truths: how will I, as some-one, *continue* to exceed my own being? (*E* 45/49–50).

And the answer to this question is stated equally clearly in the book on Saint Paul: what is required, Badiou asserts, is to 'extract from its mythological kernel a formal and entirely secularized conception of grace. The whole point is to know if any existence whatsoever can, breaking with the cruel flow of ordinary time, encounter the material chance to serve truth, and thus to become, in its subjective division, and beyond the human animal's duty to survive, an immortal' (*SP* 70). He then amplifies this argument in the following terms: 'it is our task to found a materialism of grace by means of the idea, at once simple and powerful, that any existence can one day be pierced through by what happens to it, and devote itself from then on to that which is valid for all, or, as Paul magnificently puts it, "make oneself everything to all" ' (*SP* 70).

Now, in one sense, this weaving of religious motifs into the fabric of Badiou's ethical thought is scarcely surprising, since such intertwining has been a recurrent feature of post-Kantian ethics – at least in the mainstream European tradition. It is rendered more problematic, of course, by Badiou's posture of atheism. But I do not intend to pursue here the question of whether *any* concept can be unambiguously secularized, even through a slow, anonymous process of semantic transformation, let alone by authorial fiat. I want simply to indicate that the invocation of the notion of grace by Badiou is not at all capricious – since it provides an answer to what Badiou presents as *the* central question in his ethics of truths: 'how will I, as some-one, *continue* to exceed my own being?' Furthermore, Badiou is far from being the first modern ethicist to seek to reconfigure the notion of grace. For the tradition stretching back to Kant, which spurns happiness as the direct goal of ethics and proposes a notion of the good that transcends human powers, yet also rejects any assurance of divine moral assistance, and often even the very idea of the divine, is necessarily forced into some such reworking. If the Good, as Badiou asserts (reminding us that Nietzsche, too, belongs in this lineage), is the 'superhumanity of humanity', then how on earth are we to get beyond ourselves, solely by our own effort, in order to attain it? Tracing some landmark responses to this question may help us to appreciate the distinctiveness – and, I would argue, some of the perils – of Badiou's approach.

VI

Kant's crucial reflections on grace, in his *Religion within the Limits of Reason Alone*, arise from two considerations: firstly, a sense of the severity of the moral law, which requires that the maxim of my action should be strictly universalizable, purged of any trace of self-interested bias; secondly, the claim that, though an awareness of moral duty is integral to our status as human persons, we have all nonetheless made what Kant presents as a non-temporal, character-defining choice to prioritize, at least on occasion, the incentives arising from our sensuous nature. For Kant, there thus arises the apparently intractable problem of how human beings can transform an 'intelligible character' which has been essentially corrupted by this primordial choice.[11] Kant introduces the notion of grace, in other words, at the point where freedom faces the task of breaking its self-imposed shackles, where a human nature moulded by a propensity for evil somehow has to achieve its own reorientation towards the good. Since we know that we *ought* to transform our moral disposition, and since duty makes no sense without the corresponding capacity, Kant suggests that reason is entitled to a 'reflective faith': 'She holds that, if in the inscrutable realm of the supernatural there is something more than she can explain to herself, which may yet be necessary as a complement to her moral insufficiency, this will be, even though unknown, available to her good will.'[12] For Kant, however, there can be no assurance of a moral revolution assisted by grace. Indeed, he insists that 'we can admit a work of grace as something incomprehensible, but we cannot adopt it into our maxims for either theoretical or practical use'.[13] In other words, the notion of grace should in no sense be taken as permission to relax our own moral efforts and – strictly speaking – the only beings who could be said to merit grace are those who would no longer need it.

For Kant, then, we can have no knowledge of the workings of grace, indeed we cannot even understand how it might be possible – it remains only an object of faith. Furthermore, as we have seen, Kant holds us responsible for what many more recent thinkers would no doubt regard as the ineluctable imperatives of our animal nature. He does not depict the alternative of good and evil in terms of a simple opposition between nature and freedom, but rather in terms of a contrast between two *uses* of freedom. Our natural endowment, our innate drives for self-preservation, sex, propagation and the care of children (our 'disposition to animality'), and our aspiration to equal recognition within a community (our 'disposition to humanity'), do not *intrinsically* run counter to the moral law (awareness of which is expressed in our 'disposition to personality').[14] In Kant freedom is confronted not with the stubbornness of nature, but with a paradox of its own making. In view of this, Badiou's position might well appear closer to that of a thinker who, while declaring allegiance to Kant's transcendental idealism, also reflects the pressures of modern naturalism – Arthur Schopenhauer.

Certainly, Schopenhauer's anti-theological animus, his description of spontaneous human egoism, and his sense of the inevitable subordination of our reflective capacities to the powerful promptings of the instincts, accord well with Badiou's characterization of the human being as a 'mortal and predatory animal'. In contrast with Kant's stress on the imputability of every action, Schopenhauer does not hold us *responsible* for the fact that, like the rest of the natural world, we are essentially driven by a blind, endlessly-striving metaphysical 'will'. Yet, for Schopenhauer, too, there *is* a possibility of breaking out of this bondage, namely through the self-suppression of the will. Yet how can the will turn against itself? Only through our rising 'to survey the whole of life independently of the impression of the present moment.'[15] But how in turn is this possible? Schopenhauer explains:

> Now since [. . .] that *self-suppression of the will* comes from knowledge, but all knowledge and insight as such are independent of free choice, that denial of willing, that entrance into freedom is not to be forcibly arrived at by intention or design, but comes from the innermost relation of knowing and willing in man; hence it comes suddenly as if flying in from without. Therefore the Chuch calls it the *effect of grace*; but just as she still represents it as depending on the acceptance of grace, so too the effect of the quieter is ultimately an act of the freedom of the will.[16]

Schopenhauer's discomfiture is palpable: if 'Necessity *is the kingdom of nature; freedom is the kingdom of grace*',[17] then the transition from one to the other is deeply paradoxical, achieved through a freedom which this very transition is to bring into being. In this respect, Schopenhauer's metaphysics of the will puts him in a more difficult position than Kant, whose insistence on the primacy of practical reason sets a limit to our knowledge of ultimate reality. For as Kant points out in his own defence in the *Religion*, grace is really no more mysterious than freedom itself, which, 'though containing nothing supernatural in its conception, remains, as regards its possibility, just as incomprehensible to us as is the supernatural factor which we would like to regard as a supplement to the spontaneous but deficient determination of freedom'.[18]

Where does Badiou lie between these two poles? As I have suggested, his metaphysical vision, if this is not too contentious a term, seems to lies closer to Schopenhauer. For as he repeatedly makes clear, we cannot even speak of a 'subject' prior to the happening of the truth-event; there is only a 'some-one', an 'animal of the human species' (*E* 41/44). In consequence, the truth-event can only be experienced as an irruption which carries me 'beyond' my animal and mortal self. The ethics of a truth enjoins: 'Do all that you can to persevere in that which exceeds your perseverance. Persevere in the interruption. Seize in your being that which has seized and broken you' (*E* 43/47). But this exhortation also highlights the contrast between Badiou and Schopenhauer. For, in the arch-pessimist's work, to be touched by grace is to turn away from the perspective that constitutes the world of representation, in ascetic self-denial: 'we see the world melt away with the abolished will, and retain before us only empty nothingness'.[19] Hence, we can say that, for Schopenhauer, we may *experience* grace, as the dissolution of an oppressive phenomenal reality, but this is not an experience of *engagement* or activism. One the contrary, since our practical interests are inevitably expressed in instrumental form, they perpetuate the very world of suffering from which we long to escape. Badiou, by contrast, fuses the transformative experience, the truth-event, and the orientation to practice. And it is precisely this which should give cause for alarm. Indeed, one might wonder whether Badiou's ethics should not be regarded as a form of 'fanaticism' in the Kantian sense – the articulation of an 'imagined inward experience' of being touched by grace.[20]

For Kant, the finite human being cannot leap the gap between moral capacity and moral command.[21] The human agent remains ever-conscious of the distance between her finite constitution and what is required of her: a distance which will always appear in the form duty. Badiou evokes experiences of exaltation, of aesthetic or scientific discovery, of passionate love or political engagement, in which I am '*directly* seized by fidelity' and become 'the Immortal that I am capable of being' (*E* 47/51). But in Kant, immortality remains no more than a figure, a horizon, a postulate: an expression of the conviction that, if our moral striving is to make any sense, we cannot regard the gap between delivery and demand as entirely without prospect of closure. Furthermore, for Kant the conviction of being in receipt of grace was dangerous enough in the religious domain. How much more worrying then, when Badiou, while (inconsistently) excluding the religious domain as a field of possible truth-events, exports the structure of an experience of grace into other fields, including the arena of politics.

In one sense, one can understand Badiou's motivation, of course. For, as he writes, prevailing conceptions of ethics 'designate above all the incapacity, so typical of the contemporary world, to name and strive for a Good. We should go even further, and say that the reign of ethics is one symptom of a universe ruled by a distinctive combination of resignation in the face of necessity together with a purely negative, if not destructive, will' (*E* 29/30). Faced with such a discouraging situation, confronted by what Adorno, in his lectures on moral philosophy, termed the 'overpowering machinery of external reality', one natural response would be to seek to recover the dynamizing force of ethical commitment, compressed in moments of transformative experience. Yet, the result, at least in Badiou's case, is a posture which falls too easily into a well-established paradigm: contempt for the banality and complacency of a society devoted to commerce and material well-being, the celebration of a heroic contrast between everyday communication, dismissed as the circulation of a mindless mulch of 'opinion', and the irruption of existentially galvanizing truths. The lineage can be traced, in the modern philosophical tradition, via the Heidegger of *Being and Time*, at least as far back as Fichte's secular sermons.

VII

I began by evoking the oscillation of recent cultural criticism between an exuberant assertion of pluralistic fragmentation and a renewed awareness – 'depressive' in an almost Kleinian sense – of the constraints of ethical obligation. I suggested that this alternation could itself be seen as an index of the moral situation of the present. For, as Jürgen Habermas has remarked, 'The more moral consciousness comes to be based on universalistic value-orientations, the greater become the discrepancies between indisputable moral requirements on the one hand, and organizational constraints and resistances to changes on the other.'[22] The worry raised by Badiou's conception of ethics is that, rather than patiently thinking through this impasse, it seeks to resolve it by a *coup de force*, simply combining the two extremes of the oscillation. The retreat into particularity here takes the form of the exaltation of participation in the singularity of the truth-event. Fidelity to this participation is now read as ethical, but is not susceptible to any independent assessment of its validity, to any mediation or communication. Yet the truth-event is also construed as raising a universal claim, even though it cannot anticipate wider recognition for any other than contingent reasons (for Badiou, as we have seen, 'there is no authority before which the result of a truth procedure can be made to appear'). This is not to say that the experiences that Badiou seeks to approach, through his conceptualizations of 'grace' and the 'truth-event', have no ethical relevance. But, like those glimpses beyond the reciprocal compulsion of subject and object which Adorno evokes with the term 'metaphysical experience',[23] such moments of vulnerability, such adumbrations of transcendence, can only *open the way* for new ethical responses.[24] At one point in his lectures on moral philosophy, Adorno states: 'If you were to press me to follow the example of the Ancients and make a list of cardinal virtues, I would probably respond cryptically by saying that I could think of nothing except for modesty.'[25] Ethical orientations, he implies, if they are to offer any hope of coherent action, must spring not from a sense of election and exaltation, but rather from a combination of resolution and reserve – an awareness, which Kant of course also shares, of the fragility of our individual powers, and the enormity of what justice and humanity demand.

9

AN ETHICS OF MILITANT
ENGAGEMENT*

Ernesto Laclau

ı

I find Alain Badiou's ethical reflections most congenial. There are three aspects of them, in particular, which I find clearly appealing and close to my own theoretical approach. In the first place, his attempt to articulate ethics within an emancipatory project. Against the prevailing contemporary trend, which presents ethics as a purely *defensive* intervention – that is, as a reaction to the violation of human rights – Badiou roots his ethics in an essentially affirmative discourse. Secondly, the universality of the ethical address does not depend, for Badiou, on the presumed universality of its place of enunciation: on the contrary, ethics is constitutively linked to the fidelity to an event which is always concrete and situated. Finally, Badiou scrupulously avoids the temptation to derive the ensemble of moral norms from the ethical as such – the former belongs, for him, to what is countable within a situation which is strictly heterogeneous vis-à-vis the latter.

My own theoretical approach is, from this point of view, at least comparable to Badiou's, and the fact has not gone unrecognized. Slavoj Žižek, for instance, writes:

> A series of obvious differences notwithstanding, the theoretical edifices of Laclau and Badiou are united by a deep homology. Against the Hegelian vision of the 'concrete universal', of the reconciliation between Universal and Particular (or between Being and Event) which is still clearly discernible in Marx, they both start by asserting a constitutive and irreducible gap that undermines the self-enclosed consistency of the ontological edifice: for Laclau, this gap is the gap between the Particular and the empty Universal, which necessitates the operation of hegemony (or the gap between the differential structure of the positive social order – the logic of *differences* – and properly political antagonism, which involves the logic of *equivalence*); for Badiou, it is the gap between Being and Event (between the order of Being – structure, state of situation, knowledge –

*I would like to thank Peter Hallward for his careful reading of the draft version of this chapter and for his many comments which helped me more clearly and precisely to present my argument.

and the event of Truth, Truth as Event). In both cases, the problem is how to break out of the self-enclosed field of ontology as a description of the positive universe; in both cases, the dimension which undermines the closure of ontology has an 'ethical' character – it concerns the contingent act of *decision* against the background of the 'undecidable' multiplicity of Being; consequently, both authors endeavour to conceptualize a new, post-Cartesian mode of *subjectivity* which cuts its links with ontology and hinges on a contingent act of decision.[1]

In spite of these many real points of convergence, there are also, however, several aspects in which our respective approaches fundamentally diverge, and it is these that I shall address in the following pages. The fact that our approaches are indeed comparable, however, has its advantages: opposite theoretical decisions can be presented as alternative routes whose divergence is thinkable out of what had been, up to that point, a relatively shared theoretical terrain. One last preliminary remark: I will mainly refer, in what follows, to Badiou's ethics, without any comprehensive discussion of his ontology, a task in which I hope to engage in the not too distant future.

Let us first recapitulate some basic categories of Badiou's theory. The main distinction, from his perspective, is that between *situation* and *event*. Situation is the terrain of a multiplicity corresponding to what can be called, in general terms, the field of objectivity. Being is not one – oneness is, for Badiou, a theological category – but multiple. Presentable or consistent multiplicity corresponds, essentially, with the field of knowledge, of the countable, of the distinct. The ensemble of objective distinctions corresponds to a structuring principle that Badiou calls the *state* of the situation. What we usually call morality – the normative order – is part of this state and is organized by this structural principle. A distinction has to be established here between *presentation* of a situation in which structuration – order – shows itself as such, and *representation*, the moment in which not *structure* but *structuring* comes to the fore. The event is grounded on that which is radically unrepresentable within the situation, that which constitutes its *void* (a category to which we will come back later). The event is the actual declaring of that void, a radical break with the situation that makes visible what the situation itself can only conceal. While knowledge is inscription of what happens within pre-given objective categories, *truth* – the series of implications sustained in the wake of an event – is *singular*: its evental nature cannot be subsumed under any pre-existing rule. The event is, thus, incommensurable with the situation, its break with it is truly foundational. If we tried to define its relation with the situation we could only say that it is a *subtraction* from it.

The ethical is intimately linked to the notion of event. Once the event takes place, the visibility that its advent makes possible opens an area of indeterminacy in relation to the ways of dealing with it: either we can stick to that visibility through what Badiou calls a *fidelity* to the event – which involves transforming the situation through a restructuring which takes the proclaimed truth as its point of departure – or we can negate the radically evental character of the event. When it involves the perversion or corruption of a truth, this latter option is *evil*. In Badiou's account evil can take one of three main forms: the form of *betrayal* (the abandonment of fidelity to the event), the form of the *simulacrum* (the replacement, through naming, of the void in the fullness of the community), and the form of a dogmatic *totalization* of a truth.

At this point we have to address a series of interrelated questions. Is an event, which defines itself exclusively through ability to subtract itself from a situation, enough to ground an ethical alternative? Is the distinction void/fullness a solid enough criterion for discriminating between event and simulacrum? Is the opposition situation/event sufficiently clear-cut as to ascribe to the evental camp everything needed to formulate an ethical principle? My answer to these three questions will be negative.

It makes sense to start with a consideration of the three forms of evil to which Badiou refers. The main question is: to what extent does he smuggle into his argument something that he had formally excluded at its very beginning? As we said, the basic ontological opposition that he establishes is that between situation and event, whose only ground is given by the category of 'subtraction'. This also sets up the parameters within which the distinction is thinkable. We have to forget everything about the material, ontic contents of the situation and reduce it to its purely formal defining principle (the organization of the countable, the differential, as such). In that case, however, the only possible content of the event as pure subtraction is the presentation or declaration of the unrepresentable. In other words, the event also can only have a purely *formal* content. As a result, the fidelity to the event (the exclusive content of the ethical act) has to be, as well, an entirely formal ethical injunction. How, in that case, to differentiate the ethical from the simulacrum? As Badiou himself makes clear, the simulacrum – as one of the figures of evil – can only emerge in the terrain of truth. So if Badiou is going to be faithful to his theoretical premises, the distinction between event and simulacrum has also to be a formal one – i.e. it has to emerge from the form of the event as such independently of its actual content.

Is Badiou true to his own theoretical presuppositions on this point? I don't think so. His answer to the question of the criterion distinguishing event from simulacrum is that the event addresses the *void* of a situation. 'What allows a genuine event to be at the origin of a truth – which is the only thing that can be for all, and can be eternally', he writes, 'is precisely the fact that it relates to the particularity of a situation only from the bias of its void. The void, the multiple-of-nothing, neither excludes nor constrains anyone. It is the absolute neutrality of being – such that the fidelity that originates in an event, although it is an immanent break within a singular situation, is nonetheless universally addressed' (*E* 65/73). The simulacrum – Nazism, for instance – relates to the situation as plenitude or substance. According to the logic of a simulacrum, the pseudo-event 'is supposed to bring into being, and name, not the void of the earlier situation, but its plenitude – not the universality of that which is sustained, precisely, by no particular characteristic (no particular multiple), but the absolute particularity of a community, itself rooted in the characteristics of its soil, its blood, and its race' (E 64–5/73).

What is wrong with this solution? Several things – to which we will refer later – but especially one which, to some extent, anticipates the others: the distinction truth/simulacrum cannot ultimately be formulated because it does not have any viable place of enunciation within Badiou's theoretical edifice (at this stage of its elaboration, at least.)[2] There are only two places of enunciation within Badiou's system: the situation and the event. Now, the situation is no possible locus for a discourse discriminating between true and false events, between void and fullness, because the void is precisely that which the situation cannot think. But that place of enunciation cannot be constituted around the event either. The 'truth' that, over time, develops the implications of the event cannot contribute a discriminating capacity between true and false events that the event itself does not provide. All that the subjects engaged in a truth procedure can do, *once they accept the event as a true one*, is to be clear about what perverting an event would consist of – but this by itself does not establish a criterion for distinguishing truth from simulacrum. *It is only by appealing to a third discourse which is not itself easily integrated into Badiou's theoretical system that the distinction truth/simulacrum can be maintained.* This is hardly surprising: if the event constitutes itself through a pure and simple subtraction from a situation conceived as a given contingent embodiment of the formal principle of counting (such that its concreteness has to be strictly ignored) there is no way for the subjects affirming that event to discriminate between types of interruption of that situation – let alone of attributing a differential ethical value to those types.

It is clear that, on the basis of the asserted premises, we cannot advance beyond establishing the formal components of a militant ethics, and that we cannot legislate anything concerning the content of the latter – except by smuggling a third (as yet untheorized) discourse into the argument. This appeal to a third discourse as a sort of *deus ex machina* is not peculiar to Badiou alone. Žižek's analysis of Nazism proceeds along similar lines. It starts by subscribing to Badiou's distinction: 'In contrast to this authentic act which intervenes in the constitutive void, point of failure – or what Alain Badiou has called the "symptomal torsion" of a given constellation – the inauthentic act legitimizes itself through reference to the point of substantial fullness of a given constellation (on the political terrain: Race, True Religion, Nation ...): it aims precisely at obliterating the last traces of the "symptomal torsion" which disturbs the balance of that constellation.'[3] The analysis of Nazism which follows from these premises offers few surprises:

The so-called 'Nazi revolution', with its disavowal/displacement of the fundamental social antagonism ('class struggle' that divides the social edifice from within) – with its projection/externalization of the cause of social antagonisms into the figure of the Jew, and the consequent reassertion of the corporatist notion of society as an organic Whole – clearly *avoids* confrontation with social antagonism: the 'Nazi revolution' is *the*

exemplary case of a pseudo-change, of a frenetic activity in the course of
which many things did change – 'something was going on all the time' –
so that, precisely, something – that which *really matters* – would *not*
change; so that things would fundamentally 'remain the same'.[4]

The advantage of Žižek's over Badiou's formulations is that they make quite
explicit that third silent discourse which is present in Badiou's texts only
through its theoretical effects. Žižek makes no bones about the nature of his
exercise: he robustly asserts a crude theory of 'false consciousness' which makes
it possible for him to detect the fundamental social antagonisms, what 'really
matters' in society and how things could change without any meaningful
change taking place.[5] What is wrong with all this? Not, obviously, the concrete
content of his assertions – I agree with most of it – but the role that those
assertions play in his theory and, in a more subtle way, also in Badiou's theory.
For they are a set of ontic assertions the ambition of which is to establish
distinctions between *ontological* categories. 'Situation', 'event', 'truth', 'generic
procedure', have an ontological status in Badiou's discourse.[6] Likewise the 'void'
and its opposite, i.e. a full particularity convoked as the substance of a situation.
So, in that case, how are we to determine which is the true void of a concrete
situation? There are only two possibilities: either to reabsorb, in a Hegelian
fashion, the ontic into the ontological – a solution that Žižek flirts with but
that Badiou most scrupulously tries to avoid; or to name the void through the
axiomatic postulation inherent to a truth procedure – in which case there seem
to be no available means of discriminating between true and false events, and
the principle of the distinction between event and simulacrum collapses.

A third solution is conceivable: that the *marks* of a true event are already
ontologically determined (or, if you like, transcendentally preconstituted). For
Badiou these marks exist and are inscribed in the *exclusive* alternative of either
relating to a particular situation from the bias of its void, or naming the
presumed 'fullness' of a certain situation. If we could demonstrate that such an
alternative is truly exclusive and that it is constitutively inherent to any possible concrete situation, our problem would be solved.

This demonstration is, however, impossible. Let us look at the matter from
the two sides of this potential polarity. From the void, in the first place. What
figures as void is always, for Badiou, the void of *a* situation. Whatever counts as
void, or as nothing, is scattered throughout a situation and is necessarily
included in every sub-set of a situation; since there is nothing 'in' the void that
might serve to identify or locate it, any such operation is impossible. Each
situation, however, contains a minimally identifiable element, a group or
individual located on the 'edge' of whatever counts as nothing for the situation
– an element that counts only as an indiscernible 'something', with no other
identifying characteristics. This element, for Badiou, has no elements of its own
in common with the situation, i.e. no elements that the situation itself can
recognize or discern. The inhabitants of this liminal space are presentable in
two very different ways, the articulation of which is crucial for the question that
we are discussing. Firstly, they can be *named* in a *referential* way: the *sans-papiers*

in today's France, the working class in capitalist society, the death of Christ in Saint Paul's discourse in its opposition to Hebrew Law and Greek wisdom, etc. In the second place, however, that name remains *empty* because what it designates, and proclaims through the event, does not correspond to anything that is representable within the counting of the situation – it would be, to use a different terminology, a signifier without a signified.

The problem which immediately arises concerns the precise way these two dimensions are to be linked. If referential designation and non-representabilty within the situation did exactly overlap with each other, there would be no problem: the edge of the void would be precisely located in a site defined by the parameters of the situation. But there are neither logical nor historical reasons to make this simplifying assumption. Let us suppose that a society is experiencing what Gramsci called an *organic crisis*: what confronts us, in that case, are not particular sites defining (delimiting) what is unrepresentable within the general field of representation, but rather the fact that the very logic of representation has lost its structural abilities. This transforms the role of the event: it does not simply have to proclaim the centrality of an exception vis-à-vis a highly structured situation, but has to reconstruct the principle of situationality as such around a new core.

This, in my view, radically changes the void/situation relationship. It is precisely at this point that my approach starts to differ from Badiou's. Within Badiou's system, there is no way that the void can be given any content, as it is and remains empty by definition. The 'evental site', on the other hand, always has a certain content. This is what we call 'referential designation'. This distinction makes perfect sense within the set theory approach within which Badiou operates. The possibility that we have raised, however – that the logic of representation might lose its structuring abilities – raises questions which can hardly be answered within Badiou's system. For in that case what becomes uncountable in the situation is the principle of countability as such. So the truth procedure in which its subjects engage themselves consists, in one of its basic dimensions, in reconstructing the situation around a new core. The consequence is that there is no longer any question of a linear development of the implications of the event: the latter has to show its articulating abilities *by going beyond itself*, so that the drastic separation between evental site and void has to be necessarily put into question. Consequently some filling of the void – of a special kind which requires theoretical description – becomes necessary. (Needless to say, the very idea of such a filling is an anathema for Badiou: any filling of the void is, for him, evil.)

How might this filling proceed? Badiou thinks that the void, having no members of its own (in the situation presented by set theory it figures as the empty set) does not belong to any particular situation – which means that it is included in them all – but that, as far as human situations are concerned, the subjects of a truth that affirms the event address universality pure and simple. This means, indistinct humanity – in the sense that Marx for instance asserted that the proletariat has only his chains. I can only go half way along this argument. There are two insurmountable difficulties. The first is that the category of the void – of the empty set Ø – is only empty when it operates within mathematics. When it is transposed to social analysis it is filled with certain contents – thinking, freedom/consciousness, 'only chains', etc. – which are far from being empty. What we have here is a hopelessly metaphorical exercise by which emptiness is equated with universality. It only takes a moment to realize that the universal content is not empty. We are simply confronted with an attempt at an ethical defence of universality which proceeds through an illegitimate appeal to set theory. So much for Badiou's claim that any filling of the void is evil. In the second place, we are sometimes presented with the argument that the subjects of a truth have means of differentiating between truth and simulacrum – criteria such as strict equality, universality, indifference to all qualities and values etc. But it is clear that the validity of these criteria entirely depends on accepting as a starting point the equation between void and universality. So the argument is perfectly circular.

Let me be clear: mine is not an objection to universality as such but to Badiou's way of theoretically constructing it. In one sense it is true that a radical interruption of a given situation will interpellate people across and beyond particularisms and differences. Every revolutionary break has, in that respect, universalizing effects. People live for a moment the illusion that, because an oppressive regime has been overthrown, what has been overthrown is oppression *as such*. It is in that sense that the void, in Badiou's sense, not having any distinctive content, addresses something which is beyond all particularity *as particularity*. But the other side of the picture, the moment of referential designation, is still there, doing its job. For – and at this point I definitely disagree with Badiou – I do not think that the particularism inherent in that local reference can be simply eliminated from the picture as a site having only relations of exteriority with the void. The *sans-papiers*, as an indiscernible element within their situation, *may* come to articulate a position that holds true for all members of that situation (e.g. 'Everyone who is here is from here'), but they are also constituted as political subjects through a series of particular demands which could be granted by an expansive hegemony of the existing situation and, in that sense, individual *sans-papiers* may come to be counted in their turn, i.e. become normal members of the situation.

The conclusion is obvious: the frontiers between the countable and the uncountable are essentially unstable. But this means that there is no locus, no site within the situation, which has inscribed a priori within itself the guarantees of universality: that is, there is *no natural name* for the void. Conversely, no name is a priori excluded from naming it. Let us give an example. The Solidarnosc movement started as a set of particular demands of a group of workers in Gdansk. However, as those demands were formulated in a particularly repressive context, they became the symbols and the surface of inscription of a plurality of other demands which were uncountable within the situation defined by the bureaucratic regime. That is, it was through the articulation between themselves that these demands constructed a certain universalism which transcended all particularities. This especially applies to the central symbols of Solidarnosc: a certain remnant of particularism cannot be eliminated from them, but because those symbols served to represent a large set of democratic equivalential demands, they became the embodiment of universality as such. It is through this equivalence/transcendence between particularities that something like the name of the void can be constructed. This is what in my work I have called hegemony: the process by which a particularity assumes the representation of a universality which is essentially incommensurable with it.

Two capital conclusions follow from this argument: (1) universality has no a priori sites of emergence, but it is the result of the displacement of the frontier between the countable and the uncountable – i.e. of the construction of an expansive hegemony; (2) if articulation is given its proper central role, naming the void is constitutively linked to the process of its filling, but this filling can only proceed through an uneasy balance between universality and particularity – a balance which, by definition, can never be broken through the exclusive domination of either of its two poles. Filling a void is not simply to assign to it a particular content, but to make of that content the nodal point of an equivalential universality transcending it. Now from the point of view of our original problem, which was the determination of a true event (whose precondition was the naming of a pure void – i.e. a universality not contaminated by particularity), this means that such a pure universality is impossible. Its place is always going to be occupied/embodied by something which is less than itself.

Let us now move to the other side of the polarity: the particularistic filling of the void that Badiou and Žižek discuss in connection with Nazism. Let us remain within that example which, being extreme, presents the best possible terrain for Badiou to argue his case. Badiou cannot be accused of trying to make his case easy: on the contrary, he stresses without concessions the structural parallels between event and simulacrum. '"Simulacrum" must be understood here in its strong sense', he admits:

> all the formal traits of a truth are at work in the simulacrum. Not only a universal nomination of the event, inducing the power of a radical break, but also the 'obligation' of a fidelity, and the promotion of a *simulacrum of the subject*, erected – without the advent of any Immortal – above the human animality of the others, of those who are arbitrarily declared to belong to the communitarian substance whose promotion and domination the simulacrum-event is designed to assure. (*E* 66/74)

How does Badiou establish, on these premises, the distinction between event and simulacrum? Not surprisingly, through a drastic opposition between the *void* and what stands as the *substance* of the community – precisely the distinction that we tried to undermine. 'Fidelity to a simulacrum – unlike fidelity to an event – regulates its break with the situation not by the universality of the void, but by the close particularity of an abstract set (the "Germans" or the "Aryans")' (*E* 66/74). To assess the viability of Badiou's solution we have to ask ourselves some questions which are the opposite of those we were dealing with in the case of the void: to what extent is the particularism of the Nazi discourse incompatible with any appeal to the universal (to the void)? And to what extent does the abstract set that regulates the break with the situation (the 'Germans', the 'Aryans', etc.) function in the Nazi discourse as a particularistic instance?

Let us successively consider these two questions. Regarding the first there can be no doubt at all: the void is as much addressed in the Nazi discourse as in any socialist one. Let us remember that the void is not in our view universality in the strict sense of the term but that which is uncountable in a given situation. As we have argued, and I think Badiou would agree, it does not have a single and precise site in a critical situation, when the very principles of counting are threatened and the reconstruction of the community as a whole around a new core comes to the fore as a fundamental social need. That was exactly the situation that prevailed in the crisis of the Weimar Republic. There was not then a clash between an uncountable presence and a well-structured situation (between a proclaimed event and the state of the situation), but a fundamental destructuring of the community which required that the named event became, from its very inception, a principle of restructuration. It was not a matter of substituting a fully-fledged existing situation by a different one deriving from a new principle subversive of the status quo, but of a hegemonic struggle between rival principles, between different ways of naming the uncountable to see which one was more capable of *articulating a situation* against the alternative of anomie and chaos. In this sense there is no doubt that the void as such was clearly addressed in Nazi discourse.

What, however, about the particular set (blood, race, etc.) that Nazism convoked as the event breaking with the situation? Is not this particular communitarian substance incompatible with the universality of the void (of the empty set)? We have to consider the matter carefully. In our discussion of the naming of the void we have distinguished between the referential designation of the edge of the void and the universality of the content that that site embodies. We have also argued that that universality will depend on the extension of the chain of equivalences which is expressed through that name. This means that no name having a certain political centrality will ever have a univocal particular reference. Terms which formally name a particularity will acquire, through equivalential chains, a far more universal reference while, conversely, others whose denotation is apparently universal can become, in certain discursive articulations, the name of extremely particularistic meanings. This means that: (1) there is no name of a pure, uncontaminated universality (of a pure void); (2) a purely particular name is also impossible.[7] What we have earlier called hegemony consists, precisely, in this undecidable game between universality and particularity. In that case, however, the distinction between true event and simulacrum collapses: it is simply impossible to conceive evil as a result of a particularistic invocation against the universality of truth. For the same reason, the sharp distinction between generic set and constructible set cannot be maintained either as far as society is concerned.

Does this mean that the very notion of evil has to be abandoned, that everything goes and that it is not possible to pass an ethical judgement about phenomena such as Nazism? Obviously not. The only thing that *does* follow from our previous argument is that it is impossible to ground ethical options at the abstract level of a theory dominated by the duality situation/event, and that these categories – whatever their validity in other spheres – do not provide criteria for moral choice. This also means that the terrain in which these criteria can emerge is going to be a much more concrete one. This much Badiou himself would be ready to accept: truth for him is always the truth of a situation. In that case, however, what I have called the silent third discourse implicit in his approach – the one that would actually provide him with a legitimate position of enunciation for his discourse on evil – needs explicitly to be brought to the fore. This operation, nonetheless, is not possible without introducing some changes in Badiou's theoretical apparatus. This is the question that I will address next.

II

Let us summarize our argument so far. Badiou, quite correctly, refuses to ground ethics in any a priori normativism – the latter belonging, by definition, to the situation as a countable *given*. The source of ethical commitment should be found in the implication or consequences drawn from the event conceived as *subtraction* from that situation. In that case, however, any distinction between true and false events cannot be based on what events actually proclaim – firstly, because that would smuggle into the argument the normativism which was axiomatically excluded and, secondly, because it would require a judging instance external to both situation and event (what we have called a 'third discourse'). The latter is what makes Žižek's argument hopelessly eclectic, and it is what Badiou tries to avoid. Things being so, the only course open to him is to attempt to ground the distinction event/simulacrum in the very structural differentiations that his dualistic ontology has established. He finds this ground in the duality void/plenum. This does not entirely eliminate the problem of the third discourse, for Badiou has still to explain why to give expression to the void is good while to give it to the plenum is bad, but at least a step in the right direction has been taken. The cornerstone of the argument thus relies on the distinction void/plenum being unambiguous. But, as we have seen, Badiou's distinction is untenable. Firstly, because, as we have argued earlier, the void – as far as the category is applicable to a human situation – is not for Badiou really empty but has already a certain content – the universal. And, secondly, because the arrangement of the elements of the situation brought about by the subject out of the generic inconsistency revealed by the event requires, if the notion of 'arrangement' is going to make any sense, some consistency between the universality *shown* by the event and the new arrangement resulting from the subject's intervention. In what does this 'consistency' consist of? One possibility is that it is a logical consistency. But Badiou – and also myself – would reject this possibility because in that case the gap between event and situation would be cancelled and the notion of an ontology grounded in multiplicity would no longer make any sense. The *only* other alternative is that the consistency between event and new arrangement results from a *contingent* construction – and it necessarily has to be so, given that it starts from the terrain of a primordial inconsistency. This simply means that the consistency of the new arrangement is going to be, through and through, a constructed one. Ergo 'truth procedure' and 'contingent construction' are interchangeable terms. Now, what else is this but *filling in* the void? If my argument is correct, the distinction void/plenum falls – or at least establishes between its two poles a far more complex system of mutual displacements than Badiou's sharp dichotomy allows.

What we will now go on to argue is that, paradoxically, the blind alley we are discussing is not unconnected to what is perhaps the most valuable feature of Badiou's ethics: his refusal to postulate any kind of a priori normativism. This refusal, however, has been accompanied by the *assertion* of some ontological presuppositions which are the very source of the difficulties that we are dealing with. Let us make one last remark before embarking on this discussion. Of the three figures of evil to which Badiou refers, only the first – the distinction between truth and simulacrum – is intending to discriminate between true and false event. The second, as Badiou himself recognizes, would be seen as evil not only from the perspective of the true event but from that of the simulacrum (a fascist as much as a revolutionary would consider evil any kind of weakening of the revolutionary will). As for the third figure, it presents problems of its own that we will discuss presently.

As I said at the beginning, I do not intend in this essay to discuss in any detail the complex – and in many respects fascinating – ontology developed by Badiou. But some reference to it is necessary, given that his ethics strictly depends on his ontological distinctions. The most important categories structuring the latter are as follows. Situation and event, void and plenum, we have already explained. Let us add that, the situation being essentially multiple, a new category – the 'state of the situation' – has to be introduced to bring about a principle of internal stabilization – i.e. the possibility that the structuring resources of situation can themselves be counted as *one*. The borders between the situation and its void are conceived in terms of 'edges', that is 'sites of the event'. The latter, although belonging to the situation, will provide a certain degree of infrastructure to an event should one take place – I am calling it infrastructure in a purely topographical sense without, obviously, any kind of causal connotation.

I have already raised the possibility of some displacements within Badiou's categories which could go, I think, some way in the direction of solving some of the difficulties that his ethical theory presents at the moment. I will now review, in sequence: (1) the precise nature of those displacements; (2) the extent to which they put the ethical argument in a better terrain; (3) the consequences that they would have – if accepted – for Badiou's ontological perspective.

I have attempted an initial deconstruction of the stark opposition void/ plenum. I have suggested that the edge of the void is not a precise place within an otherwise fully ordered (countable) situation, but something whose very presence makes it impossible for a situation to be entirely structured as such. (It is like the Lacanian real, which is not something existing *alongside* the symbolic, but which is *within* the symbolic in such a way as to prevent the symbolic from being fully constituted.) In that case, however, a distinction has to be introduced between the *situation* and what we could call with a neologism the *situationness*, the former being the actually ontic existing *order* and the second the ontological principle of *ordering* as such. These two dimensions never fully overlap with each other. This being the case, the *event* – whose unpredictability within the situation, asserted by Badiou, I fully accept – has from its very inception the two roles that we have mentioned earlier: on the one hand, to subvert the existing state of the situation by naming the unnameable; on the other, I would add, to restructure a new state around a new core. Mao's long march succeeded because it was not only the destruction of an old order but also the reconstruction of the nation around a new core. And Gramsci's notion of a 'becoming state' of the working class – against any simplistic notion of 'seizure of power' – moves in the same direction. In that case, however, situation and event contaminate each other: they are not separate locations within a social topography, but constitutive dimensions of any social identity. (One central consequence of this assertion is, as we will see, that the event loses, in some respects, the exceptional character attributed to it by Badiou.)

The same goes for the duality event/site of the event. (The site would be, for instance, in Christian discourse, Christ's mortality, while the event would be his resurrection.) For Badiou there is an essential exteriority between the two. It is only at that price that the event can be truly universal – i.e. it can reveal the void that does not belong in any part of the situation although it is necessarily included in all of them. In the Christian notion of incarnation, again, no physical quality anticipated, in the particular body of Mary, that she was going to be the mother of God. I cannot accept this logic. As in the previous case, the relationship between event and site of the event has to be conceived as one of mutual contamination. The demands of the *sans-papiers* are clearly, *in the first instance*, particular and not universal demands. So how can some kind of universality emerge out of them? Only insofar as people excluded from many other sites within a situation (who are unnameable within the latter) perceive their common nature as excluded and live their struggles – in their particularity – as part of a larger emancipatory struggle. But this means that any event of universal significance is constructed out of a plurality of sites whose particularity is equivalentially articulated but definitely not eliminated. As we tried to show earlier with the example of Solidarnosc, one particular site can acquire a special relevance as locus of a universal equivalent, but even at that site the tension between universality and particularity is constitutive of the emancipatory struggle.

The consequence of this is clear: a hegemonic universality is the only one that any society can achieve. The infinity of the emancipatory task is very much present – it is not a question of denying it in the name of a pure particularism – for the struggle against an oppressive regime can be constructed, through equivalential chains, as a struggle against oppression in general, but the particularism of the hegemonic force (however diluted its particularity might be) is still there producing its limiting effects. It is like gold, the function of which as general equivalent (as money) does not cancel the oscillations inherent to its nature as a particular commodity. There is a moment in Badiou's analysis in which he almost approaches the hegemonico-equivalential logic that we are describing: it is when he refers to 'investigations' (*enquêtes*) as militant attempts to win over elements of the situation to the event (*EE* 334). But his attempt is rather limited: it is not conceived by him as the *construction* of a wider evental site through the expansion of equivalential chains, but as a process of total conversion in which there is either 'connection' or 'disconnection' without possibility of any middle. Although the result of this piece-by-piece construction is as much for Badiou as for me a widening of the evental site, there is not in his account any deepening of the mechanisms underlying the operations of 'connection' and 'disconnection'. In the end, the process of conversion, seen at its purest in the case of religion, remains, for Badiou, the model paradigm for any description of the process of winning over.

So where are we left, as far as our ethical question is concerned, if we accept this set of displacements of Badiou's categories (and I am sure Badiou would not accept them)? Firstly, it is clear that all ground for the distinction between truth and simulacrum has collapsed. That ground – in Badiou's discourse – was given by the possibility of a radical differentiation between void and plenum. But it is precisely that distinction that does not stand once the filling of the void and the naming of it have become indistinguishable from each other. However, this very collapse of the distinction opens the way to other possibilities that Badiou's stark dichotomy had closed. For the edge of the void not only has no precise location (if it had it would have a *proper*, unambiguous name) but names the absent fullness of the situation – it is, if you want, the presence of an absence, something which can be *named* but not *counted* (i.e. which cannot be represented as an objective difference). If, on top of that, we accept that the void is constitutively included in any situation – and this is something I very much agree with, from a different theoretical perspective – the possibility of *naming* it, which Badiou quite rightly sees as its only possibility of discursive inscription, *would be to attribute to a particular difference the role of naming something entirely incommensurable with itself – i.e. the absent fullness of the situation.*[8] In that case, naming the void and naming the plenum become indistinguishable from each other. The only other possibility, that the site of the event *qua* site determines what the event can name, is excluded *de jure* by Badiou's argument – and, anyway, it would again raise the spectre of the 'third discourse'. In that case, however, blood, race, the nation, the proletarian revolution or communism, are indifferent ways of naming the void/plenum. Let us be clear: from a political viewpoint it makes, of course, which signifier will name the void makes all the difference. The problem, however, is how discursively to construct such a political differentiation. Badiou's implicit answer would be that – *malgré lui* – the void has potentially a certain content: the universal. For me – given the subversion that I have attempted at the ontological level of the distinction truth/simulacrum – this solution is not available. In what follows, I will present an outline of what is, for me, the right way of dealing with this problem.

How to get out of this impasse? In my view the answer requires two steps. Our first step involves the full recognition that, under the label of the 'ethical', two different things have been put together which do not necessarily overlap – in fact they usually do not. The first is the search for the unconditioned, i.e. that which would fill the gap between what society is and what it ought to be. The second is the moral evaluation of the various ways of carrying out this filling role – as far, of course, as this filling operation is accepted as a legitimate one (which is not the case with Badiou). How do these two different tasks interact with each other? A first possibility is that the distinction between the two is denied. Plato's search for the 'good society' is at one and the same time the description of a society which is both without gaps or holes and morally good. Aristotle's *Nicomachean Ethics* pursues a similar conjunction of spheres. The problem emerges when it is perceived that the filling function can operate through many different fillers and that there is no way of determining the latter through the mere logical analysis of the former. To return to our previous terminology: the void undermines the principle of countability in society (what we have called the situationness of the situation) but does not anticipate how to choose between different states of the situation. In a society experiencing an organic crisis the need for *some kind* of order, whether conservative or revolutionary, becomes more important than the concrete order fulfilling this need. In other words: the search for the unconditioned prevails over the evaluation of the ways of achieving it. Hobbes' sovereign drew its legitimacy from the fact that it could bring about *some* order, regardless of its content, against the chaos of the state of nature. Or again: what in those cases is the object of ethical investment is not the ontic content of a certain *order* but the principle of *ordering* as such.

It is not difficult to realize that a militant ethics of the event, as opposed to the situationally determined normative order, has to privilege this moment of rupture over the ordering resources of the situational dimension. But with implacable logic, this leads to a total uncertainty about the normative content of the ethical act. We can easily end in Žižek's exaltation of the ruthlessness of power and the spirit of sacrifice as values in themselves.[9] Badiou tries to avoid this pitfall through a strict distinction between void and plenum. But, as we have shown, this is an untenable distinction. In order to avoid this cul-de-sac we have to perform a first ascetic operation, and strictly separate the two meanings that the label ethics embraces in an unhappy symbiosis: 'ordering' as a positive value beyond any ontic determination and the concrete systems of social norms to which we give our moral approval. I suggest that we should restrict the term 'ethics' to the first dimension. This means that, from an ethical point of view, fascism and communism are indistinguishable – but, of course, ethics no longer has anything to do with moral evaluation. So, how can we move from one level to the other?

It is here that our second step has to be taken. The ethical as such, as we have seen, cannot have any differentiating ontic content as its defining feature. Its meaning is exhausted in the pure declaring/filling of a void/plenum. This is the point, however, in which the theoretical effects of deconstructing Badiou's dualisms can be brought into operation. We have already explained the basic pattern of that deconstruction: the contamination of each pole of the dichotomies by the other. Let us go to the ontic/ontological distinction that we have established between situation and situationness. There is no event which is exhausted, as far as its meaning is concerned, in its pure breaking with the situation – i.e. there is no event which, in the very movement of this break, does not present itself as a potential bearer of a new order, of situationness as such. This implies that the meaning of the event *per se* is suspended between its ontic content and its ontological role or, to put it in other terms, *that there is nothing which can proceed as a pure subtraction*. The breaking moment involved in an event – in a radical decision – is still there, *but the site of the event is not purely passive*: going back to Saint Paul, there would have been no resurrection without death.

Where does this leave us as far as ethical theory is concerned? At this point: the ethical as such – as we have defined it – has no normative content, but the subject which constitutes itself through an ethical act is not a pure, unencumbered subject, but one whose site of constitution (and the lack inherent in it) are not done away with by that ethical act (the event). That is, the moment of the ethical involves a *radical investment*, and in this formula its two terms have to be given equal weight. Its radicalism means that the act of investment is not explained by its object (as far as its object is concerned, the act proceeds truly *ex nihilo*). But the object of the investment is not a purely transparent medium either: it has a situational opaqueness that the event can twist but not eliminate. To use a Heideggerian formulation, we are *thrown* into the normative order (as part of our being thrown into the world) so that the subject who constitutes him/herself through an ethical investment is already part of a situation and of the lack inherent in the latter. Every situation deploys a symbolic framework without which even the event would have no meaning; the lack implies that, since the symbolic order can never be saturated, it cannot explain the event out of its own resources. 'Events' in Badiou's sense are moments in which the state of the situation is *radically* put into question; but it is wrong to think that we have purely situational periods interrupted by purely evental interventions: the contamination between the evental and the situational is the very fabric of social life.

So the answer to the question of how we can move from the ethical to the normative, from the unconditional assertion inherent in any event to the level of moral choice and evaluation, is that such a choice and evaluation have largely been already made before the event with the symbolic resources of the situation itself. The subject is only partially the subject inspired by the event; the naming of the unrepresentable in which the event consists involves reference to an unrepresented within *a* situation and can only proceed through the displacement of elements already present in that situation. This is what we have called the mutual contamination between situation and event. Without it any winning over by the event of elements of the situation would be impossible, except through a totally irrational act of conversion.

This gives us, I think, the intellectual tools to solve what would otherwise be an aporia in Badiou's analysis. I am referring to the issues related to what is for him the third form of evil – the attempt to totalize a truth, to eradicate all elements of the situation which are foreign to its implications. That this totalitarian attempt is evil is something I am fully prepared to accept. The difficulty lies in that, in Badiou's system, there are no adequate theoretical resources to deal with this form of evil and, especially, with the alternative social arrangement in which situation and event are not in a relation of mutual exclusion. What does it exactly mean for a truth not to attempt to be total? Badiou's partial answer in terms of a necessary recognition of human animality is certainly less than convincing. For what a truth which is less than total will be confronted with is other opinions, views, ideas, etc., and if the truth is *permanently* non-total it will have to incorporate into its form this element of confrontation – which involves collective deliberation. Peter Hallward has quite rightly pointed out, in his introduction to the English edition of Badiou's *Ethics*, that it is difficult, given Badiou's notion of an event, to see how this element of deliberation can be incorporated into his theoretical framework.[10] I would add: it is not difficult, it is impossible. For if the proclaimed truth is self-grounded, and if its relation with the situation is one of pure subtraction, no deliberation is possible. The only real alternatives as far as the elements of the situation are concerned are total rejection of the truth (disconnection) or what we have called conversion (connection) whose mechanisms are not specified. In these circumstances, that the truth does not attempt to be total can only mean that deliberation is a deaf dialogue in which the truth just reiterates itself in the expectation that, as a result of some miracle, radical conversion will take place.

Now if we move to our own perspective, which involves the contamination between situation and event, the difficulty disappears. Firstly, social agents share, at the level of a situation, values, ideas, beliefs, etc. that the truth, not being total, does not put entirely into question. Thus, a process of argumentation can take place that justifies the situational rearrangements in terms of those situational aspects that the truth procedure does not subvert. Secondly, the void requires, in our view, a filling, but the filler is not a necessary one – that is why the event is irreducible to the situation. In that case the process of connection ceases to be irrational as far as it presupposes an identification which proceeds out of a constitutive lack. This already involves deliberation. But, thirdly, the edges of the void are, as we have seen, multiple, and the event is only constructed through chains of equivalences linking a plurality of sites. This necessarily involves deliberation conceived in a wide sense (involving partial conversions, dialogues, negotiations, struggles, etc.). If the event only takes place through this process of collective construction, we see that deliberation is not something externally added to it but something belonging to its inherent nature. The aspiration to make of truth a total one is evil as far as it interrupts this process of equivalential construction and turns a single site into an absolute place of the enunciation of truth.

There is one last point we have to deal with. We have suggested a series of displacements of the categories informing Badiou's analysis. Can these displacements take place within the general framework of Badiou's ontology – i.e. within his attribution to set theory of a grounding role in the discourse concerning being as being? The answer is clearly negative. Let us cast our question in a transcendental fashion: how must an object be so that the type of relation that we have subsumed under the general label of 'contamination' becomes possible? Or, what amounts to the same thing: what are the conditions of possibility of such a relation? Let me be clear that we are not speaking about any regional ontology; if something such as an 'articulation', or an 'equivalential relation', or the 'construction of the universal through its hegemonic taking up by some particularity' is going to take place at all, the very possibility has to be given at the level of an ontology dealing with being qua being – especially if, as we think, these operations are not superstructural expressions of a hidden deeper reality but the primary terrain of the constitution of objects.

Now, it should be clear that set theory would find serious difficulties in dealing with something such as a relation of articulation, especially if it is grounded in the postulate of extensionality. Needless to say, I am not advocating the return to any kind of intensional grounding which would present all the difficulties which are well known since Russell's paradox. As far as set theory is concerned extensionality is fine. What I am putting into question is that set theory could play the role of a fundamental ontology that Badiou attributes to it. I think that set theory is just one way of constituting entities within a much wider field of ontological possibilities. If we take the equivalential relation, for instance, it involves an articulation between universality and particularity which is only conceivable in terms of *analogy*. But such a relation cannot be properly thought within the framework of Badiou's mathematical ontology. The same happens with the ensemble of phenomena known in psychoanalysis as 'overdetermination'. And I insist that it is not possible to sidestep this incompatibility by attributing it to the level of abstraction at which we are working[11] (set theory operating at such a level that all the distinctions on which our theoretical approach is based would not be pertinent or representable). The true issue is that the emergence of any new field of objectivity presupposes ontological possibilities which are the task of philosophy to uncover.

Is there a field that is more primary than that uncovered by set theory which would allow us properly to account *ontologically* for the type of relations that we are exploring? I think there is, and it is *linguistics*. The relations of analogy through which the aggregation constructing an eventual site are established are relations of *substitution*, and the differential relations constituting the area of objective distinctions (which define the 'situation', in Badiou's terms) compose the field of *combinations*. Now, substitutions and combinations are the only possible forms of objectivity in a Saussurean universe, and if they are extracted from their anchorage in speech and writing – that is, if the separation of form from substance is made in a more consequent and radical way than Saussure's – we are not in the field of a regional but of a general or fundamental ontology.

I would even add something more. This ontology cannot remain within the straightjacket of classical structuralism, which privileged the syntagmatic over the paradigmatic pole of language. On the contrary, once equivalential relations are recognized as constitutive of objectivity as such – i.e. once the paradigmatic pole of substitutions is given its proper weight in ontological description – we are not only in the terrain of a linguistic ontology but also of a rhetorical one. In our previous example of Solidarnosc the 'event' took place through the aggregation of a plurality of 'sites' on the basis of their *analogy* in the common opposition to an oppressive regime. And what is this substitution through analogy but a metaphorical aggregation? Metaphor, metonymy, synecdoche (and especially catachresis as their common denominator) are not categories describing adornments of language, as classical philosophy had it, but ontological categories describing the constitution of objectivity as such. It is important to see that this does not involve any kind of theoretical nihilism or anti-philosophy[12] because it is the result of a critique which is fully internal to the conceptual medium as such and is, in that sense, a strictly philosophical enterprise. Many consequences follow from taking this path, including the ability to describe in more precise conceptual terms what we have called the contamination (a better term might perhaps be overdetermination) between the evental and the situational.[13]

The huge question that remains is the following: could the ensemble of relations that I have described as rhetorical be absorbed and described as a special case within the wider categories of set theory, so that the latter would retain their ontological priority; or, rather, could set theory itself be described as an internal possibility – admittedly an extreme one – within the field of a generalized rhetoric? I am convinced that the right answer implies the second alternative, but this demonstration will have to wait for another occasion.

10

COMMUNISM AS SEPARATION

Alberto Toscano

Ordinary reality is a space of placements, a partitioned order, a network of relations,[1] in short, a law-bound structure of representations. Thought is a two-fold operation: the separation, out of this structure, of an immanent excess and the rigorous application of this excess, this real kernel of illegality, back on to representation, to unhinge and transform its coherence.

This elementary image of thought – as a separation of and from reality, as the dysfunction of representation – has always been the crux of Badiou's work, yet it has also been subjected to a radical recasting, dividing his work into two distinct figures, of *destruction and subtraction*.[2] I would like to examine here the motivation behind this division, and to propose the thesis that it is on the basis of an exacting and unvarying commitment to a certain idea of what it is to think – an idea whose origin is exquisitely political – that Badiou has found it imperative to split his own thought in two, or, to use a formula that I will attempt to elucidate in the course of this essay: to split separation itself.

If thought is co-extensive with a practice of separation, what is it that comes to be separated? Or, if separation works out of the element of order and representation, what is the real – in the Lacanian sense – that emerges from this operation? The key to Badiou's entire intellectual enterprise is that *separation is aimed at bringing forth the inseparate*; that what cannot be assigned a part, that is, represented as an item within the structure of reality, is precisely what the operations which I have here summarized under the term 'separation' are designed to produce. A corollary to this affirmation is that in and by separation thought as capacity presents itself, or, which amounts to the same, that thought is the production of what cannot be 'taken apart', what cannot be represented as a part, the name of which is *the generic* and which constitutes the cornerstone of Badiou's doctrine, at least as it has come to be formulated in *Being and Event*.[3]

Yet the generic is a relatively late name in Badiou's philosophy, preceded by the name of the inseparate as a political project: communism. To consider the persistence, in Badiou's thinking, of the idea of communism, together with its rupture, or immanent destruction, is to understand what lies behind destruction and subtraction as the two principal figures of the thought of separation. Moreover, it is the only path allowing for the genuine comprehension of what might otherwise appear as a simple provocation, the idea that the highest task of thought (and of politics) lies in the production of Sameness – and not in the contagions of hybridity, the call of alterity or the experience of difference.

Admittedly, this path is rife with peril, the name of 'communism' eliciting, with almost physiological inevitability, the most ardent reactions, be they of hostility, or – rather seldom these days – of enthusiasm (and, in this case, not necessarily for the 'right' reasons, as the often unsavoury spectacle of parliamentary communism testifies). Let us at once dispel or displace these reactions by considering, following Badiou himself, what divides the name of communism and allows for its philosophical consideration.

In a dense and iconoclastic pamphlet from 1991,[4] Badiou considers the significance for the thinking of politics of the then recent demise of the USSR. His verdict is stark: rather than constituting a veritable event this is but a second death, the death of the atrophied institutionalized body of communism, already bereft of any driving political subjectivity, of any sustained experimental invention of forms of organization, of watchwords and principles. No state, he argues, could function as the emblem of the politics of emancipation that once took communism as its name. This is not a matter of opinion but the consequence of a vital distinction within political ontology, between immanent and precarious processes of political subjectivation, on the one hand, and their fatal representation in the structures of the state, on the other. This distinction, which in Badiou's vocabulary is bound to the one between presentation and representation, is nevertheless not my immediate concern. The veritable *pièce de résistance* in this argument is the affirmation, in the wake of its incessantly represented death (of its death in representation, to follow Badiou), of the *eternity of communism*.

We enter here into the terrain of what Badiou, in some of his most recent work, names *metapolitics*.[5] Metapolitics is one of the figures taken by philosophy's qualified dependence on its conditions, and defines the effects upon thought as such, as registered and configured by philosophy on the basis of singular sequences of non-philosophical subjectivation, the generic procedures that Badiou has divided into science, art, politics and love. The metapolitical – as opposed to the strictly intra-subjective (militant) or the represented (statist) – name of communism is constituted by a determination, for thought as such, extracted by philosophy from the aleatory invention and organization of the politics of equality. The product of this extraction is an 'eternity'. Let us listen to Badiou himself:

> The obstinate militant tenacity, elicited by an incalculable event, to sustain the aleatory being of a singularity without predicate, of an infinity with no immanent hierarchy or determination, what I call the generic, [...] is – when its procedure is political – the ontological concept of democracy, or of communism, it's the same thing. [...] [It is] the philosophical, and therefore eternal, concept of rebellious subjectivity. [...] Every political event which founds a truth exposes the subject that it induces to the eternity of the equal. 'Communism', in having named this eternity, cannot be the adequate name of a death (*DO*, 13–15).

That we are not in the presence of a nostalgic apologetics – the *ressentiment* of the defeated – will become clear in a moment, as we register the profound effects of Badiou's suspension of the destructive figure of politics, and of his stark diagnosis of Marxist-Leninism as the properly metaphysical stage of political ontology. For now, it is important to note that it is in such a meta-political procedure – the philosophical extraction of a concept from the travails of subjectivation – that much of Badiou's often misapprehended platonism lies. Eternity is thought here not as the intuition of an archetype, impassively anticipating its precarious manifestations, but as the fixation of a concept. Produced by the living thought of politics, punctuated by datable events and sequences, and bequeathed to posterity – as that which every singular political procedure reaffirms and rearticulates – the concept in this instance is that of 'the eternity of the equal'.

As Badiou himself notes in *D'un Désastre obscur*, this 'formal' eternity (not the eternity of a transcendent substance but precisely that of the *idea* of communism) had already been the object of a co-authored tract of his (with François Balmès), *De l'Idéologie*, in the guise of a theory of communist invariants.[6]

Still within the categorial ambit of the Marxist-Leninist tradition, the theory of communist invariants is essentially articulated around two arguments: (1) Aspirations for radical equality, for the annihilation of property and the state, are present throughout the history of politics, revealed in the intermittence of revolts, in the specific figures of the antagonism between domination and the dominated.[7] They are essentially disjoined from any economic teleology and constitute the spontaneous thought of the masses in the face of the structured objectivity of exploitation, as represented by the dominant ideology. There is, in other words, an 'immediate intelligence' of communism, which constitutes the antagonistic thought of the masses, the force of their resistance, and which is *unrepresentable* from the point of view of the state. (2) These communist invariants are only *realized* with the constitution of the proletariat, that is, with the advent of that figure that signals the transformation of the masses (and not the aristocracy, the bourgeoisie, etc.) into the revolutionary class. The communist invariants, which until then had been structurally destined to defeat – expressed in the language of domination and serving the needs of *another* class – are now themselves directed by the party and guided by the divisive analysis of class. This conjunctural opportunity is, in the eyes of Badiou and Balmès, absolutely new, and bound to the fact that the invariants are no longer a demand of equality heterogeneous to the order of representation, but, albeit foreclosed, are structurally *transitive* to this order. In other words, with the advent of capitalism the unrepresentable force that had driven revolt up to that point is capable, by means of the antagonistic conjunction of masses, class and party, of assuming its role as the foreclosed *source* of order, of *taking power* in the clear knowledge that 'resistance is the secret of domination'.

Now, this contemporary figure of revolt, crystallized in what the authors refer to as the 'communism of production', is entirely sustained by the historico-political notion of *realization*, whereby the unrepresentable excess that has always driven revolt can constitute itself not just as an intermittently recurring force, but, through class-antagonism and the appropriation of production, emerge as a transitional representation of the unrepresentable, as a dictatorship of the proletariat. While this position is not the 'classical type' of a classist politics – as testified to by the eternity of the invariants and the decisionist character of the antagonism directed by the party, which evacuates the tele-ological dimension of classism, the idea of the party as 'midwife' of communism – it does accord to class a crucial role, to wit that of providing the dialectical articulation of the unrepresentable demands of resistance ('the eternity of the equal') and the law which structures and orders representations (in this case the ideological expression of the relations obtaining under capitalism). The tran-sitivity of the excess (in the guise of resistance) to the structural totality (the capitalist mode of production and its ideological component) is of the essence here; it sustains, in the domain of historical becoming, what Badiou will later refer to as the Marxist hypothesis, which posits the task of egalitarian politics as the domination of non-domination.

In *De l'Idéologie*, Badiou and Balmès had written of the 'logical power' of the proletariat, its singular constitution, under the direction of the party, as the representative of the unrepresentable, as the capacity to dominate the passage to non-domination. Badiou will examine this logical power in terms of a theory of the subject in his eponymous book of 1982. The effects of this examination upon the idea of a communism of production will prove considerable, leading the notion of a realization of revolt to what can be seen as its point of extreme and ultimately unsustainable coherence.

Once again, the question is the following: how does the unrepresentable demand for non-domination, the invariance of communism, constitute itself as antagonistic to the structure of representation? How is political separation effected? In other words, what are the operations whereby a political subject comes to be? (A subject being, for Badiou, nothing if not the finite support of the irruption of the unrepresentable.) To understand this matter it is essential to consider the nature and the extent of the transitivity obtaining between structure and subjectivation, or between representation and revolt. Unlike in *De l'Idéologie*, in *Théorie du sujet* there seems to be no remnant of the Marxist-Leninist thesis of an appropriation of production. Indeed, there is no separation of production and ideology which would allow for the constitution of the former as autonomous domain; every being is constitutively split between itself and its indexical localization by representation – what Badiou here calls the *esplace*, the space of placements. It is only this localization, this place, which is allowed to appear; being 'itself', which is the real of the *esplace*, is unrepre-sentable, it is – in Lacanese – a lack-of-being [*manque-à-être*] (or, in Badiou's jargon, the *horlieu*, the out-of-place). 'Subject' names the organized capacity of this 'lack-of-being', this hidden force behind the structured process of locali-zation, to *turn* on the structure, to force representation to include its real.

The absence of any distinction between production – which would constitute the substance and power of the masses – and representation, means that the only way for 'the eternity of the equal' to be attested is by purifying itself of the indexes of representation, of its inclusion in the totalizing order of places. It might appear that in this model there is no place for the notion of transitivity, whether the logic of the latter be that of expression or that of appropriation. This impression would nevertheless be incorrect. Badiou's theory of the subject does in fact contain a notion of transitivity but it is one 'woven' out of antagonism. This antagonism is to be understood in two ways: (1) the *structural* antagonism between place and force that constitutes determination as domination, as the indexing of every force to its proper place within the system of representation; (2) the *subjective* antagonism of a force bent on destroying its place, by crossing the limit imposed by determination and thus limiting representation itself, what Badiou, with some irony, calls 'the labour of the positive' (*TS* 30).

Indispensable to this figure of the thinking of non-domination – let us name it the *communism of destruction* – is 'the eternal antecedence of the subject to itself' (*TS* 163), the idea that the force that organizes itself as the destruction of representation 'was', always already, the real of representation itself, its foreclosed being. It is precisely because this transitivity is only given when the excess of the real turns on representation, and not on the basis of any autonomy of the masses that could be either assumed or appropriated (just as one would be said to appropriate the means of production), that its figure is a destructive one. The political subject proves its antecedence to itself by disarticulating the space of placement, and singularly by destroying its own place. Or: the masses are revealed as an antagonistic class by the organized destruction which is the only *raison d'être* of the party (let us not forget that party and subject are, for the Badiou of the *Théorie du Sujet*, quasi-synonymous terms). This communism of destruction can be seen as the ultimate, and perhaps terminal, figure of the politics of transitivity, a figure in which the absence of any actually existing autonomy from the domination of representation means that the transitivity of the subject to the structure can only be revealed by the never-ending destruction of the latter.

With the publication of *Can Politics Be Thought?* (1985) Badiou signals a break, at once philosophical and political, with the very idea of a dialectical transitivity between the politics of non-domination and the system of representation. At the heart of this rupture is a thorough rethinking of the very place of the Two in political subjectivity, no longer to be configured as destructive antagonism but rather as a discontinuous and event-bound subtraction.[8] What happens to the idea of communism in this break, and in the series of works that draw out its considerable consequences for politics and ontology?

The first thing to note is that this break is not an intra-philosophical one, but follows from the assumption of the end of a sequence of political militancy, from what Badiou calls the destruction of Marxism (in this regard, the question that guides this essay could also be formulated as: what is a communism which separates itself from Marxism?). In other words, the supplementation of the theory of the subject with a theory of the event is motivated by the intellectual necessity of holding true to the eternity of the equal whilst forgoing the tenets of transitivity. What, after all, is the 'function' of the event, if not that of allowing us to think the dysfunction of representation, the interruption of domination, without the compulsion of postulating the antecedence of the (political) subject to itself? Or, in more strictly political terms, to think the possibility of a communist politics, a politics of equality, which is not based on antagonism as the motor of representation?

It is precisely because Badiou's untiring conviction, to which all of his work testifies, is that the highest task of thought is to think communism – that is, to separate and configure the unrepresentable out of the structures of representation – that both the communism of production and the communism of destruction must be subjected to vehement criticism. What is deserving of the epithet 'metaphysical' in these doctrines is the idea that politics is somehow inscribed in representation, that what is foreclosed by domination is nevertheless endowed with a latent political force; which is to say, that the political subject which emerges out of the labour of the positive, whether this be the appropriation of production or the limitation and destruction of place, is its own obscure precursor. Even and especially in its destructive figure, the communism that depends on the transitivity of its subject to the structure of domination – a transitivity defined by antagonism as the foreclosed motor of representation – is cursed by its adherence to representation: it is forced both to manifest itself only in and by destruction *and* to endow itself with a representative, a referent, precisely in order to dominate non-domination (the decades of debate over the dictatorship of the proletariat are the history of this lure). Here lies the metaphysical impasse of the Marxist-Leninist figure of communist politics.

The idea of communism that appears in Badiou's work in the wake of his deconstruction of transitivity in politics[9] – an idea of communism which, by way of contrast to the other two, I would like to call that of the *production of communism*[10] – is essentially carried by a transformation in the very nature of separation, an emancipation from the dialectics and the secret teleologies of antagonism.

In this regard, the concept of unbinding, *déliaison*, bears an immense function, both critical and ontological.[11] It affects the ontological basis of the communist imperative to think politics from the side of the unrepresentable. The weakness or instability of Marxist-Leninism lies, in Badiou's eyes, precisely in the idea that a bond – the bond of class – could, via the antagonism concentrated by the party-form, undo binding as such.[12] The impasse of the destructive or dialectical figure of separation is constituted by its obstinate reliance, in order to sustain its attack on the domination of representation, on what Badiou calls 'entities of reference', objective crystallizations of antagonism.[13] Without these referents, and without the ontological support that they are accorded by the dialectical self-antecedence of the political subject, the movement of destruction, of the irruption of the unrepresented into the order of representation, is drained of all de facto consistency.

If, in the domain of emancipatory politics, 'the hypothesis of a domination of non-domination'[14] has been linked to the movement of destruction, it is to the extent that non-domination itself has been reduced to the fleeting real that flashes in the bloody interval between, on the one hand, the party's domination of an antagonistic struggle, and, on the other, the dominant structures of the socio-political order that demand to be destroyed. It is from this antagonistic, or negative, determination of the politics of non-domination that the 'double bind' of the communism of the twentieth century emerges. The primary imperative is: 'Act so as to realize non-domination!' But within this ontology of antagonism, 'the real, conceived as both contingent and absolute, is never real enough not to be suspected of semblance'.[15] Whence derives the second, 'binding', imperative: 'Suspect everything as an agent of domination!' The only resolution of this double bind – and it is indeed an incessant bind, so much so that it could almost be characterized as the veritable motor of much political action – is given by the continuous purification of both the subjective support of the party and the structure of representation itself. This movement of purification, whereby the only proof of the real of communism is provided by the step-by-step elimination of all instances of determination, provides the veritable form of *terror*, the notion that the unrepresentable is only given as a sort of infinite persecution of everything that dominates (e.g. classifies, ranks, places, divides, etc.) social being. It follows that the passive body of this destructive subjectivation – the party(-state) – can only persevere by perpetually sundering itself and laying waste to the intimate traces of the old order.

In order to avert the outcome of this lethal oscillation between the monolithic bond and the fury of destruction, whilst trenchantly holding on to 'the eternity of the equal', Badiou poses that the very material of politics is not to be sought in a consistent instance of antagonism (i.e. class), but precisely in the radical inconsistency, the infinite dissemination of what the order of representation forecloses. In this regard, communism is to be revitalized by traversing a certain nihilism, by giving up on the idea that its movement is inscribed in the structure of representation (the lure of class antagonism as the motor of history) or that it can refer to the consistency of a representative – however transitory – of the unrepresentable (the hypothesis of a dictatorship of the proletariat). So, while the thesis of unbinding – posing that the real of politics and representation is radically multiple and non-hierarchical, *ergo* that emancipation is devoid of a substantial or embodied referent that would precede the invention of a practice – provides a far more unequivocal basis in abstract ontology for the idea of communism, it simultaneously removes any notion of a dialectical relation (be it genetic and/or destructive) between this real and the social reality in which it is indexed, partitioned or regulated. It is crucial to understand that Badiou's hostility to a communism based on any variety of socio-economic immanence rests on the conviction that the eternity of the equal is not of the order of a new bond, of a new system of relations, but is an attempt to think and practise, in the specific domain which is that of politics, the radical demand of a singularity without predicate, of a multiplicity not ordained into property or determination. This is why all 'anticipations' of politics must be abandoned, why all political concepts that would make communism transitive to the genesis of order and representation must be forsaken. This is not only the case for socio-economic totality, for community,[16] or for the continuity of struggles,[17] but also for the terminal operation of transitivity – destruction –

the production of a political substance through the infinite task of purifying representation.

At base, Badiou's diagnosis tells us, the metaphysical weakness as well as the very real disasters of communism are to be ascribed to a certain relationship to the political instance of representation, the state. This relationship is determined by the idea that the task of a communist thought and practice is to traverse the state by means of the analysis of class antagonism, with the aim of forcing communist subjectivity into the articulations of representation. But if antagonism is not the motor of political representation, what operation – that is, what form of subjectivation – can present the real of representation, can organize the communist demand to separate the inseparate out from its domination by the partial and hierarchical order of representation? What is certain, above all, is that the abandonment of class antagonism as the dialectical support of communist subjectivity affects it with a radical intransitivity to representation as well as with a discontinuity in its manifestations. In other words, the eternity of communism is now to be understood as a formal invariant (all forms of political subjectivity are communist) but not as a material one (there is no spontaneous drive to communism, which would be the precursor of its fullblown organized political subjectivation).

Though exclusion of the real remains a structural constant of representation, the figure of the Two, of the separation of the inseparate, is, each and every time, a singular invention. The rare and non-cumulative nature of political subjectivation is thus the consequence of the critical abandonment of the structural function of antagonism. Communism is here bereft of any assurance, and most importantly of any teleology – even the dark admixture of teleology and decisionism proposed by the figure of destruction. Since unbinding is an ontological given, albeit a foreclosed one, and not a force that must be liberated from representation, the problem of communism becomes precisely that of producing the inseparate; which is to say, it is neither that of realizing it nor that of expressing it. One of Badiou's key metapolitical theses is that this production must take place *at a distance* from representation, at a distance from the state. What is at stake is precisely a non- or a-dialectical relation between the effective thinking of communism and the structures of domination, a relation which can no longer rely on antagonism as the hidden principle of the latter.

This theme introduces us to the crucial distance between Badiou's metapolitical inscription of his own 'politics without a party' and what he himself defines as the political project of 'generic communism', namely:

> an egalitarian society of free association between polymorphous workers, in which activity is not regulated by technical or social decrees and specializations, but by the collective mastery of necessities. In such a society, the state is dissolved as a separate instance of public coercion. Politics, inasmuch as it expresses the interests of social groups, and aims at the conquest of power, is itself dissolved. Thus, every communist politics has as its proper aim its own dissolution in the modality of the

end of the separate form of the state in general, even if the state in question is a democratic one.

Badiou juxtaposes this 'Leninist' vision, founded on 'the ultimate end of politics [as] the in-separate authority of the infinite, or the coming to itself [*advenue à soi*] of the collective as such', to the idea of politics as a 'singular collective practice at a distance from the state', a politics in which the collective is a production of the formalizing power of political prescription.[18] While we are keenly aware of the reasons behind Badiou's deconstruction of substantial or teleological varieties of communism, we must remark that the 'formal' criteria of this singular collective practice cannot – 'downstream', as it were – avoid the encounter with the materiality of 'necessities'. In other words, bereft as it may be of any transitivity to the dynamics of the social or any latency of the political subject, such a practice cannot but result in an *actual* production of communism, albeit a communism whose image can never be given in advance. While Badiou is indeed proposing something like politics for politics' sake (whence its autonomy as a generic procedure), the universalizable and egalitarian determination of such a politics cannot but have effects, 'communist' effects in the real.

Needless to say, this new image of communism also entails a new image of domination. The state, no longer split by antagonism (by its function as the placement or indexing of force), is in ontological excess of presentation, and forecloses the inconsistency or the void at the heart of reality; in specifically political terms, it forecloses unbinding as the real of social existence. As Badiou writes, 'the state is not founded on a social bond that it would express, but on unbinding, which it prohibits' (*EE* 125). Properly political subjectivation – politics as a truth procedure – begins with this real, with the infinity of unbinding, but, and this is essential, *it cannot rely on the internal dynamics of representation* to assure the possibility that unbinding may itself be applied back on to the bound structures of representation. Having abdicated the principle of (class) antagonism, politics thus depends on a wager on the dysfunction of representation, on holding true to the decision that something in representation has faltered, that at the edges of order the real of unbinding has made an irruption. It is therefore as the precarious point of a dysfunction of representation that the concept of the event allows for the construction of communism in the absence of structural antagonism.

In the dysfunction of which the event is the signal, political thought finds the rare chance to uphold, by means of the invention of principles and practices specific to the locus of this dysfunction, the eternity of the equal as the boundless capacity for universality. The invariants of *De l'Idéologie* make a 'formal' return here, in the sense that every political truth, for Badiou, puts to the test the axiom that thought (i.e. the capacity to separate oneself from the hierarchies and determinations of representation) is the thought of all, that, in the vocabulary of Maoism, 'the masses think'. Yet, in contradistinction to the transitive, antagonistic forms of communism (of production and of destruction) this position effectively removes the substantiality of the collective. The collective, it states, is a consequence of political subjectivation; it is the *effect*, on a situation, of the radically egalitarian demand that thought be universalizable.

The collective is thus not the starting-point of unbinding, whose ontological status is strictly pre-political, but the product of a two-fold process: on the one hand, the measurement of the infinite excess of the state, that is, of the untrammelled domination of representation prior to subjectivation; on the other, the constitution, on the basis of the event as dysfunction, of a *generic part* of the situation. To illustrate this formal delineation of political subjectivity, it is useful to consider its effects on the political concept of mass movement.

In the transitive forms of politics, the mass movement provides the 'spectacular' proof, not only that the hidden basis of political representation is antagonistic, but that the very motor of the dynamic of representation is constituted by the foreclosed power of the people and its drive to equality; in brief, that 'the masses make history'. The problem of political organization is precisely that of realizing – that is, of *dividing* – this force.[19] Whence the directive function of the party, as a power capable of appropriating and annulling representation, together with the operations that produce it.

This figure is deeply transformed in Badiou's work after 1985. While mass movements do remain a privileged site for the irruption of the real, providing what Badiou will call the 'inconsistent consistency of the multiple in historical presentation',[20] they are no longer continuous with political collectives, as the substantial precursors of political subjectivity. The mass movement, far from being this substance, is the problematic and pre-political sign that unbinding gnaws away under the hierarchical determinations of representation. The step from this manifestation of the unbound infinity of situations to the collective production of equality is instead founded on the two moments of separation which characterize political subjectivity: distance (or freedom) and subtraction (or equality).

Rather than being immanent to representation by way of antagonistic destruction, the production of communism depends on setting out a political space separate from that of the state, from its hierarchies and determinations. This space is constituted by fixing a stable measure to the otherwise errant excess of state domination. The means for this measurement is the political function of *prescription*. A statement, drawn from the event-dysfunction, obliges the state to demonstrate its exclusion of presentation, its foreclosure of unbinding. In the practice of Badiou's *Organisation politique*, this prescription can take the form of a political principle such as 'everyone who works here is from here', a principle that manifests (in the repression, reluctance or indifference of the state) the (often abyssal) space which separates the order of representation from the communist demand that the subordination of thought and being to hierarchy and partition be suspended – a demand which in this case is anchored in the need to disqualify, once and for all, the so-called 'problem of immigration' and its nefarious exclusion of the principle of equality.

However, this moment of distance – the freedom of a political space at a remove from the state – would be but a sort of dualistic hysteria were it not for the construction, within this space, of an actual equality. If it is really to substitute antagonism as the key to subjectivation, the political function of distance must therefore be conjoined to the production of equality, to 'the production of some real under the egalitarian maxim'[21] (i.e., the maxim that thought is the thought of all). This production entails that, to use the terminology of *Being and Event*, a generic part be constructed by 'avoiding' the determinations imposed by the excess of the state. This generic part, made up of an infinite sequence of finite inquiries (of finite 'avoidances' of what the structure of representation would itself recognize as a part), is the precise concept of the separation of the inseparate, that is, of the real of a situation as it results from a truth procedure.[22] It is the real of a situation – it is its *truth* – to the extent that its only being consists in belonging to it; because it is woven out of inquiries at least one of which always avoids capture (domination) as a recognizable part. Equality is produced as a part whose only property is that of being *of* a situation, a part with no other trait but that of pure belonging to determine, to *separate* it.

We can see then how subtraction proves to be double: first, it is conceived as the unbound real of representation, as the unbinding which is subtracted from the order of representation, what representation cannot allow to appear; second, it is the procedure whereby this unbinding is configured at a distance from representation, by systematically subtracting it from this order, by constituting a generic part out of the systematic avoidance of the laws of representation. The distance between these two subtractions – the one foreclosed and ontological, the other enacted in subjectivation – sets out the temporality of subjectivation and accounts for the fact that the truth of being is always produced, and, moreover, that its dependence on the work of inquiries upon representation means that it is irrevocably situated (each of the inquiries is finite) at the same time as integrally universalizable (the truth of being is always that of a pure belonging, of a singularity not indexed by domination). With regard to politics, it is only this second subtraction that allows us to move from the infinite of unbinding to the equality of the same, in the space measured out by prescription; it completes the formal parameters of a communist politics, 'what singularizes the political procedure'.[23] Politics remains ineluctably 'against the state' – truth is still of the order of the Two, representation is forced to make place for the generic – but this opposition is no longer the engine of subjectivity. On the contrary, it is what subjectivity must create as the space of freedom and the collective 'body' of equality. Antagonism is a consequence, not a condition.

'The generic is *egalitarian*, and every subject, ultimately, is under the injunction of equality [*est ordonné à l'égalité*]'.[24] That is, every subject takes the *form*, regardless of the names that call it forth, of a communist subject. Yet far from providing the subject with any density or substance, in light of Badiou's theory of the subject this means that there is nothing in the order of domination – that is, neither its production nor its representation – to guarantee the success, *or even the existence*, of a communist politics. Suspended to the event of dysfunction, to the freedom of prescription and the local inquiries into the generic, communism is presented here as bereft of the 'fiction' that it is

somehow inscribed in the dynamics of the social. Or, equality is only eternal –
as a formal requirement of every true instance of political subjectivation – to the
very extent that it is nowhere latent. Alas, it is of the essence of Badiou's
proposal that at this point metapolitics – that *philosophy* – abandon any pretence
of anticipating the precarious and situated fate of the production of communism. It is here that, in the words of *D'un Désastre obscur*, politics really
begins, and everything remains to be invented (*DO* 56).

11

ON THE SUBJECT OF THE DIALECTIC

Bruno Bosteels

I

To date there seem to have been two fundamental approaches to the philosophy of Alain Badiou. The first, drawing mainly on the ontological meditations in *Being and Event*, studies the renewed possibility of thinking of being as pure multiplicity; the second seeks to define the truth of an event by turning to one or more of the four conditions of philosophy that are science, politics, art and love. Badiou himself distinguishes these two possibilities in his closing argument at the first international conference devoted to his work, which was held a few years ago in Bordeaux: 'The one takes as its point of departure the formal theory of being, mathematics as ontology, and the difficult concept of the situation; the other sets out primarily from the event and its consequences in the order of a generic truth.'[1] Each of these approaches, in turn, entails a specific set of references, not only in Badiou's own body of work but also in relation to other major thinkers, both in France and abroad. The first approach finds its most daunting interlocutors among the likes of Deleuze and Heidegger, if not more directly in the contributions to set theory made by Cantor, Gödel and Cohen, while the second is more likely to seek the company of Lacan, Althusser, Mallarmé or Beckett – not to omit Marx, Lenin and Mao: 'Again, the first finds critical support in logic, in set theory, or in the delicate relation between inconsistent multiplicity and its thinkable presentation as consistent multiplicity. The other points to the Lacanian subject, or to emancipatory politics, or to the theory of artistic procedures.'[2] Fundamentally, while the first approach remains within the bounds of ontological reason alone, the second calls upon an account of truth as part of an axiomatic theory of the subject.

As Badiou himself seems to be increasingly aware, however, this division of labour concerning the two dominant approaches to his work – like two halves of a mystical shell – may well lose sight of the most important contribution – perhaps even the rational kernel – of his entire philosophy, that is, the way in which he enables us to think of the emergence of a new and profoundly transformed multiple as the result of the articulation of a singular truth on to an existing state of things. This articulation, which I will argue can be seen as dialectical in a sense that is today more controversial and untimely than ever before, is precisely what any reader will miss who concentrates either on the ontological theses *or* on the theory of the subject, so as to put being firmly on the one hand and the event firmly on the other. Many critics, first and foremost among them Slavoj Žižek and Peter Hallward, argue that this is precisely what Badiou himself ends up doing, when in his later work, after abandoning a more traditional dialectical view, he sets up a rigid divide similar to the Kantian (or even Sartrean) opposition between the world of phenomena and the realm of things in themselves (or between being for-itself and being in-itself). But I would argue that there are too many elements in Badiou's own work, and not only in the earlier books from before the so-called mathematical turn, that resist this interpretation. Not the least indicative among these is the fact that one of Badiou's most openly declared philosophical enemies has always been and continues to be Kant, just as from a more political standpoint Badiou repeatedly makes an argument against this type of opposition, whether 'leftist' or 'statist', that would leave being and the event utterly and completely unrelated, or absolutely disjoined. In what follows, then, I would like to see if there is anything to be gained if we call the logic behind this argument 'dialectical' in keeping with a long-standing tradition of post-Hegelian thought. But the term itself is, in a way, inessential: what matters is the conceptual argument and the operations it calls for.

On the most basic and general level, what this argument for a dialectical reading of Badiou's work involves is precisely a mode of thinking that does *not* seek to distinguish being on the one hand from the event on the other, but rather to articulate them together within one and the same plane – even if this means passing through the paradoxes of an impasse that would seem to signal the end of all normal relations and mediations. As Lenin reminds us after reading Hegel's *Science of Logic*: ' "On the one hand, and on the other", "the one and the other". That is eclecticism. Dialectics requires an all-round consideration of relationships in their concrete development but not a patchwork of bits and pieces.'[3] Even the effort by way of an uncompromising contrast merely to juxtapose the two approaches mentioned above, one restricted to the austere formal science of being as pure multiple of multiples and the other almost mystically enthralled by the pristine truth of an event belonging only to itself, is unable to catch hold of what I have tentatively called the rational kernel of Badiou's philosophy. This kernel, to be sure, is never fully self-present but rather always happens to be split from within. As Badiou writes half-jokingly at the beginning of *Théorie du sujet*: 'In Hegel, there are two dialectical matrices, and this is what makes the famous story of the shell and the kernel a doubtful enigma. It is the kernel itself that is fissured, as in the case of those peaches, actually irritating to eat, of which one bite of the teeth breaks the hard inner core into two pivoting halves' (*TS* 21). Similarly, what is needed is a full-blown account of the divided articulation between the normal order of being and the truth of a haphazard event that constitutes the rational kernel of the dialectic according to Badiou.

Badiou has no interest in formulating a simple external opposition – let us say following the model of two parallel lines which will never meet except at an illusory and ever-retreating point on the horizon that at once would signal the

fact of their disastrous coincidence – between being as the dispersed inconsistency of pure multiples, on the one hand, and, on the other, truth as tied to
the secularized miracle of an unprecedented event. If this were indeed the case
then the objection that Badiou remains profoundly Kantian – an objection first
raised by Deleuze in his correspondence with Badiou, many years after Badiou
himself, then still a Maoist, had levelled this same objection even more
aggressively against Deleuze and Guattari themselves – would be entirely to the
point.[4] But this objection minimizes the importance of several key moments in
Badiou's theory. Between the structured situation of a given multiple and the
various figures of subjectivity that actually make a truth happen, the real issue
is to account for how and when one can impact the other, for how long, and to
what effect, or with what type of consequences. Ultimately, this is nothing
more and nothing less than the question of change – of how a given situation
can be changed in the event of a radically new and unpredictable truth. As
Badiou says in a recent interview: 'Really, in the end, I have only one question:
What is the new in a situation?' He goes on:

> My unique philosophical question, I would say, is the following: Can we
> think that there is something new in the situation, not the new outside
> the situation nor the new somewhere else, but can we really think of
> novelty and treat it in the situation? The system of philosophical answers
> that I elaborate, whatever its complexity may well be, is subordinated to
> that question and to no other.[5]

Something new actually *can* occur, there *can be* something new under the sun
when there happens to be an excess in the situation, but this excess, which on
rare occasions adds something new and discontinuous to the situation, must
nevertheless be thought from within this situation itself, and not from some
unfathomable transcendent beyond or some prior and long-lost origin. To think
of the transformative capacity of a truth from within a given situation, however,
also requires an account of the givenness of this given, and thus the new must
be thought together with the old.

Even many years after his Maoist period, indeed, this articulation of the old
and the new in the end remains the pivotal question for Badiou:

> Even when there is event, structure, formalization, mathematics, multi-
> plicity, and so on, this is exclusively destined, in my eyes, to think
> through the new in terms of the situation. But, of course, to think the
> new in situation, we also have to think the situation, and thus we have to
> think what is repetition, what is the old, what is not new, and after that
> we have to think the new.[6]

In fact, with this question of the changeover between the old and the new, we
are once again close to one of Lenin's key concerns in his notes on Hegel's *Logic*.
Change develops 'not only as decrease and increase, as repetition', Lenin writes,
but also 'as a unity of opposites', and it is this second conception alone that

defines the dialectic insofar as it 'furnishes the key to the "leaps", to the "break in continuity", to the "transformation into the opposite", to the destruction of the old and the emergence of the new'.[7]

If we consider the title of Badiou's most encompassing work to date, *Being and Event*, it is therefore the peculiar articulation *between* the two orders that really matters, and the fact that this articulation actually amounts to a non-relation should not lead us immediately to conclude that it has no dialectical dimension. As Badiou says in the same interview quoted above: 'I would like to insist that, even in the title *Being and Event*, the "and" is fundamental', but this should not be seen too quickly as hiding a simple underlying opposition. Badiou adds:

> It is not the opposition between the event and the situation that interests me first and foremost. That is not the focus of my interest. Besides, from this point of view, I have always complained about being read in a way that is askew, or about being read only for the first chapters and then nobody reads the core of the proposal. Because, in my eyes, the principal contribution of my work does not consist in opposing the situation to the event. In a certain sense, that is something that everybody does these days. The principal contribution consists in posing the following question: What can we deduce or infer from this from the point of view of the situation itself?[8]

Badiou's current investigations, in fact, continue to map out the logic of change in such a way as to bypass even more explicitly the simple if not merely miraculous opposition between being and event, between situation and event:

> The reader will notice that I can henceforth consider 'site' and 'evental multiplicity' to be identical – thus avoiding the banal aporias of the dialectic of structure and historicity – and that I avoid any recourse to some mysterious nomination. Moreover, instead of the rigid opposition between situation and event, I unfold the nuances of transformation, from the mobile–immobile modification all the way to the event properly speaking, by passing through the neutrality of facts.[9]

Thus, unlike what happens in Heidegger's *Being and Time* but with numerous family resemblances and clear conceptual ties to Sartre's *Being and Nothingness*, the value of the pivotal term in the title of *Being and Event* is as much disjunctive as it is conjunctive. It is not a question of retrieving a deeper hermeneutic proximity or overlap (the idea that being qua being always already 'is' or 'gives itself' as event, as the event of originary temporalization, which at once would amount to an ontologization of the event), nor of rendering a primordial dualism (whereby being and event would remain forever separate as two 'dimensions' or 'realms' completely isolated from one another in an inoperative externality) but of formalizing the axioms by which the two are articulated through a gap or deadlock (through the 'impasse of being' itself as that which a subject, in the event of a truth that conditions it, retroactively 'forces' into existence).

It is at this point that the reader of Badiou's earlier work might have expected a full account of this formalization to include some reference or other to dialectical modes of thinking. Even as late as in *Can Politics Be Thought?*, Badiou suggests the possibility that the keywords of his philosophy lay the groundwork for a renewal of the dialectic: 'I hold that the concepts of event, structure, intervention, and fidelity are the very concepts of the dialectic, insofar as the latter is not reduced to the flat image, which was already inadequate for Hegel himself, of totalization and the labour of the negative' (*PP* 84). The concepts of event, structure, intervention and fidelity, of course, continue to form the backbone of Badiou's current work. What, then, is the fate of the dialectic in this context? What are the consequences, for anyone intent not just on understanding but on working *with* this philosopher's thought, of a sustained confrontation with the history and theory of dialectical thinking?

III

The question that I want to pose is not only whether Badiou can teach us what it means to think dialectically again, but also to what extent a dialectical interpretation might help us avoid, or at least reconsider, some of the misconceptions surrounding Badiou's own work. For most readers, the answer to both sides of this question typically involves the notion of a radical breakaway from the dialectic – a break that would occur sometime in the mid to late eighties and that not surprisingly would be in tune with the larger crisis and ultimate demise of Marxism-Leninism and the collapse of the Soviet Union. Badiou, the argument then goes, was indeed a staunch defender of the materialist dialectic up until and including *Théorie du sujet*, a most obscure and often misunderstood seminar written under the heavy influence of French Maoism as much as of Mallarmé and Lacan. But after *Can Politics Be Thought?*, and most definitely so starting with *Being and Event*, he is supposed to have destroyed, or at least to have bypassed, the last metaphysical and essentialist remnants of this belief in the dialectic, including its reformulation by the most fervent followers of the thought of Chairman Mao.[10] Mathematics, briefly put, is thought to have replaced dialectics in the more recent and widely read works by Badiou.

There are certainly good reasons to accept this reading. Thus, in *Abridged Metapolitics*, to give but one recent example, Badiou seems to reject all forms of dialectical thinking as being inherently misguided – unable as they are to think politics *from within*, as would be the true task of the metapolitics he calls for, rather than to think merely *about* the essence of the political, which for him has been the principal occupation of all hitherto existing political philosophies. The dialectical mode of thinking politics would thus appear to be the first victim of Badiou's proposal for a metapolitical orientation in philosophy, despite the fact that, little more than a decade ago and while using the same keywords of situation, event, intervention, and so on, he had posited that politics could be thought through the concepts of a renewed dialectic.

Badiou seems to be especially influenced in this regard by his friend and fellow ex-Maoist Sylvain Lazarus, whose *Anthropologie du nom* receives an extensive, though not entirely uncritical, review in a key chapter from *Abridged Metapolitics*. Both authors refuse to tie the possibility of thinking politics to a dialectical articulation between objective and subjective conditions, or between the socio-economical sphere and its concentration as the political act proper, in the orthodox Leninist sense. 'Dialectical', in this context, is considered to be roughly equivalent to 'historicist', 'classist', and 'positivist', all of which would designate a dominant yet obsolete figure of political intelligibility: a 'saturated' historical mode of politics, to use the term coined by Lazarus. The suspicion is that an attempt such as the dialectical one to name the entity *in relation to which* the possibility of a political sequence emerges, whether this is done in terms of history or society, in terms of time or totality, runs the risk of dispersing the singularity of such a sequence on to two or more heterogeneous fields. The outcome of such attempts do typically involve some mediation or other of subjective and objective factors – with Lenin's vanguard party as the organizational form needed to close the gap between the two.[11] For Badiou, who on this point agrees fully with his friend Lazarus, a sequence in politics must rather be thought in interiority, from within what they term an homogeneous multiplicity, through the categories, places and prescriptions that are the material index of its momentum, without making the nature of the political process transitive to any fixed combination of data, be they social being and consciousness, the mental and the material, or discursive and non-discursive practices. Subtracted from the realm of objectivity, politics would also no longer be subordinated to the overarching sense of history: 'Such is the principal gain of the disjunction between politics and history, and of the abolition of the category of time: the grasping in thought of a political sequence remains an homogeneous operation, whether regarding a politics that is "ongoing" or one that is over and done with, even if the protocols to be followed in each case are different' (*AM* 58). Very little, if anything, it would seem, can be said in this context in favour of a dialectical understanding of Badiou's recent thought.

Badiou and Lazarus do suggest, however, that the dialectic as heterogeneous articulation can be found mainly in the field of the social sciences, among historians and political scientists. Their diagnosis thus leaves room for another dialectic, one capable of thinking through the material rupture produced by a political intervention, for instance, without having recourse to the form of the party nor to the idealist circulating terms of time and social movement, the co-presence of which is typically called upon to overcome an underlying heterogeneity of social being and consciousness. In particular, Badiou quotes Lazarus, who allows for a strange margin of uncertainty when evaluating the exact status of the dialectic and negativity in Hegel's very own formulation, carefully separated from the historicist dialectic of the social sciences (*AM* 60).

Hegel's shoes, supposing that he himself has indeed long been put back on his feet, are apparently still waiting for someone to fill them. Or perhaps it would be more accurate to suggest that the poor man's footwear, after having been so amply filled for over two centuries with everything from the most profane to the sublime, desperately needs to be emptied – voided in favour of a new understanding of the dialectic precisely in terms of void and excess rather than of totalization, of scission and the symptomal torsion of split identities, instead of as negation and the negation of negation, and of the breakdown of representation instead of as the elusive self-presentation of the concept. Hegel must be split, rather than put upside down. 'Thus, at the heart of the Hegelian dialectic we should disentangle two processes, two concepts of movement', Badiou adds in *Théorie du sujet*: '(a) A dialectical matrix covered by the term alienation; the idea of a simple term that unfolds in its becoming-other, in order to come back into its own as accomplished concept. (b) A dialectical matrix whose operator is scission, under the theme: there is no unity other than split. Without the least return to self, nor any connection between the final and the inaugural' (*TS* 22). The question, then, is not *whether* Hegel should be revived at all but rather *which* Hegel. Or else, but this question is related to the first: *which* of his shoes should we fit, the left one or the right one? The one from the *Science of Logic* or the one from *The Phenomenology of Spirit*?

Badiou first aligned himself with French Maoism via Hegel, by retrieving Hegel's *Logic* (together with Lenin's *Philosophical Notebooks*) against both Althusser's ferocious anti-Hegelianism and the vogue for Hegel's *Phenomenology* that Kojève had inspired in the likes of Bataille, Sartre and Lacan.[12] More recently, in personal interviews, he still fondly compares *Being and Event* to the *Logic*, while considering *Théorie du sujet* more akin to the *Phenomenology*. This is neither trivial nor purely immodest: a full understanding of a possible role for the dialectic in Badiou's thought certainly stands or falls with an adequate articulation of the differences and relations between these two major books, along the lines of what happens with Hegel. Each of these by itself, however, is still one-sided. Perhaps, then, to return to the earlier question, we should say that both of Hegel's shoes, perhaps like Van Gogh's ill-fated peasant boots, are left ones, and that the painful task ahead of us is to put them on at the same time.

Even *Abridged Metapolitics*, in this sense, is perhaps much closer than would first appear to the dialectical premise behind *Can Politics Be Thought?*. In order to bring out this proximity we need a mode of thinking that allows us to reflect how a break with all that is, by prescribing what can be – not in some bold messianic or anarchist future but in the sober immediacy of a wager on the here and now – nevertheless continues to be a homogeneous situation. And yet this homogeneity should not come to designate an ever so slightly transfigured and exalted perpetuation of the status quo. How can such a simple and yet para-doxical situation be thought as a multiple that is both new and yet homo-geneous? Or, to use a slightly different formulation, how can we think of an excess or supplement to the situation that in truth is still immanent to this situation itself?

In spite of the declared obsolescence of the dialectic between subjective and objective factors, between consciousness and social being, or even between theory and practice, I want to argue that this logic of emergent truths calls for a new set of dialectical categories, the categories required for a dialectic of the new. As Badiou adds in the interview quoted above: 'At least in this regard I remain more profoundly Hegelian. That is, I am convinced that the new can only be thought as process. There surely is novelty in the event's upsurge, but this novelty is always evanescent. It is not there that we can pinpoint the new in its materiality, but that is precisely the point that interests me: the materiality of the new.'[13] Picking up on this last point, I would go so far as to posit that what is needed to grasp the materiality of the new is actually a renewal of the materialist dialectic. Ever since the fall of the USSR, many philosophers and ideologues have been quick to redeem a certain Marx – and even a certain idea of communism – from the stuffy archives of vulgar or orthodox Marxism. Perhaps the time has come, though, when the stakes should be shifted in a different direction and philosophy should come to the rescue of dialectical materialism as well. In fact, if the practice of theory or philosophy is defined by carefully working through and against received opinions, then nothing can be more urgent indeed than to resist the mindless consensus that is only all too happy to sacrifice the slightest hint of dialectical and materialist thinking, if this is the price to be paid in order to present oneself as the proud rediscoverer of the truth of a certain Marx.

IV

Before we take a closer look at *Being and Event* in order to analyse how this case could be made for the recent works, there is still another way of approaching the legacy of dialectical thinking in Badiou. This would involve a closer reading of *The Century*, his recent lecture series at the Collège International de Philosophie. These lectures seem to want to come to terms once more with the possibility, or even the desirability, of a renewal of the dialectic. In fact, this has been a task that the past century imposed on itself: 'The century offers the figure of a non-dialectical juxtaposition of the two and the one. The question here consists in knowing what the century's final account is regarding dialectical thinking' (*LS* 50). Badiou insists that much of the twentieth century has been dominated by what Deleuze would have described as so many cases of 'disjunctive synthesis', that is, non-dialectical or even anti-dialectical solutions to the problem of articulating not only the old and the new, the end and the beginning, but also truth and semblance, life and the will, historicism and vanguardism. The highest aim was to come face to face with the real in an instantaneous act or ecstatic break, rather than in an internal overcoming of contradictions. In fact, it is precisely the absence of any dialectical sublation that seems to have been compensated for by sheer violence, by the passion of the real that characterizes so many artistic and political sequences in the century: 'Violence comes in at the point of the disjunction. It substitutes itself for a missing conjunction, it functions like a forced dialectical link in the place of the anti-dialectic' (*LS* 27). Only on a few occasions in these lectures does Badiou directly express interest in a more properly dialectical understanding of truth as process over and against the primacy of the act, but in general he clearly prefers to dwell on the century's most radical experiments in disjunction and delinking.

In view of this shifting evaluation, one initial conclusion could be that the decline, or the outright obsolescence, of dialectical thinking is primarily due to the exhaustion of certain theoretical and philosophical models – from Hegel's *Logic* to Lukács' *History and Class Consciousness* and Sartre's *Critique of Dialectical Reason* to Adorno's *Negative Dialectics*. Badiou of course identified himself very strongly with the theory of the dialectic for a long time, starting with his two early pamphlets *Théorie de la contradiction* and *De l'Idéologie*, through the running commentary on a Maoist text by Zhang Shiying in *Le Noyau rationnel de la dialectique hégélienne*, all the way to the above-mentioned statement in *Can Politics Be Thought?* Instead of resulting from a sense of theoretical exhaustion, however, the notion that the dialectical mode has reached its moment of closure could also be attributed to those practices and experiments from the past century, be they political or artistic, that failed to realize this tradition of thought – a tradition that otherwise could still be worth fighting for. Is the violence of disaster, then, inherent in the dialectical system or method as such, or does its failure leave the promise of a true dialectic largely intact? And pending the answer to this question, are there practical or theoretical alternatives to the predominance of those tragically unresolved, and most often extremely violent, disjunctive syntheses as diagnosed by Badiou in *The Century*?

v

Rather than bidding farewell to all forms of dialectical thinking and confining them to the dustbin of history where they might waste away together with the concepts of the class struggle and the dictatorship of the proletariat, perhaps we should consider that Badiou's most important work to date, notwithstanding the overwhelming predominance of mathematics, opens with a clear tipping of the hat to the dialectical system and method. Let me recall that *Being and Event* from the outset is meant to provide the ontological substructure that was supposedly missing, or in any case insufficiently articulated, in Badiou's earlier attempt at a synthesis of his thinking in *Théorie du sujet*. Whereas this earlier work merely seemed to suppose that there is such a thing as subjectivation, the later one seeks to make this supposition compatible with the thesis that mathematics *is* ontology as the science of being qua being. Recourse to the mathematics of set theory, from Cantor to Cohen, more specifically, would provide a formal alternative to the poetic ontologies of Heideggerian origin, while at the same time laying out a theory of the subject compatible with the interventionist doctrines of Marx and Freud, of Lenin and Lacan. Badiou immediately foresees that this ambitious plan to render the discourse of being compatible with a theory of the subject will remind certain readers of the worst outgrowths of those state-sponsored efforts that sought to forge dialectical materialism into the official philosophy of Marxism. Speaking in retrospect of the thesis that 'there is' subjectivation, as outlined in *Théorie du sujet*, Badiou notes, in the introduction to *Being and Event*:

> The compatibility of this thesis with a possible ontology worried me, because the force – and the absolute weakness – of the 'old' Marxism, of

dialectical materialism, had been to postulate such a compatibility in the guise of the generality of the laws of the dialectic, i.e., in the end, in the guise of the isomorphism between the dialectic of nature and the dialectic of history. For sure, this (Hegelian) isomorphism was stillborn (*EE* 10).

The isomorphism, or the simple homology, between nature and history, between history and consciousness, between society and politics, or between substance and subject, cancels out the possibility of thinking of the truth of an event from within a homogeneous multiplicity, or according to an immanent excess. To avoid this risk and remain strictly within the realm of thought, of the subject without an object, many readers will have concluded that after *Théorie du sujet*, or at the very latest after *Can Politics Be Thought?*, dialectics was to have been replaced by mathematics, as would happen in *Being and Event* – whereby the baby was perhaps thrown away together with the bathwater. However, I want to argue not only that the principal theses in this last book continue to be strongly reminiscent of the laws of the dialectic, provided of course that these laws or axioms are properly reformulated, but also, and perhaps even more importantly, that a failure to grasp the exact nature of the dialectic contained in these theses will continue to lead to the kind of misunderstandings or ill-conceived objections that already haunt the reception of Badiou's philosophy as a whole.

Being and Event, to begin with, makes several references to the 'dialectic of void and excess' (*EE* 126–7). By this is meant, in the first place, that the void constitutes the sole ontological foundation: the void, or mathematically speaking the empty set, is the only proper name of being. From the void in a given situation we can surmise that what counts, or what is counted as one, as someone or as something, in and of itself is strictly speaking an inconsistent multiplicity, and that only an operation of counting turns this inconsistency into a consistent number of somethings. The random multiplicity that 'precedes' this counting operation, however, can never be thought as such, except retroactively, in the rare event of a certain miscount. Thus, the void can somehow be made to appear only through the excess of the counting operation over and above itself. Badiou, to be precise, distinguishes between two such operations: the first, which he calls presentation, counts as so many ones all the *elements* that belong to a given set, e.g. the citizens of a nation, while the second count, or representation, recounts the first one by counting as so many ones all the *parts* or subsets of the initial set, e.g. the various racial, ethnic or gendered sub-groups of the nation's citizenry. The first count defines the basic structure of a situation, while the second seeks to guarantee its metastructure, or what is also called the state of the situation. Badiou's dialectic of void and excess then holds that there is always an excess of parts over elements, of inclusion over belonging, of representation over simple presentation. While this theorem is trivial in the case of finite sets, further developments in set theory reveal that in an infinite situation this excess is properly immeasurable, there being no well-defined means by which to determine by how much the power set, or the set of all sub-sets that are included in a given set, will exceed the number of elements that belong to this set to begin with. In fact, only a subjective decision can put a measure on this excess – a decision, that is, loyal to the event that exposed the excess in the first place. It is thus the doctrine of the event, by which the void of a situation is revealed and, through a breakdown of the count, a fleeting glimpse of being as pure multiple is offered, that somehow links the ontology of set theory to the theory of the subject.

There are various reasons why this fairly straightforward argument can be seen as dialectical in a new and unexpected sense. Let me point out a few of these reasons, which together give us the possible elements (or the parts and elements) of a materialist dialectic:

1. Dialectical thinking, if this is still the appropriate label, continues to be defined in terms of scission and the torsion of scission, and not in terms of alienation and the overcoming of alienation. 'In concrete, militant philosophy, it is thus indispensable to announce that there is only one law of the dialectic: One divides into two', Badiou had written in a Maoist passage from *Théorie du sujet*: 'Dialectics states that there is a Two and proposes itself to infer the One as moving division. Metaphysics poses the One, and forever gets tangled up in drawing from it the Two' (*TS* 32, 40). To a certain extent, this law still applies to Badiou's later philosophy, following *Being and Event*. Thus, rather than the simple opposition between being and event, what really matters is the split *within* being between presentation and representation. When Žižek presents this prior split as some kind of discovery and a possible blind spot in Badiou's thinking, he is merely repeating the very kernel of the latter's ontology, which is at the same time its immanent deadlock; and, far from presupposing some wild vitality of pure presentation, this impasse of being is nothing but the result of formal counting operations that are impossible to fix. Likewise, an event is not only defined by purely belonging to itself in a manner that could be considered sovereign or absolutist, but it is an event *for* a situation, as indexed by its site. Even the formal matheme of the event inscribes this originary scission. Nothing can take away the fact that an event can occur only at a site that is symptomatic of the situation as a whole. Finally, a truth procedure consists in a *torsion* of the divided situation back upon itself, starting from the site of the event and moving in the direction of a generic extension of its truth as applicable to all. These are the concepts that a dialectical reading should reconsider: not just being and event, but scission, site, and torsion – the split within being between belonging and inclusion, the site of an event that makes this an event for a specific situation, and the forced return to this situation from the point of view of its generic extension.

2. Dialectical thinking does not consist in establishing a mechanical homology or isomorphism between subject and object, but in articulating both through the formal paradox of an impasse, as in the interplay of void and excess. Badiou, in this regard, can be said to participate in a larger trend in post-Marxism (in his case we should rather say post-Maoism), which holds not only that the subject is split but also, and more importantly, that a subject is needed to bring out the constitutive impasse of the structure that would have defined objectivity. The immeasurable excess of the state of a situation over this

situation itself formalizes the fact that a structure is exceeded by its redoubling in a metastructure. However, this point of the real in ontology, which bars the objective order from achieving a well-ordered closure, requires at the same time a decision that is nothing if not subjective. Partly by retrieving a conclusion from *Théorie du sujet* (according to which 'the real is the *impasse* of formalization; formalization is the place of the *passe-en-force* of the real' [*TS* 40]), Badiou sums up the trajectory of *Being and Event* as follows: 'The *impasse* of being, which causes the quantitative excess of the state to wander beyond measure, is in truth the *passe* of the Subject' (*EE* 471). A subject is called for to put a measure on the exorbitant power of the structure over itself. The structural fact of the impasse of being is already mediated by subjectivity; without the intervention of a subject faithful to the event, the gap in the structure would not even be visible.

3. The dialectic of substance and subject can be phrased even more explicitly in orthodox terms as the 'leap' or 'turnabout', the 'transformation into the opposite' from quantity to quality. Echoes from Hegel's *Umschlag* can also be heard, in other words, in Badiou's idiosyncratic use of the Lacanian *passe*. 'There is an insurmountable excess of the subsets over the elements' which is such that 'no matter how exact the quantitative knowledge of a situation might be, we cannot estimate, except via an arbitrary decision, "by how much" its state exceeds it', Badiou writes in a key passage from *Being and Event*. 'The fact that at this point it is necessary to tolerate the almost complete arbitrariness of a choice, and that quantity, this paradigm of objectivity, leads to pure sub-jectivity, that is what I would like to call the Cantor-Gödel-Cohen-Easton symptom' (*EE* 113, 309–11). The mathematics of set theory, far from being incompatible with the dialectic, thus strangely enough ends up confirming one of its principal laws. As Hegel himself observed: 'It is said, *natura non facit saltum*; and ordinary thinking when it has to grasp a coming-to-be or a ceasing-to-be, fancies it has done so by representing it as a *gradual* emergence or disappearance', to which the author of the *Logic* responds 'that gradualness explains nothing without leaps' – a view enthusiastically endorsed by Lenin in the margins of his *Philosophical Notebooks*: 'Leaps! Breaks in gradualness! Leaps! Leaps!'[14] In fact, to grasp how opposites, by leaps and breaks in the gradualness of nature, all of a sudden pass over into one another and come to be identical is one of the most orthodox definitions of the task of the dialectical method: 'Dialectics is the doctrine of the *identity of opposites* – how they can be and how they become – under which conditions they become identical, transforming one into the other – why the human mind must not take these opposites for dead, but for living, conditioned, mobile, transforming one into the other.'[15]

4. The break with nature as a gradual and well-ordered structure at the same time implies that, for such a break truly to happen, the initial situation will have had to become historical. Badiou's dialectic, if this is indeed the label we want to use, avoids most of the aporias of historicity and structure, of liberty and causality, that still haunted much of the work of Althusser, for instance, in his polemic with Sartre. Badiou acknowledges the canonical importance of this polemic as one of the last in which the political options seemed clear, such that philosophy could aim to subsume them in the direction of a foundation. As he

writes in *Can Politics Be Thought?*: 'The last debate in this matter opposed the tenants of liberty, as founding reflective transparency, to the tenants of the structure, as prescription of a regime of causality. Sartre against Althusser: this meant, at bottom, the Cause against the cause' (*PP* 10). It was Badiou's Maoism that enabled him to bring together the doctrine of structural causality with a subject's commitment to the Cause. But this was possible only because over-determination, upon closer inspection, already signalled that place, similar to the site of an event, where history seizes a given structure, or to put it the other way around, where a structural impasse becomes historicized. If we were to continue using the orthodox vocabulary, we might say that this is the point where the materialist dialectic already carries within it the logic of historical materialism. Thus, in *Being and Event*, one of the central chapters is devoted to answering the question of what turns a situation into a historical one, and the break between nature and history – between the well-ordered sameness of being and the irruption of a supernumerary event on the edges of the void – is as important in this later book as was the break earlier between structure and history in *Théorie du sujet*. It should also be said, however, that Badiou has only recently begun to supplement his formal definition of what constitutes a his-torical situation, that is, a situation marked by the site of an event, with the actual study of a few of those sites and situations. *The Century* already provides at least in part a historical counterweight for the more abstract materialist dialectic put forth in *Being and Event*, and even more recently Badiou has devoted two special lectures, respectively to the Cultural Revolution and the Paris Commune,[16] in which he proposes, against all odds, to think through the links between history and politics – to think the historicity of politics. Much more work certainly needs to be done along these lines if we are fully to grasp how, in the doctrine of being and event, we are not reduced to a stance that is either structural or historicist; rather, we are bound to consider both at the same time in their immanent dialectic.

If *Being and Event*, like Hegel's *Logic*, seems more structural and abstract in this regard, we should nevertheless not forget that at the centre of this book the concept of a historical situation is already defined from within the parameters of structural-ontological mathematics. Similarly, if *Théorie du sujet*, like *The Phe-nomenology of Spirit*, seems to stick more closely to concrete experiences, we should also not forget that the structural gap between inclusion and belonging, which forms the ontological impasse of being, is also already defined in this book as the abyssal ground for an intervening doctrine of the subject.

5. There is one final aspect that should be considered by those critics who fail to perceive any possibility for a more dialectical understanding of Badiou's philosophy, and who in fact reproach him for ending up with a rigid if not miraculous and thoroughly anti-dialectical series of oppositions between being and event, knowledge and truth, the human animal and the immortal subject, and so on. I am referring of course to the ongoing efforts on Badiou's own part, from his Maoist period all the way to the most dense ontological meditations, to counter precisely such oppositions with a staunch critique of what in the old days he would have called the twin 'deviations' of leftism and statism – of

adventurism and opportunism. We do not even have to go back to *Le Noyau rationnel de la dialectique hégélienne* (1978) to find a summary of this critique, since even as late as in *Being and Event* (1988), in a pivotal meditation on 'The Intervention', Badiou warns us against the temptation to put the event in a set all by itself, as a singleton utterly disjoined from the situation. Such would be the temptation of what he proposes to call 'speculative leftism', which is nothing but a mirror-image of 'statism', that is, the way in which the state systematically tries to reduce the erratic novelty of a political event, for instance, to the rabble-rousing discontent of the mob, of foreign agitators, and so on. 'The terms that are registered by the state, guarantee of the count-for-one of the parts, are finally the site and the putting-into-one of the name of the event', Badiou claims: 'This is certainly a Two (the site as such counted as one, and a multiple put into one), but the problem is that between these two terms *there is no relation whatsoever*.'[17] The connections between an event and its site remain an enigma from the point of view of the state, with the result that both are merely juxtaposed as being essentially unrelated in their duality. However, we do not fare much better at the other end of the ideological spectrum when the event, rather than being foreclosed by the state, is hypostasized into a radical beginning. 'Speculative leftism imagines that the intervention is authorized only by itself, and breaks with the situation with no other support than its own negative will', Badiou concludes: 'Speculative leftism is fascinated by the ultra-one of the event, and thinks it is possible in its name to deny all immanence to the structured regime of the count-for-one. And since the ultra-one has the structure of the Two, the imaginary of a radical beginning inevitably leads, in every range of thought, to a Manichean hypostasis' (*EE* 232–3). If Badiou's philosophy indeed falls prey to either or both of these two positions, then the least his critics should recognize is the fact that his work would have provided them with all the tools necessary to set up the proper traps.

VI

Even if we accept the need to articulate being, event, site, subject, intervention and so on in such a way as to avoid the extremes of leftism and statism, the reader may still be reluctant to call this articulation a new dialectic. Why give a stale blood transfusion to a horse that may have been beaten to death several decades ago? 'The point is to be clear about the subject of the dialectic', as Badiou writes in *Can Politics Be Thought?*: 'The dialecticity of the dialectic consists precisely in having a conceptual history and in dividing the Hegelian matrix to the point where it turns out to be essentially a doctrine of the event, and not the guided adventure of the spirit. A politics, rather than a history' (*PP* 84). For Badiou, dialectics ultimately means a form of thinking that relates to the truth of a situation, not by way of a mediation but through an interruption, a scission, or a cut in representation. The outline for a renewal of the materialist dialectic in *Can Politics Be Thought?* in this sense remains valid for the arguments that have come out of *Being and Event*: 'Dialectical thinking will be recognized first of all by its conflict with representation. Such thinking tracks down the unrepresentable point in its field, from which it turns out that one touches upon the real' (*PP* 86). Tracking down the immanent point of excess in representation, however, is still insufficient, unless this point of the real is taken up as the paradoxical leverage for a subject's emerging capacity for truth: 'A dialectical form of thinking thus makes a *hole* in the disposition of knowledge (of representations), on the occasion of a symptomatic breakdown, which it *interprets* according to the *hypothesis of a capacity* in which the *après-coup* of a subject will have asserted itself' (*PP* 89). For Badiou, this is the unique strength of Marx, who listened to the popular uprisings of 1848 and responded in the future anterior with the hypothesis of a proletarian political capacity, just as Freud at the turn of the century listened to the hysterical interruptions of the familiar discourse on sexuality and love in order to respond with the intervening doctrine of psychoanalysis. But today, can we still hold that one divides into two? 'This question of the thought of the Two has as its horizon the destiny of dialectical thought: in the end, is the category of contradiction in the Hegelian, Marxist and Sartrean heritage still pertinent or not to the conceptualization of difference?' Badiou himself asks in another conversation, to which he responds: 'I think the question is still open.'[18]

VII

I began this argument by outlining the two most common approaches to Badiou's work. Both of these approaches, though, remain in a sense internal to one and the same hermeneutic, dominated by the concern to read the texts themselves in the right way. The aim in both cases remains a form of exegesis, which as always seeks somewhat desperately to stabilize the correct reading of a thinker. It would be a completely different matter, however, to take on the risk of an intervention by rethinking a specific situation in light of this thinker's conceptual apparatus. Žižek, of course, for many years has tried to combine both of these options, relying heavily on Badiou's concepts in his own analysis of the current moment, while at the same time being extremely critical, even to the point of generating a set of misunderstandings of his own, whenever he enters in a more exegetical discussion of Badiou's philosophy as a whole. But otherwise, for reasons that are at least in part due to the complexity of the major texts, this philosopher has been the subject mainly of studies of the explanatory kind. The difficult task that seems to me to lie ahead involves taking up the transformative and critical kind, by way of separate and localized interventions in the present that would attempt to think through our actuality in the terms provided by Badiou. This is, after all, the hope expressed by the author himself, in the introduction to *Being and Event*: 'The categories which this book lays out, and which run the gamut from the pure multiple to the subject, constitute the general order of a form of thinking that is such that it can be *practised* throughout the extent of our contemporary frame of reference. They are thus made available to serve the procedures of science as much as those of politics or analysis. They attempt to organize an abstract vision of the requirements of our age.'[19] In this sense, though, nearly everything still remains to be done.

12

FROM PURIFICATION TO SUBTRACTION: BADIOU AND THE REAL*

Slavoj Žižek

In his recent book *The Century* (2004), Alain Badiou identifies as the key feature of the twentieth century the 'passion of the Real {*la passion du réel*}'. In contrast to the nineteenth century of the utopian or 'scientific' projects and ideals, plans about the future, the twentieth century aimed at delivering the thing itself, at directly realizing the longed-for New Order. Or as Fernando Pessoa put it:

> Do not crave to construct in the space
> for which you think that it lies in the future,
> that it promises you some kind of tomorrow.
> Realize yourself today, do not wait.
> You alone are your life.

The ultimate and defining experience of the twentieth century was this direct experience of the Real as opposed to everyday social reality – the Real in its extreme violence as the price to be paid for peeling off the deceiving layers of reality. Already in the trenches of the First World War, Ernst Jünger celebrated face-to-face combat as the model of an authentic intersubjective encounter. Such authenticity resides in the act of violent transgression, from the Lacanian Real – the Thing Antigone confronts when he violates the order of the City – to the Bataillean excess.

As Badiou describes it, this passion for the Real in the last century tended to lead it down one of two paths: that of purification and that of subtraction. In contrast to purification which endeavours to isolate the kernel of the Real by violently peeling off the imaginary reality that conceals it, subtraction starts from the Void, from the reduction of all determinate content, and then tries to establish a minimal difference between this Void and an element which functions as its stand-in. Along with Badiou himself, it is Jacques Rancière who has developed this approach in terms of a politics of the 'empty set', a politics of the 'supernumerary' element which belongs to the set but has no distinctive place

---

* Substantial portions of this chapter appeared in slightly different form in the foreword to the second edition of Žižek, *For They Know Not What They Do: Enjoyment as a Political Factor* (London: Verso, 2002).

in it. What, for Rancière, is politics proper? A phenomenon which, for the first time, appeared in Ancient Greece when the members of demos (those with no firmly determined place in the hierarchical social edifice) not only demanded that their voice be heard against those in power and that they be included in the public sphere on an equal footing with the ruling oligarchy and aristocracy: even more, they, the excluded, those with no fixed place within the social edifice, presented themselves as the representatives, the stands-in, for the Whole of Society, for the true Universality. We – the 'nothing', we who are not counted in the social order – we are the people, we are All against others who stand only for their particular privileged interest.[1] In short, political conflict designates the tension between the structured social body in which each part has its place, and 'the part with no-part' which unsettles this order on account of the empty principle of universality, of what Balibar calls *egaliberté*, the principled equality of all men qua speaking beings. Such for instance are the *liumang*, 'hoodlums', in present feudal-capitalist China, those who (with regard to the existing order) are displaced and freely float, lacking a fixed work-and-residence, lacking also any cultural or sexual identity and registration.

Politics proper thus always involves a kind of short-circuit between the Universal and the Particular, the paradox of a 'singular Universal', of a singular which appears as the stand-in for the Universal, destabilizing the 'natural' functional order of relations in the social body. For both Rancière and Badiou, this identification of the non-part with the Whole, of the part of society with no properly defined place within it (or that resists its allocated subordinated place within it) with the Universal, is the elementary gesture of politicization, discernible in all great democratic events from the French Revolution (in which the Third Estate proclaimed itself identical to the Nation as such, against aristocracy and clergy) to the demise of ex-European Socialism (in which dissident 'forums' proclaimed themselves representative of the entire society against the party *nomenklatura*). In this precise sense, politics and democracy are synonymous: the basic aim of anti-democratic politics always and by definition is and was depoliticization, i.e. the unconditional demand that 'things should return to normal', the restoration of each individual to his or her particular job.

The same point can also be made in anti-statist terms: those who are subtracted from the grasp of the state are not accounted for, counted in, i.e. their multiple *presence* is not properly *represented* within the One of the state. In this sense the 'minimal difference' is that between the set and this surplus-element which belongs to the set but lacks any differential property that would specify its place within its edifice: it is precisely this lack of specific (functional) difference which makes it an embodiment of the pure difference between the place and its elements. This 'supernumerary' element is thus a kind of 'Malevitch in politics', a square on a surface marking the minimal difference between the place and what takes place, between background and figure. Or, in the terms proposed by Ernesto Laclau and Chantal Mouffe, this 'supernumerary' element emerges when we pass from *difference* to *antagonism*. Since, in it, all qualitative differences inherent to the social edifice are suspended, it stands for the 'pure' difference as such, for the non-social within the field of the social. Or to put it in the terms of the logic of the signifier, in it, the Zero itself is counted as One.

Is this shift from purification to subtraction not also the shift from Kant to Hegel? From tension between phenomena and Thing to an inconsistency/gap between phenomena themselves? The standard notion of reality is that of a hard kernel which resist the conceptual grasp. What Hegel does is simply take this notion of reality *more literally*: 'hard' or non-conceptual reality is something which *emerges* when notional self-development gets caught in an inconsistency and becomes non-transparent to itself. In short, the limit is transposed from exterior to interior: there is Reality because and insofar as the Notion is inconsistent, doesn't coincide with itself ... In short, multiple perspectival inconsistencies between phenomena are not an effect of the impact of the transcendent Thing – on the contrary, the Thing is nothing but the ontologization of the inconsistency between phenomena. The logic of this reversal is ultimately the same as the passage from the special to the general theory of relativity in Einstein. While the special theory already introduces the notion of the curved space, it conceives of this curvature as the effect of matter: it is the presence of matter which curves the space, i.e. only an empty space would have been non-curved. With the passage to the general theory, the causality is reversed: far from causing the curvature of the space, matter is its *effect*. In the same way, the Lacanian Real – the Thing – is not so much the inert presence which 'curves' the symbolic space (introducing gaps and inconsistencies in it), but, rather, the effect of these gaps and inconsistencies.

So there are two fundamentally different ways for us to relate to the Void, best captured by the paradox of Achilles and the tortoise: while Achilles can easily overtake the tortoise, he cannot ever reach her. We either posit the Void as the impossible-real Limit of the human experience which we can only indefinitely approach, the absolute Thing towards which we have to maintain a proper distance – if we get too close to it, we get burned by the sun – our attitude towards the Void must then be thoroughly ambiguous, marked by simultaneous attraction and repulsion. Or else we posit it as that through which we should (and, in a way, even always-already have) pass(ed). Therein resides the gist of the Hegelian notion of 'tarrying with the negative' which Lacan rendered in his notion of the deep connection between death drive and creative sublimation: in order for (symbolic) creation to take place, the death drive (the Hegelian self-relating absolute negativity) has to accomplish its work of, precisely, emptying the place and thus making it ready for creation. Instead of the old topic of phenomenal objects disappearing/dissolving in the vortex of the Thing, we get objects which are nothing but the Void of the Thing embodied, or, in Hegelese, objects in which negativity assumes positive existence.

In religious terms, this passage from the Impossible-Real One (Thing), refracted/reflected in the multitude of its appearances, to the Twosome is the very passage from Judaism to Christianity: the Jewish God is the Real Thing of Beyond, while the divine dimension of Christ is just a tiny grimace, an imperceptible shade, which differentiates him from other (ordinary) humans. Christ is not 'sublime' in the sense of an 'object elevated to the dignity of a

Thing', he is not a stand-in for the impossible Thing-God. He is rather 'the Thing itself', or, more accurately, 'the Thing itself' is nothing but the rupture/ gap which makes Christ not fully human.

Properly understood, the Real is thus not *another* Centre, a 'deeper', 'true' focal point or 'black hole' around which the symbolic formations fluctuate; it is rather the obstacle on account of which every Centre is always displaced, missed. The Real is not the abyss of the Thing which forever eludes our grasp, and on account of which every symbolization of the Real is partial and inappropriate; it is rather that invisible obstacle, that distorting screen which always 'falsifies' our access to external reality, that 'bone in the throat' which gives a pathological twist to every symbolization, on account of which every symbolization misses its object. The Real is the disavowed X on account of which our vision of reality is anamorphically distorted, in keeping with the basic logic of Freud's interpretation of dreams: the real kernel of the dream is not the dream's latent thought, which is displaced/translated into the explicit texture of the dream, but the unconscious desire, which inscribes itself through the very distortion of the latent thought into the explicit texture.

Or again, the Real is *simultaneously* the Thing to which direct access is not possible *and* the obstacle which prevents this direct access; the Thing which eludes our grasp *and* the distorting screen which makes us miss the Thing. More precisely, the Real is ultimately the very shift of perspective from the first to the second standpoint. Recall Adorno's well-known analysis of the antagonistic character of the notion of society: in a first approach, the split between the two notions of society (Anglo-Saxon individualistic-nominalistic and Durkheimian organicist notion of society as a totality which pre-exists individuals) seems irreducible, we seem to be dealing with a true Kantian antinomy which cannot be resolved via a higher 'dialectical synthesis', and which elevates society into an inaccessible Thing-in-itself. However, in a second moment, one should merely take note of how this radical antinomy which seems to preclude our access to the social Thing *already is the thing itself* – the fundamental feature of today's society *is* the irreconcilable antagonism between Totality and the individual. Don't we find exactly the same shift at the very core of the Christian experience? It is the very radical separation of man from God which unites us with God, since, in the figure of Christ, God is thoroughly separated *from himself*. The point is thus not to 'overcome' the gap which separates us from God, but to take note of how *this gap is internal to God himself*.

In short, reality is not exhausted by the mere interplay of appearances, there is indeed a Real – however, this Real is not the inaccessible Thing, but the *gap* which prevents our access to it. So when Nietzsche affirms that truth is a perspective, this assertion is to be read together with Lenin's notion of the partisan/partial character of knowledge (the (in)famous *partij'nost*): in a class society, 'true' objective knowledge is possible only from the 'interested' revolutionary standpoint. This means neither an epistemologically naïve reliance on the 'objective knowledge' available when we get rid of our partial prejudices and preconceptions and adopt a 'neutral' view, nor the (complementary) relativist view that there is no ultimate truth, only multiple subjective perspectives. Both terms have to be fully asserted: there *is*, among the multitude of opinions, a *true* knowledge, but this knowledge is accessible only from an 'interested' partial position.[2]

I

One should be careful, then, not to miss the fundamental philosophical gesture of Alain Badiou. As a materialist, in order to be thoroughly materialist, he focuses on the *idealist* topos *par excellence*: how can a human animal forsake its animality and put its life in the service of a transcendent Truth? How can the 'transubstantiation' from the pleasure-oriented life of an *individual* to the life of a *subject* dedicated to a Cause occur? How is a free act possible? How can one break the network of the causal connections of positive reality and conceive of an act which begins by and in itself? In short, Badiou *repeats within the materialist frame the elementary gesture of idealist anti-reductionism*. Human Reason cannot be reduced to the result of evolutionary adaptation; art is not just a heightened procedure of providing sensual pleasures, but a medium of Truth, etc. And lest we suppose this gesture is also aimed at psychoanalysis (is not the point of the notion of 'sublimation' that the allegedly 'higher' human activities are just a roundabout way to realize a 'lower' goal?), the same effort is at work in the great achievement of psychoanalysis: its claim is that sexuality itself, sexual drives which pertain to the human animal, cannot be accounted for in evolutionary terms.[3] This makes clear the true stakes of Badiou's gesture. In order for materialism truly to win over idealism, it is not enough to succeed in the reductionist approach and demonstrate how mind, consciousness, etc. can nonetheless somehow be accounted for within the evolutionary-positivist materialist frame. On the contrary, the materialist claim should be much stronger: it is *only* materialism which can accurately explain the very phenomena of mind, consciousness, etc. And conversely, it is idealism, which always-already 'reifies' them, which is 'vulgar'.

Badiou identifies four possible domains in which a Truth-Event can occur, four domains in which subjects emerge as 'operators' of a truth procedure: science, art, politics, love. This theory of the four 'conditions' of philosophy allows us to approach in a new way the old problem of the role of philosophy. Often, however, other disciplines take over (at least part of) the 'normal' role of philosophy. In some of the nineteenth-century nations like Hungary or Poland, it was literature which played the role of philosophy (that of articulating the ultimate horizon of meaning of the nation in the process of its full constitution). In the United States today – given the predominance of cognitivism and neurologically based studies in philosophy departments – most of 'Continental Philosophy' takes place in Comparative Literature, Cultural Studies, English, French and German departments. (As they are wont to say these days: if you analyse a rat's vertebra you are doing philosophy, if you analyse Hegel you belong to CompLit.) In Slovenia during the 1970s, 'dissident' philosophy took place in sociology departments and institutes. The other extreme is also possible, when philosophy itself takes over the tasks of other academic (or even non-academic) practices and discipline: again, in the late Yugoslavia and some other Socialist countries, philosophy was one of the spaces of the first articulation of 'dissident' political projects, it effectively was 'politics pursued by other means' (as Althusser put it apropos of Lenin).

So where did philosophy play its 'normal role'? Germany is the usual answer. However, is it not already a commonplace that the extraordinary role of philosophy in German history was grounded in the belatedness of the realization of the German national political project? As Marx realized early on, taking his cue from Heine: the Germans had their philosophical revolution (German Idealism) because they missed the political revolution (which took place in France). Is there then a norm at all? The best examples are perhaps those anaemic academic philosophies like neo-Kantianism one hundred years ago in Germany or French Cartesian epistemology (Leon Brunschvicg, etc.) during the first half of the twentieth century – moments in which philosophy was at its most stale, established, 'dead', irrelevant. (No wonder that, in 2002, Luc Ferry, a neo-Kantian, was nominated the Minister of Education in the new centre-right French government.)

What if, then, there is no 'normal role' at all? What if it is the exceptions themselves that retroactively create the illusion of the 'norm' they allegedly violate? What if not only does exception prove to be the rule in philosophy, what if philosophy itself – the need for authentic philosophical thought – arises precisely in those moments when (other) parts-constituents of the social edifice cannot play their 'proper role'? What if the 'proper' spaces for philosophy *are* these very gaps and interstices opened up by the pathological displacements in the social edifice? The first great merit of Badiou is thus that, for the first time, he has systematically deployed the four modes of this reference of philosophy (to science, art, politics and love).

II

Here, however, a first critical reflection imposes itself. One is tempted to risk the hypothesis that Badiou's first three truth procedures (science, art, politics) follow the classic logic of the triad of True-Beautiful-Good: the science of truth, the art of beauty, the politics of the good. So what about the fourth procedure, love? Is it not clear that it sticks out from the series, being somehow more fundamental and 'universal', always liable to break out of line? There are thus not simply four truth procedures but three-plus-one – a fact perhaps not emphasized enough by Badiou himself (although, apropos sexual difference, he does remark that 'women' tend to colour all other truth procedures through love). What is encompassed by this fourth procedure is not just the miracle of love, but also psychoanalysis, theology, and philosophy itself (the *love* of wisdom). So is love not Badiou's 'Asiatic mode of production' – the category into which he throws all truth procedures which do not fit the other three modes? This fourth procedure also serves as a kind of underlying formal principle or matrix of all of them (which accounts for the fact that, although Badiou denies to religion the status of truth procedure, he nonetheless claims that Paul was the first to deploy the very formal matrix of the Truth-Event).[4] And insofar as Badiou recognizes that the science of love – this fourth, excessive, truth procedure – is psychoanalysis, one should not be surprised to find that Badiou's relationship with Lacan is the nodal point of his thought.

How, exactly, does Badiou's philosophy relate to Lacan's theory? One should begin by accepting unequivocally that Badiou is right to reject Lacan's 'anti-philosophy'. In fact, when Lacan endlessly varies the motif of how philosophy tries to 'fill in the holes', to present a totalizing view of the universe, to cover up all the gaps, ruptures and inconsistencies (for instance, in the total self-transparency of self-consciousness), and of how, against philosophy, psycho-analysis asserts the constitutive gap/rupture/inconsistency, etc., he simply misses the point of what the most fundamental philosophical gesture is: not to close the gap, but, on the contrary, to *open up* a radical gap in the very edifice of the universe, the 'ontological difference', the gap between the empirical and the transcendental, where nothing of the two levels can be reduced to the other. As we know from Kant, transcendental constitution is a mark of our (human) finitude and has nothing to do with 'creating reality'; on the other hand, reality only appears to us within the transcendental horizon, so we cannot account for the emergence of the transcendental horizon from within the ontic self-development of reality.[5]

However, this general statement does not allow us to dispense with the work of a more detailed confrontation. It is Bruno Bosteels who has provided the most detailed account to date of the difference between Badiou's and the Lacanian approach.[6] What the two approaches share, Bosteels recognizes, is the focus on the shattering encounter of the Real, on the 'symptomal torsion' at which the given symbolic situation breaks down. But what then happens at this point of the intrusion of utmost negativity? Badiou's approach turns on the difference between *impasse* and *passe*; for Lacan, by contrast, the ultimate authentic experience (the 'traversing of fantasy') would seem to be nothing more than that of fully confronting the fundamental impasse of the symbolic order. This tragic encounter of the impossible Real *is* the limit-experience of a human being: one can only sustain it, one cannot force a passage through it. The political implications of such a stance apparently speak for themselves: while Lacan enables us to gain an insight into the falsity of the existing state, this insight is already 'it', there is no way to pass through it, every attempt to impose a new order is denounced as illusory. 'From the point of the real as absent cause', Bosteels notes, 'any ordered consistency must necessarily appear to be imaginary insofar as it conceals this fundamental lack itself.'[7] Is this then not the arch-conservative vision according to which the ultimate truth of being is the nullity of every Truth, the primordial vortex which threatens to draw us into its abyss? All we can do, after this shattering insight, is return to the semblance, to the texture of illusions which allow us to temporarily avoid the view of the terrifying abyss, humbly aware of the fragility of this texture...

So for Lacan, Truth would be this shattering experience of the Void – a sudden insight into the abyss of Being, 'not a process so much as a brief traumatic encounter, or illuminating shock, in the midst of common reality', whereas for Badiou Truth is what comes afterward: the long arduous work of fidelity, of enforcing a new law on to the situation.[8] It is thus a matter of deciding between 'a vanishing apparition of the real as absent cause (for Lacan) or a forceful transformation of the real into a consistent truth (for Badiou)'. Bosteels concludes that

> the problem with [Lacan's] doctrine is precisely that, while never ceasing to be dialectical in pinpointing the absent cause and its divisive effects on the whole, it nevertheless remains tied to this whole itself and is thus unable to account for the latter's possible transformation. [. . .] Surely anchored in the real as a lack of being, a truth procedure is that which gives being to this very lack. Pinpointing the absent cause or constitutive outside of a situation, in other words, remains a dialectical yet idealist tactic, unless this evanescent point of the real is forced, distorted, and extended, in order to give consistency to the real as a new generic truth.[9]

Bosteels goes on to recall here Badiou's opposition between Sophocles and Aeschylus. Not only Lacan, but also psychoanalysis as such, in its entire history, was focused on the Sophoclean topic of the Oedipus' family: from Oedipus confronting the unbearable Thing, the horror of his crime, the horror impossible to sustain (when one becomes aware what one did, one can only blind oneself), to Antigone's fateful step into the lethal zone between the two deaths (which provokes Creon's superego rage destined to conceal the void of the Thing). To this Sophoclean couple of superego/anxiety, Badiou opposes the Aeschylean couple of courage and justice: the courage of Orestes who risks his act, the justice (re-)established by the new Law of Athena.

III

Convincing as this example is, one cannot avoid asking the obvious question: isn't this new Law imposed by Athena the patriarchal Law based on the repression of what then returns as obscene superego fury? The more fundamental issue, however, is: is Lacan really unable to think a procedure which gives being to the very lack itself? Isn't this again the work of *sublimation*? Doesn't sublimation precisely 'give being to this very lack', to the lack as/of the impossible Thing, insofar as sublimation is 'an object elevated to the dignity of a Thing'?[10] This is why Lacan links death drive and creative sublimation: death drive does the negative work of destruction, of suspending the existing order of Law, thereby, as it were, clearing the table, opening up the space for sublimation which can (re)start the work of creation. Both Lacan and Badiou thus share the notion of a radical cut/rupture, 'event', encounter of the Real, which opens up the space for the work of sublimation, of creating the new order. The distance which separates them is to be sought elsewhere – where? Here is how Bosteels describes the modality of the truth procedure:

Setting out from the void which prior to the event remains indiscernible in the language of established knowledge, a subjective intervention names the event which disappears no sooner than it appears; it faithfully connects as many elements of the situation as possible to this name which is the only trace of the vanished event, and subsequently forces the extended situation from the bias of the new truth as if the latter were indeed already generally applicable.[11]

The key words in this faithful rendering of Badiou's position are the seemingly innocent 'as if'. In order to avoid the Stalinist *désastre*, which is grounded in the misreading of the new truth as directly applicable to the situation, as its ontological order, one should only proceed *as if* the new truth is applicable ... Can we imagine a more direct application of the Kantian distinction between constitutive principles (a priori categories which directly constitute reality) and regulative *ideas*, which should only be applied to reality in the *as if* mode (one should act as if reality is sustained by a teleological order, as if there is a God and immortal soul, etc.). When Badiou asserts the 'unnameable' as the resisting point of the Real, the 'indivisible remainder' which prevents the 'forceful transformation' to conclude its work, this assertion is strictly correlative to the *as if* mode of the post-eventual work of forcing the real: it is because of this remainder that the work of truth cannot ever leave this conditional mode behind. It is no accident then that Badiou recently reaffirmed one of his definitions of Evil:[12] the total *forcing* of the Unnameable, the fully accomplished naming of it, the dream of total Nomination ('everything can be named within the field of the given generic truth procedure'), whereby the fiction (the Kantian regulative Idea?) of the accomplished truth procedure is taken for reality (it starts to function as constitutive). According to Badiou, what such forcing obliterates is the inherent limitation of the generic truth procedure, its undecidability, indiscernibility ... : the accomplished truth destroys itself, the accomplished political truth turns into totalitarianism. The ethics of Truth is thus the ethics of the respect for the unnameable Real which cannot be forced.

How can we avoid the Kantian reading of this limitation? Although Badiou rejects the ontological-transcendental status of finitude as the ultimate horizon of our existence, is his limitation of the truth procedure not ultimately grounded in the fact that it is the *finite* subject, the operator of the infinite truth procedure, who, in an act of pure decision/choice, proclaims the Event as the starting point of reference of a truth procedure (statements like 'I love you', 'Christ has arisen from the dead')? Although Badiou subordinates the subject to the infinite truth procedure, the place of this procedure is silently constrained by the subject's finitude.[13] Significantly, Badiou, the great critic of the notion of totalitarianism, resorts to this notion here in a way very similar to the Kantian liberal critics of 'Hegelian totalitarianism'.

This brings us to the central tension in the relationship between Badiou and Lacan, which can best be traced through the way each of them relates to Kant. According to the predominant doxa, Lacan (in his late work, at least) is much closer to Kant that to Hegel, elaborating a kind of transcendental 'critique of pure desire', while Badiou is supposed to be staunchly anti-Kantian. A more careful reading, however, exposes Badiou's unexpected Kantianism. So when Bosteels claims that 'there is something more than just awkward in the criticism according to which Badiou's *Being and Event* would later get trapped in a naive undialectical, or even pre-critical separation of these two spheres – being and event, knowledge and truth, the finite animal and the immortal subject',[14] one can only add: yes, and that 'more' is that this criticism is *valid*. Already for Kant, there is no subjective purity (such a position is accessible only to a saint, and, due to its finitude, no human being can attain this position): the Kantian subject is the name for an interminable ethical work, and purity is just the negative measure of our everlasting impurity (when *we* accomplish an ethical act, we cannot ever pretend or know that we were effectively not moved by some pathological motivation). It is Badiou who is thus deeply Kantian in his gap between the 'eternity' of, say, the idea of justice, and the interminable work of forcing it into a situation. And what about Badiou's repeated insistence that 'consequences in reality' do not matter, that – apropos of the passage from Leninism to Stalinism, for example – one cannot conceive of Stalinism as the revealed truth of Leninism? What about his insistence that the process of truth is not in any way affected by what goes on at the level of being? For Badiou, a certain truth procedure ceases for strictly inherent reasons, when its sequence is exhausted – what matters is *sequence*, not *consequence*. What this means is that the irreducible impurity has its measure in the eternity of the pure Truth as its inherent measure: although the Idea of egalitarian Justice is always realized in an impure way, through the arduous work of forcing it upon the multiplicity of the order of being, these vicissitudes do not affect the Idea itself, which shines through them.

The key to Badiou's opposition of Being and Event is the preceding split, within the order of Being itself, between the pure multiplicity that beings present insofar as they belong to a situation (and which can be articulated by a mathematical ontology) and their re-presentation according to the prevailing state of that situation. The whole of what any situated multiplicity presents cannot be entirely represented by the state of that situation, and an event always occurs at the site of this surplus/remainder which eludes the grasp of the state. The question is therefore that of the exact status of this gap between the pure multiplicity of presentation and its representation by the state(s). Again, the hidden Kantian reference is crucial here: the gap which separates the pure multiplicity of the Real from the appearing of a 'world' whose coordinates are given in a set of categories which predetermine its horizon is the very gap which, in Kant, separates the Thing-in-itself from our phenomenal reality, i.e. from the way things appear to us as objects of our experience.

The basic problem remains unsolved by Kant as well as by Badiou: how does the gap between the pure multiplicity of being and its appearance in the multitude of worlds arise? *How does being appear to itself?* Or, to put it in 'Leninist' terms: the problem is not whether there is some reality beneath the phenomenal world of our experience. The true problem is exactly the opposite one – how does the gap open up within the absolute closure of the Real, within which elements of the Real can appear? Why the need for the pure multiplicity to be re-presented in a state? When Bosteels writes that the state of a situation is 'an imposing defence mechanism set up to guard against the perils of the void', one should therefore raise a naive, but nonetheless crucial, question: where does this need for defence come from? Why are we not able simply to dwell in the void? Is it not that there already has to be some tension/antagonism operative within the pure multiplicity of Being itself?

Badiou's oscillation apropos of the Event is crucial here: while linking the Event to its nomination and opposing any mystical direct access to it, any Romantic rhetorics of immersion into the Nameless Absolute Thing, Badiou is nonetheless continuously gnawed by doubts about the appropriateness of nominations (apropos of Marxism, for example, he claims that we still lack the proper name for what effectively occurred in the revolutionary turbulences of the last centuries, i.e. that 'class struggle' is *not* an appropriate nomination). This deadlock appears at its purest when Badiou defines the 'perverse' position of those who try to behave as if there was no Event. Badiou's 'official' position is that the Event is radically subjective (it exists only for those who engage themselves on its behalf). How, then, can the pervert ignore something which is not there at all for him? Is it not that the Event must then have a status which cannot be reduced to the circle of subjective recognition/nomination, so that those who, *within* the situation from which the Event emerged, ignore the Event, are also affected by it? In short, what Badiou seems to miss here is the minimal structure of historicity (as opposed to mere historicism), which resides in what Adorno called 'the power of the New to bind us [*die Verbindlichkeit des Neuen*]'.[15] When something truly New emerges, one cannot go on as if it did not happen, since the very fact of this innovation changes all the coordinates. After Schoenberg, one cannot continue to write musical pieces in the old Romantic tonal mode; after Kandinsky and Picasso, one cannot paint in the old figurative way; after Kafka and Joyce, one cannot write in the old realist way. More precisely: of course, one can do it, but if one does it, these old forms are no longer the same. They have lost their innocence and now look like a nostalgic fake.

We can return at this point to Bosteels' basic reproach, according to which psychoanalysis

> collapses into an instantaneous act what is in reality an ongoing and impure procedure, which from a singular event leads to a generic truth by way of a forced return upon the initial situation. Whereas for Žižek, the empty place of the real that is impossible to symbolize is somehow already the act of truth itself, for Badiou a truth comes about only by forcing the real and by displacing the empty place, so as to make the impossible possible. 'Every truth is post-evental', Badiou writes.[16]

We can dispel a first misunderstanding here if we remember that, for Lacan, the Event (or Act, or encounter of the Real) *does not itself occur in the dimension of truth*. For Lacan also, 'truth is post-evental', although in a different sense than for Badiou: truth comes afterwards, as the Event's symbolization. Along the same lines, when Bosteels quotes the lines from my *Sublime Object* about 'traversing the fantasy' as the 'almost nothing' of the anamorphic shift of perspective (as the unique shattering moment of the complete symbolic alteration in which, although nothing has changed in reality, all of a sudden 'nothing remains the same'), one should not forget that this *instantaneous reversal is not the end but the beginning*, the shift which opens up the space for the 'post-evental' work. To put it in Hegelese, it is the 'positing of the presupposition' which opens the actual work of positing. (There should be no need to mention the obvious fact that, in the psychoanalytic treatment, truth is not an instant insight, but the 'impure' process of working-through which can last for years.)

Nowhere is the gap which separates Badiou from Lacan more clearly evident than apropos of the famous four discourses distinguished by Lacan (as the discourses of the hysteric, the master, the university and the analyst). In recent seminars Badiou has proposed his own version of the four discourses (distinguished now as those of the hysteric, the master, the pervert and the mystic). In the beginning there is the hysteric's discourse: in the hysterical subject, the new truth explodes in an event, it is articulated in the guise of an inconsistent provocation, and the subject itself is blind to the true dimension of what it stumbled upon – think of the proverbial unexpected outburst to the beloved, 'I love you!' which surprises even its author. It is the master's task properly to elaborate the truth into a consistent discourse, to work out its sequence. The pervert, on the contrary, works as if there was no truth-event, and categorizes the effects of this event as if they could be accounted for in the order of knowledge (for example, a historian of the French Revolution like François Furet who explains it as the outcome of the complexity of the French situation in the late eighteenth century, depriving it of its universal scope). To these three, Badiou adds the mystical (or anti-philosophical) discourse, the position of clinging to the pure In-Itself of the truth beyond the grasp of any discourse.

There is a series of interconnected differences between this notion of four discourses and Lacan's own matrix of four discourses.[17] The two principal differences concern the opposition of Master and Analyst. First, in Lacan, it is not the hysteric but the Master who performs the act of nomination: he pronounces the new Master-Signifier which restructures the entire field. The Master's intervention is momentary, unique, singular, like the magic touch which shifts the perspective and all of a sudden transforms chaos into the New Order – in contrast to the discourse of University which elaborates the sequence from the new Master-Signifier (the new system of knowledge).[18] The second difference is that, in Badiou's account, there is no place for the discourse of the analyst – its place is held by the mystical discourse fixated on the unnameable Event, resisting its discursive elaboration as unauthentic. For Lacan, on the other hand, there is no place for an additional mystical discourse, for the simple reason that such a mystical stance is *not a discourse* (a social link) – and the discourse of the analyst is precisely a discourse which takes as its 'agent', its structuring principle, the traumatic kernel of the Real which serves as an insurmountable obstacle to the discursive link, introducing into it an indelible antagonism, impossibility, destabilizing gap.

Such is the true difference between Badiou and Lacan: what Badiou precludes is the possibility of devising a discourse that has as its structuring principle the unnameable 'indivisible remainder' which eludes a discursive grasp. In other words, as far as Badiou is concerned, when we are confronted with this remainder we must either name it, transpose it into the master's discourse, ignore it, or stare at it in mystified awe. This means that we should turn Badiou's reproach to Lacan back against Badiou himself: it is Badiou who is unable to expand the encounter of the Real into a *discourse*, it is Badiou for whom this encounter, if it is to start to function as a discourse, must first be transposed into a Master's discourse. The ultimate difference between Badiou and Lacan thus concerns the relationship between the shattering encounter of the Real and the ensuing arduous work of transforming this explosion of negativity into a new order. For Badiou, this new order 'sublates' the exploding negativity into a new consistent truth, while for Lacan, every Truth displays the structure of a (symbolic) fiction, i.e. no Truth is able to touch the Real.

Does this mean that Badiou is right – namely in his reproach that, in a paradigmatic gesture of what Badiou calls 'anti-philosophy', Lacan relativizes truth to just another narrative/symbolic fiction which forever fails to grasp the 'irrational' hard kernel of the Real? One should first recall here that the Lacanian triad Real-Imaginary-Symbolic reflects itself within each of its three elements. There are thus three modalities of the Real: the 'real Real' (the horrifying Thing, the primordial object, from Irma's throat to the Alien), the 'symbolic Real' (the Real as consistency: the signifier reduced to a senseless formula, like the quantum physics formulas which can no longer be translated back into – or related to – the everyday experience of our lifeworld), and the 'imaginary Real' (the mysterious *je ne sais quoi*, the unfathomable 'something' on account of which the sublime dimension shines through an ordinary object). The Real is thus effectively all three dimensions at the same time: the abyssal vortex which ruins every consistent structure; the mathematized consistent structure of reality; the fragile pure appearance. And, in a strictly homologous way, there are three modalities of the Symbolic – the real (the signifier reduced to a senseless formula), the imaginary (the Jungian 'symbols'), and the symbolic (speech, meaningful language) and three modalities of the Imaginary – the real (fantasy, which is precisely an imaginary scenario occupying the place of the Real), the imaginary (image as such in its fundamental function of a decoy), and the symbolic (again, the Jungian 'symbols' or New Age archetypes). Far from being reduced to the traumatic void of the Thing which resists symbolization, the Lacanian Real thus designates also the senseless symbolic consistency (of the 'matheme'), as well as the pure appearance irreducible to its causes ('the real of an illusion'). Consequently, Lacan not only *does* supplement the Real as the void of the absent cause with the Real as consistency; he also adds a third term, that of the Real as pure appearing, which is also operative in Badiou in the guise of that 'minimal difference' which arises when we subtract all fake particular difference – from the minimal 'pure' difference between figure and background in Malevitch's *White Square on White Surface* up to the unfathomable minimal difference between Christ and other men.

If we go back now to Badiou's distinction, in *The Century*, between the purifying and subtractive versions of 'the passion of the real': should we not supplement Badiou's two passions of the Real (the passion of purification and the passion of subtraction) with that of scientific-theoretical *formalization* as the third approach to the Real? The Real can be isolated through violent purification, the shedding away of false layers of deceptive reality; it can be isolated as the singular universal which marks the minimal difference; and it can also be isolated in the guise of a formalization which renders a subjectless 'knowledge in the Real'. It is easy to discern here again the triad of Real, Imaginary, Symbolic: the Real attained through violent purification, the Imaginary of the minimal difference, the Symbolic of the pure formal matrix.

The political consequences of this deadlock are crucial. In *The Century* Badiou seems to oscillate between the plea for a direct fidelity to the twentieth century's 'passion of the real', and the prospect of passing from the politics of purification to a politics of subtraction. While he makes it fully clear that the horrors of the twentieth century, from the Holocaust to gulag, are a necessary outcome of the purification-mode of the 'passion of the Real', and while he admits that protests against it are fully legitimate (witness his admiration for Varlam Shalamov's *Kolyma Tales*), he nonetheless stops short of renouncing it. Why? Because *fully to follow the logic of subtraction would force him to abandon the very frame of the opposition between Being and Event.* Within the logic of subtraction, the Event is not external to the order of Being, but located in the 'minimal difference' inherent to the order of Being itself. The parallel is strict here between Badiou's two versions of the 'passion of the Real' and the two main versions of the Real in Lacan, i.e. the Real as the destructive vortex, the inaccessible/impossible hard kernel which we cannot approach without risking our own destruction and the Real as the pure *Schein* of a minimal difference, as another dimension which shines through in the gaps of an inconsistent reality. If Badiou were to accomplish this step, he might, perhaps, choose to conceive of the twenty-first century as the displaced repetition of the twentieth century: after the (self-)destructive climax of the logic of purification, the passion of the Real should be reinvented as the politics of subtraction. There is a necessity in this blunder: subtraction is possible only after the fiasco of purification, as its repetition, in which the 'passion of the Real' is sublated, freed of its (self-)destructive potential. But short of taking this step, Badiou is left with only two options: either to remain faithful to the destructive ethics of purification, or to take refuge in the Kantian distinction between a normative regulative Ideal and the constituted order of reality.

What all this means is that there is a Kantian problem with Badiou which is grounded in his dualism of Being and Event, and which needs to be surpassed. The only way out of this predicament is to assert that the unnameable Real is not an external limitation but an *absolutely inherent* limitation. Truth is a generic procedure which cannot comprise its own concept-name, a name that would totalize it – as Lacan put it, 'there is no meta-language' (or Heidegger: 'the name for a name is always lacking') and this lack, far from being a limitation of language, is its positive condition. It is only because and through this lack that we have language. So, like the Lacanian Real which is not external to the Symbolic but rather makes it non-all from within (as Laclau puts it: in an antagonism, the external limit coincides with the internal one), the unnameable is inherent to the domain of names. This is why, for Badiou as for Heidegger, poetry is the experience or articulation of the limits of the potency of language, of the limits of what we can force through and with language. *This* and only this is the proper passage from Kant to Hegel: not the passage from limited/ incomplete to full/completed nomination ('absolute knowledge'), but the passage of the very limit of nomination from the exterior to the interior. The true materialist solution is thus that the Event is *nothing but* its own inscription into the order of Being, a cut/rupture in the order of Being on account of which Being cannot ever form a consistent All. There is no Beyond of Being or other-than-Being which inscribes itself into the order of Being – there 'is' nothing but the order of Being. If we adapt again the paradox of Einstein's general theory of relativity: an Event does not curve the space of Being through its inscription into it – on the contrary, an event is *nothing but* this curvature of the space of Being. 'All there is' is the interstice, the non-self-coincidence, of Being, i.e. the ontological non-closure of the order of Being.

Badiou's counter-argument to Lacan (formulated by Bosteels, among others) is that what really matters is not the Event as such, the encounter with the Real, but its consequences, its inscription, the consistency of the new discourse which emerges from the Event ... One is again tempted to turn this counter-argument against Badiou himself, against his 'oppositional' stance of advocating the impossible goal of pure presence without the state of representation. We should indeed gather the strength to 'take over' and assume power, rather than merely persist in the safety of the oppositional stance. If one is not ready to do this then one continues to rely on state power as that against which one defines one's own position. What this means at the ontological level is that, ultimately, we should reject Badiou's notion of mathematics (the theory of pure multiplicity) as the only consistent ontology or science of Being: if mathematics is ontology, then, in order to account for the *gap* between Being and Event, we will either have to remain stuck in dualism *or* dismiss the Event as an ultimately illusory local occurrence within the encompassing order of Being. Badiou is anti-Deleuze, on this point, but he remains within the same field: while Deleuze asserts the substantial One as the background-medium of multiplicity, Badiou opposes the multiplicity of Being to the One-ness of the singular Event. Against either notion of multiplicity, we should assert that the ultimate ontological given is the gap which separates the One from within.

Back now to the political dimension: is, then, the opposition of purification and subtraction not ultimately that of state power and resistance to it? Is it that, once the party takes state power, subtraction reverses back into purification, into the annihilation of the 'class enemy', a purification all the more total the more subtraction was pure (since the democratic-revolutionary subject was devoid of any determinate property, to have any such property makes its bearer seem suspect ...)? The problem is thus: how to pursue the politics of subtraction *once one is in power*? How to avoid the position of the Beautiful Soul stuck into the eternal role of 'resistance', opposing Power without effectively wanting to subvert it? The standard answer of Laclau (and also of Claude Lefort) is: democracy. That is to say, the politics of subtraction is democracy itself (not in its concrete liberal-parliamentary guise, but as the infinite Idea, to put it in Badiou's Platonist terms). In democracy, it is precisely the amorphous remainder without qualities which takes power, with no special qualifications justifying its members (in contrast to corporatism, one needs no particular qualifications to be a democratic subject). Furthermore, in democracy, the rule of the One is exploded from within, through the minimal difference between place and element. In democracy, the 'natural' state of every political agent is opposition, and exerting power is an exception, a temporary occupation of the empty place of power. It is this minimal difference between the place (of power) and the agent/element (which exerts power) that disappears in premodern states as well as in 'totalitarianism'.

Convincing as it may sound, Badiou is fully justified in his rejection of this easy way out. Why? The problem with democracy is that, the moment it is established as a positive formal system regulating the way a multitude of political subjects compete for power, it has to exclude some options as 'non-democratic', and this exclusion, this founding decision about who is included in and who is excluded from the field of democratic options, is not itself democratic. This is no mere matter of formal games with the paradoxes of meta-language, since, at this precise point, Marx's old insight remains fully valid: this inclusion/exclusion is overdetermined by the fundamental social antagonism ('class struggle'), which, for that very reason, cannot ever be adequately translated into the form of democratic competition. The ultimate democratic illusion – and, simultaneously, the point at which the limitation of democracy becomes directly palpable – is that one can accomplish social revolution painlessly, through 'peaceful means', by simply winning elections. It is this illusion that is formalist in the strictest sense of the term: it abstracts from the concrete framework of social relations within which the democratic form is operative. Consequently, although there is no profit in ridiculing political democracy one should nonetheless insist on the Marxist lesson, confirmed by the post-Socialist craving for privatization, about political democracy's reliance on private property. In short, the problem with democracy is not that it is democracy but that it is a form of state power involving certain relationships of production. Marx's old notion of the 'dictatorship of the proletariat', reactualized by Lenin, points precisely in this direction, trying to provide an answer to the crucial question: what kind of power will there be after we take power?

In this sense, the revolutionary politics of the twenty-first century should remain faithful to the twentieth century's 'passion of the Real', *repeating* the Leninist 'politics of purification' in the guise of the 'politics of subtraction'.

However, although Lenin may appear to stand for the originating moment of the politics of purification, it would be more accurate to perceive him as the neutral figure in which both versions of the 'passion of the Real' still co-exist. Are not the factional struggles within revolutionary parties (and, one is tempted to add, within psychoanalytic organizations) always struggles to define a 'minimal difference'? Recall Lenin's insistence, in the polemics at the time of the split between Bolsheviks and Mensheviks, on how the presence or absence of one single word in the party statute can affect the fate of the movement for decades in advance: the accent remains here on the most 'superficial' small difference, on the shibboleth of an accent in the formulation, which is revealed to have fateful consequences in the Real.

13

WHAT IF THE OTHER IS STUPID? BADIOU AND LACAN ON 'LOGICAL TIME'

Ed Pluth and Dominiek Hoens

When May 1968 broke out, Lacan's notorious reaction was to suggest that the students were simply looking for another master. He later went on to argue that revolution meant going around in circles.

It might seem surprising then that someone like Badiou, who tries to theorize political acts and revolutions, is determined to draw so much from Lacanian theory. As always, however, it is important not to confuse influence and adherence: Badiou takes Lacan's suspicion seriously, and this is precisely what enables him to come up with a nuanced and detailed account of genuine acts. In what follows we will show how Badiou, in order to develop his own theory of the act, draws on a short article by Lacan of 1945: 'Logical Time and the Assertion of Anticipated Certainty: A New Sophism'.[1] Badiou discusses this text in two successive chapters of *Théorie du sujet*. We will begin with a presentation of Lacan's text, and then of Badiou's commentary on it.

In our second part, we will go on to argue that both Badiou and Lacan are in fundamental agreement about the nature of an act, and that both use the situation described in 'Logical Time' to illustrate a unique dimension pertaining to certain kinds of acts. The act in 'Logical Time' is of a type that other theories of the act do not account for: it is neither a conclusion drawn from instrumental reason (if you want X do Y) nor an act that comes from a pure spontaneity. Instead, it possesses something Lacan calls 'anticipatory certitude'.

While Lacan mentions in the original edition of the article that it is a fragment of a larger, unpublished, *Essai d'une logique collective*, and he makes explicit political references in other texts from that period, he never worked out the ethical and political implications of 'Logical Time'.[2] In our third section we will suggest that Badiou, by contrast, successfully uses 'Logical Time' to make some important ethical distinctions, which we will approach through the Kantian distinction between enthusiasm and *Schwärmerei* (fanaticism).

I

In his text, Lacan analyses a logical problem.[3] A prison warden can free one of three prisoners, and decides to subject them to a test. He shows them five discs – three white and two black – and tells them that he is going to put one disc on each of their backs. They cannot see which it is, and are not allowed to communicate in any way with the other prisoners. The first to come up to him and tell him what colour disc he has on his back will be freed. But the warden adds another condition. The conclusion must be based on logical, and not simply probabilistic reasons. That is, the prisoners cannot just make a lucky guess, but must give sound reasons for why they have come to their conclusion.

The warden proceeds to put a white disc on each prisoner's back. How do they come to the right solution? Let's give the three prisoners names – A, B, and C – and let's adopt A's perspective. A sees two whites, and knows there are five discs in play: three white and two black. If A saw two blacks, then he would know right away that he is white. But A sees two whites. From this situation, nothing can be concluded directly. So, he is forced to make a hypothesis. He supposes that he is black, and then considers what B and C would see, and what kind of hypothesis they would make in this case. If A is black, and if, for example, B supposes that he were black, then C, according to B, would be able to leave immediately, because C would see two blacks. Now, C does not leave immediately, so B should arrive at the conclusion that he is white (supposing A is black). But B also does not leave, so A is able to conclude that he is white.

In *Théorie du sujet*, Badiou formalizes these lines of reasoning as R1, R2 and R3 (268). R1 is what C would conclude if A and B were black: 'I am white.' C can come to this conclusion immediately without making any hypotheses, and that is why Lacan calls it 'the instant of the glance'. R2 is what B would consider if A were black and C white: 'if I were black, then C would leave immediately. C does not leave immediately. So, I am white.' R3 is what, finally, A thinks if, as in the situation actually being considered, both B and C are white: 'Since neither A nor B leave, my initial hypothesis that I am black is incorrect. So I am white.'

A's line of reasoning goes through all three of these moments: R1, R2, R3. To describe the process that A goes through, Lacan distinguishes among three 'times': the instant of the glance, the time for comprehending, and the moment of concluding. The instant of the glance lasts as long as it takes to notice what is given in the situation: each prisoner sees two white discs. The time for comprehending lasts as long as it takes to make a line of reasoning. The most difficult and most interesting time is the moment of concluding.

Given this way of approaching the situation in 'Logical Time', one might think that the prisoners are able to reach a conclusion just by following through a line of reasoning. This is not the case, for the simple reason that A's line of reasoning depends on B and C's supposed hesitation. But this is just a supposition: B and C are not hesitating, they are just standing still. A cannot deduce anything about what B and C are thinking from the fact of their immobility. This is why Lacan thinks that something entirely different happens in the moment of concluding.

What happens to A while he is going through his line of reasoning is a moment of anxiety, what Lacan calls 'the ontological form of anxiety' ('Logical Time' 13). He is not anxious about losing the game, but anxious that he simply will not be able to make a conclusion. Why is this the case? If A realizes that he can come to a conclusion if he interprets the other's standing still as a hesitation, then he also realizes that the others must not move. If the others head for the door of the prison, he can no longer use B and C's hesitation as an element in his line of reasoning.

What A realizes is that he urgently has to end his thinking process and head for the door. So he jumps to a conclusion that closes the time for comprehending, and makes that time retroactively meaningful. It is important to note here that in the moment of concluding A does not make an additional step on the level of thinking, but that he can and has to end his thinking by an act.

Is A sure of his act? He is sure that it is necessary to act, but cannot be sure of the soundness of his reasoning. This is the moment of what Lacan calls anticipatory certitude. By this he means that A leaps ahead to a conclusion whose ground or reason can only be verified after the act. This verification is provided by what happens after he has come to a conclusion: the other two prisoners head for the door at the same moment, which makes him doubt his conclusion. This doubt progressively disappears in two halts that follow after the moment of the conclusion. There are two halts after the moment of conclusion because there are three prisoners. For reasons we needn't go into further here, the number of halts that occur depends on the number of prisoners. The halts provide real evidence for what, in the line of reasoning, were only suppositions. During the halts, what was subjective about the line of reasoning gets de-subjectified, and becomes a shared, intersubjective truth. Beginning with an uncertain, singular decision A reaches a certain and 'universal' truth.

Badiou gives a more or less straightforward recap of Lacan's essay in *Théorie du sujet*, before arriving at his main objection: 'Logical Time' is an account of subjective action which allows for 'neither anticipation nor retroaction'.[4] As Badiou would have it, the moment of conclusion in Lacan's essay is nothing but a decision which flows out of the line of reasoning: 'either the subjective calculus is ruled through and through algebraically, or there is a hasty subjectivation and a subjective process of certitude' (*TS* 270). These two possibilities exclude each other. If a subjective calculus, a line of reasoning, leads to a conclusion, there is neither a hasty subjectivation nor a subjective process of certitude following the conclusion. Against Lacan's logical, algebraic perspective, Badiou wants to show how one should not overlook the importance of haste in the intersubjective process. Using Lacan's own terminology to express his point, Badiou writes that 'haste, not inferable from the symbolic, is the mode in which the subject exceeds [the symbolic] by exposing himself to the real' (*TS* 272).

What Badiou means is that Lacan makes the moment of conclusion derive from an 'algebra', or from a symbolic process. If that were the case, there would be no reason for A to doubt his conclusion when the others get up. Since he does doubt, it is clear to Badiou that the conclusion must have been uncertain and anticipatory. Only, he does not find a good explanation for this doubt in Lacan's reading. As he puts it, 'there must be something that Lacan is not telling us' (*TS* 269). Lacan just notes that there is doubt, without saying why. Badiou takes the further step of saying that, given Lacan's approach to the prisoner's problem, *there should not be any doubt*. This is because the prisoners are taken to be identical, in terms of their intelligence and rational agility.

Badiou argues that the only way to save anticipation and the retroactive nature of certainty is to reject this equivalence. A is always entitled to ask himself the following question: 'what if the other is stupid?' (*TS* 270). Confronted with this possibility, A would indeed experience a moment of doubt at the first halt. The others are moving too, and A would fear that he was perhaps too hasty in his conclusion. If the others are stupid then it is possible that A is not white, because his conclusion was based on the time he supposed it takes for them to conclude they are white. If this time is longer, since they might be stupid, then A has reason to doubt his conclusion at the first halt, and wonder whether he is black.

Badiou situates haste after the moment of conclusion, portraying it as a kind of question A asks himself: 'Wasn't I too hasty? Wasn't there something I overlooked?' By considering the possibility that the others are stupid, Badiou thinks haste and anticipation can be introduced into what would otherwise be the machine-like unfolding of a logical process. According to Badiou, Lacan's text tries to make the right point about the act – it should possess an anticipatory certitude – but it does not set about doing so correctly.

As we have seen, anticipatory certitude is precisely what Lacan underlines in his reading of the prisoner's problem. But there is an important difference between Lacan and Badiou's accounts. Whereas Badiou locates haste at the first halt, Lacan places it in the moment of conclusion itself. On Lacan's account, the fact that A does not suppose that the others are stupid, but think just as he does, is actually what makes A experience an anxiety about the others leaving him behind, which would make it impossible for him to make any conclusion. The supposed equivalence leads Lacan to find the moment of the act itself hasty. In this way, we see that haste for Lacan is not about doubting one's conclusion after it has been made: haste is a constitutive feature of the conclusion itself.

Despite this difference between Badiou and Lacan, they both want to stress the same point: anticipatory certitude is a hallmark of this type of act. It is the specific character of such an act that we will go on to discuss in more detail now, so as to suggest how 'Logical Time' helps free Badiou from a possible criticism: the criticism that his theory embraces a decisionistic, Romantic and subjective ethic.

II

In what way is the moment of conclusion anticipatory? The act precedes the certainty that should have led up to the act. As we have seen, from the situation as it is no sound conclusion can be reached. A does not have enough information to make a conclusion. The best he can do is make a hypothesis and give some meaning to the fact that the others are standing still. As we have seen, he interprets the standing still of the others as a hesitation. Yet A cannot be sure: and as the clock ticks, another factor is introduced. By considering that the others might be getting ready to conclude, A realizes that he also has to conclude. A has to conclude so that he can use the other's standing still as a reason for his act: once they move, his line of reasoning will no longer hold true.

By acting, A retroactively gives his line of reasoning a sense. We see here that his act is not based on a line of reasoning, although it does emerge from a line of reasoning. This means that the act is an element of the line of reasoning itself. The term 'conclusion' for characterizing this act is thus a bit misleading. It is not a conclusion that follows from premises: The term 'conclusion' should be taken in a different way. The 'conclusion' is simply something that brings the time of comprehending to a close.

The fact that the act is anticipatory also allows the singular nature of the act to be desubjectified. This is clear from what happens during the two halts. By acting, without being sure, A suddenly has something to doubt when the others move, as Badiou emphasizes. This doubt allows the act to be verified, because what happens is that A, for the first time, sees real hesitations from the others, rather than hesitations that A simply supposes or reads into the situation: B and C doubt their conclusion too and stand still. This standing still can be unambiguously interpreted as a hesitation since it interrupts their initial movement.

This verification process has two important results. For A himself, it desubjectifies his line of reasoning, in the sense that he now sees objective evidence for the hypothesis he made about what the other prisoners were thinking. Secondly, the singular or subjective conclusion A initially makes can now take on a properly universal form. When the act was made, A had the following, hasty, reason for it: 'I have to conclude that I am white out of fear that the others will leave me behind, making any conclusion impossible.' After the two halts and the verification process they induce, everyone can formulate the simple truth: 'we are three whites because there were two halts'. As Badiou notes in his recent book *The Century*, 'as soon as it's a matter of creative action, the real is only accessible through the subsumption of an "I" by a "we" '.[5]

It is important to point out that this anticipatory kind of act is neither an act that simply follows from a line of reasoning, nor is it an act that is purely spontaneous and *ex nihilo*. The act contains aspects of both. There is a line of reasoning, and there is a spontaneity. But here, the line of reasoning creates a void of uncertainty out of which the act will come. Badiou points out that an act is a real that interrupts the symbolic, but it would not be right to understand the act as an absolute break with the line of reasoning. The act is not a cut in the line of reasoning, or a break with the line of reasoning. As an interruption in the line of reasoning, the act is both part of it and something that suspends its logic, which also allows for it to be resumed after the act (as we have seen, the halts take up the line of reasoning again in a different dimension: the dimension of intersubjective truth). Badiou is right to point out, in Lacanese, that the act is real. He has the further virtue of pointing out that the act is not just real.

What would it mean for the act to be simply an eruption of the real? Actually, there is no pure eruption of the real! It is always already contaminated with names. If the real just happens then it happens without happening, like a trauma, as something which takes place without time and place, without name. To jump ahead a bit to one of the points we will make about Badiou's ethics: to remain faithful to the negative qua negative would be to betray the negative. Only by elaborating on the negative is one actually being faithful to it. In psychoanalytic terms, a symptom remains faithful to a trauma precisely because it elaborates on the trauma by interpreting it and naming it. Without this elaboration there would be nothing but inhibition or anxiety. Indeed, the real without name is simply anxiety, and not an act.

It is worth comparing what Slavoj Žižek has to say about the act here.[6] Consider this passage, in which Žižek claims that an act is not something that emerges from a line of reasoning: 'is not [. . .] a suspension of the principle of sufficient reason(s), however, the very definition of the *act*?' This suggests that there are no reasons for an act. It is difficult to see how an act would be anything other than spontaneous and *ex nihilo* on this account. And indeed elsewhere, Žižek writes, 'the act as real is an event which occurs *ex nihilo*'.[7] In the theory of the act that we find in Badiou and Lacan, however, the relation between the act and the line of reasoning is more complex.

By emphasizing the negative nature of an act, Žižek wants to do justice to what is 'real' about an act. Žižek is right to stress this, but by neglecting the importance of an act's involvement with the symbolic, Žižek seems to be saying that the real of an act happens without the symbolic. Our point is that the real is not without the symbolic, and the act is not without the line of reasoning. For example, in an act, as 'Logical Time' teaches us, the real emerges at a particular place and at a particular moment, one actually prepared by the line of reasoning. So again, it is important to point out that while the act is not a product or result of the line of reasoning, it is not without a relation to it.[8]

Another virtue of the theory of the act that can be drawn from 'Logical Time' is its emphasis on the procedural nature of an act. And oddly, it appears that here Badiou is being more Lacanian than Žižek! For Žižek the act is a moment, whereas Badiou and Lacan show how an act is a process: in fact, they understand the moment of concluding as the beginning of a process. The moment of concluding should not be seen as the act itself without the doubt and the verification process that occur in its wake. Badiou develops the implications of this point elsewhere, with his notions of a truth-process and a generic procedure.

In our view it is Badiou rather than Lacan who develops the ethical and political implications of 'Logical Time'. In doing so it seems to us that he re-elaborates the Kantian distinction between enthusiasm and fanaticism.[9]

Enthusiasm transgresses the limits of reason but in a reserved, modest way: someone who is enthusiastic sees something beyond the limits of a given situation, something which is not yet there, without being sure of its possible realization. The fanatic, on the contrary, seems to neglect the fact that he or she is transgressing the limits of reason, and assumes that he or she has a direct grasp on what is outside reason. And even if what is beyond reason is to be realized, for the fanatic it can only happen by chance or a divine intervention and not by testing and perhaps even changing the idea during a truth-process.

At the end of his treatment of 'Logical Time', Badiou introduces some ethical notions that he elaborates on later in *Théorie du sujet*. Pointing out that 'haste is divisible', he proceeds to discuss two ethical modes in which haste can appear, which to our ears sound very much like the distinction between enthusiasm and fanaticism. On the one hand, prisoner A can leave 'without thinking of the other's qualitative difference' (*TS* 273). Speaking in the first person, Badiou puts it this way: 'my passion for being free leads me to be confident only in the shortest algorithm, intolerant of any interruption' (*TS* 273). In this case, A would not be bothered by the fact that the other prisoners get up when he does: A is certain of his conclusion and the line of reasoning that led up to it. This kind of confidence is later in *Théorie du sujet* called 'belief [*croyance*] (*TS* 337). In the context of 'Logical Time', it appears as a belief in one's line of reasoning, or as a belief that justification for the moment of concluding already exists: this is just like our fanatic, who believes he or she has a direct grasp on what is beyond reason.

Another kind of haste can be found in the confidence that characterizes courage. Badiou describes this as something supported by a 'strategic antici-pation that is not able to succeed in founding a certitude' (*TS* 274) – except, of course, retroactively! This kind of haste seems to us to be very close to what is meant by enthusiasm. The enthusiast knows he or she is making claims that cannot be proved, but is courageous enough to proceed and is confident that the claim is true and that sufficient reasons for it will show up. The enthusiast is by definition modest. He or she has neither the modesty of someone who decides nothing ('I cannot decide, there are not enough premises, I don't have enough information, my knowledge is too limited', etc.) nor the modesty of the fanatic who says that he or she is sure about a claim but that it is only a subjective point of view and that, of course, others may have another opinion (the con-temporary, liberal ideology of tolerance, where everything is 'an interesting opinion'). The enthusiast is modest in making a claim precisely because of how he or she is positioned 'on the way to' truth. Or put differently, the enthusiast leaves the gap between the singular decision and a universal truth open until the situation changes in such a way that the singular can be universally assumed as 'a given'.

IV

There are several problems with 'Logical Time', however, and they have to do with the artificiality of the situation described there. For one thing, the whole story is essentially teleological: the prisoners make a decision for themselves which subsequently turns out to be true. Badiou's critique focuses on this problem: it is as if the situation is a logical machine moving inexorably to the *correct* conclusion. Secondly, the decision the prisoners make is true because it is fully adequate to the situation: that is, their claim is true because they made the right statement about the colour on their back. This seems to suggest that truth is first of all something out there that the prisoners have to figure out. Badiou's own notion of truth is quite different. He would say that what the prisoners arrive at here is a merely 'veridical' statement, a correct opinion, one that is able to be confirmed in their situation, whereas 'truth' is not something that can be confirmed (*EE* 365–9).

Furthermore, the situation is limited by the way it is set up, and in particular by the fact that there are only two possibilities: either one is white or black. A's entire reasoning process is based on these two possibilities. Whatever claim A then makes can already be verified within the terms of the situation. While we have been trying to point out the similarities between Badiou's theory of decision or intervention and the situation in 'Logical Time', the two don't quite match, and the reason for this is very simple: there is no event in 'Logical Time'. In the absence of an event, it is difficult to see what the act is based on. Elsewhere in Badiou's theory, of course, decisive acts, or truth-processes, are contingent upon events. By contrast, an event seems radically excluded from the situation of 'Logical Time', because there are only two signifiers, or two names, available (black or white), and they fully describe all the elements of the situation among which one has to choose.

Apart from these problems inherent to the situation described in 'Logical Time', the situation there does allow both Badiou and Lacan to show the importance of a singular moment of acting which precedes an intersubjective verification process. This implies that the individual decision might be mistaken. What is important is what follows. Using the distinction between enthusiasm and fanaticism again, we see that there are two modes of acting: the enthusiast can enthusiastically make mistakes, but what will always differentiate the enthusiast from the fanatic is the way he or she fails. The fanatic resembles a prisoner who might have learned the truth from a whisper in his ear by the prison warden. Like this prisoner, the fanatic does not go through the anxious moment of the act. As Badiou formulates it, 'only the intervener will know if there was something that happened'.[10] A fanatic is not actually intervening, because he or she has not made a decision and therefore does not participate in a truth process. Only someone who has decided can put a decision to the test. This reminds us of one of the commonly acknowledged features of enthusiasm: enthusiasm is contagious, it needs others with whom it can share its 'divine insight'. The fanatic does not need others because in the end he or she is completely satisfied with a mystical union with supersensible truths.

Put in these terms, of course, no one would want to be a fanatic: fanaticism is pathological. Therefore, to avoid fanaticism, one might be inclined to think of the undecidable as something which ought to be preserved in its undecidability. The question then is whether such an advocate of the undecidable is really so very different from the fanatic. Whereas the fanatic immediately embraces revelations that cannot be discussed, thereby negating the undecidable directly, the advocate of the undecidable would, in 'Logical Time', remain forever positioned in that uncomfortable, anxious moment of conclusion, never acceding to a process of verification, in fear of doing injustice to the truth-moment of anxiety. The enthusiast goes *through* the truth-moment of anxiety, and remains faithful to that moment precisely by replying to it: by replying to it with an act. As Lacan puts it in his unpublished Seminar on anxiety: 'to act is to pull a certitude out of anxiety'.[11]

v

At the opening of his discussion of 'Logical Time', Badiou declares that what is at stake for him is the fixing of an 'irreducible gap' between his theory and Lacan's. We have shown that when it comes to an understanding of the act, both thinkers are quite similar. Where Badiou differs from Lacan is in his ability to draw explicit ethical and political lessons from the kind of act described in 'Logical Time'. In political terms, Badiou's conclusion implies adherence to a familiar Leninist principle:

> When the popular insurrection bursts out, it is never because the calculable moment of this insurrection has come. It is because there is nothing left for it but to rise up, which is what Lenin said: there is a revolution when 'those on the bottom' no longer want to continue as before, and the evidence imposes itself, massively, that it is better to die standing than to live lying down. [Lacan's] anecdote shows that it is the interruption of an algorithm that subjectivates, not its effectuation (*TS* 272–3).

Any revolutionary act must work with the troubling undecidability inherent to a symbolic universe, and *acts* precisely as a reply to the real of an event. But as we have shown, Badiou nonetheless emphasizes the necessary struggle or work to be done to name this event. This process of naming eventually creates a new symbolic order whose operational closure, to use Lacanian terminology, will be ensured by other master signifiers.

14

THE FIFTH CONDITION

Alenka Zupančič

Alain Badiou's philosophy is undoubtedly one of the most powerful conceptual proposals of contemporary thought. It is also a daring proposal, very much in line with Badiou's fundamental and emphatic affirmation of philosophy as such – where the word 'affirmation' can be taken in its Nietzschean sense. This is to say that, in spite of Badiou's continuous – explicit or implicit – polemics with and against 'modern sophists', his philosophical enterprise can in no way be reduced to a reaction to these 'bad' others. Of course, philosophy has its conditions: mathematics, politics, art and love. Yet, these are 'just' conditions, they do not provide a foundation for philosophy. Should any of the above-mentioned generic procedures be transformed from a condition to the foundation of philosophy then this gives rise to what Badiou calls a 'suture' that can lead to a suspension of philosophy, i.e. to its abandoning itself to one of its conditions. One could thus say that there is also a fifth condition of philosophy: philosophy has to pull itself away from the immediate grip of its own conditions, while nevertheless remaining under the effect of these conditions.

Although emphatically opposed to fashionable statements about the end of philosophy (and history), Badiou nevertheless suggests that something *did* happen to (or in) philosophy after Hegel. In a certain sense, Hegel *was* the 'last philosopher'. Badiou says as much when he states: 'if philosophy is threatened by suspension, and this perhaps since Hegel, it is because it is captive to a network of sutures to its conditions, especially to its scientific and political conditions, which forbade it from configuring their general compossibility' (*MP* 45/64). According to this account, philosophy after Hegel did not die, it rather suspended itself by delegating its functions to one or another of its conditions: to science (the 'positivist suture'), to politics ('political suture') and then, as a kind of reaction to these two sutures, to art ('poetical suture'). Since Hegel, philosophy thus mostly took place in the element of its own suppression, to the advantage of one of these procedures (science, politics, art). This is also why, according to Badiou, all great philosophers after Hegel were in fact anti-philosophers (Nietzsche, Marx, Wittgenstein, Heidegger . . .). From this perspective, the eleven chapters of Badiou's *Manifesto for Philosophy* could indeed be read as a reversal of Marx's eleventh thesis on Feuerbach: for quite some time, philosophers were trying to change the world, or to justify it (a frequent consequence, according to Badiou, of the positivist suture), or else to merge

with it through a poetical experience of Existence and of the Unspeakable ...
and the time has come for philosophers to start to philosophize!

Of course, this in no way implies that philosophy should be, for instance,
'apolitical'. On the contrary, no real philosophy is at liberty to choose to be
apolitical or indifferent to any of the four generic procedures that constitute its
conditions. Nevertheless, it operates in a certain distance from them. This
distance is not a distance of disengagement, it springs from the following
fundamental axiom: 'Philosophy is not a production of truth but an operation
that starts out from truths' (CS 66). As Peter Hallward notes, for all its
ambition Badiou's philosophy cultivates a certain modesty with respect to its
conditions.[1] Truths are produced elsewhere: within the four generic procedures,
the origin of which is always an event (in the Badiouian sense of the word).
Philosophy is thus defined as a conceptual space where the generic procedures,
are 'configured' and 'composed'. Philosophy does not establish any truth, but it
has at its disposal a place of truths; it does not utter any truths, it utters a
thinkable conjuncture of truths. In one sense, philosophy is a scene (or stage) of
truths. It is precisely this scene or space that disappears whenever philosophy
abandons itself to one of its conditions. Badiou recently coined a very telling
expression, 'la passion du réel', the passion of the real, and one could perhaps say
that it is precisely such passion of the real that tempts modern philosophy to
abandon itself to one of its conditions, i.e. to look for a direct access to (the
production of) truth.

On this level, there is an interesting resemblance between Badiou's project
and the project of so-called critical (or Kantian) philosophy, with its two
fundamental preoccupations or claims: the interrogation of the conditions of
possibility of philosophy and the consequent restriction of philosophy to a
clearly delimited field. The anecdotal aspect of this resemblance, at least, is
perfectly obvious. Kant himself had his 'anti-philosopher': David Hume.
Hume's objection to the notion of causality could be understood as undermining the reign of the One as guarantor of the link between cause and effect,
thus opening the way, to use Badiou's terms, for the authority of the multiple.
The reaction to Hume that shaped the conditions of thought in Kant's time was
two-fold: a dogmatic repetition of the old views which refused to *hear* what
Hume was saying, and the rise of scepticism or, if one prefers, of sophism. Kant
states himself to be weary of both – of dogmatism since it teaches nothing, and
of scepticism since it amounts to an abdication of philosophy that, as he puts it
very nicely, 'does not even promise us anything – even the quiet state of a
contented ignorance'.[2] Kant decides to carry out his philosophical project,
much as Badiou does, 'in proximity' to the anti-philosophy of Hume, i.e. by
acknowledging his gesture of dethronement of the One, without accepting its
sophistic implications as necessary. He starts off by defining the conditions of
possibility of philosophy, insisting that his proposal, although it might look
extremely ambitious, 'arrogant and vainglorious', is in fact 'incomparably more
moderate' than both dogmatic and sceptical claims.[3] For sceptics, 'these pre-
tended *indifferentists*, however they may try to disguise themselves by substituting a popular tone for the language of the Schools, inevitably fall back, in

so far as they think at all, into those very metaphysical assertions which they profess so greatly to despise'.[4] It is tempting to compare this passage with Badiou's discussion of the great contemporary sophists who, although they are the rare thinkers of our time, remain caught in the same paradox:

> It is never really modest to declare an 'end', a completion, a radical impasse. The announcement of the 'End of Grand Narratives' is as immodest as the Grand Narrative itself, the certainty of the 'end of metaphysics' proceeds within the metaphysical element of certainty, the deconstruction of the concept of subject requires a central category – being, for example – whose historial prescription of which is even more determinant, etc. [...]. The contrite prosopopeia of abjection is as much a posture, an imposture, as the bugle blaring cavalry of the Spirit's second coming. The end of the End of History is cut from the same cloth as this End (*MP* 11/30–31tm).

Kant's own response to the proclaimed impasse or dead end of philosophy is, first, to establish the conditions of the possibility of philosophy, and then to assign to philosophy its proper field, preventing it from sliding either into *Schwärmerei* or into sophistic play. If philosophy steps out the field that defines it and constitutes its scene or space it can head only for disaster. On this level, i.e. concerning the very philosophical gesture involved in the Kantian project on the one hand and in Badiou's project on the other, the similarities seem to be more than just superficial.

However, it is not the purpose of this chapter to compare Badiou and Kant. Neither is it to establish whether the Kantian gesture was purely restrictive or else if it had the power of effectively re-inaugurating philosophy under new conditions, or in the face of the reconfiguration of its conditions. (Given the subsequent development of German idealism I would be rather inclined to opt for the second suggestion.) My question concerns the philosophical impact, in the context of the contemporary configuration of philosophy, of the key elements that constitute Badiou's own definition of philosophy. Philosophy is only possible: (1) under the four conditions which philosophy itself declares us such; (2) by maintaining a distance towards these conditions, which is to say by resisting a suture of philosophy to any of its conditions or by renouncing the claim that philosophy is itself a production of truth. This is what I've called the 'fifth condition'.

According to Badiou himself, it is especially this second point that constitutes what is mainly at stake in the contemporary dividing line of philosophy. Most modern philosophers are ready to subscribe (and thus to abandon) 'their' philosophy to one of its conditions. One could say that in this case they are, strictly speaking, no longer philosophers, but thinkers. In his book on Saint Paul, Badiou points out how names that designate the four generic procedures are being systematically replaced by other names which aim at effacing the procedures of truth involved in them: culture instead of art, technique instead of science, management instead of politics, sexuality instead of love. One could add to this list: thinkers instead of philosophers. Except that thinkers, in the above-defined sense, are precisely those who usually fight against such re-nominations, especially those concerning the generic procedures to which they themselves subscribe their thought. In this sense 'scientific thinkers' would be the last to fail to distinguish between science and technology, 'poetic thinkers' the last to confuse culture and art, engaged 'political thinkers' the last to abandon the name politics in favour of management ... On the other hand, more than a few of those who, in recent decades, were happy to be called 'philosophers' have indeed embraced these re-nominations as signs of modernity, progress and the ongoing secularization of society. This is probably why Badiou maintains, more or less explicitly, that modern anti-philosophy (and its 'thinkers') have been for quite some time the only guardians of the philosophical flame, so to speak. If philosophy did not die, but has continued to live in the element of its own suspension, this is largely the merit of anti-philosophy, i.e. of thinkers.

Now 'thought' (*la pensée*) is not a special prerogative of philosophy, it belongs essentially to all generic procedures or procedures of truth. In this sense, philosophy could be said to be the 'thought of thought', and in this respect Badiou is in fact closer to Hegel than to Kant. His attempt to delimit a field of philosophy proper does not consist in inviting philosophy to restrain itself from certain kinds of statements, forbidding it to go beyond a certain limit: the space of philosophy is not created by drawing limits around its field, but simply by affirming the very space of reflexivity of thought. To say that philosophy proper is the thought of thought does not mean or imply that it is in the position of the Other of the Other. Quite the contrary: philosophy takes place within the constitutive (and inherent) reflexivity of thought. The relation of philosophy to its conditions is not simply that of certain conditions that have to be satisfied in order for philosophy to be possible. Although this is also true to a certain extent, the main accent of Badiou's proposal is elsewhere: it is the *thinking within* (the dimension of truth produced by) its conditions that constitutes the condition of philosophy. Philosophy is work that takes place at a distance from its conditions, yet within the realm of these conditions.

One way of understanding more precisely the conceptual stakes of this 'fifth condition' leads to an interesting question that we have so far left unanswered. We saw that Badiou himself maintains that something did happen in the nineteenth century, 'just after Hegel' (*MP* 49), something that changed the course (as well as the 'nature') of philosophy. But what? Could one try to determine what exactly happened? Badiou does not address this question directly. He often hints, however, that it has to do with a destitution of the One, i.e. with the replacement of the 'authority of the One' with the 'authority of the multiple'. He also hints that (the development of) capitalism had an important role in this: 'It is obviously the only thing we can and must welcome within Capital: it exposes the pure multiple as the foundation of presentation; it denounces every effect of One as a simple, precarious configuration; it dismisses the symbolic representations in which the bond [*lien*] found a semblance of

being' (MP 37/56). One could say that what happened in the nineteenth century is that a slow but massive shift took place from one dominant social bond
to another. Yet what is at stake in this shift of the social bond is not simply the
alternative between or the replacement of One with multiple.

In order to appreciate this properly it is important to determine what exactly
the expression 'authority of the One' refers to. There is, first of all, an important
difference between what Badiou calls the 'authority of the One' and what he
calls the 'count for one'. The latter is simply the condition of any thinkable
situation or thing: whereas the purely multiple is inconsistent and is a pure
'excess beyond itself', all consistent thought supposes a structure, a counting-
for-one, such that every presented or presentable multiple is consistent. Every
presentable multiple is presented, in other words, precisely as a *set* or consistent
being-together of a certain collection of elements. In this respect, the counting-
for-one (and with it the notion of 'one') is perfectly compatible with the notion
of pure multiplicity. However, excess beyond itself, which is the very being of
Being as purely multiple, also takes place on the level of what is already
counted-for-one, i.e. on the level of presentation, within a set, or within what
Badiou calls a 'situation' (which is just another word for 'set'): it takes place as
the excess of the parts of a given multiple or set over its elements: if we have a
multiple of, say, five elements, the possible combination of these elements – i.e.
the number of the 'parts' – exceeds by far the number of elements (more
precisely, this number amounts to two to the power of five). This excess, that
Badiou also calls *l'excès errant*, a 'wandering excess', is one of the crucial notions
of his ontology, for he holds 'the wandering [*errance*] of the excess to be the real
of being' (MP 61/81). What he calls the 'state' of a situation (playing on the
double meaning of this word) involves the operation whereby this excess itself is
counted-for-one, and thus fixed (or made consistent). The count-for-one itself,
which takes place on the level of presentation, is thus counted-for-one. This is
what Badiou also calls *representation*, or meta-structure.

Now, what is involved in the expression the 'authority of the One' is
something quite different than the count-for-one which makes any multiplicity
presentable or intelligible, as well as something other than a 'state'. Badiou
usually employs the statement 'the One is not' as synonymous with 'God is not',
or else as directly synonymous with the 'death of God'. Yet at the same time he
also identifies this statement with what is involved in his own fundamental
ontological stance: a multiple is always a multiple of multiples (of multiples, of
multiples ...), and the eventual 'stopping point' can in no way be a 'one' but
only a *void*. However, I would maintain that the 'One is not' (in the sense of
'God is not') cannot be situated on the same level as the positing of a void as
'the stuff that being is made of'. The reason for this is that – as Badiou himself
points out[5] – 'God is dead' is not an ontological statement but a statement that
belongs to an eventual horizon or, more precisely, to its closure. In other words, I
would suggest that we take the formulation 'authority of the One' to refer to a
structurally as well as historically determinable social bond, and not as primarily referring to a conceptual choice between One and multiple.

The 'authority of the One' is a social bond which roughly corresponds to what Lacan conceptualized as the discourse of the Master. The Master's discourse is not exactly a 'state' in Badiou's sense. In it, the wandering excess is fixed, not by being counted as one, but by being subjected and attached, as Other, to the agency of the One. The authority of the One is not based upon a totalization of a multiple, it is not a 'forcing' of the multiple by the One. It is based upon relating the One and Other in the element of their pure disjunction. The Master's discourse functioned so well and so long because it succeeded in transforming the 'weakest' point of a given multiple (the point of its very inconsistency) into the strongest lever, as well as the source, of its own power. What was entirely mobilized or absorbed in the One was not the colourful multiplicity of Being, but the point of its potential generic power: its loose end, the point on account of which no multiplicity can be intrinsically 'counted as One'. The important thing to remember in relation to the Master's discourse (or the authority of the One) is that the agent of this social bond is not the excessive multiplicity counted-for-one, it is not a unified *totality* of the excessive multiplicity, but an (empty) signifier of its impossible totalization. In other words, the way multiplicity is attached (and fixed) to the One is that the One gives body to, or incarnates, the constitutive void of the multiple. This is how the master signifier, as *agent* of this social bond, fixates the excess, assigns it its place and keeps it there.

What happens with the destitution of the authority of the One is that the bond between the One and multiple, the bond that was there in their very disjunction, dissolves. The result is that the excess, as the very real of Being, emerges as a free-floating element and appears in a form of a 'passionate detachment'. For what happens is not that excess loses its signifier or representation (since it never really had one), what it loses is its attachment to the One. One could say that a spectre of excess starts haunting the society, in its different spheres; and its 'spectral' form is in no way insignificant. The Master's discourse (or, if one prefers, the authority of the One) is a social bond in which this excessive element is, if one may say so, in the 'ideal' place, in the service of the hegemonic power of the One, which reigns by *assuming* the very excessiveness of excess. What happens with the destitution of this bond is, so to speak, that the ghost of excess escapes from the bottle. This process could be said to have started with the French Revolution, to have reached its full extent in the nineteenth century, and to have continued through a part of the twentieth century. The nineteenth century in particular was deeply haunted by this excessive element in all possible forms, from the conceptual to the phantasmagoric. Perhaps no single phrase can capture, so to speak, the spirit of the thought of this period (regardless of different schools and orientations) better than this: *there is something rotten in the State of Things*. Some thinkers of the time attributed this rot to the still-remaining pockets of the authority of the One, believing that redemption would come only with their definitive elimination. Others, on the contrary, saw the origin of discontent in the very destitution of the authority of the One. But we can say, without oversimplifying things, that virtually all serious thinkers sought to think at a maximal proximity to, if not in a direct confrontation with, this excess. A 'tarrying with the excess' thus became the most prominent figure of thought. Utopias, designed to eliminate social and other injustice, mostly proposed to achieve this by eliminating this very excess. To a certain extent, even Marx was tempted by the possibility of eliminating, once and for all, the excessive, disharmonious element of society – the element in which he himself recognized its truth, its real and its symptom. As for Nietzsche, one could say that a 'tarrying with the excess' constituted the very core of his writings, although he certainly did not seek to eliminate it. In his recent book, *On the Psychotheology of Everyday life: Reflections on Freud and Rosenzweig*, Eric Santner develops a reading of these two authors around the central notion of a 'constitutive "too muchness"'[6] which corresponds perfectly to the notion of 'wandering excess'. In literature, the explosion of a 'wandering excess' is even more directly perceptible: the undead dead, spectral, unplaceable figures and 'Things', from *Frankenstein* to *Dracula*, passing through all kinds of phenomena that Freud treated under the title of *Das Unheumliche*, the uncanny. Not to mention that one of the most popular serials of the middle of the nineteenth century was Eugène Sue's *The Wandering Jew* (*Le Juif errant* – another name for *l'excès errant?*).

And at the same time this (wandering) excess was increasingly becoming recognized as, precisely, the real of being, and also as the locus if its truth. If, for modern (anti-)philosophy, Hegel became one of the most criticized (if not directly loathed) of philosophers it is precisely since it seems that, in his speculative edifice, everything adds up: there are no loose ends, no scars ('the wounds of the spirit heal without scars'), no cracks. In short: no wandering excess. Philosophy in general did not escape this mocking contempt: there are more things in heaven and earth than are dreamt of in (our) philosophy. Or, in another version of this objection: instead of disclosing it, philosophy conceals the real of being, its cracks and its critical points. Freud liked to quote the last verses of the following Heine poem that summarizes this objection splendidly:

> Life and the world's too fragmented for me!
> A German professor can give me the key.
> He puts life in order with skill magisterial,
> Builds a rational system for better or worse;
> With nightcap and dressing-gown scraps for material
> He chinks up the holes in the universe.[7]

The post-Hegelian philosophy (or, if one prefers, anti-philosophy) started off with this fundamental claim: symbolic representations which were traditionally considered as access to the truth and to the real of Being in fact alienate us from Being and deform it (or our perception of it). And classical philosophy (or 'metaphysics') was suddenly recognized as the queen of this representative misrepresentation.

Indeed, if one were to name one central issue that distinguishes the rise of modern thought it is perhaps none other than precisely the issue of representation (and the question of the One and/or Multiple is part of this issue), its profound interrogation, and the whole consequent turn against (the logic of) representation. This is perhaps most perceptible in (modern) art, which frontally attacked the notion of art as representation. Gérard Wajcman was right when he defined the central problem of modern art as follows: 'How to find access to the world in some other way than through image? How to aim at the world, at the real, without at the same time interposing the screen of representation?'[8] In politics, this also was a central issue: who represents people and how they can be properly represented? Why are some represented and some not? And what if the very idea of representation is the source of society's evils and its alienation? The realm of politics is especially interesting in this respect since the introduction of a 'representative' system coincided with the very questioning of its pertinence. Something similar took place in respect to the generic procedure of love: a simultaneous demand that love be properly represented by the institution of marriage (the new imperative that one should marry out of love), and a massive 'observation' that this is in fact impossible, i.e. that marriage can never truly represent the real of love.

It was this general interrogation of representation and, to put it simply, the conviction that the real of being escapes representation (or else is falsified, distorted by it), which drew philosophy towards embracing the immediacy of one or another of its conditions. Paradoxically, Badiou emphatically shares this view of representation, although he is as emphatic in rejecting the consequences that philosophy drew from it. Philosophy embraced the immediacy of its conditions since this immediacy seemed to be the only bond remaining between thought and being. It is not so much that philosophy was seized by a passion for a direct access to the production of truths (as I suggested earlier) as it is that this direct access seemed to remain the *only possible* bond between philosophy and the ontological layer of its conditions. The either/or of modern (anti-)philosophy sprang from what appeared as the very impossibility of a position that could satisfy Badiou's 'fifth condition' (again, that philosophy has to pull itself away from the immediate grip of its conditions, while nevertheless remaining under these conditions). Before, the scene for such composing of truths was provided by the faith in representation. I use the word 'faith' deliberately, since the correlation of an object and its representation presupposed an Other vouching for this correlation and its unchangeableness. This Other (or, perhaps better, this other One), by *fixing* the relationship between, for instance, words and things, corresponds to what Badiou calls representation as meta-structure. For this is exactly one of the ways we could resume Badiou's distinction between presentation and representation: presentation involves naming the things (or 'elements'), whereas representation involves fixing the relationship between things (or elements) and 'their' names.

For Badiou, representation also constitutes the crucial operation of the institution of a state, and as such he views it as repudiation of a truth procedure. Hence Badiou's principled position *against* representation and the state – a position he adopts while remaining, at the time, well aware of the difficulty of simply putting an end to all representation (or all state). Badiou acknowledges that the state is co-original to any situation, which is to say that 'there is always both presentation and representation' (*EE* 110). The end of representation and the 'universality of simple presentation' (an egalitarian counting-for-one) remains a goal that bears some resemblance to the Kantian notion of a 'regulative idea', i.e. an idea that cannot be realized but in view of which one orientates one's engagement in reality. This question of presentation and representation (and their distinction) is indeed a very difficult one, and constitutes a perhaps not yet entirely worked-out aspect of Badiou's conceptual edifice. At the same time, it is undoubtedly one of its central aspects. If nothing else, it is essential for the very possibility of philosophy (its 'fifth condition'), for it seems that philosophy as composition and configuration of truths (produced elsewhere) cannot exactly be said to be a 'simple presentation'. More: could one not say that what comes the closest to philosophy as simple presentation is precisely what Badiou calls modern anti-philosophy? Philosophy as presentation *is* nothing other than philosophy abandoning itself to its conditions, philosophy as an immediate part of procedure(s) of truth (or else as a sophistic game of endlessly surfing on the waves of the 'wandering excess').

So are we then supposed instead to embrace representation as the meta-structure which alone could guarantee a space or scene for philosophy proper? Of course not; this would be falling back to the essentially premodern (or pre-Hegelian) position.

The answer – which I will only try to sketch or roughly indicate here – rather lies in acknowledging something that Badiou strangely refuses to acknowledge or at least to adopt. Something that happened in linguistics and gained a definite form in psychoanalysis (more precisely, in the Lacanian 'use' of linguistics). Something that can in no way be dismissed as yet another expression of the 'linguistic turn' and even less as a 'poetic turn'. Something that is as important for contemporary philosophy as is Cantor's secularization of the infinite: an entirely new conception of representation. A conception which is not that of representation as meta-structure, and does not involve the idea of the signifier (or 'name') representing an object for the subject. A conception which strikingly meets Badiou's own demand of 'destitution of the category of object' while preserving the category of the subject (cf. *MP* 72–3/91–2). A conception that finds its most concise formulation in Lacan's statement: 'a signifier represents a subject for another signifier'. This was a major breakthrough of contemporary thought, a breakthrough that could in fact provide philosophy with its 'fifth condition', i.e. its own distinctive conceptual space. For in this conception, representation is not a 'presentation of presentation' or the state *of* a situation but rather a 'presentation within presentation' or a state *within* a situation. In this conception, representation is itself infinite and constitutively not-all (or non-conclusive), it represents no object and does not prevent a continuous un-relating of its own terms (which is how Badiou defines the mechanism of truth). Here, representation as such is a wandering excess over itself; representation *is* the infinite tarrying with the excess that springs not simply from what is or is not represented (its 'object'), but from this act of representation itself, from its own inherent 'crack' or inconsistency. The Real is not something outside or beyond representation, but is the very crack of representation.

The problem of representation as meta-structure, and the consequent imperative to restrain oneself from representation or to pull oneself away from the 'state', is something that belongs to a different ontology than the ontology of the purely multiple, of infinity and of contingency. It could only concern a universe in which the evental statement 'God is dead' for whatever reason does not hold true. In an infinite contingent universe (or 'situation'), by contrast, there is no necessity for the 'counting of the count itself' to be situated on a meta-level. It can very well be situated on the same level as the counting-for-one itself, only separated from it by an irreducible interval (and it is this interval that Lacan calls the Real). Moreover, this is precisely what *makes* a situation 'infinite'. What makes it infinite is not the exclusion of any operation of representation (which would 'want' to count it for one and thus to close it upon itself) but its inclusion. What makes any particular 'presentation' infinite is precisely that it already *includes* representation.

This conception also allows for an effect of unification (or fixation) taking place, yet a different one from what Badiou calls 'state'. Lacan links it to his notion of the 'quilting point' (*point de capiton*). This unification of a (potentially) infinite set is not the same as in the case of meta-structure. S_1 as '*point de capiton*' is not a meta-signifier in relation to S_2, to the virtually infinite battery of signifiers and their combinations that Lacan also calls 'knowledge'. S_1 quilts this set not by counting the count itself, but by 'presenting' the very impossibility of an immediate coincidence of the two counts, i.e. by presenting the very gap between them. In other words, S_1 is the signifier of the impossibility of the two (counting and counting the count itself) to be One. It is the signifier of the very gap or interval or void that separates them in any process of representation: a void that is precisely the cause of the infinite layering of representation. For Lacan, the Real of being is this void or interval or gap, this very non-coincidence, whereas the wandering excess is already its result. S_1 presents this void by naming it, it does not represent it. Lacan's S_1, the (in)famous 'master signifier' or 'phallic signifier' is, paradoxically, the only way to write that 'the One is not' and that what 'is' is the void that constitutes the original disjunction in the midst of every count-for-one. The count-for-one is always already two. S_1 is the matheme of what one can describe as 'the One is not'. It writes that 'the One is not' by presenting the very thing that prevents it from being One. This is what S_1 says: the One is not; yet what is is not a pure multiple, but two. This is perhaps Lacan's crucial insight: if there is something on which one could lean in order to leave the 'ontology of the One' behind, this something is not simply the multiple, but a Two.

This, of course, is directly related to the point in which Badiou recognizes a major contribution of psychoanalysis to the conditions of philosophy: psychoanalysis is the first (consistent) thought of the generic procedure of love. Which is to say that it is the first thinkable articulation of 'a Two that would neither be counted for one nor would it be the sum of one + one. A Two that would be counted for two in an immanent way (. . .), where Two is neither a fusion nor a sum; and where Two is thus in excess over that what constitutes it, without there being a Third [term] to join it.'[9]

This singular notion of the Two is very much related to the question of representation, i.e. of the possibility for the 'counting the count itself' to be situated on the same level as the count (and not on a meta-level), yet dislocated in relation to it. For this is precisely what it implies to think a 'Two that would be counted for two in an immanent way'.

Badiou was not only the first philosopher explicitly to conceptualize this singular notion of the Two in philosophy, he also reminded psychoanalysis of the production of this truth that it sometimes tends to forget. By conceptualizing it within philosophy, i.e. within the space of a 'general compossibility' of truths, he gave contemporary philosophy one of its most precious concepts which, although it comes from a singular generic procedure, has its universal value and is in no way limited to that procedure. I would also add that with this concept, Badiou addresses the question of representation from a new and different angle, an angle which avoids the difficulties sketched out above and which, at the same time, directly concerns the conditions of philosophy.

If philosophy is to take place within the space of the infinite process of truth without itself being a process of truth, if it is to be situated on the same level as generic procedures yet at a certain distance from them (i.e. dislocated in relation to them), then it has to rely precisely on such an 'immanent count-for-two' as is at work in a Badiouian conception of the Two.

This would imply, of course, that one of the four conditions of philosophy (love, with its immanent count-for-two) is also its 'fifth condition', the condition that defines the very relationship of philosophy with its conditions and keeps it from merging with them, as well as from appearing as their independent sum. As a thought that operates within the field of four generic procedures of truth, without simply merging with this field and becoming indistinguishable from it, philosophy presupposes a *scène du Deux*, a 'stage/scene of the Two'. In other words, in the configuration of conditions of philosophy, one of its conditions – the immanent count-for-two, which Badiou recognizes in the figure of love – has itself to be counted-for-two.

15

WHAT REMAINS OF FIDELITY
AFTER SERIOUS THOUGHT

Alexander García Düttmann

'La danse mimerait la pensée encore indécidée.'[1]

One manner and, in a sense, perhaps the only manner of relating to a philosopher's thought is to consider it an event, and to do so not just in the realm of
ideas, but in one's own comportment, worthy not just of serious thought, but of
an active and militant fidelity, of a faithfulness which both constitutes and
reflects the event. For how could I grasp what is at stake in a thought, how
could I seize what a thought does or does not to provide me with a hitherto
unknown sense of the world, raising or lowering the stakes, if I were not faced
with a choice or a decision which affects me as much as it affects the thought
itself, and which leaves no space for the equanimity of an impartial evaluation?
In philosophy, but also in art, science, politics and love, the mutual implication
of event and fidelity points towards the relevance of experience for thinking, for
a certain intelligibility at the heart of love, politics, science and art. Here,
experience stands for involvement and concern. It designates the instantaneous
traversal of a world opening up in the moment of decision. Is a true believer –
one who adheres to a philosophical doctrine, for example – a personification of
fidelity? My definition of a true believer will transpire in the answer I give to
this question. There is a definition according to which true believers devote
their intelligence to a cause, but tend to sever it from imagination. They
relinquish fidelity by subordinating imagination to the understanding.

We cannot understand fidelity, Alain Badiou shows, without a notion of
what it means for something to take place as an event. For fidelity depends on
the unexpected appearance of a singularity that cannot be accounted for in a
given situation – I may accept a rule, but in doing so I am not being *faithful* to
the rule I follow. Fidelity also depends on the capacity of resisting its own
regulation and institutionalization. Without such resistance, which finds its
resources in singularity itself, fidelity would amount to a merely functional
verification, to a sterile confirmation, to a dogmatic repetition, and would cease
to be a commitment. It would no longer run the risk of betrayal. Conversely, to
have a notion of what it means for something to take place as an event, an
understanding of fidelity is required. An event that would not be constituted by
the very fidelity it calls for, an event that could be identified as the object to

which fidelity attaches itself and that for this reason would not be brought about by a faithful intervention, an event that would be added to a situation as a further element, could not interrupt the way of the world and would turn into a mere fact, into a given elucidated by 'calculations internal to a situation'.[2] Thus fidelity and event imply one another in an infinite process in which ultimately they cannot be distinguished. A sudden illumination that could dispense with fidelity (*SP* 16) would be less an event than a redemption of the world or a release from it, an entering into the event itself, as it were.

Badiou conceives of fidelity in terms of an eventful faithfulness to an event. Such fidelity does not simply rely on an event to provide the preposition essential to its expression with an object or a sense of direction. It rather makes the event happen in the first place, thus acquiring its sense of direction in the movement it triggers.* Fidelity is as singular as the event itself and cannot be shared except by those who behave faithfully. It does not aim at establishing a universal consensus (*AM* 33) and does not let itself be referred to as an existing and identifiable pattern of behaviour, as a subjective capacity or as a virtue attributed to what the philosophical tradition labels as a subject (*EE* 258). There is no such subject who would be capable of fidelity in principle or who would deserve being called faithful on the basis of an attribution of qualities, since the implication of fidelity in the event demands that the subject emerges from fidelity. In order to constitute a kind of 'support' (*E* 39) for fidelity, the subject must already be faithful to an event. Consequently fidelity impedes a subject from gaining a dispassionate awareness or knowledge of a collective commitment. Fidelity and faithfulness, the two terms which in English translate *fidélité*, each highlight one important aspect of the concept as used by Badiou. The objectivity fidelity connotes indicates that *fidélité* is not merely the

---

* *Competing fidelities* – 'What? Fidelity makes the event happen in the first place? Badiou denies this categorically. What makes an event happen is chance combined with the structural foreclosure of the site.' – 'You are right, of course. Later on in my short text I shall refer to the very end of the section on fidelity which can be found in *Being and Event*. Here, Badiou says that fidelity is all the more "real", the more it appears to be in the same supplementary position as the event considered in relation to a situation. Does this not imply that there is a point at which it proves impossible to distinguish between event and fidelity, and at which fidelity must itself be conceived of as an event – "as a second event" (*EE* 265)? If I am right, event is *also* a name for fidelity. It is on such an understanding that I base my argument, or rather: that I attribute the claim I wish to make myself to Badiou, too. You could say that in the passage to which I allude Badiou merely points towards a limit at which fidelity ceases to be fidelity. When fidelity turns into an event, it no longer makes sense to speak of fidelity. Hence, in your eyes, Badiou tells us that fidelity always moves between two limits. Each limit indicates its disappearance, as it were. On the one hand, fidelity must not become too institutionalized, on the other hand it must beware from coming too close to the limit at which it is in danger of becoming indistinguishable from an event. Would such an interpretation not be much more consistent with Badiou's general usage of the concept of fidelity? Certainly. But since we must also distinguish fidelity from a verification, a confirmation, a repetition, and think of it in terms of a commitment; since, in order for us to use the concept of fidelity meaningfully, we must also keep in mind that fidelity needs to "appear innovative [*faire figure d'innovation*]", I am suggesting that we might draw a *positive* consequence from the possibility of fidelity becoming indistinguishable from an event. Don't forget that Badiou does not explicitly reject this possibility. My suggestion, then, consists in the following claim: to maintain that fidelity turns into yet another event can be interpreted as meaning that fidelity is constitutive of the event and that, without fidelity, the event would not happen. I do *not* wish to reduce fidelity to a mere event. In analysing fidelity as that which is preceded by an event *and* as that which is constitutive of an event, or which makes it happen in the first place, I am trying to do justice to the concept of fidelity as we tend to use it, *and* to follow Badiou in the course of an active interpretation.'

disposition of a subject, while the subjectivity that faithfulness connotes indicates that *fidélité* is nevertheless a radical commitment. *Fidélité* is a radical commitment precisely to the extent that it is *not* a subjective disposition.

However, the immanence of fidelity cannot be entirely closed upon itself or else its incommensurability would erase the event and the faithful behaviour itself. This is why, without quite knowing it, I am always confronted with the pressing question of whether I am faithful here and now, at this very moment; that is, before I can even *try* to take hold of faithfulness cognitively and refer to myself as a faithful or unfaithful subject, as a subject whose fidelity would be evidence of an event. It is as if the question proved to be all the more pressing the more the answer must precede it, the more the application of criteria reveals itself to be misguided, not only because external criteria mistake a singular form of fidelity for an instance of a general rule but also because internal criteria, supplied by the singularity of a faithful comportment, still entail an objectification. The instant I confront the question of fidelity and ask myself whether I am indeed faithful, I step outside of faithfulness altogether. I stop being faithful, though I do not therefore become unfaithful: 'There is no failure, there is only a ceasing' (*AM* 142). An event consists in my relation to it as much as it allows for this relation. Yet once an event and my relation to it are transformed into objects of knowledge, once fidelity becomes a memory of an event whose existence it presupposes and whose presupposed existence limits the usages which can be made of the event's name (*PM* 214), once it relates to the event as to a promise (*CT* 20, 23) and once its manifestations are comprehended as so many interpretations of an object or as so many views of a subject, fidelity vanishes. It keeps escaping all attempts that seek to justify it in hindsight. Hence, to maintain that I am confronted with the pressing question of fidelity when I cannot be, is a way of conveying a disquieting insight. On the one hand, fidelity would not be a commitment if it did not defy its identification; on the other hand, fidelity would abolish itself and resemble a symptom of delusion or madness if it did not test itself against the possibility of its own failure. In other words, fidelity must be an event, or remain indistinguishable from an event, and it must also mark its essential difference from the event to which it relates, or trace the outline of a more or less recognizable behaviour.

In Badiou's work this difficulty in conceiving of fidelity is acknowledged twice, for both the thought that there is more than just one form of fidelity and the thought that fidelity always involves a fidelity towards fidelity testify to it. Fidelity is intrinsically multiple, but each of its multiple forms is dependent on another. When, in a meditation on Pascal, Badiou states that those who are faithful to an event split into a conservative majority and an avant-garde minority, into those who refuse to recognize that the event has taken place and those who do not, he distinguishes between two forms of fidelity (*EE* 241). What are the implications of this distinction, the ones to which Badiou draws attention and the ones he leaves unmentioned? An anticipatory fidelity relates to an event as if it belonged to past and future at the same time, as if it had already taken place precisely because it has not yet taken place. The temporal structure of such fidelity exposes it to confusion. The event, a 'pure beginning'

(*SP* 52) which does not prove anything and which cannot be proven other than by a faithful decision or by a naming which carries the name beyond its own linguistic particularity and thus safeguards the event's intrinsic 'unnameability' (*SP* 49; cf. 81, 118), threatens to be mistaken for something in need of verification. When it falls prey to this sort of confusion, anticipatory fidelity solidifies into what Badiou refers to as a 'prophetic disposition' (*EE* 289). Still, a rupture would not occur without preparation and anticipatory fidelity reveals itself to be essential for an event to take place – in the instant of a faithful decision. Fidelity can only ever overcome itself.

Now to the extent that the event has not taken place and that the representation of an expected outcome (*SP* 102) must vigilantly be prevented, anticipatory fidelity functions as a fidelity towards fidelity. But must it not undergo a radical transformation? When, rather than risking a decision, it holds on steadily to an announcement, or to a sense of an impending rupture, it is in danger of betraying the event, stifled by its own perseverance. Fidelity cannot and should not avoid venturing forward. In so doing, however, in betraying itself for the sake of the event it anticipates, it always risks a decision which may be premature or powerless. Then the event, which fidelity aims to recognize by way of a confirmation and a creation, does not take place. Faced with such undecidability, fidelity seems once again to demand a fidelity towards fidelity, an awareness of the necessity to take a risk and to make a decision which does not sacrifice fidelity or which sacrifices fidelity only to fulfil its paradoxical purpose of preparing for a rupture. Insofar as the awareness of this necessity is necessarily limited and cannot substitute for the act of deciding and recognizing, for the surprise of the event's unexpected taking place, fidelity towards fidelity is much in the same position as fidelity. Hence fidelity appears to be constantly in search, in lack or in excess of itself.

Anticipatory fidelity is the complement of an 'institutional' fidelity (*EE* 265) which preserves the actuality of the event, as it were, by proceeding to the connection of elements in a situation considered from the viewpoint of an 'evental supplement' (*E* 38). While anticipatory fidelity can turn into a 'prophetic disposition', which perpetuates a promise and impedes the happening of an event, institutional fidelity can turn into a 'canonical disposition' which completely absorbs the disruptive effects of the event (*EE* 289).

But if it precedes and survives itself in the guise of anticipatory and institutional fidelity, where can fidelity be found, exactly? It would seem that fidelity is all the more 'real' (*EE* 265) the more it, too, amounts to an event and opposes the representation of its being (*EE* 261); that is, the less it waits for an event to take place and the more remote an event is (*SP* 119), or the more disparate the elements it connects are (*EE* 265) and the less it can be told apart from a fidelity towards fidelity. For fidelity and fidelity towards fidelity ultimately converge in the faithful decision which commits perseverance, the perseverance characteristic of a 'human animal', to 'that which breaks with or gets into the way of this very perseverance' (*E* 43), to the interrupting, fugitive, anarchic indiscernibility of event and fidelity. If fidelity towards fidelity denotes the risk of fidelity, if it signals the externality of a fidelity which cannot be an event without at the same time relating to an event, if, in view of a fidelity to come, it indicates a necessary and irreducible temporal tension, then this impossible point of convergence is neither the point where 'human animals' achieve immortality by seizing their self-preservation nor the point at which their mortality is corroborated. But do not the examples Badiou cites, from fidelity towards Plato in philosophy and fidelity towards Schoenberg in art to fidelity towards May 1968 in politics (*E* 39), suggest a rather predictable and hence rather conservative approach? Only inasmuch as fidelity is lacking and remoteness is understood in the light of a conventional idea of rarefication.

Badiou, in his meditation on Pascal, focuses on the necessity of deciding for or against an event taking place or having taken place. In the absence of criteria of recognition and judgement, and under circumstances of undecidability which translate into both the impossibility of the event taking place and the impossibility of the event not taking place, there is nothing left but the intervention of a decision which is itself torn between a fidelity which stands for 'confidence', 'belief', 'faith', 'credence' (*EE* 241) and a fidelity which is dashed to pieces on the 'rock of nihilism'. But since one cannot relate to an event from the outside, since in order to relate to an event one must already be faithful to it and faithful to this fidelity, a decision for or against an event taking place has always already been made, as Badiou points out. One relates to an intervening decision by ratifying or rejecting it, not by actually making it, not by making it at the present moment. The polemical dimension of a decision which calls an event into existence (*CT* 54, 99) resides in the unavoidability of relating to it in one way or another. However, if speaking of a decision and an intervention entails that it must be possible in principle to decide that an event has not taken place (*PM* 97), and to contest the existence of an event acknowledged by others – then a recognition must be sought at the heart of fidelity, a recognition which Badiou in one instance qualifies as 'subjective' and 'immediate' (*SP* 23). It is by virtue of such a recognition that the avant-garde minority faithful to an event becomes entangled in an interminable struggle for recognition, in a struggle for confirmation and establishment of that which has been recognized and at the same awaits recognition.[3] Just as there cannot be a fidelity which does not depend on a fidelity towards fidelity, on a kind of loyalty, perhaps, there cannot be an immediacy whose assertive force is not diverted immediately or whose axiomatic effects are not disrupted. Badiou's invectives against an 'ethics of difference' based on a 'recognition of the other' (*E* 21) may prove legitimate, but they do not absolve him from conceiving of a struggle for recognition. Such a struggle would be serious and violent since it would occur between 'judgements of existence' (*CT* 54) and would originate *within* these judgements themselves. Yet to the extent that I cannot recognize an event and behave faithfully without asking myself a question and letting the other ask me a question, a question as to whether I should recognize the event and behave faithfully or not, a question as to whether I have recognized the event and do behave faithfully or not, the struggle for recognition in which fidelity gets caught up from the start must also be a struggle for the providing of reasons, no matter how unfathomable the disjunction between logic and existence, creation and reflection, positing and justifying.

What remains of fidelity, then, in the wake of Badiou? Perhaps the thought that fidelity is *seeing* embodied.** Let's dance now.

** *Competing fidelities* – 'Doesn't Badiou's mathematical orientation block any comparison with phenomenology?' – 'You are right, of course. When I wrote this sentence and emphasized the word you incriminate, the last thing on my mind was a hint at phenomenology. Doubtless this was philosophically naive, especially in such a charged context. First I had chosen a different word. But then a friend pointed out to me that *discerning*, in English, is often associated with taste. So after giving it much serious thought we decided that *seeing* would be less contextually and idiomatically marked, and convey the meaning I wished to express much better. In allowing us to establish a relation, fidelity shows us that there is no view from nowhere. Oh, I almost forgot – at the end of the preceding paragraph I mention logic and existence in loose reference to Hegel, not to Badiou's terminology!'

16

BADIOU'S POETICS

Jean-Jacques Lecercle

The first paradox is trivial enough. It concerns the philosophical detractor of language who waxes eloquent in his denunciation of the despised medium. For philosophy, like poetry, is clearly an exercise of and in language. This reminds us of Deleuze's essay, 'L'Epuisé', which deals with Beckett's late television plays, where language there is none, but where Deleuze deals with the situation not only in terms of Beckett's language, but also of three different types of language.[1]

To be sure, Badiou belongs to that line of philosophers (rather rare these days) who resist the overwhelming importance of language for philosophy. He does this in two ways (*C* 119–22). He upholds the position of truth against the modern sophistry of the poststructuralists and postmodernists, and he rejects the linguistic turn taken by philosophy, both in the Wittgensteinian version (where all philosophical problems are grammatical problems) and in the Heideggerian, hermeneutic, version. So for him my first paradox is no paradox. Philosophy operates by subtraction, and what the subtraction mainly achieves is a breaking of the surface of language, the surface upon which the Sophist has established himself (*C* 81). This abandonment of language as a field of philosophical enquiry is a small price to pay for avoiding the position of the Sophist, for whom there are no truths, but only techniques of utterance and sites for enunciation, and for whom there is nothing but a multiplicity of language-games, since being is inaccessible to thought (*C* 74). So avoidance of the paradox is easy: all we have to do is carefully to separate natural language, a hindrance to philosophy, from the language of ontology, that is of mathematics.

Is this merely a restatement of Carnap's familiar positivist position? It is not: Badiou does not use the contrast between natural and artificial languages, and, more importantly for us, quite unlike Carnap he raises the question of the poem: perhaps there is a way, after all, of saving language for philosophy, through a celebration of poetic practice.

This seems in fact to be Badiou's real answer: the operation of subtraction separates philosophical discourse from the poem. This is a Platonist gesture, the recognition of the constitutive diaphor (*diaphora*), or discord, between philosophy and poetry, between the poem and philosophical argument. We can express this through a correlation with Greek names, for this philosophical battle was fought

long ago on the Aegean, and we, on this distant Northern sea, have merely
inherited it: *poiesis* v. *dianoia* (the vaticinating celebration of being is opposed to
the slow and painful argumentative path that ascends to first principles [cf. *PM*
33]), *pathos* v. *logos* (the poem is a site for the expression of affect, the philosophical text deals with argument and logic).

This solution to our first paradox, which separates a reasonable or purified use
of language from its poetic uses, is essentially Plato's solution and it justifies his
expulsion of poetry from the ideal *polis*. But it is still unsatisfactory, not least
for Badiou: it tends to reduce the poem to an exercise in sophistry (*PM* 34). For
Badiou is, in this respect, singularly placed. Hence my second paradox.

The second paradox notes that Badiou, the arch anti-Sophist, who almost
single-handedly resists the linguistic turn, is, as a novelist and playwright, a
technician of poetic language, even if he is not exactly a linguist. Besides, he
shares with contemporary Sophists, the likes of Lyotard, Derrida, etc., a keen
interest in literature: he is no exception to the rule that today a philosopher has
to invade the field of the literary critic and enthuse over literary texts. So we
find Badiou writing essays, even books, on literature and art (a book on Beckett,
his *Petit Manuel d'inesthétique*, etc.). He obviously has a great book on Mallarmé
in him, which he has come close to publishing (*C* 108, footnote). And like all
these philosophers, he has constructed his own idiosyncratic canon, a number of
poets whose names appear again and again in his work: Hölderlin, Mallarmé,
Celan, Pessoa (Badiou is one of the rare writers to celebrate the greatness of the
Portuguese poet of the many aliases). But in his awareness of the philosophical
importance of the poem, Badiou is in good company: Plato is not immune to a
form of this second paradox, when he reaches the level of the first principles.
When he finds himself *epekeina tes ousias*, beyond substance, he has recourse to
the archetypal poetic techniques of myth and metaphor (*PM* 36): in such
rarefied regions, philosophy is naturally combined with poetical speech [*dire*].

An elementary solution to the second paradox consists in producing a
symmetrical position to that of the philosopher who becomes a surrogate poet:
the position of the poet as surrogate philosopher. If, when the limits of argumentative thought, of *dianoia*, have been reached, philosophy waxes poetic, then
we may call for a moment when, once the vaticinating impulse of the poem has
been exhausted, the poem abandons *pathos* for *logos*. We may wish for a poetry of
pure *logos*, the only object of which is the contemplation of ideas, the production of truths. Such a poem Badiou finds in the works of Mallarmé, a poem
that presents itself as thought. So let us rehearse the not unproblematic progression towards the climax of the modern poem in Mallarmé.

II SAVING THE POEM FOR THOUGHT

It all begins, inevitably, with Parmenides: the first philosophical argument
takes the form of a poem, the founding philosopher is also a poet. This is where
the separation must operate: the first move in philosophy is the desacralization
of the poem, the interruption of the revelling in *pathos*, its substitution with
rational argument, a violent form of intervention. Here is how Badiou describes

the process: 'Philosophy demands that the authority of *deep* saying [*proféthe*]
be interrupted by lay argument' (*C* 94). A brief parenthesis on Badiou's language: it is precise and rather laconic, difficult but crystal clear – a form of
linguistic asceticism; or again, the philosopher mistrusts language, but he has
style (and my heart goes out to his translators).

From this violent intervention, three types of relationship between philosophy and poetry emerge. First comes the Romantic tradition, from Parmenides
to Heidegger, where poetic language is the natural site for authenticity and the
disclosure of being and truth. This is clearly the wrong path, as it is the path
that resists the separation between the two modes of language. Second comes
the aesthetic tradition that begins with Aristotle, where the poem is no longer a
source of knowledge but has become the object of the theoretical gaze of the
philosopher, on a par with natural phenomena, and no longer concerned with
truth but only with verisimilitude. This path, too, is clearly wrong: it fails to
do justice to the power of the poem. Third comes the Platonist gesture of
exclusion, which rejects the poem because of its very power, of its charm in the
etymological sense. Such a gesture recognizes the extraordinary power of poetry
and constantly re-enacts the movement of separation that constitutes philosophy, thereby also recognizing, through a form of Freudian denial, that philosophy and poetry, at least at the beginning, if not in principle, are inextricably
mixed. The three positions are sometimes called by Badiou 'artistic schemata':
Plato's schema is didactic insofar as it asserts that art is incapable of truth but
exerts considerable charm, and must therefore be kept under close surveillance.
In an interesting, and faintly ironic twist, Badiou notes that the contemporary
version of this schema is the Marxist position towards art (*PM* 20), captured at
its didactic best in Brecht.

Badiou's own poetics can be described as an effort to reach a fourth position,
which would maintain the separation between the poem and philosophical
discourse but would accept that the poem is the site for the production of truths
(we remember that, for Badiou, truths always come in the plural: the concept of
Truth is empty). Such a position may be expressed through a *third paradox*, this
time an entirely positive one.

On the one hand, the poem is a site for truth, and as such a *condition* for
philosophy. If philosophy, as Badiou claims, is a procuress of truths (he uses the
word *maquerelle*, with its fine eighteenth-century connotations), the poem creates any number of ravishing young persons, of either sex, for philosophy to
thrive upon.

On the other hand, philosophy operates as a *deposition* of poetry: it demands of
the poem that it should abandon its auratic search of or revelling in meaning, it
demands the abandonment of all forms of pathos. Thus, Deleuze is duly criticized
for taking his aesthetics seriously, that is literally, for constructing an aesthetics
on the extraction of blocks of affects from affections, of percepts from percep-
tions, and for sharply separating concepts from percepts and affects. The tables
have been turned: it is Deleuze who accomplishes the Platonist gesture of
separation between philosophy and the poem, whereas Badiou's deposition
relieves such separation in the Hegelian sense, which explains the proximity of

philosophy to myth and metaphor, and also the distance between *logos* and *pathos*: deposition operates through the de-aesthetization of the poem, the separation between the presence of the idea, which the poem captures, and the pathos of bodily affection, which it must discard.

In this type of poetics, a great deal is demanded of literature: what the poem must renounce, what is deposed in it, is all that seems to concern the poem's relationship to language.

Here is Badiou in an essay tellingly entitled 'The Philosophical Recourse to the Poem': 'Philosophy must and shall establish itself at this subtractive point where language is articulated to thought [*s'ordonne*] without the prestige and mimetic incitements of image, fiction or narrative' (*C* 101). Two pages later, he adds comparison and rhythm to this list. But of course Badiou is aware that not only the poem, but philosophy itself, have recourse to all those techniques of language. The difference between the poem and philosophy (deposition is merely the inscription of the necessity of this difference) lies in the fact that, in philosophy, such techniques are precisely *located* at the place where a truth emerges that punctures meaning and defies interpretation. What is demanded of the poem, in order for it to condition philosophy, is that, in resisting the charm and incitement of fiction, image and narrative, it should choose truth, which does not make sense, against meaning, which all too readily makes conventional sense, and thereby fosters interpretation. For what fiction, narrative and metaphor produce in their literary pervasiveness is a plurality, or a surfeit, of interpretations.

Hence the poetry that Badiou calls for, and finds in Mallarmé. Such poetry has two singular characteristics: it is a poetry of *logos*, a poetry concerned with thought, and it is a poetry capable of naming the event, of extracting from the advent of the event not affects and percepts but truths (where it appears that Badiou's poetics is the inverse of Deleuze's aesthetics).

It is easy to see why language is a problem in Badiou's poetics, why its importance for poetry, as indeed for philosophy, is obvious and crucial, but deeply paradoxical. For language is always, at first at least, the language of the situation, in which the event cannot be named, in which the truths that follow from the event cannot be formulated. And yet the unnameable event *must* be named, and a new language, adapted to that naming, must be forged. It is a violent process. The language of the poem is paradoxical because it is the site of a violent birth: in order to attempt to name the unnameable, the poem must break and reconstruct language. There are revolutions in language, as there are in society. 'Mallarmé' is the name for this new operation of the poem. And indeed Badiou's poetics seems to be a reformulation of Mallarmé's poetic programme, as expressed by the famous phrase, *donner un sens plus pur aux mots de la tribu* ('give a purer meaning to the words of the tribe').

III MALLARMÉ

As we have seen, Mallarmé is a constant preoccupation in Badiou's work (in *Conditions* he states that Mallarmé is 'the emblem of the relationship between poetry and philosophy' [C 108]). So I shall indulge in a brief reading of his essay, 'Mallarmé's Method'.

We immediately encounter our *fourth paradox*. Badiou's method of reading poetry is, on the face of it, singular. On the one hand, the poem, qua thought, has nothing to do with semantics and meaning, and everything with 'negation' and with syntax. On the other hand, much to the surprise (and perhaps the indignation) of the literary critic, he begins with a prose translation of the poem.

Here is Badiou explaining what he is doing:

> The guiding thread of the clarification [of the poem] is syntactic and not concerned with interpretation or semantics [...]. In the philosophical appropriation of Mallarmé's poem, which presupposes the recovery of that which is lacking (the thought, under the sign of Truth, of the operations of thought), we must always begin with a 'translation', which is merely the explication [*mise à plat*], or punctuation, of the syntactic development of the poem (C 109).

And this is exactly how Badiou begins his reading (one has the feeling that this is how a reading of a Mallarmé poem *always* begins, if the reader is honest with herself). In the first section of his essay, he reads the poem beginning with '*A la nue accablante tu*', and his syntactic parsing explains, quite rightly, that *tu* is the past participle of the verb *taire*, not the second person singular pronoun. Unfortunately this indispensable, if limited, exercise, Mallarmé's syntax being notoriously contorted, soon turns into simple translation: the second poem he reads, '*Ses purs ongles très haut*', being the object of a prose summary (C 114). This translation is glorified with the title of 'prose preparation that allows us a first grasp of the poem': an unfortunate term, in that it suggests that the finished product consists of a layer of poetic language painted over a prose preparation of meaning.

For the literary critic that I am, this is deeply problematic. To come back to the first line of the first poem, nothing is made of the presence of the personal pronoun in the first line of the second stanza, in exactly the same position in the line ('*Quel sépulcral naufrage (tu / le sais)* ...), nor of the presence of '*nue*' in the first line, with the assonance between '*nue*' and '*tu*', and the at least possible ambivalence between the noun ('*nue*' means 'cloud') and the adjective (the feminine form of 'naked'). This type of analysis, a fine example of which, and one close to Badiou, can be found in Jean-Claude Milner's 'Tombeau de Mallarmé', has one striking characteristic: it is incompatible with semantic glossing.[2]

Of course, Badiou is aware of all this, and he is a philosopher, not a literary critic (this does not mean that we must ultimately condone his practice as reader of poetry). The question, therefore, is: what is he trying to achieve? I shall suggest a number of propositions.

The first thing to note is that this poetics is not an aesthetics. This is how he defines his 'inaesthetics', on the first page of his *Petit manuel d'inesthétique*: 'By "inaesthetics", I mean a relationship between philosophy and art which, as it posits that art is in itself a site for the production of truths, does not claim to make art in any way an object for philosophy. Against aesthetic speculation, inaesthetics describes the strictly intra-philosophical effects induced by the independent existence of a number of works of art' (PM 7).

This gives us a frame for a number of positive propositions about art *in its relation to philosophy*, that is, art as it must be in order to condition philosophy (and conversely, philosophy as it must be in order to be conditioned by art: the relationship is not one-sided).

The first proposition is that syntax is essential to the constitution of the poem. The contrast between semantics and syntax is a constant in Badiou's reflections on the poem: in this, he follows Mallarmé, whom he is fond of quoting on the subject ('we must have a guarantee: syntax' [C 109]). In his *Petit manuel d'inesthétique*, he compares Mallarmé and Pessoa for their *syntactic machination* (PM 70): the poem disturbs the natural flow of reading and delays interpretation, a constant but mistaken urge; it does this in order to give time to the Idea to work through the immediate image. In his answer to the Polish poet Czeslaw Milosz, who deplores the hermeticism of modernist poetry, Badiou insists on the crucial function of such syntactic convolutions. This is of considerable interest for the literary critic, even if the claim is still largely programmatic: our task is to develop such intuitions of the philosopher.

The second proposition is specific to Mallarmé's poems. In his reading, Badiou identifies three types of 'negation'. The first is the *vanishing* that marks the absence of the event in the site of its emergence. Thus, in the first poem that he comments upon, the absent word, 'shipwreck' (*'le naufrage'*), names the event, and is represented in the text by a chain of metonyms of which it is the absent source. The second is the *cancellation*, which is a mark of the undecidability of the event. The traces left by the shipwreck on the surface of the sea might have been left by a vanishing siren: the vanishing of the ship is thus itself cancelled. The third is the foreclosure (*forclusion*) that marks the absence of even the slightest trace, the paradoxical marking of the impossibility of the mark, the forceful absence of the radically unnameable. The foreclosed terms are that which no poetic truth can force into expression: the subject (the poet), the end (of the poem, of the subject: death), the material worked upon (language itself is foreclosed in the poem: you can poetically express any number of things, but not language). The literary critic might be entitled to read this as a characterization of style: the forcing out (*forçage*) of language when taken to its limits, towards the point where it vanishes into mere gibberish or silence. Except of course, there is no lyrical revelling in the ineffable in Badiou's poetics: such negations, such absences, are structural. A poetics of truth has the clarity and asceticism of rational structure, and the absence of the relevant term is part of the argument of the poem.

As a result of this, and this is my third proposition, the poem is no lyrical celebration of affect or disclosure of meaning, but an *operation*: neither a description nor an expression (PM 50). Such 'operation', when the reader has to accomplish it in her turn, is the inverse of interpretation: it does not claim to offer a key to the meaning of the poem that is being read, it provides an entry into the poet's syntactic machination. Let the poem itself operate: this is what the surface hermeticism of the text demands. The term 'operation' is chosen advisedly: it radically cuts off any reference to affect and the ineffable. A poetry of *logos* is a poetry of operations – not strictly mathematical ones, but certainly as rational as those of mathematics.

My fourth proposition is that this defines a poetics of purity and void. The 'purer sense' that the poem, in Mallarmé's famous phrase, gives the words of the tribe is a reaching out for the purity of what he calls 'the Notion', what the philosopher calls the Idea. Neither elegy, nor hymn, nor lyrical outburst, the poem is a reaching out for the purity of the Idea (this is the poetic version of the operation of subtraction). These are the four words in which Badiou sums up the 'singular operations of poetry *qua* thought', to be found in Mallarmé, Rimbaud, Hölderlin and Beckett: 'dis-objectivation, dis-orientation, inter-ruption and isolation' (*CT* 122). As we can see, such poetics relies on negation in the same sense as negative theology does, or in the sense that the Real in Lacan can only be grasped through negative description (it is senseless, indif-ferent, impossible, etc.). In the same vein, a truth for Badiou is undecidable, indiscernible, unnameable and generic (the last term is as negative as the others: it means that no characteristic of such truth may be expressed in the prevailing encyclopaedia).

IV PROBLEMS

It is easy to see why this poetics exerts such a strong fascination on the literary critic (I should perhaps say, 'on this literary critic'). It is equally easy to see why it is a source of unease to him. I shall try to give expression to both.

This poetics is fascinating: it makes for what are undoubtedly strong read-ings, of Rimbaud, for instance (*Conditions* has an essay entitled 'Rimbaud's method'), or of Mallarmé. In spite of the initial operation of translation, the readings of the Mallarmé poems are compelling. Suddenly the words of those hermetic poems come alive (I almost wrote: 'make sense', which is exactly what, according to Badiou, they do not), and a coherence emerges, around the con-cepts of event, naming and fidelity (*PM* 213–14). But can we go further? Can we find interest in this reading for the literary critic, independently of the philosopher?

The interest of such reading is that it ascribes its true power to poetry. Badiou is fond of the French phrase *à la hauteur de*. 'Penser *à la hauteur de Pessoa*' (*PM* 62): what is this 'height' which the philosopher must share with the poet? It is the singular power of language. We must beware of the traps of translation here, lest we fall back into the sophistic celebration of language which Badiou wishes to avoid at all costs. His phrase is *'les puissances de la langue'* (*PM* 43) – the vocabulary is not entirely consistent, since a few lines later this *'puissance'* becomes *'pouvoir'*. But the general drift is clear: *potentia* is not merely power, and *langue* is certainly not language. In Mallarmé, such power is identified as the power eternally to state the disappearance of what presents itself, in other words to capture the emergence of the event. Such *hauteur* enables us to understand why the poem is indeed a condition of philosophy.

But other poetics, not least the Romantic tradition that gives all power to language, ascribes similar, if not greater, importance to the poem. So there is something else that, in Badiou's poetics, deeply satisfies the literary critic. It is a poetics of the anti-lyrical, of the impersonal, as opposed to the effusions of an affected subject (what Deleuze contemptuously calls his 'dirty little story' – and by which, unlike Badiou, he means what psychoanalysis is looking for). Badiou's poetics does not take as its elementary unit of poetic thought the single work or the personal author, but what he calls the artistic configuration, which is the true site for the emergence of the event and the production of truths. In this, Badiou shares the modernist poetics one can find in his contemporaries, Foucault or Deleuze.

Badiou's originality, however, is the articulation of the two seemingly independent words, 'poem' and 'thought'. This is of special interest to the literary critic, at least if he takes his task seriously, and holds, as I do, that literature *thinks*. Badiou is the thinker of poetry as thought. And as such he has truly found a fourth path, or site, for the relationship between poetry and philosophy, beyond the aporia of the contrast between *pathos* and *logos*, between auratic or lyrical vaticination and the exclusion of thought from poetry or poetry from thought. Badiou is one of the rare people, perhaps the only one, capable of making a decision, of solving the paradox the two terms form by firmly excluding one of them, the unexpected one, and turning the other, *logos*, into the very stuff that poetry is made of.

Yet, fascinated as the literary critic is, sometimes to the point of enthusiasm, he cannot conceal a feeling of unease. Let me propose three reasons for this.

The first may be entirely contingent. We can formulate it in a *fifth paradox*. Badiou appears to be a novelist whose thinking about art well-nigh ignores the novel. Apart from a few references to the artistic configuration of the novel, culminating in Joyce, and giving the impression that it is now exhausted, the Badiou canon seems to be entirely composed of poets (this is a major difference with Deleuze). Since what must be deposed from poetry in order for it to think is the mimetic, characterized as the combination of image, fiction and narrative, there seems to be no place for the novel in Badiou's poetics: where poetry is concerned with truth, the novel is concerned with fiction and make-believe. In other words, the novel is an Aristotelian genre. But I think such a view would be deeply mistaken. Truths in Badiou are generic in yet another sense: artistic truths are situated in a genre. So his poetics is not a general aesthetics, not even a poetics of literature, but a poetics of the poem as a specific site for specific truths, which are different from the truths of the novel. After all, Badiou is singular among contemporary philosophers in that he is not only a philosopher but also has a recognized artistic position, at least in the field of drama: a notable dramatist himself (in this, his only rival, and predecessor, is Jean-Paul Sartre), he is also a well-known theorist of the theatre, whose positions are at the centre of lively discussion (a trace of this may be found in his *Petit manuel d'inesthétique*, in the shape of 'Theses for the theatre' [*PM* 113–20], the first of which, in a move that is by now familiar to us, states that 'the theatre thinks'). There remains a nagging suspicion, however, that for Badiou the novel is not the literary genre where literature thinks *par excellence*. But this remark can only be provisional, and calls for a detailed critical analysis of Badiou's practice as a novelist.

The second source of unease concerns the treatment of syntax. Here the objection is stronger. My feeling is that Badiou's treatment of syntax is not yet *à la hauteur* of Mallarmé's formula on syntax as guarantee. The limited examples he provides in his essay reduce syntactic analysis to mere parsing, which in turn opens the way for semantic glossing, which is the reality behind the 'prose preparation' of the poem. Let us call this the *sixth paradox*: syntax here is merely another name for semantics; that is, the name for the imposition upon the poem of a single, because true, interpretation of the text. But this need not be so. I have already alluded to the concept of *forçage*, 'forcing language by the advent of "another" language, a language both immanent and created', as Badiou puts it (*PM* 41): this opens up vistas of a truly syntactic analysis of the poem, in which for once Badiou would be close to his philosophical other, Deleuze, whose definition of style is based on a broad concept of a-grammaticality, and who tries to define what he calls the 'intensive line of syntax'.[3]

With the obvious exclusion from Badiou's commentary of the question of the signifier, we come to my last source of unease and our *seventh paradox*. Badiou, as we have seen, freely translates, and into prose at that, what is almost untranslatable into another language, or at least demands the strongest poetical gifts on the part of the translator: as a poet to be translated, Mallarmé is a Benjaminian creature. Hence, if Badiou's reading of the work of art, in terms of immanence and singularity (*PM* 21), entirely satisfies the student of literature, his reading of Mallarmé's poems is barely an *explication de texte*, at least as we literary critics know it (it belongs to another sub-genre, the *philosophical* not-so-close commentary, always a form of exploitation when practised on a literary text). Hence our *paradox number eight*: it is because Badiou takes the poem as his privileged object (an entirely convincing move) that the limitations of what remains a prosaic reading clearly emerge. The answer to this, in Badiou's terms, might be that you cannot name the unnameable, that in which a truth reaches its limits (*PM* 42): what Badiou looks for in the poem is precisely this, which lies beyond the signifier. In Deleuze's aesthetics, a similar movement induces him to define style in terms not only of a-grammaticality but of a striving towards silence or a change of medium. Badiou's position, at least, is entirely coherent: the unnameable is not the ineffable.

The general irony of Badiou's readings of poetry is of course that they are such strong and decisive readings that they leave a lot of space for other readings, as the poem spectacularly exceeds the truth that Badiou's reading extracts from it.

V CONCLUSION

Perhaps my first paradox (the language-hater who waxes eloquent) was not so trivial after all. Resisting the linguistic turn involves consequences for the construction of a poetics. One aspect of Badiou's importance as a thinker of poetry is that he does not shy from an apparently impossible task: how to construct a poetics while at the same time downplaying the role of language (its independence, its materiality, its non-transparency). Badiou's grandeur lies in the extraordinary coherence and single-mindedness of his philosophical position: he is concerned with being and the event, not language and its games. The advantage of such a position is that it is a point of resistance to the postmodern invasion. The price to pay is a return to what seems to me to be an essentially modernist poetics (witness his canon), i.e. to an artistic sequence whose heyday is definitely in the past, and whose potential may now be exhausted.

17

AESTHETICS, INAESTHETICS, ANTI-AESTHETICS*

Jacques Rancière

I would like to propose here some rudimentary means for identifying the as yet Unidentified Flying Object that has recently landed on our soil, proffering as its sole letters of introduction these two sentences: 'By "inaesthetics" I mean a relation between philosophy and art such that, while positing that art is itself the producer of truths, it in no way claims to turn art into an object for philosophy. By way of contrast to aesthetic speculation, inaesthetics describes the strictly intra-philosophical effects brought about by the independent existence of some works of art' (*PM* 7). Both these sentences deploy an initial question. They affirm the proposition proper to Alain Badiou, that of a relation which is also a non-relation between these two things, each of which relates only to itself. But they also situate this singular proposition within a config-uration that enjoys widespread consensual support in contemporary thought. Between the analytical denunciation of speculative aesthetics and the Lyotardian denunciation of aesthetic debility, a whole range of discourses these days are in agreement on the dominant theme of the necessity of effecting a radical separation between those practices that are proper to art and the pernicious enterprise of an aesthetic speculation that ceaselessly denatures the idea of art by trying to appropriate it.

Consequently, in order to identify inaesthetics, it is first necessary to grasp the logic that inscribes its singularity within this common anti-aesthetic consensus. To do this one must try from the outset to identify the reason for this consensus itself. It seems to me the latter can be summarized as follows: the denunciation of the aesthetic 'denaturation' of art is a way of guaranteeing its 'nature', or if you prefer, the univocity of its name. It pre-emptively ensures that there is well and truly a univocal concept of art, effectuated in the autonomous singularity of works and encountered in a specific experience. In short, the denunciation of the aesthetic usurpation ensures that there is something proper to art. It ensures the identification of that propriety. This implies, furthermore, that what goes by the name of aesthetics is what then problematizes what is

---

*This chapter, translated by Ray Brassier, was first published as 'Esthétique, inesthétique, anti-esthétique', in *Alain Badiou: Penser le multiple*, ed. Charles Ramond (Paris: L'Harmattan, 2002), pp. 477–96.

proper to art, i.e. the univocity of its concept, the relation between its unity and the plurality of arts, and modes of acknowledging its presence.

There are broadly speaking three principal philosophical attitudes concerning the identification of art and the arts. I shall briefly recall them here, more or less in line with the recapitulation that opens Alain Badiou's text on 'Art and Philosophy' (*PM* 9–15). The first, which is associated with the name of Plato, can be summarized thus: there are *arts*, which is to say ways of putting forms of knowledge into practice via the imitation of models, and there are *appearances*, or simulacra of the arts. There are true and false imitations. In this order of things the notion of *art* as we understand it is nowhere to be found. Which is why it makes no sense to bewail the fact that Plato 'subordinated art to politics'. For as a matter of fact Plato does not subordinate art to anything. More radically still, he *knows* nothing of art. What he knows is the poem insofar as it educates, and it is of the poem that he asks: to what ends and by what means does it educate? Art is then disjoined from truth, not just in the sense in which the true is opposed to the simulacrum, but in the sense whereby the very distinction between truth and simulacrum leaves no identifiable space for art.

The second form – which, for brevity's sake, we will call Aristotelian – identifies art in the pair *mimesis/poeisis*. As far as this form is concerned, among the arts, among the ways of doing in general, there are certain arts that perform specific tasks: they make imitations, which is to say, assemblages of represented actions. These arts are withdrawn not only from the usual evaluation of artistic products according to their usefulness, but also from the legislation that truth exercises over discourses and images. Art does not exist here as an autonomous notion. But there does exist a criterion of discrimination within the general realm of the *tekhnai*, namely the criterion of imitation, which functions in three ways. It is first of all a principle of classification that allows one to distinguish from among the arts a specific class equipped with its own criteria. But it is also a principle of internal normativity specified through principles, rules, criteria of recognition and appreciation that allow one to judge whether or not an imitation is genuinely art, whether it conforms to the rules of good imitation in general and those of an art or specific genre of imitation in particular. Lastly, it is a principle of distinction and comparison that allows one to separate and compare the various forms of imitation. This is how I will define what I call a representative regime of art, i.e. a regime in which art in general does not exist but where there do exist criteria of identification for what the arts do, and of appreciation for what is or is not art, for good or bad art.

Finally, there exists a third form of identification, which could be called the properly *aesthetic* identification or aesthetic regime of art. This regime deserves to be called aesthetic because the identification of art it carries out no longer operates by way of a specific difference within the realm of various ways of doing and by way of criteria of inclusion and evaluation that allow one to judge these conceptions and executions, but instead by identifying a mode of sensible being proper to artistic products. The latter are identified as belonging to the mode of being of a sensible datum that differs from itself, a mode that has become identical with a way of thinking that also differs from itself. In this mode of identification art indeed finds itself identified as a specific concept. But this takes place through the defection of every criterion that might separate its particular ways of doing from other ways of doing. For this is precisely what *mimesis* was: not that obligation to resemblance with which our schoolchildren and quite a few of their teachers stubbornly persist in identifying it, but a principle of discrimination at the heart of human activity, one that delimits a specific realm and that allows us to include objects and to compare classes of objects within it. *Mimesis* separated what was art from what was not art. Conversely, the new definitions, the *aesthetic* definitions in which the autonomy of art is affirmed, all variously say the same thing and affirm the same paradox: henceforth, art is to be recognized by its characteristic indistinction. The products of art make manifest in sensible mode that quality of the *made* that is identical with the un-made, that quality of the *known* that is identical with the un-known, or of the *willed* that makes it identical with the un-willed. In short, what is proper to art, and finally nameable as such, is its identity with non-art. And it is in this respect that, henceforth, the notion of truth positively pertains to art. Not because art alone is held to be capable of truth, according to the thesis that Badiou unfairly ascribes to German Romanticism, but because art is art only insofar as this category pertains to it. And it pertains to it because art is what testifies to a passing of the idea through the sensible, in the differing of a sensible datum from the ordinary regime of the sensible. In this regime, there is art because there is an eternity that passes, because the new modality of the eternal is that of passing.

There follows this consequence: if eternity merely passes, its effect is in no way identifiable with the effectuation of a determinate form within a specific materiality. It always consists in the difference between what passes and that through which it passes. As a result, thought's immanence to the sensible is immediately doubled. Form is the form of a pure passage and at the same time a moment in a history of forms. The principle of the idea's immanence to sensible presence is thereby immediately converted into a principle of division. The only thing that prevents the idea from becoming submerged in the situation within which it manifests itself is the fact that it is always ahead of or lagging behind itself, according to a stricture encapsulated by the famous Hegelian dilemma: if art is a thing of the past for us, it is because, generally, its presence is a past presence, and because in what was supposed to be its present it was in fact something other than art. It was a form of life, a communal mode, a religious manifestation.

Thus, the aesthetic identification of art as the manifestation of a truth through the passage of the infinite within the finite originarily links that passage to a 'life of forms', a process of formation of forms. And in this process what vanishes are all criteria for differentiating between the forms of art and the forms of life of which it is the expression, along with all criteria for differentiating between the forms of art and the forms of thought that ensure its proper grasp. The same holds for the principles that allowed for differentiating between arts and ultimately for the very difference between art and non-art. In a word, art's aesthetic autonomy becomes just another name for its heteronomy.

The aesthetic identification of art provides the principle for its generalized disidentification. The latter begins with Vico's discovery that Homer was a poet because he wasn't a poet at all. It continues in the Balzacian assertion that the great poet of the new era is not a poet but a geologist, but also in the indiscernibility between Balzac's own great novels and the stock-in-trade stuff he wrote in order to put food on the table. It carries on in Rimbaud's quest for the gold of the new poem in asinine rhymes and idiotic paintings, or in the constant risk that a sentence penned by Flaubert threatens at any moment to turn into a phrase coined by Paul de Kock;[1] it persists, likewise, in those unidentified objects, the prose poem and the essay – in that essay on Sainte-Beuve, for example, which turns into a pseudo-biographical novel and concludes with a theory that is not its true theory. I will not continue further with the indeterminable list of these disorders in the identifications of art. I have only given 'literary' examples because 'literature' is the name under which disorder first affected the art of writing before going on to spread its confusions in the realm of the so-called plastic arts and so-called theatrical arts.

In due course a defence against this modern disorder was invented. This defence is called *modernism*. Modernism is that conception of art which affirms its aesthetic identification whilst refusing those forms of dis-identification through which the latter is effectuated. Modernism endorses the autonomy of art but refuses its heteronomy (which is nothing other than the other name of its autonomy). Modernism sought to make this inconsistency seem consistent through the invention of an exemplary fable that serves to bind the homonymy of art to the self-contemporaneity of the modernist era. This fable simply identifies the modern revolution in art with the discovery of art's pure and finally unveiled essence. It assimilates the retreat of mimesis to an insurrection through which, in the course of the preceding hundred years, the arts would seem to have liberated themselves from the representational obligation and thereby rediscovered the end proper to art, hitherto perverted and reduced to the status of a mere means, itself subordinated to an external end. The aesthetic identification of art is thereby brought back to the autonomization of each art, henceforth devoted to demonstrating art's one and only power, in each case identical with the revelation of those powers of thought immanent to the materiality of each specific art. Thus, literary modernity would consist in the exploitation of the pure powers of language, freed from the obligation to communicate; pictorial modernity would consist in a painting freed from the depiction of naked women or warhorses, a painting able to conquer the powers intrinsic to the bi-dimensional surface and the materiality of coloured pigment; musical modernity would be identical with a twelve-tone language, freed from every analogy with expressive language, etc. In this way something 'proper to art' is identified, something which each art realizes with its own means, which are very different from those of its neighbour. And in this way the global distinction between art and non-art is also assured. The trouble is that this identification of that which is proper to art in general with what is proper to the particular arts insofar as they keep to their allotted places becomes harder and harder to defend when confronted with the reality of those mixtures which have characterized artistic development for at least a century now, and this despite the regular discovery of new 'New Laocoons'.[2] This is why the claim on behalf of what is 'proper to art' is increasingly made in a negative mode by denouncing everything that muddies the distinction between art and non-art, and especially by denouncing the imprisonment of art by the discourse on art in general, and by philosophical discourse in particular. Contemporary 'anti-aesthetics' thereby proves to be the final, defensive phase of modernism, stubbornly trying to tear what it identifies as art's 'propriety' away from its inclusion in that aesthetic regime of art which allows art to exist only at the cost of disappropriating it.

How might we now go about situating *inaesthetics* within the anti-aesthetic consensus, itself understood as the present phase in the modernist configuration of the conception of art? We can certainly discern in Badiou's problematization of art some of the characteristic traits of modernism: the espousal of an artistic modernity understood in terms of anti-mimesis, in the sense of a subtraction from every obligation to imitate an external reality; the assertion that the truths of art are absolutely proper to it, and so the careful delineation of a border between art and the discourse on art; finally, the affirmation of a watertight separation between the arts. But these modernist assertions are not put together according to the usual figure of modernism. Badiou refuses, for instance, the notion that the specificity of the arts resides in their respective *languages*. It resides, he affirms, in their *Ideas*. And although the hero of his conception of art is the Telquelian hero of literary modernity, the Mallarmé of the virginal night of *Igitur*, of the *Coup de dés* and the *Sonnet en X*, it is not the essence of language – whether pure or opaque – that he identifies on the page of the latter but the passage of the Idea. In a word, Badiou's undoubted modernism is a twisted modernism. The supposedly unitary and modern essence of art 'as it is in itself' is twisted, and even twisted twice over by Badiou's core philosophical project, by what could be called his ultra-Platonism, as encapsulated in the notion of a Platonism of the multiple.

The twist that straightforward modernism thereby undergoes at the hands of Badiou must itself be understood in the context of the attempts which, for a long time now, have tried to reconcile the Platonist condemnation of images with the assertion that there is something proper to art. Historically, these attempts have taken two major forms. There was the mimetic form, whose formula Panofsky summarizes in *Idea* and which consists in bringing false imitation back to true imitation by turning the artist into a contemplator of the eternal Idea who makes its reflection shine in sensible appearances. This pictorial neo-Platonism of the resemblance between the image and the Idea is not a position that Badiou could endorse. For him, it is not a question of redeeming art by providing the Idea with sensible *analoga*, by allowing the eternity of the model to be reflected upon the surface of the painting. For Badiou, to be a genuine Platonist, to be so in a modern way, is to make the Platonic eternity of the Idea come forth in the radicalization of anti-*mimesis*. It is to make the Idea without resemblance come forth within that which is absolutely dissimilar to it, in precisely that which Platonism absolutely challenges and which challenges it interminably in return: the opacity of situations and the make-believe of theatre. The Platonism of the immortal Idea's triumph over everything sensible and mortal is only valid for Badiou if its demand can be incarnated in the figure of a caricatural Arab, a shameless hedonist, bruiser and liar.[3] In a word, Platonism here is only valid as the identity of Platonism and anti-Platonism.

But this Platonism of the identity of opposites only distinguishes itself from neo-Platonism by virtue of its filiation with a second 'Platonism of art': the Platonism of the aesthetic age, elaborated in post-Kantian Romanticism and Idealism, which lets the Idea come forth as passage within the sensible and lets art be its witness. It depends on the aesthetic identification of the Idea with the double difference that obtains both between thought and itself and between the sensible and itself, one which determines the passage of the Infinite within the finite. Badiou has to assume the kinship between his 'Modernist Platonism' (*PM* 12) and that aesthetic determination of art which, rigorously understood, shatters the modernist paradigm. It is in vain that he tries to rid himself of it in the text which we quoted above on 'Art and Philosophy' by ascribing the aesthetic identification of art to Romantic theory specifically and by summarily assimilating Romanticism to Christology (which is to say, following another summary assimilation, to a foetid, pity-laden bias toward the mortal, suffering body). These hasty amalgams leave untouched the problem they are supposed to resolve. In fact, the issue here is not the choice between the mortal body and the eternity of the Idea: what is at issue is how we are to define the status of the *passing* or passage of this eternity itself.

With Badiou, everything is always played out around what constitutes the core image of Romantic art according to Hegel, which is to say, not the cross but the empty sepulchre – emptied of an Idea which has re-ascended into heaven, never to return. What matters is not the struggle between death and immortality. That particular struggle is over. It is a question of knowing *where* the Resurrected, for whom one looks in vain here, has gone. The Hegelian account conceives of the status of art and truth in such a way that each is put ceaselessly behind or ahead of itself, such that for instance the eternity of a statue is ensured by the impossibility for a religion to think the eternal, and the soaring of a cathedral spire is composed of the impossibility for a thought which has found the Eternal to endow it with a sensible form. It is not a morbid eulogy of suffering flesh that is at issue here but the voyage of an eternity still caught between the muteness of stone and the return into itself of thought. Around the empty sepulchre crowd the shadows of everything that threatens the Idea's Platonic/anti-Platonic passage through art: the glorious rather than suffering body of the Church or community, the becoming-philosophy of the poem, the becoming-image and imagery of the advent of the Eternal, the becoming-museum and becoming-archaeology of art ... – in short, all those forms of the Idea's absorption into the sensible and of the sensible's absorption into the Idea that provide the currency for the aesthetic identification of art.

In Badiou, every analysis of a poem or work of art brings us back to this primitive scene and replays it in the same way. In each case, it will be a matter of making immortality appear upon the empty sepulchre, in place of every vanished body but also of every idea that has re-ascended into heaven, an immortality present in the words and iridescent wings of the Angel who each time announces that once again the Idea has revealed itself in its passing: the angel of the Resurrection, the angel of the Annunciation, who attests, like the Rimbaldian genius, that he will return again in order to testify once more to the ever-renewed event of the Idea's advent. It is a matter of making the passing itself remain, of rendering the inconsistency of the passage of the Idea perpetually consistent by preventing it from losing itself, whether in the muteness of things or in the interiority of thought. The passage of the Infinite must be separated from its aesthetic site, from the life of forms, from the Odyssey of spirit estranged from itself.

Badiou then has to apply the cutting edge of Platonic separation within the realm of aesthetic indiscernibility, so as to distinguish the forms of art and those of life, the forms of art and those of the thought of art, the forms of art and those of non-art. At the heart of the Platonic Romanticism which affirms that art is anti-mimetic, that it pertains to truth and that truth passes, he has to invoke another Platonism, that new Platonism which, by pluralizing truth into so many discrete truths, highlights the ever-renewed eternity of the act which consumes the sensible without remainder. He wants to make eternity pass into the ever-renewed separation that lets the Idea shine in the vanishing of the sensible, to affirm the absolutely singular yet always similar character of the advent of the Idea by preventing its inscribed cipher from becoming lost in the muteness of stone, the hieroglyph of the text, the décor of life or the rhythm of the collective. He wants this not so much in order to preserve a realm that would be proper to poetry or to art, but to preserve the educational value of the Idea. For to be a Platonist is also to maintain that the question of the poem is ultimately an ethical and political one, that the poem or art is educational. Platonist aesthetics in general paradoxically maintain that there is a way of learning or accessing the truth that is proper to art. But this can be understood in two ways. In the first place there is Romantic *Bildung*, the identification of the forms of art with the forms of a life that is to be cultivated. Badiou's ultra-Platonism counters this with the claim that there is only one thing that educates: the contemplation of Ideas. But the entire paradox of his modernist Platonism lies here: the reason why Badiou stands at the furthest remove from the modernist faith in the autonomy of art is also the reason why, in an equivocal companionship, he is obliged to reiterate some of the fundamental propositions of that faith. He has to affirm the existence of something proper to art or the poem, which modernity has finally uncovered in its purity, affirm that this proper is the manifestation of a self-sufficient truth entirely separate from every discourse on art, and finally affirm also that this something which is 'proper to art' is always the proper of *an* art. He has to do this not because of the ordinary modernist faith in the 'language' proper to each art, but because it is the condition for the separation through which what is attested is the idea alone, the idea which educates through its exhibition. And he has on occasion to do this at the price of a paradoxical position: that of reproducing the very divisions of *mimesis* in order to ensure the anti-mimetic principle of separation.

I have in mind here for instance Badiou's constant opposition between the

thought that is immanent to the Mallarméan poem and Mallarmé's own pronouncements concerning poetry, which ultimately boils down to the classic
opposition between verse and prose. But the aesthetic regime of the arts and
Mallarmé's poetics deprive this opposition between prose essay and verse poetry
of any discriminatory pertinence: 'Crise de vers' is not a text by Mallarmé *about*
poetry, it is Mallarméan poetry, neither more nor less so than the 'Sonnet en X',
which is at once and indissociably a poem and a statement *about* poetry. I also
have in mind this assertion about the identity between modernity and anti-
mimesis, which quite noticeably exceeds the evidence provided for it: 'The
modern poem is the opposite of a mimesis. Through its operation it exhibits an
Idea of which the object and objectivity are merely pale imitations' (*PM* 38–9).
Here the gesture that imposes the cut quite noticeably exceeds the discriminatory power of the statement. The latter does little more in effect than
reiterate the founding idea of the mimetic regime, that of poetry's superiority
over history, as asserted in chapter IX of Aristotle's *Poetics*. And the two
Mallarméan lines used to illustrate it ('Le matin frais s'il lutte/Ne murmure point
d'eau que ne verse ma flute') say no more than these two other lines by La Fontaine,
which I am in the habit of using precisely as a typical illustration of this
mimetic regime: 'Les charmes qu'Hortésie étend sous ses ombrages/Sont plus beaux dans
mes vers qu'en ses propres ouvrages'. The formula that wishes to oppose *mimesis* and
anti-mimesis in fact renders them indiscernible.

Once again, what finds expression here is not just the usual modernist *doxa* of
anti-representation. Prior to any criterion of distinction, it is the affirmative
character of the operation of truth, the affirmative character of disappearance
that is initially asserted. It is not so much from *mimesis* as from *aisthesis*, from
the aesthetic identification of the passage of truth, that Badiou strives to preserve the Mallarméan poem. Against every incarnation of the Idea which would
engulf it in sensible matter, Badiou wants to highlight the Idea as pure subtraction, as the pure operation of the wholesale disappearance of the sensible.
But he also wants to allow this subtraction to escape from every vanishing and
let it remain as an inscription. In other words, he wants to ensure the problematic coordination of two principles. Firstly, the Idea is a subtraction.
Secondly, every subtraction is the inscription of a name. There is art insofar as
there is naming. So the relevant principle in Badiou is not that of art but that of
the poem. For him, the essence of art is that of the poem. It consists in
inscribing, in forever conserving the disappearance as such rather than the
disappeared. Which is why ultimately only two arts are required in Badiou's
system of the arts: the poem as affirmation, as inscription of a disappearance,
and theatre as the site wherein this affirmation turns into mobilization.

As a result, Badiou has to try to guarantee the status of the poem as linguistic
inscription – a difficult operation since it contravenes that dispersion of the
poem which is proper to the aesthetic regime of the arts and of which Mallarmé
is an eminent theoretician. Similarly, the text that fixes Badiou's conception of
dance is in fact a settling of scores with Mallarmé in the name of Mallarmé. The
latter, in a famous text, characterized the art of the dancer as 'a poem freed from
the apparatuses of the scribe'. This is a paradoxical assertion, Badiou tells us,

'because the poem is by definition a trace, an inscription, and singularly so in the Mallarméan conception of it' (*PM* 104). I would say for my part that this definition and this singularity are in fact Badiou's and his alone. For the poem is continuously uttered and deployed by Mallarmé not as a trace {*trace*} but as a *line* {*tracé*} – the deployment of an appearing and a disappearing in terms that resemble the 'subject' of the poem: the motion of a fan, a mane of hair, a curtain, a wave, the golden rustling of fireworks or cigarette smoke. It is this deployment in analogy that constitutes the poem as effectivity of the Idea.

There follows from this a consequence which Mallarmé sometimes accepts and sometimes refuses in order to maintain the 'lucidity' of the poem, the lucidity of thought put into words. This consequence is the possibility that the poem might be 'freed from the apparatuses of the scribe', that it might consist in the same way in which the illiterate dancer's legs translate the daydream of the spectator, of which she knows nothing, but who 'lays at her feet' its flower. It is the possibility that the poem might unfold in steps, be deployed in materials, diffracted into sounds, reflected in the gold of the auditorium, bounce on the silk of the stoles. It is from all these slippages of disappearance, all the glitterings of the iridescence of the angel's wings, all these dispersions of its message that Badiou wants to safeguard Mallarmé. To that end, he alters both the meaning and the letter of the text. Mallarmé, addressing his double the spectator-dreamer, showed the latter how the writing of the ballerina's footsteps analogized 'the nudity of *your* concepts'. Badiou transforms this analogical relation between two thoughts into a metaphor for a thought which is 'without relation to anything other than itself' (*PM* 105). Consequently, dance expresses the nudity of *concepts* in general rather than of *your* concepts: the way in which the mere arrangement of bodies becomes capable of welcoming the passage of an idea. A hierarchy of the forms of art is thereby established which ensures the status of art – and primarily of the poem – as producer of educative truths. Of course, to do this, one has to purge the Mallarméan corpus of all those things – those fans, postal addresses or verses for accompanying glazed fruits – which make up the bulk of it. It is further necessary that the arrangement of the poem not be the curve delineated by its verse lines but the protocol of the succession, substitution and inscription of its names. Finally, the Mallarméan poem must be placed under the jurisdiction of a double affirmation ensuring both the irreducible autonomy of the poem and the need for a philosophy capable of 'discerning its truths'. The poem first thinks itself non-reflexively (thereby excluding any poem of the poem and any 'speculation' concerning it); the poem then *subtracts* this thought which is its own and in the process gives rise to the properly philosophical task, that of discerning the truths it subtracts – a task that has become the preserve of a philosophy rid in this way of all competition.

But what exactly is it that is thereby *discerned*, which, ultimately, means *named*? It is always the status of the poem as affirmation and at the same time metaphorization of the advent of the Idea. If Badiou calls dance a metaphor of thought, a manifestation of the capacity of bodies for truth, we might say that in his work the general status of artistic manifestation consists in signifying and symbolizing the passage of an idea, in showing that a body is capable of it, that a site is capable of harbouring it, a group of being seized by it. To my mind Badiou thus plays in a rather peculiar way with art's symbolic character, understood in the Hegelian sense: he distributes the arts on the basis of a beginning, dance, which is assigned the task of showing that there can be thought in bodies. It does this by showing that earth can become air, and in Badiou this metamorphosis is already called a *naming*.[4] And then at the summit of all the arts he places the poem as inscription of a name. To do this he has to tie the poem to the assertion of the name, and tear its words away from that fate which makes them circulate between fossils and hieroglyphs, between glorious body and the fluttering of a fan, between idiotic paintings and songs of the people – a fate to which, from Novalis to Proust or from Balzac to Mallarmé and Rimbaud, the poem is remorselessly driven by its aesthetic regime, which also drives it through music, painting and dance, and likewise through typography, the decorative arts or pyrotechny.

This is how Badiou brings the poem back to the Platonic order of the *logos*. He turns this *logos* into a maxim capable of arousing the courage of thought in general. The poem is thereby turned into an orientation for thought, and Badiou's taste for the maxims which he extracts from poems, and endows with a general value, is well known – for example: '*Nous t'affirmons, Méthode* [We affirm you, Method]' or '*Sur les inconsistences s'appuyer* [Seek a foothold in inconsistencies]'. But at the same time he excludes the possibility that the poem be self-sufficient in orienting thought. This task is reserved for philosophy: it is philosophy that discerns the orientations dictated by the poem. This implies that the inscription of the name and the declaration of the maxim are posited as effects of the poem-form – which is to say, of an apparatus of naming – and that this apparatus be posited as the *thought* that the poem subtracts [*soustrait*]. Following good Althusserian logic, philosophy is then summoned in order to discern the truths encrypted in the poem, even if this means miraculously rediscovering its own, which it claims to have been divested of. So for example philosophy recognizes that the 'duty' of the 'family of the iridized'[5] is nothing but the 'duty of thought', that the duty of thought lies in 'deciding at the point of the undecidable', and that it is precisely this requirement which is at stake in the question of knowing whether a steamship has sunk in the vicinity or whether the foam merely attests to the flight of a siren come to laugh in our faces (*À la nue accablante tu*). At a stroke, the Mallarméan poem, which is already an allegory of the poem, in the form of a 'tail-swipe' of the Idea, becomes in Badiou an allegory of the form of the event in general and of the courage of the thought that withstands its ordeal in particular. Which also means that in this regard it is comparable with every other poem which allows itself to be bent to the same demonstration, to be assigned the same task of speaking twice, to say the same event of the Idea twice: the first time as a maxim, the second time as an enigma.

What Badiou actually effects through this double saying of the poem is thus a repositioning of the symbolic gap. He wants to separate the poem – hence thought and its courage – from the Romantic quagmire whereby it gets bogged down in the humus of fossils – or conversely, from the Symbolist evanescence of fluttering fans. He claims to deliver the poem from its obligation to be 'poem of the poem' and philosophy from its obligation of being a philosophy of the poem. But this deliverance is a lure. For according to his analysis, the enigma comes down to the metaphor through which philosophy recognizes 'the thought of the poem', the thought of the event of truth in an image, which it finds twice said by the poem: in the affirmation of the maxim and in the transparency of the metaphor, which only a shallow stream, ceaselessly crossed, serves to separate. The knot [*nouage*] – or in Badiou's own vocabulary, the suture – through which philosophy is tied to the poem is then brought about through its very denial. The poem only says what philosophy needs it to say and what it pretends to discover in the surprise of the poem. This denial of the knot, this knotting carried out through denial, is not a matter of mere oversight. It is the only way of ensuring the necessary and impossible coincidence of two contradictory requirements: the Platonist/anti-Platonist requirement of a poem that teaches us about the courage of truth on the one hand, and the modernist requirement of the autonomy of art on the other.

We are now in a position to extend what Badiou tells us about dance to the whole of his system. In delineating the principles of dance, he emphasizes that it is not 'dance itself', its technique and history, which is in question, but dance 'insofar as philosophy shelters and harbours it' (*PM* 99). For Badiou, there can be truths of dance only insofar as it takes shelter in philosophy, which is to say, through the connection [*nouage*] of dance and philosophy. It will be objected that this proposition is specific to dance and that, for Badiou, dance is precisely not an art; as a result philosophy can and must tie itself to dance in order to extract from its *movements* the *signs* of an inherent disposition to truth within bodies. But it is possible to tackle the problem the other way round and ask ourselves about the place of this 'art which is not art'. We may wonder then whether Badiou's own classification of the arts is not designed precisely in order to ensure art's inviolable 'propriety' and the purity of each art by quarantining and marginalizing the connection of art with that which is not art – whether it be philosophy or the misery of the world. We might wonder, likewise, whether it is not at these very margins that tensions emerge which are capable of calling into question the connection of Platonism and modernism encapsulated in the term 'inaesthetics'. The system of the arts in Badiou appears as a well-guarded fortress, guarded by those to whom it shows the door – *its* door – those who are lumbered with all the misery of non-art and the equivocations of connection [*les équivoques du nouage*], and who thereby preserve the void of the central place wherein the poem's virginal purity is enthroned.

Perhaps these obscure negotiations about boundaries provide the occasion for a new comparison between Badiou's thought and the modernist forms of the identification of art. As we have seen, this tension is noticeable in the texts on dance. On the one hand, the philosophical 'shelter' provided for the latter is a way of thrusting the blade of separation right into the heart of the Mallarméan analogy between the dance and the poem. But at the same time, the connection thereby *declared* of the 'movements' of an art and of the 'concepts' of philosophy undermines the entire edifice of denial. It rebounds on to the 'centre' and forces a new consideration of the *aesthetic* connection of the productions of art and the forms of the thought of art. And the new concepts which Badiou has recently added to his system, whether it be the general notion of *configuration* in order to think the subject of art, or the specific notion of *impurification* which he applies to cinema, are simply so many ways of reconsidering the divisions of modernist thought. It is surely not insignificant that the notion of configuration, first introduced in relation to cinema, obliges a repositioning of the relations between poem and thought and calls into question the 'evental' theory of the poem. Significantly, the first example of configuration/subject that the *Handbook of Inaesthetics* presents us with is that of 'tragedy', which Badiou presents as beginning with the event named Aeschylus and as reaching with Euripides its point of saturation. This poetic configuration is quite clearly a configuration of connection [*de nouage*]: it is 'Greek tragedy' sheltering under the concepts which philosophy, from Schelling to Nietzsche and Heidegger, has provided for it, i.e. Greek tragedy as philosophical concept – but also as raw material for the modern art named 'theatrical directing' [*mise en scène*].

But probably the clearest example of this muddying of modernist oppositions is to be found in cinema and its 'impurity'. Badiou assigns to cinema an exemplary role in the patrolling of that border between art and non-art which I mentioned earlier, one wherein its function is that of a sort of doorman/bouncer/filter. But for Badiou cinema is also the specific witness to a crisis – or in his vocabulary, saturation – in the modernist paradigm of the separation between art and non-art. There have been, he tells us, two great ages of cinema: a representational Hollywood age and a modern age of anti-narrative, anti-representational cinema. It would certainly be possible to argue about this sequence, which applies a simple division of *mimesis* from *anti-mimesis* only at the price of occluding the anti-representational paradigm in accordance with which cinema, before its standardization by Hollywood, declared itself to be an art at the price of setting aside the great aesthetic schema of the Idea's direct – unnamed – presence in the movement of bodies and images, which its theoreticians had drawn from Mallarmé and dance. The fact remains that this division leads Badiou to consider contemporary cinema as belonging to a third age in which there is no paradigm prescribing cinema's artistic character. In a word, what he describes is what others would call a postmodern age of cinema (and 'postmodernism' is in fact nothing but the disillusioned recognition of the inconsistency of the modernist paradigm, in a word, the weary version of anti-aesthetic spleen). But what is interesting is that this diagnosis obliges Badiou tacitly to call into question the very division between representational and anti-representational eras by affirming that art's internal divisions do not pertain to cinema because it is not really an art, or else because it is an entirely particular art: an impure art, or an art of impurity, the art of mixture in general, the one which is made up of the mixture of other arts (novel, music, painting, theatre). On the one hand, then, Badiou reiterates André Bazin's thesis. On the other hand, he radicalizes it. Cinema is not just made up of the mixture of other arts. Its own proper, defining characteristic consists in *impurifying* them.

It is possible to recognize in this assignation of cinema's own improper 'propriety' a highly specific form of the exclusion of the impure, which in fact means the exclusion of aesthetics as regime of art, regime of the indistinction of art and arts. Badiou assigns an art of the borders the task of containing all these 'impurifications', all these slippages which – ever since Mallarmé and a few others established its programme of thought – have invaded the realm of arts, muddying the borders between the exhibition of speech and dance or the circus, between painting and sculpture, photography or lightshows. It is fairly obvious that the cinematographic 'impurification' has many precursors. First there was opera, invented as a restoration of Greek tragedy and capable of both becoming the total work of art and of lending its name to 'soap opera'. Then there were all the impurifications of dramatic art – stagings of texts and stagings of props, boxing rings, circus rings, symbolist or biomechanical choreographies – through which theatre, named either as theatre or as directing [*mise en scène*], declared itself an autonomous art. We know that, historically, these impurifications provided the testing ground for many of the ways cinema was to explore montage, acting and the visual. But Badiou assigns all these inventions to a very determinate place by making theatre the pure 'site' for the 'formula', and by making the process of theatrical directing the haphazard ephemeralization through which the eternity of the Idea present in the text is turned into a collective summoning of latent courage. By thematizing the impurity of cinema Badiou acknowledges the constitutive impurity of this aesthetic regime of the arts (which is the only thing that ensures the singularity of art) but only so that he can immediately drive it out to the margins of art.

The same stakes are present in the other function Badiou assigns to the impure art of cinema: that of purging whatever of non-art can be purged. The 'formal' impurification of the other arts is in effect, according to him, the means through which cinema purges itself of its own impurity – thus it purges for instance all the imagery, all the visual stereotypes that constitute its raw material. Cinema conceived in this way divides into two: it is art insofar as it purges itself of the visual stereotypes that constitute it as a spectacle in Debord's sense, a form of the commerce of images and the free-flow of social stereotypes of visuality – today for example, the stereotypes of pornography, speed, catastrophe or the virtual. But precisely because of this, it carries out the purging of non-art in general. It acts as frontier and intersection by filtering whatever of non-art is capable of passing into art.

Here once again, Badiou encounters a general law of the aesthetic regime, even if he acknowledges it only in cinematography and pushes it out to the borders of art. What he says of cinema could equally be applied to literature – which Badiou, as a *theoretician*, only identifies under the name of the poem. Understood in its constitutive impropriety, the latter has been the site of a similar negotiation of the indiscernible border, which always needs to be redrawn, between art and non-art. In reference to cinematographic impurity, Badiou himself alludes to those 'idiotic paintings' in which Rimbaud sought the gold of the new poem. Among the examples I cited earlier, I would invoke Balzac here and the way in which he 'impurifies' the fine flow of narrative prose by importing into it an 'impurification' of painting, by drawing a story from a genre portrait in the Dutch manner (whose importance in the aesthetic connection of thought and image was emphasized by Hegel and others). We also know how this impurification of prose by painting and of painting by prose in Balzac serves a process of purification, always at the limits of the indiscernible, which reworks and repositions the stereotypes of the serialized novel, but also the stereotypes of that mode of imaginary visuality illustrated by the *physiologies* of his time, the presentation that society gives of itself and of the distribution of types that constitute it. Badiou's characterization of the duality of cinema in terms of art and non-art, impurifier and purifier, opens on to the whole long history of exchanges between art and non-art that defines the aesthetic regime of art. Even as it tries to ward off aesthetics, perhaps inaesthetics thereby enters into a new dialogue with it. It puts back into play, if not into question, the operations through which it sought to challenge the logic of the aesthetic regime of the arts.

Returning now to my initial question, and keeping a clear distance from the terms of its 'letter of introduction', my conclusion is that *inaesthetics* is the shared name, the homonymous and equivocal name for three processes through which Badiou's modern Platonism confronts the equivocations of the homonymy of art. Firstly, 'inaesthetics' names the operations of dissimulation, the operations that dissociate the logic of art's aesthetic regime, through which the 'Platonism of the multiple' is constructed as the thought of art. It names the operations through which the 'truths' of art – which is to say, of the poem first and foremost – are torn from the indistinction of the metamorphic universe in which the aesthetic regime connects the forms of art, the forms of life, and the forms of the thought of art. Secondly, 'inaesthetics' designates the twisted necessity whereby those dividing lines through which the Platonism of truths hides its affinity with aesthetic Platonism come to coincide with the dividing lines through which *modernism* seeks to guarantee that which is 'proper to art' against its aesthetic indistinction. It names the way in which art's Platonic heteronomy comes to be adjusted to the modernist dogmas of art's autonomy and play its part in that anti-aesthetic resentment which is the eventual result of the modernist guarantee. But perhaps 'inaesthetics' also designates a third process, one through which the first two are at once accomplished and undermined. It designates the movement whereby the attempt to delimit the places of art, to delimit what is not-yet-art and distinguish between art/non-art, undermines the very end it was supposed to secure and releases what it was supposed to shut away by retying art to non-art and to the discourse on art. Inaesthetics would then no longer just be the translation of modernism's anti-aesthetic consummation into Badiou's terms. It could be the name for something that reopens the question of what is 'proper' to art and the homonymy of art. Against the tide of anti-aesthetic resentment and postmodern inanity, it would be the site and occasion for challenging the modernist configuration of Badiou's conception of art, for reconsidering the misleading evidence for the identification of art and its homonymy.

AFTERWORD

SOME REPLIES TO A DEMANDING FRIEND

Alain Badiou

At the heart of all the objections put forward by this incomparable reader, translator, companion and critic, this harsh and tender friend, Peter Hallward, there lies the intersection of two problems:

1. Isn't it too abstract to reduce the diversity of empirical worlds to a collection of pure multiples? Do we do not thereby fall back upon a dogmatic distinction between, on the one hand, the simple being of things, and, on the other, the qualities and relations which alone can *identify* these things?
2. Isn't it necessary, from the outset, to think the *relation* between the pure presentation of what is (its multiple being) and the situation (or world) in which what is comes to be presented (or presents itself)? In other words, to think the relation between presentation and representation? Or, in the terms I've come to adopt in my most recent work: to think the relation between objective 'atoms' and the worlds in which they constitute the being of appearance, or appearing?

These fundamental questions subtend a whole host of more concrete queries. For example: What is the status of the empirical sciences (physics and biology)? When dealing with issues relating to our collective existence, can we really concern ourselves with exclusively political sequences? Are there not slow evolutions in which the role of institutions, customs, generations – in brief, of the state – is of crucial significance? But you have just read all this in Hallward's introduction, in his own style.

I do not intend to treat these questions here one by one, nor do I wish to enter into subtle counter-arguments. After all, could I do any better than I already have done in my books? I believe it is more important to axiomatize my *intentions*; I am perfectly aware of the paradoxical violence of the statements I uphold, and will explain why I continue steadfastly to uphold them. I will do this in five points.

I

It is very important to grant a statement from the very beginning of *Being and Event* its full scope: ontology *is a situation*. Or, if you prefer: ontology is a world. This means that the mathematical theory of pure multiplicity in no way claims to inform the way we might think everything that is presented in the infinity of real situations, but only the thinking *of presentation as such*. This is what I call, adopting the vocabulary of the philosophical tradition, being *qua being*. Whatever else we do, we must not disregard the *qua*. It is obvious (for me as much as for Aristotle) that if you think the planet Mars from within the ontological situation, then you will give priority to determining what grounds a certain identity between Mars and Jupiter, and not to what indicates their differences. We might even say that, strictly speaking, you are thinking *nothing* about the planet Mars. What you are theorizing is rather the general possibility of multiple-presentation. Considered '*qua* being', it is certainly the case that the planet Mars activates a possibility immanent to the mathematical theory of pure multiplicities. You will only arrive at the exact nature of this possibility by taking the planet Mars as your starting-point, and certainly not by beginning from mathematized ontology, in which 'Mars' simply doesn't exist at all. In other words, in its being Mars is ultimately a pure multiple, but we cannot determine this singular multiple that is Mars (insofar as we can think it in terms of its being as such) by moving from mathematical theory to the identification of this singularity. We must proceed the other way around; we must move from an acknowledgement of the appearing of Mars in a world (whose scale, or 'transcendental regime' [*le transcendental*], we can establish) to its ontological determination. Nonetheless, the fact that this determination is ultimately mathematical leaves a trace. This trace consists in the simple fact that scientific physics must be mathematized. At bottom, when Galileo says that the world 'is written in the language of mathematics' he is not saying anything different.

II

By conceiving of things this way I can also establish, in passing, the status of those 'sciences' which are not 'hard sciences', namely biology (in its current form) and the disparate collection of the human sciences. My argument is very simple. To the extent that they have any material effect these disciplines are technical knowledges; for the rest they are nothing but ideologies. That knowledges and techniques exist is an established fact pertaining to the encyclopaedia of situations. To account for this fact there is no need for the intellectual apparatus of ontology, since we are dealing here only with the diversified legislation of worlds, and therefore with the laws of the transcendental. Biology, for the time being, is thus nothing but a collection of findings [*trouvailles*] anarchically correlated to a powerful apparatus of experimentation, an apparatus that enables, for example, the blind statistical testing of the effects of a given molecule or the role of a given protein in a particular physiological sequence. The ideological component is very important here (just look at the intrusion into research of 'ethical' concerns of religious origin, or at the conservative social organization of medicine, or at ecological obscurantism). Nevertheless, ideology does not dominate the discipline absolutely, since the technical apparatus does produce real effects that can be repeated and controlled, especially in the therapeutic domain. In the human sciences, by contrast, with the exception of their small quasi-formalized component (which thereby touches upon the being of objects: phonology in linguistics, the foundations of Marxist economics, perhaps a part of the anthropological theory of kinship, perhaps also a segment of psychoanalysis), ideology is largely dominant, and is currently oriented towards the economic, military and 'moral' maintenance of parliamentarian capitalism, presented as a commendable end of History.

I would like to reserve the name of science for truth procedures which, setting out from a worldly situation whose dimensions and scale of which are established, touch on the being of appearing [*l'être de l'apparaître*]. In other words, what qualify as sciences are only those disciplines in which the power of being leaves the following indisputable trace: the obligation of mathematic formalism. Let me add that sciences are *not* the only truth procedures (my approach is not scientistic). The power of the multiple and its empty 'heart' can also be summoned through the *creation of sensory forms* (art), through *the axiomatization (or organization) of the resources of the collective in its confrontation with the state* (politics), and through *the systematic play, carried to infinity, of pure difference* (love). In at least these ways the human species of animal can serve as the material for truths. Among these four kinds of truth, science is distinguished by the way it combines the mathematical resource of the letter (the mark [*stigmate*] inscribed by ontology) and the theoretically controlled experimental apparatus (the mark inscribed according to the transcendental constraints specific to this or that world).

III

As regards the intrinsic articulation between a presented multiplicity and the world in which it is presented (or presents itself), my current schema is rather complicated. It is not true that in the objective determination of worlds (I call 'object' a multiple that is 'there' in a determinate world), the relation of objects to other objects of the world is not taken into account. Indeed, the function that assigns to every multiple the degree of intensity of its appearing is fundamentally a *differential* function. It identifies a given multiple through the systematic comparison of the intensity of its appearing-in-the-world (its being-there) with the intensity of all the other multiples that are co-present in the world. That this comparison is ultimately quantitative (an order of degrees) conforms to everything that science (precisely) tells us: the correlation of worldly phenomena with the purity of their being is *marked* by the necessity of *measurements*. In certain respects it is not false to say, as the Pythagoreans did, that everything is number. Is not matter itself reducible to energy-fields of quantifiable intensity? Likewise, in the conception of the appearing of multi-plicities that I propose, we have intensities that can be compared. The structure of order and the comparison of degrees simply exhibit the rationality of intensive measurement, the single law of appearing.

To pit the 'qualitative' against the reign of number has always been the rhetorical strategy of anti-scientific obscurantism. To be sure, there is a *truth* of pure qualities (in visual art, for example). But this is a generic creation, and not a logical given of worlds. The pure logic of appearance is marked in its form by the underlying mathematicity of the being of what appears.

I might add that the main theorem of this whole theory demonstrates the existence of a crucial link between appearance and being, namely the retro-action, on to a pure multiple, of the transcendental structurings of a world. Using the pure relational logic of topoi, we can actually demonstrate that, when it is caught up in a determinate world, a multiple receives an intrinsic *form*. Without doubt, the exploration of this form is the most difficult part of my forthcoming *Logiques des mondes* – just like the theory of truth as a generic sub-set is the most difficult part of *Being and Event*. I hope nevertheless that it receives the attention it deserves since I think, if I may say so, that it is a rather beautiful theory! It shows both that every object is composed of atoms and that every 'homogeneous' part of an object can be synthesized (i.e. enveloped by a dominant term). All this allows me to construct a bridge between the philo-sophy of being-there – a major preoccupation of our time ever since Heidegger, if not Hegel – and the most demanding mathematization (in this case, the theory of sheaves [*faisceaux*], the most contemporary form of the link between algebra and geometry).

IV

It is true that the binary opposition affirmed in *Being and Event* between 'situation' and 'state of the situation', or between presentation and repre-sentation, posed some tough theoretical problems. Nonetheless, to maintain that the relation of simple presentation (belonging, marked by $\in$) is a form of immanence absolutely distinct from representation, or from the sub-set (inclusion, marked by $\subseteq$), is all the more essential since I believe it is this scission of immanence (the existence of two incommensurable forms of being-in) that radically distinguishes my ontology from that of Deleuze: vitalism, including Spinoza's version of vitalism (the philosophy of the power [*puissance*] of being), requires the absolute unity of Relation.

I remain determined, therefore, to combine the ontological maintenance of the binary opposition with the logical introduction of all sorts of nuances in the ways whereby a multiple is presented in a world. I do not pretend that this combination is easily made. In the end, it rests on my first point: ontology is a world. Now as it happens, for a number of crucial reasons (which in the end boil down to the necessarily absolute character, as far as the *concepts* are concerned, of the opposition between being and nothingness), *the logic of the ontological world is binary*. In other words, the world of ontology is a classical one (a classical world is one whose transcendental regime is a Boolean algebra, i.e. it is a world that validates the logical principle of the excluded middle). To the extent that it is thought ontologically, a multiple is thus forced to sustain a stark opposition between its presentation and its representation. To the extent that it is thought logically, that is, relative to the world in which it is declared to be 'there', a multiple – now apprehended as an object – is inscribed, in its denumerable relation to all the possible degrees of intensity of appearance, as a potentially infinite *variation*.

In the end, all of this comes down to *the binomial of being and existence*. Much of what Hallward resists with respect to the rigidity of the doctrine of being is in any case at least nuanced if not reduced in the correlated doctrine of existence (a multiple 'exists' relative to a given world, whereas a multiple 'is' relative to the world of ontology – i.e. of mathematics – alone).

Let us hazard the following formulation: being is what existence becomes when the world is mathematics (ontology).

v

Within this framework, I can now try to sketch a reply to the questions concerning history, *longues durées*, institutions, etc. A world is the set of the objective variations that constitute it. From this point of view, certainly, there are always modifications, in one direction or another, which are so many displacements of relative intensities. I have never said that every transformation or becoming is a truth procedure and consequently dependent upon a founding event and a fidelity to this event. But what does require a founding discontinuity, together with the ethic of a truth, is a sequence that involves change *in the transcendental evaluations themselves*. It is true that in *Being and Event*, in which the main preoccupation is with thinking the being of truths (and of subjects), the opposition might seem to be between pure conservation (situation, encyclopaedia) and becoming (inquiries, subjects, the generic). In *Logiques des mondes*, I can rationally distinguish four figures of transformation: a modification (which is the mode of being of the objects of the world), a fact (which is a transcendental novelty, but one endowed with a low degree of intensity), a singularity (a transcendental novelty whose intensity is strong, but which has few consequences), and an event (a singularity with consequences of maximal intensity). By playing on these four figures and their interrelations it is perfectly possible to think all the types of evolution internal to a world, and to see that, in order to arrive at a new type of existence with regard to a given problem (the status of sexual difference, the future of Palestine, the resurrection of music after serialism, etc.), it is necessary to possess, at one and the same time: a certain transcendental regime of intra-worldly modifications, the shock of an event, the constitution of a new subject, the rule-bound consequences of this constitution, and so on. These are the resources required by a concrete analysis of change.

Having said that, the aspect of such changes that matters to the philosopher is the aspect that involves construction of a truth. Why? Because this construction remains unthinkable if we limit ourselves to the logic of the interests of the human animal, which means: to the logic of the (very many) worlds inhabited by this crafty, cruel and obstinate animal. In other words, because only this construction is trans-human. All I am doing here, in fact, is corroborating some very old speculative statements. Plato: philosophy is an awakening, ordinary life is nothing but a dream. Aristotle: we must live as immortals. Hegel: the absolute works through us. Nietzsche: we must free the overman within man.

Philosophy must always watch over itself, so as not to become an anthropology, and in particular an anthropology of finitude. Yes, that is its task: to guard us from every establishment of an anthropology of finitude. The tools I propose are those that the epoch forces us to forge in order to keep up this guard, this watch. The mathematical ontology of the multiple, the categorial logic of worlds, the ray of appearance, evental intensity, the generic sub-set of a truth, the subject of truth ... These are so many available means to focus our thought on all that the human animal can do, over and above that which it commonly thinks itself capable of doing, on this paradoxical capacity that has no other reason to come to light (through a difficult fidelity) than the desire, forced by an evental outside, to move beyond the resignation of established beliefs.

Lin Piao, today a largely forgotten character and one who met a grievous fate, used to say, in order to stigmatize as 'revisionist' the established and bureaucratic communism of the Russians: 'in the end, the essence of revisionism is the fear of death'. If we understand by 'death' the key signifier of every anthropology of finitude (which might take the form, as it does today, of the 'body', or of the 'intimate' – these mediocre deaths), then we will say: 'The essence of philosophy is the struggle against revisionism.'

I leave you with this definition; its consequences are not negligible.

Translated by Alberto Toscano

NOTES

INTRODUCTION

1   Alain Badiou, 'Platon et/ou Aristote-Leibniz' (1995): pp. 62–3.
2   Jean-Paul Sartre, *L'Existentialisme est un humanisme* [1946] (Paris: Gallimard 'Folio', 1996): pp. 32–3.
3   Perhaps the most striking and certainly the most radical example of an analysis of an eventaI sequence inspired in part by Badiou's conception of things (despite obvious philosophical differences) is Christian Jambet's *La Grande Résurrection d'Alamût* (Lagrasse: Verdier, 1990; see in particular p. 192, n. 228).
4   For an especially clear account see Badiou, 'Mathématiques et philosophie' (2003).
5   Badiou, 'Logologie contre ontologie' (1996): 113–14.
6   To be more precise: Badiou's ontology seeks to avoid both the presentation of being as a sort of transcendent object independent of its articulation *and* the idea that being is nothing more than the presupposition of a formalist axiomatics. On the one hand, 'the apodicity of mathematics is guaranteed directly by being itself, which it pronounces' (*EE* 13), such that mathematics is not merely 'a matter of thought, it is a matter of realities' (*NN* 11; cf. 261); on the other hand, true thought does not encounter such realities as external objects (in accordance with Kantian restrictions) but thinks them directly, adequately (roughly in accordance with Platonic or Spinozist notions of adequation).
7   Joseph Dauben, *Georg Cantor: His Mathematics and Philosophy of the Infinite* (Cambridge, MA: Harvard University Press, 1979), pp. 147, 294–7.
8   See *EE* 71–2. Though being cannot be exposed as multiple, Badiou can nevertheless show that the decision to characterize being as multiple is *necessary* once we have concluded that being cannot be thought as one (*EE* 37–8).
9   Again, since 0 is a natural number, this description applies only to the set of positive integers {1, 2, 3 ...}. The fact that in the set of natural numbers 0 itself must be the element at the edge of the void raises one of the most difficult issues in *Being and Event*: the elusive distinction between the void as such and its *name* or mark (cf. *EE* 80–1, 103–4), a distinction complicated by the fact that Badiou presents the void as nothing other than 'the proper name of being' (*EE* 68–9). This is one of several mathematics-related topics that Anindya Bhattacharyya is exploring with rare precision in his forthcoming study of Badiou's ontology.
10 Badiou, *La Commune de Paris: une déclaration politique sur la politique* (2003). The Haitian war of independence that began in 1791 would be another highly pertinent example of a somewhat similar sequence. Cf. Peter Hallward, 'Haitian Inspiration: Notes on the Bicentenary of Haiti's Independence', *Radical Philosophy* 123 (January 2004): 2–7.
11 Badiou, *La Commune de Paris*, p. 14. Badiou's own readings of Lenin as a theorist of political *subjectivity*, of course, generally privilege this same gap (see for instance *TS* 63–4, 187–8, 246–7; *DI* 33; *La Distance politique* 2 [Feb. 1992], 9). (*La Distance Politique* is the journal of the Organisation Politique, which Badiou founded with Natacha Michel and Sylvain Lazarus in the mid-1980s; for details consult http://www.organisationpolitique.com.)
12 I go into some of these same questions in more detail in my *Subject to Truth*, chapter 13. The most notable defence of Badiou as a dialectical thinker has been proposed by Bruno Bosteels (see his contribution to the present volume); although I certainly stand by the general thrust of my non-relational interpretation, Bos-

teels' argument is strong enough to oblige me to qualify one or two aspects of this interpretation here.

13 Badiou contrasts this position with Paul Ricoeur's tacitly Christian conception of forgiveness, whereby whatever evil you might commit, in the end 'you are worth more than what you do' (Badiou, 'Le Sujet supposé chrétien de Paul Ricœur' [2003], p. 8).

14 Badiou, 'L'Etre, l'événement et la militance' (1991), p. 21; 'Saisissement, dessaisie, fidélité' (1990), p. 21; cf. AM 36.

15 Badiou, 'Ontology and Politics' (1999), in Infinite Thought, p. 179.

16 Bruno Bosteels is right to point out in his contribution to this volume that in Subject to Truth (p. 413, n. 53) I misrepresent, referring to L'Etre et l'événement p. 230, the non-relation between an event and its site: the reference in question in fact applies only to the way an eventual sequence will look from the perspective of the state. (With great regret, I've since realized that I made a similar error in Subject to Truth, p. 25, where I quote a passage of Théorie du sujet that refers to 'extreme' renunciation of the world: although Badiou is unequivocally hostile to any ethic adapted to the prevailing way of the world, his 'Promethean' alternative also seeks to avoid a merely tragic posture of isolation from the world). These errors are inexcusable. I still think that there is a good case for saying that there's no relation between the occurring of an event and the site in which it occurs (or the multiplicity that it is), but clearly not on the basis of this particular passage of Being and Event: see below, question 5. Bosteels and I might agree at least on this: a somewhat different understanding of the event – which as things stand is the only available link between consistency and inconsistency, albeit one that vanishes as soon as it appears – may allow for the conception of a more dialectical or relational version of militant truth.

17 Badiou, 'Philosophy and Psychoanalysis' (1999), Infinite Thought, p. 86.

18 Badiou, 'Platon et/ou Aristote-Leibniz' (1995), p. 72. Hence the 'unicity' of the void, where 'unicity' means: given a certain property, only one being can be conceived as having that property. As Badiou notes, this applies to $\emptyset$ and ω_0 as much as to a monotheistic notion of God (EE 560).

19 Badiou, La Commune de Paris (2003), p. 29.

20 EE 113. Is it enough to say then that only in the wake of a truth can we distinguish something from nothing or someone from no one, that only an event can open the way for a new dialectic between consistency and inconsistency, when in each case 'what allows a genuine event to be at the origin of a truth, which is the only thing that can be for all, and that can be eternally, is precisely the fact that it relates to the particularity of a situation only from the bias of its void, [which] is the absolute neutrality of being' (E 65; cf. EE 431; PM 88)? On the apparently irreducible gap between the void (or inexistence) and substance (or existence) see also François Wahl's sophisticated reading of Being and Event in Charles Ramond (ed.), Penser le multiple, pp. 177–82.

21 On Badiou's refusal of the linguistic turn see in particular EE 317–25; CT 123–5.

22 Badiou has recently dismissed biology, for instance, as a 'rampant empiricism disguised as science', while noting how easily physics can open the door to 'spiritualism' if not 'obscurantism' (Badiou, 'Mathématiques et philosophie' (2003), p. 14). In a related sense: though the logic of forcing that Badiou adapts from Cohen applies clearly enough to matters of pure conviction or inspiration, it is less obviously adapted to empirical situations (for instance to the first of Badiou's own illustrations in Being and Event, which turns on the possible existence, as anticipated by Newtonian astronomy, of a new planet in our solar system [EE 440]).

23 'L'Entretien de Bruxelles' (1990), p. 19; AM 82–3; EE 374.

24 'It is more interesting and more attuned to the necessity of the times', says Badiou in response to Oliver Feltham's question, 'to think that all situations are infinite

[. . .]: it is a conviction, not a deduction' (Badiou, 'Ontology and Politics', *Infinite Thought*, p. 182; see also Zupančič's contribution to the present volume).

25   Cf. Paul Cohen, *Set Theory and the Continuum Hypothesis* (New York: W. A. Benjamin, 1966), p. 112; Mary Tiles, *The Philosophy of Set Theory* (Oxford: Blackwell, 1989), p. 186.

26   Badiou, rev. of 'Gilles Deleuze: *Le Pli: Leibniz et le baroque*' (1990), p. 180.

27   *EE* 232–3: see also Bosteels' contribution to this volume. I admit that, though its formulation remains sketchy in *Being and Event*, I did not pay sufficient attention to the constraints of this temporality in *Subject to Truth*. I admit too that, as Bosteels and Toscano have pointed out (in recent correspondence), the theory of periodization presented in *Théorie du sujet* and preserved to some extent in *Can Politics Be Thought?* does open the door to a more nuanced, more cumulative conception of events (e.g. the October Revolution as a partial reprise of the Paris Commune), and judging from the early drafts of *Logiques des mondes* it seems that Badiou may soon return to explore the matter in terms that attenuate the characterization of events as random and haphazard. He seems more willing now to soften the previously rigid opposition between situation and event and to provide in its place a more subtle model of transformation that includes ordinary occurrences or 'facts' of the situation, a more developed conception of the eventals site, a more ramified typology of 'singularities', and so on.

28   Badiou, 'Being by Numbers' (1994), p. 118; cf. *CT* 69; *SP* 119.

29   After Benjamin, after Foucault, this is a question that Françoise Proust in particular began to develop in the years before she died (in December 1998); see her *De la Résistance* (Paris: Le Cerf, 1997) and her interview with Daniel Bensaïd, 'Résister à l'irrésistible', in *Art, culture, politique*, ed. Jean-Marc Lachaud (Paris: PUF, 2000), pp. 149–60. See also Bensaïd, *Résistances: Essai de taupologie générale* (Paris: Fayard, 2001), pp. 35–45, along with his contribution to the present volume.

30   See for instance Jean-Paul Sartre, *Critique de la raison dialectique* [1960] (Paris: Gallimard, 1985), p. 76; Sartre, *Situations IX* (Paris: Gallimard, 1972), pp. 101–3.

31   See in particular Bernard Stiegler, 'Technics of Decision', *Angelaki* 8 (2) (August 2003): 151–68.

32   *E* 39; cf. *EE* 444; *SP* 80–1, 89.

33   What Badiou most admires about those who chose to resist the Nazi occupation is precisely that their choice involved no deliberation, i.e. that – like every true decision – it had effectively been made in advance, as a matter of necessity (*AM* 9–17).

34   See for instance a 1997 interview with Miep Gies, online at http://teacher.scholastic.com/frank/tscripts/miep.htm. The question of what motivates a subject, of what is at stake when a subject is mysteriously *seized* by an event, is one that has been asked in different ways by Simon Critchley ('Comment ne pas céder sur son désir?', in Ramond (ed.), *Penser le multiple*, pp. 210ff.) and Sam Gillespie ('Get Your Lack On', a talk presented at the University of Middlesex, 29 March 2003). Gillespie proposes a useful comparison between fidelity and the late Lacanian notion of drive.

35   Pierre Macherey, 'Le Mallarmé d'Alain Badiou', in Ramond (ed.), *Penser le multiple*, pp. 405–6: see also Zupančič and Rancière's contributions to the present volume.

36   Compare Badiou's position here with the approach long defended by Noam Chomsky, for example (cf. Chomsky, *Understanding Power*, ed. Peter R. Mitchell and John Schoeffel [New York: New Press, 2002], pp. 63–4).

37   The declaration is quoted in Badiou, *La Commune de Paris*, p. 16.

38   'The ethics of a truth amounts entirely to a sort of restraint [*retenue*] with respect to its powers' (*C* 194; cf. *E* 63, 78).

39   These and other questions about the relation between Badiou's ontology and his onto-logy are among the many topics that have been raised at a series of workshops on Badiou's work at the University of Paris VIII over 2002–3, organized by Oliver

Feltham and Bruno Besana: much of the material presented at these workshops will be published as *Alain Badiou: de l'ontologie à la politique*, forthcoming 2004.
40 I am referring here to the unpublished draft of *Logiques des mondes*, chapter 3 ('Le Monde'); cf. CT 191–3.

CHAPTER 1

1   *EE* 235ff.; Blaise Pascal, *Pensées*, trans. A. J. Krailsheimer (Harmondsworth: Penguin, 1966; the translation follows the order established by Lafuma).
2   Blaise Pascal, *Discours sur la religion et quelques autres sujets, restitués et publiés par Emmanuel Martineau* (Paris: Fayard/Armand Colin, 1992).
3   Henri Gouhier, *Blaise Pascal: Commentaires* (Paris: Vrin, 1971), pp. 362–5.
4   Jean Mesnard, *Les Pensées de Pascal* (Paris: Sedes, 1993), pp. 269ff.
5   Edmund Husserl, *L'Origine de la géométrie*, trans. with an introduction by Jacques Derrida (Paris: PUF, 1962), pp. 48–53; Derrida, *Edmund Husserl's Origin of Geometry: An Introduction*, trans. John P. Leavey (Stony Brook, NY: Nicholas Hays, 1978), pp. 59–64.
6   Jacques Derrida, *De la Grammatologie* (Paris: Minuit, 1967), p. 34; *Of Grammatology*, trans. Gayatri C. Spivak (Baltimore: Johns Hopkins University Press, 1976), p. 20tm.
7   Jacques Derrida, *Spectres de Marx* (Paris: Galilée, 1993), p. 200; *Spectres of Marx*, trans. Peggy Kamuf (London: Routledge, 1994), p. 123tm.
8   Georges Canguilhem, *Idéologie et rationalité dans l'histoire des sciences de la vie* (Paris: Vrin, 1977), pp. 44–5. Canguilhem alludes here to Bogdan Suchodolski's article 'Les Facteurs du développement de l'histoire des sciences' (XIIe Congrès International d'Histoire des Sciences, Colloques, Textes des Rapports), *Revue de Synthèse* 49–52 (1968), 27–38.
9   Georges Canguilhem, 'Galilée: la signification de l'oeuvre et la leçon de l'homme', in *Etudes d'histoire et de philosophie des sciences* (Paris: Vrin, 1968), pp. 44–6. I discuss these texts in my article 'Etre dans le vrai? Science et vérité dans la philosophie de Georges Canguilhem', in Balibar, *Lieux et noms de la vérité* (La Tour d'Aigues: Editions de l'Aube, 1994): 163–97.
10 Thanks to the publication of Merleau-Ponty's last lectures, together with the preparatory material: Maurice Merleau-Ponty, *Notes de cours 1959–1961* (Paris: Gallimard, 1996); *Notes de cours sur 'L'Origine de la géométrie' de Husserl, suivi de Recherches sur la phénoménologie de Merleau-Ponty* (Paris: PUF, 1998).
11 Cf. Merleau-Ponty, *Eloge de la philosophie et autres essais* (Paris: Gallimard, 1989), pp. 54, 93, 121.
12 Jean Cavaillès, *Sur la Logique et la théorie de la science* (Paris: Vrin, 1987).
13 Michel Foucault, *L'Ordre du discours* (Paris: Gallimard, 1971), pp. 15–20; 'The Discourse on Language', trans. Rupert Swyer, published as the appendix to Foucault, *The Archaeology of Knowledge* (London: Tavistock, 1972), pp. 215–37.
14 Foucault, *The History of Sexuality, Volume I: An Introduction*, trans. Robert Hurley (Harmondsworth: Penguin, 1981), pp. 59–60.
15 Foucault, *The History of Sexuality, Volume II: The Use of Pleasure*, trans. Robert Hurley (Harmondsworth: Penguin, 1987), pp. 6–7.
16 Michel Foucault, review of Alexandre Koyré, *La Révolution astronomique: La Nouvelle Revue Française* 108 (1961), reprinted in *Dits et Ecrits 1954–1988, Vol. 1* (Paris: Gallimard, 1994), 170–1: 'There are sad histories of truth: those plunged into mourning by the tale of so many magical and dead errors.'
17 My hasty reference to 'the first person since Cavaillès' calls for two qualifications. First, to point out that we are still speaking only of the French environment. And second, to mention in counterpart, and remaining within that tradition, the work of Jules Vuillemin and Michel Serres, and especially Jean-Toussaint Desanti who,

in his *Idéalités mathématiques* (1968), attempted to do the opposite of what Badiou is doing: to construct a phenomenological meta-mathematics that takes as its specific object the historicity of theories.

18   See, for example, the second part of the essay on the semantic conception of truth and the foundations of semantics in Alfred Tarski, *Logic, Semantics and Meta-mathematics* (Indianapolis: Hackett, 1983).

19   Cf. Paul J. Cohen, *Set Theory and the Continuum Hypothesis* (New York: Benjamin, 1966).

20   Badiou, *Le Concept de modèle* (Paris: Maspero, 1969).

21   There could, perhaps, be no better demonstration of the profoundly different philosophical orientations of Badiou and Foucault than this terminological reversal, as it turns the utterance into a relationship with knowledge: for Foucault, 'veridicity' or 'truth-telling' is the active mode of truth which, at the heart of knowledges, unmasks and shakes their power-function; for Badiou, veridicity is a linguistic inscription that is inseparable from knowledges (in discursive 'encyclopaedias'), whilst the eventual truth marks a break with them.

22   Thomas Aquinas, translated excerpts from *Question disputée de la vérité* (Question I), in *Philosophes médiévaux des XIIIe et XIe siècles*, ed. Ruédi Imbach and Maryse-Hélène Méléard (Paris: UGE 10/18, 1986), pp. 69–94.

23   Badiou, 'Silence, solipsisme, sainteté: l'antiphilosophie de Wittengenstein' (1994).

24   See, for example, Jean Trouillard, 'Procession néo-platonicienne et création judéo-chrétienne', in *Néoplatonisme: mélanges offerts a Jean Trouillard: Les Cahiers de Fontenay* (March 1981); pp. 1–30; Stanislas Breton, *Du Principe: l'organisation contemporaine du pensable* (Paris: Aubier-Montaigne, 1971), pp. 150ff.

25   It should, however, be noted that the 'opposition in juxtaposition' of the 'X without X' thematized by Derrida on the basis of Blanchot (see in particular 'Pas', in Derrida, *Parages* [Paris: Galilée, 1986]) is always related to a *to come* or to an *advent* [*à-venir*] that has no foundations in presence; in Badiou, the 'X without X' that subtends the idea of taking 'a further step' is related to an event that has taken place or will take place.

26   Stanislas Breton, 'Dieu est dieu. Essai sur la violence des propositions tautologiques', in *Philosophie buissonière* (Grenoble: Jérôme Millon, 1989). See his profound exegesis, *Unicité et monothéisme* (Paris: Editions du Cerf, 1981).

27   Badiou and Balmès, *De l'Idéologie* (Paris: Maspero, 1976).

28   'What is the real unifying factor in this promotion of the cultural value of oppressed sub-sets [. . .]? It is, quite obviously, monetary abstraction, whose false universality is perfectly in keeping with communitarianist medleys' (*SP* 7).

29   'The fact that this revelation is of the order of a fable prevents Paul from being an artist, a scientist, or a state revolutionary, but it also denies him all access to philosophical subjectivity, which is either of the order of conceptual foundation or self-foundation, or subject to *real* truth procedures. For Paul, the event of truth disqualifies philosophical Truth just as, for us, the fictive dimension of that event disqualifies its claim to be a real truth' (*SP* 116).

CHAPTER 2

1   For an extremely clear formulation, see for example *PM* 21.

2   Anne Montavont demonstrates a use of the term *Abbau* by Husserl that makes one want to engage in an *Abbau* of the *Gestell* of the various *Abbau* of/in contemporary thought. Cf. Anne Montavont, *De la passivité dans la phénoménologie de Husserl* (Paris: PUF, 1999), pp. 215–16.

3   Aristotle, *Metaphysics*, A 982b 22.

4   Badiou, *Ahmed le philosophe* (1995), p. 101.

CHAPTER THREE

1   'We ask of materialism that it include what we require, that which Marxism, albeit unbeknown to it, has always had as its guiding thread: a theory of the subject' (*TS* 198).

2   'Platonisme et ontologie mathématique', in *CT* 103. See also 'La Mathématique est une pensée' in the same volume, especially page 49, and *EE* 49.

3   *D* 78. Badiou is perfectly consistent on this point. Fifteen years earlier, in *Théorie du sujet*, he had written: 'Every materialism posits the primitive unicity of being, implying that being's intimate constitution requires one name only. Matter is that name' (*TS* 206). A name, and not a concept. It is a question of evacuating the name 'matter' of every residue of phenomenological or conceptual idealization. Six years later, in *Being and Event*, Badiou will alight on a fittingly meaningless proper name for being in its unidealizable material constitution: that of the void or null-set, Ø.

4   This is not to say that Badiou identifies the subtraction of being with the subtraction of truth. Indeed, he explicitly warns against the dangers of doing so: 'It is this radical distinction between being and truth which my critics seem to have great difficulty grasping, especially when it becomes necessary to think the being of truths, which is entirely different from truth as truth, which is forcing [...] [But] with Cohen's theorem, mathematics allows one to establish that, even if truth is distinct from being, nevertheless, the being of a truth remains 'homogeneous' with being as being (which is to say that there is only one kind of being)' (Badiou, 'Dix-neuf Réponses à beaucoup plus d'objections' [1989]: 247–68). Since, for Badiou, being is at once and indissociably that which is consistently presented as multiple (counted-as-one) and that which is subtracted from presentation, or that which in-consists (i.e. the void as multiple-of-nothing [cf. *EE* 31–91]), truth manifests the in-consistency of a situation's suture to its being: 'Since the groundless ground of what is presented is inconsistency, a truth will be that which, from within the presented and as a part of the presented, brings forth the inconsistency which ultimately provides the basis for the consistency of presentation' (*MP* 88). It is crucial not to conflate this distinction between consistency and inconsistency with any sort of ontological difference between beings and Being. Whereas Heidegger's 'Being' is in transcendent exception to everything that is because it is *more than* anything, Badiou's void is in immanent subtraction to everything that is because it is *less than* anything.

5   Cf. *MP* 13–20, 59–70.

6   'If ontology is that particular situation which presents presentation, it must also present the law of every presentation, which is that of the errancy of the void, the unpresentable as non-encounter. Ontology will present presentation only insofar as it will theorize the presentative suture to being, which, properly conceived, is the void wherein the originary inconsistency is subtracted from the count. Thus, ontology is obliged to propose a theory of the void' (*EE* 70).

7   'The reintrication of mathematics and philosophy is the necessary operation for whoever wants to have done with the power of myths, whatever they may be, including the myth of wandering and the Law, the myth of the immemorial, and even – because, as Hegel would say, it is the manner in which the path is taken that counts – the myth of the painful absence of myths' (*C* 176).

8   'We may think the historicity of certain multiples, but we cannot think one History' (*EE* 196).

9   *MP* 37–8. Interestingly, for Badiou, axiomatic set theory figures as the apex of active nihilism: it is Cantor, not Nietzsche, who has succeeded in thinking the death of God – i.e. of the One.

10 Again, the foreclosure through which the inconsistent void subtracts itself from presentation is not to be confused with the bestowing withdrawal through which presencing withholds itself from presence (Heidegger).

11 Gilles Deleuze and Félix Guattari, *L'Anti-Oedipe: Capitalisme et schizophrénie* (Paris: Minuit, 1972), pp. 297–8.

12 All the while acknowledging the crucial dissimilarity: that the former propose a paradigm of being as plenitude (the full or intensive body of the Earth: the Deterritorialized), while the latter proposes a paradigm of being as empty.

13 'It is necessary to prevent the catastrophe of presentation which would occur were the latter to encounter its own void, which is to say, to prevent the presentative advent of inconsistency as such, or the ruin of the One' (*EE* 109).

14 Politics puts the State at a distance, the distance of its measure. The resignation that prevails in non political periods is fuelled by the fact that the State is not at a distance because the measure of its power is errant. One is a captive of the State's unassignable errancy. Politics is the interruption of this errancy, it is the exhibiting of a measure of the State's power. It is in this sense that politics is 'freedom'. The State is in effect the unlimited subordination of the parts of the situation, a subordination whose secret is the errancy of unconditional power, its lack of measure. Freedom here consists in a distancing of the State effected through the collective fixing of a measure of the excess. And if the excess is measured, it is because the collective can measure up to it. (*AM* 160)

But what if in the era of human genome sequencing and what Deleuze and Guattari call 'generalized machinic enslavement', there is simply no distance left to measure between the ubiquitous automation of Capital and the wretched ape with which it has achieved an almost perfect symbiotic intimacy?

15 *C* 206. Although my hurried exposition risks eliding the important distinction between connection [*connexion fidèle*] and forcing as two distinct moments of the truth procedure, I believe it is a mistake to think one can abstract them from the latter as separate operations. In the final section of *Being and Event* ('Le Forçage: vérité et sujet'), Badiou clearly emphasizes their inseparability:

I will call the relation implied in the fundamental law of the subject, forcing. If a term in the situation forces a statement in the subject-language, this means that the veridicality of that statement in the situation to come is equivalent to that term's belonging to the indiscernible part which results from the generic procedure. Thus, it means that this term, which is linked to the statement by the relation of forcing, belongs to truth. Or that the enquiry into the connection between this term, which has been encountered through the subject's aleatory trajectory, and the name of the event, has had a positive outcome. A term forces a statement if its positive connection to the event forces the statement to be veridical in the new situation (the situation supplemented by an indiscernible truth). Forcing is a relation that is *verifiable by knowledge*, since it bears on a term of the situation (which has been presented and named in the language of the situation) and a statement of the subject-language (the names of which have been 'assembled' using multiples of the situation). What is not verifiable by knowledge is whether or not the term that forces a statement belongs to the indiscernible. The latter is solely a function of the randomness of the enquiries. (*EE* 441)

Connection pertains to the hazardous unverifiablity of the hypothetical condition ('if term x belongs to the indiscernible'), whereas forcing pertains to the verifiability of the consequent ('then statement y about x will be verifiable'). Clearly, the truth procedure requires the indivisibility of condition and consequent, connective enquiry and forcing.

16 'If there is no formula by which to discern two terms of the situation, we can be sure that the choice to make the verification proceed via one rather than the other is devoid of any basis in the objectivity of their difference. Thus, it is an absolutely pure choice, free of any presupposition other than that of having to choose the term through which the verification of the consequences of the axiom will proceed, without there being any mark to distinguish one term from the other' (*C* 190).

17 'Clearly, the act of the subject is essentially finite, as is the presentation of indiscernibles in its being. Nevertheless, the verifying trajectory goes on, investing the situation through successive indifferences, so that what thereby takes shape little by little behind these acts delineates the contour of a sub-set of the situation or universe wherein the evental axiom verifies its effects. This sub-set is clearly infinite and remains incompletable' (C 191).

18 Thus, for example, in his *Saint Paul*, Badiou writes: 'There is no letter of salvation or literal form for a truth procedure. This means that there is a letter only for that which constitutes an automatism or a calculation. The corollary being: there is calculation only of the letter. There is a numbering only of death' (SP 88).

19 Cf. Alan Turing, 'On computable numbers, with an application to the *Entscheidungsproblem*', in *Proceedings of the London Mathematical Society*, 2nd series, no. 42 (1936–37): 544–6.

20 Cf. Turing, op. cit. This identification was arrived at independently in the same year (1936) by Alonzo Church and is now known as 'the Church–Turing thesis'.

21 Chaitin has made his results partially accessible to the lay reader (by which I mean myself) in *The Unknowable* (New York: Springer-Verlag, 1999) and *Exploring Randomness* (New York: Springer-Verlag, 2001). A more technical treatment is provided in *The Limits of Mathematics* (New York: Springer-Verlag, 1998). I ought to mention that the iconoclastic Chaitin is still a controversial figure and there are those who take issue with what they see as the excessive claims he makes on behalf of the significance of his own work. See for instance Michiel Van Lambalgen, 'Algorithmic Information Theory' in *The Journal of Symbolic Logic* 54 (1989): 1389–1400. See also Panu Raatikainen, 'On Interpreting Chaitin's Incompleteness Theorem', in *Journal of Philosophical Logic* 27 (1998): 569–86; Raatikainen, 'Algorithmic Information Theory and Undecidability', in *Synthese* 123 (2000): 217–25; Raatikainen, 'Review of *Exploring Randomness and The Unknowable*', in *Notices of the American Mathematical Society* 48:9 (2001): 992–6. Nevertheless, it seems to me that these critics are targeting Chaitin's claims about the philosophical *implications* of his incompleteness results for the foundations of mathematics, rather than the mathematical cogency of those results.

22 In other words: the length of the shortest computer program required to generate it.

23 Chaitin acknowledges M. Davis, H. Putnam, J. Robinson, Y. Matijasevic and J. Jones.

24 Chaitin shows how if the program-length complexity (H) for a finite random bit string X_n is defined as always being less than N, an infinite random bit string X will have the following property: almost all but finitely many of its prefixes X_n will be finite random strings.

25 It can be found in Chaitin's *Algorithmic Information Theory* (Cambridge, UK: Cambridge University Press, 1987).

26 Chaitin, *The Unknowable*, p. 93.

27 'If a truth is to surge forth eventually, it must be non-denumerable, impredicable, uncontrollable. This is precisely what Paul calls grace: that which occurs without being couched in any predicate, that which is trans-legal, that which happens to everyone without an assignable reason. Grace is the opposite of law insofar as it is what comes without being due [. . .]. That which founds a subject cannot be what is due to it' (SP 80–1; on the event as 'grace' see also DZ 142–3).

28 '[T]he undecidability of the Continuum Hypothesis effectively consummates set theory [. . .]. It indicates the point of escape, the aporia, the immanent errancy wherein thought experiences itself as an un-grounded confrontation with the undecidable, or – to use Gödel's vocabulary – as a continuous resort to intuition, which is to say, to decision' (CT 108). Thus, '[b]esides the multiple as presentative basis, truth requires the event as extra-one. Consequently, truth forces decision' (EE 470).

CHAPTER 4

1   Paul Cohen, *Set Theory and the Continuum Hypothesis* (NY: W. A. Benjamin, 1966), p. 151.
2   Spinoza, *Ethics*, part I, appendix.

CHAPTER 5

1   Cf. Todd May, *Reconsidering Difference: Nancy, Derrida, Levinas, and Deleuze* (University Park: Penn State Press, 1997), esp. pp. 165–82.
2   Badiou, *Deleuze: The Clamor of Being*, trans. Louise Burchill (Minneapolis: University of Minnesota Press, 2000), p. 11. Hereafter *D*.
3   Gilles Deleuze, *Difference and Repetition*, trans. Paul Patton (New York: Columbia University Press, 1994), p. 57.
4   Deleuze, *Expressionism in Philosophy: Spinoza*, trans. Martin Joughin (New York: Zone Books, 1990), p. 167.
5   Deleuze, *Difference and Repetition*, p. 36.
6   *D* 39/24, quoting Deleuze, *The Logic of Sense*, ed. Constantin Boundas, trans. Mark Lester with Charles Stivale (New York: Columbia University Press, 1990), p. 179.
7   Deleuze, *Expressionism in Philosophy*, p. 42.
8   Deleuze, 'Plato and the Simulacrum', in *The Logic of Sense*, p. 262.
9   Deleuze, *Difference and Repetition*, p. 208.
10 Deleuze, *Difference and Repetition*, p. 209.
11 Deleuze, *Difference and Repetition*, p. 207.
12 *D* 79/52. The phrase 'distinct and yet indiscernible' is taken from Deleuze's *Cinema 2: The Time-Image*, trans. Hugh Tomlinson and Robert Galeta (Minneapolis: University of Minnesota Press, 1989), p. 81.
13 May, *Reconsidering Difference*, pp. 191–2.
14 For example: '[W]e should have no more difficulty in admitting the virtual insistence of pure recollections in time than we do for the actual existence of non-perceived objects in space' (Deleuze, *Cinema 2*, p. 80).
15 Deleuze and Guattari, *What is Philosophy?*, trans. Hugh Tomlinson and Graham Burchell (New York: Columbia University Press, 1994), p. 82.
16 Deleuze, *Bergsonism*, trans. Hugh Tomlinson and Barbara Habberjam (New York: Zone Books, 1988), p. 59.
17 Deleuze, *Bergsonism*, p. 82.
18 Deleuze, *Bergsonism*, p. 38.
19 Deleuze, *Difference and Repetition*, p. 209. Badiou cites this passage in *D* 77–78/51.
20 Deleuze, *Difference and Repetition*, p. 214.

CHAPTER 6

1   Gilles Deleuze, *Foucault*, trans. Seán Hand (Minneapolis: University of Minnesota Press, 1986), p. 42. Deleuze was speaking of Virilio's relation to Foucault.
2   For one example among many, see *EE* 522: 'the latent paradigm in Deleuze is "natural" [. . .]. Mine is mathematical.'
3   Alain Badiou, 'Un, multiple, multiplicité(s)', 4. (My references are to the typescript of this text, which to my knowledge is Badiou's only direct discussion of Deleuze's theory of multiplicities; the article has since been published in *Multitudes* 1 [March 2000], 195–211).
4   See Badiou, 'Un, multiple, Multiplicité(s)': p. 4, and *D* 69/46.
5   Gilles Deleuze and Félix Guattari, *Anti-Oedipus*, trans. Robert Hurley, Mark Seem and Helen R. Lane (New York: Viking, 1977), pp. 371–2. For Badiou's appeal to

Lautréamont, see *CT* 72 and 'De la Vie comme nom de l'Etre', in *Rue Descartes* 20 (May 1998), p. 34.

6   Proclus, *Commentary of the First Book of Euclid's Elements*, trans. Glenn R. Murrow (Princeton: Princeton University Press, 1970), pp. 63–7, as cited in Deleuze, *Difference and Repetition*, p. 16 and *passim*.

7   Deleuze, *Logic of Sense*, ed. Constantin V. Boundas, trans. Mark Lester with Charles Stivale (New York: Columbia University Press, 1990), p. 54.

8   Deleuze, *Difference and Repetition*, p. 160 (emphasis added).

9   Deleuze and Guattari, *A Thousand Plateaus*, pp. 408–9.

10 Deleuze and Guattari, *A Thousand Plateaus*, p. 554 n. 23, commenting on Léon Brunschvicg, *Les Etapes de la philosophie mathématique* [1912] (Paris: Blanchard, 1972), pp. 327–31.

11 Deleuze and Guattari, *What is Philosophy?*, trans. Hugh Tomlinson and Graham Burchell (New York: Columbia University Press, 1994), p. 128tm.

12 See Carl B. Boyer, *The History of the Calculus and Its Conceptual Development* (New York: Dover, 1959), p. 267. Deleuze praises Boyer's book as 'the best study of the history of the differential calculus and its modern structural interpretation' (Deleuze, *Logic of Sense*, p. 339).

13 Giulio Giorello, 'The "Fine Structure" of Mathematical Revolutions: Metaphysics, Legitimacy, and Rigour', in *Revolutions in Mathematics*, ed. Donald Gillies (Oxford: Clarendon Press, 1992), p. 135. I thank Andrew Murphie for this reference.

14 See Penelope Maddy, *Naturalism in Mathematics* (Oxford: Oxford University Press, 1997), pp. 51–2, for a discussion of Cantorian 'finitism'.

15 For a useful discussion of Weierstrass' 'discretization program' (written from the viewpoint of cognitive science), see George Lakoff and Rafael E. Núñez, *Where Mathematics Comes From: How the Embodied Mind Brings Mathematics Into Being* (New York: Basic Books, 2000), pp. 257–324.

16 See Maddy, *Naturalism in Mathematics*, p. 28.

17 Deleuze, *Difference and Repetition*, p. 180.

18 Deleuze, *Difference and Repetition*, p. 323 n. 22. Deleuze is referring to the work of thinkers such as Georges Canguilhem, Georges Bouligand, Albert Lautman and Jules Vuillemin.

19 Deleuze and Guattari, *A Thousand Plateaus*, p. 144.

20 Jean Dieudonné, *L'Axiomatique dans les mathématiques modernes* (Paris: Congrès International de la Philosophie des Sciences, 1949), vol. 3, pp. 47–8, as cited in Robert Blanché, *L'Axiomatique* (Paris: PUF, 1955), p. 91.

21 Nicolas Bourbaki, 'The Architecture of Mathematics', in *Great Currents of Mathematical Thought*, ed. François Le Lionnais, trans. R. A. Hall and Howard G. Bergmann (New York: Dover, 1971), p. 31.

22 See Deleuze, seminar of 22 February 1972 (available on-line at <http://www.webdeleuze.com>): 'The idea of a scientific task that no longer passes through codes but rather through an axiomatic first took place in mathematics toward the end of the nineteenth century, that is, with Weierstrass [...], who makes an axiomatic of differential relations. One finds this well-formed only in the capitalism of the nineteenth century.'

23 All the citations in this paragraph are from Deleuze and Guattari, *A Thousand Plateaus*, pp. 373–4.

24 Deleuze and Guattari, *A Thousand Plateaus*, p. 361. This section of the 'Treatise on Nomadology' (pp. 361–74) develops in detail the distinction between 'major' and 'minor' science.

25 Deleuze and Guattari, *A Thousand Plateaus*, p. 486.

26 Deleuze and Guattari, *A Thousand Plateaus*, p. 362; cf. p. 144.

27 Deleuze and Guattari, *A Thousand Plateaus*, pp. 485, 486.

28 See Abraham Robinson, *Non-Standard Analysis* (Princeton: Princeton University Press, 1966). For accessible discussions of Robinson's achievement, see Jim Holt,

'Infinitesimally Yours', in *The New York Review of Books* 46: 9 (20 May 1999), as well as the chapter on 'Nonstandard Analysis' in Philip J. Davis and Reuben Hersch, *The Mathematical Experience* (Boston and New York: Houghton Mifflin, 1981), pp. 237–54. The latter note that 'Robinson has in a sense vindicated the reckless abandon of eighteenth-century mathematics against the straight-laced rigour of the nineteenth century, adding a new chapter in the never-ending war between the finite and the infinite, the continuous and the discrete' (p. 238).

29 Henri Poincaré, 'L'Oeuvre mathématique de Weierstrass', *Acta mathematica* 22 (1898–99): 1–18, as cited in Carl B. Boyer, *History of Mathematics* (Princeton: Princeton University Press, 1968), p. 601. Boyer notes that one finds in Riemann 'a strongly intuitive and geometrical background in analysis that contrasts sharply with the arithmetizing tendencies of the Weierstrassian school' (p. 601).

30 Deleuze and Guattari, *A Thousand Plateaus*, p. 461.

31 Deleuze and Guattari, *A Thousand Plateaus*, pp. 362, 367 (emphases added).

32 Badiou, 'Un, Multiple, Multiplicité(s)', p. 4.

33 Deleuze, *Difference and Repetition*, p. 170.

34 Deleuze, *Difference and Repetition*, p. 161.

35 Deleuze, *Difference and Repetition*, p. 179.

36 Deleuze, *Difference and Repetition*, p. 171.

37 The only aspect of Deleuze's treatment of mathematics that Badiou has discussed directly is Deleuze's interpretations of Riemannian manifolds, but his critiques seem to me to miss the import of Deleuze's own analyses. Badiou suggests that a Riemannian manifold not only entails 'a neutralization of difference' (whereas Riemannian space is defined differentially) and a 'preliminary figure of the One' (whereas Riemannian space has no preliminary unity), but that it also finds the 'subjacent ontology of its invention' in set theory (whereas its *invention* is tied to problematics and the use of infinitesimals). See Badiou, 'Un, Multiple, Multiplicité(s)': 10. What Badiou's comments reflect, rather, is the inevitable effort of 'major' science to translate an intrinsic manifold into the discrete terms of an extensive set – though as Abraham Robinson noted, it is by no means clear that results obtained in differential geometry using infinitesmals are automatically obtainable using Weierstrassian methods (see Robinson, *Non-Standard Analysis*, pp. 83, 277).

38 See, in particular, Deleuze, *Difference and Repetition*, p. 183, although the entirety of the fifth chapter is an elaboration of Deleuze's theory of multiplicities.

39 Manuel DeLanda, for instance, in his recent book, *Intensive Science and Virtual Philosophy* (New York: Continuum, 2002), has proposed several refinements in Deleuze's formalization, drawn from contemporary science: certain types of singularities are now recognizable as 'strange attractors'; the resolution of a problematic field (the movement from the virtual to the actual) can now be described in terms of a series of spatio-temporal 'symmetry-breaking cascades', and so on. But as Delanda insists, despite his own modifications to Deleuze's theory, Deleuze himself 'should get the credit for having adequately *posed the problem*' of problematics (p. 102).

40 *D* 32/20. Badiou characterizes Deleuze's position in explicit Neo-Platonic terms: 'It is as though the paradoxical or supereminent One immanently engenders a procession of beings whose univocal sense it distributes' (*D* 41–2/26).

41 This conflation is stated most clearly in *D* 69/46: 'the univocal sovereignty of the One'. For criticisms of Badiou's understanding of the doctrine of univocity, see Nathan Widder, 'The Rights of Simulacra: Deleuze and the Univocity of Being', in *Continental Philosophy Review* 34 (2001): 437–53, and Keith Ansell-Pearson, 'The Simple Virtual: A Renewed Thinking of the One', in his *Philosophy and the Adventure of the Virtual: Bergson and the Time of Life* (London: Routledge, 2002), pp. 97–114.

42 Deleuze and Guattari, *What is Philosophy?*, pp. 35, 202–3.

43 See Deleuze, *Difference and Repetition*, pp. xvi, 220–1: 'We tried to constitute a philosophical concept from the *mathematical* function of differen*t*iation and the *biological* function of differen*c*iation, in asking whether there was not a statable relation between these two concepts which could not appear at the level of their respective objects [. . .]. Mathematics and biology appear here only in the guise of technical models which allow the exposition of the virtual [problematic multiplicities] and the process of actualization [biological individuation].' Deleuze thus rejects Badiou's reduction of ontology to mathematics, and would no doubt have been sympathetic to Ernst Mayr's suggestion that biology can be seen as the highest science, capable of encompassing and synthesizing diverse developments in mathematics, physics and chemistry. See Ernst Mayr, 'Is Biology an Autonomous Science?', in his *Toward a New Philosophy of Biology: Observations of an Evolutionist* (Cambridge, MA: Harvard University Press, 1988), pp. 8–23.

44 Badiou, 'Un, Multiple, Multiplicité(s)', p. 6.

45 Deleuze, seminar of 22 April 1980 (<http://www.webdeleuze.com>).

46 Deleuze, 'H as in "History of Philosophy"', in his *Abécédaire* (overview by Charles J. Stivale <http://www.langlab.wayne.edu/Romance/FreDeleuze.html>).

47 Deleuze, seminar of 14 March 1978. See also the seminar of 21 March 1978: 'The abstract is lived experience. I would almost say that once you have reached lived experience, you reach the most fully living core of the abstract [. . .]. You can live nothing but the abstract and nobody has lived anything else but the abstract.'

48 Deleuze, *Bergsonism*, trans. Hugh Tomlinson (New York: Zone Books, 1988), p. 14.

49 Deleuze, *Bergsonism*, p. 14; D 57/36.

50 Deleuze and Guattari, *A Thousand Plateaus*, p. 570, n. 61; see also p. 461.

51 Deleuze, *Difference and Repetition*, p. 323, n. 21.

52 On the role of the scholia, see Deleuze, *Expressionism in Philosophy: Spinoza*, trans. Martin Joughin (New York: Zone Books, 1992), pp. 342–50 (the appendix on the scholia). On the deductive hiatuses introduced in the fifth book of the *Ethics*, see 'Spinoza and the Three Ethics', in *Essays Critical and Clinical*, trans. Daniel W. Smith and Michael A. Greco (Minneapolis: University of Minnesota Press, 1997), esp. pp. 149–50.

53 D 8/1. See also Badiou's essay on Spinoza, 'L'Ontologie fermée de Spinoza', in *CT* 73–93.

54 See Deleuze, *Difference and Repetition*, pp. 161 and 323 n. 21. Reuben Hersh makes a similar point in his *What is Mathematics, Really?* (New York: Oxford University Press, 1997), pp. 112–113: 'Euclidean certainty is boldly advertized in the *Method* and shamelessly ditched in the *Geometry*.'

55 See Deleuze and Guattari, *A Thousand Plateaus*, p. 455: 'Our use of the word "axiomatic" is far from a metaphor; we find *literally* the same theoretical problems that are posed by the models in an axiomatic repeated in relation to the State.'

56 Deleuze and Guattari, *A Thousand Plateaus*, p. 466.

57 Deleuze, seminar of 22 February 1972: 'The scientific axiomatic is only one of the means by which the fluxes of science, the fluxes of knowledge, are guarded and taken up by the capitalist machine [. . .]. All axiomatics are means of leading science to the capitalist market. All axiomatics are abstract Oedipal formations.'

58 Deleuze and Guattari, *What is Philosophy?*, p. 152.

59 Deleuze and Guattari, *What is Philosophy?*, pp. 46–7.

60 Deleuze and Guattari, *A Thousand Plateaus*, p. 266; Deleuze, *Spinoza, Practical Philosophy*, p. 128.

61 D 136/91: Badiou notes that 'Deleuze always maintained that, in doing this [conceptualizing absolute beginnings], I fall back into transcendence and into the equivocity of analogy.' See also D 97/64: 'it is essential for me that truth be thought [. . .] as *interruption*'.

CHAPTER 7

1   Alain Badiou, 'Nous pouvons redéployer la philosophie' (1993), 2.
2   Truth is a matter of 'acts', explains Peter Hallward in his book *Subject to Truth*, pp. 154–5; see also Eustache Kouvélakis, 'La Politique dans ses limites, ou les paradoxes d'Alain Badiou', in *Y-a-t-il une pensée unique en philosophie politique?*, special issue (no. 28) of *Actuel Marx* (2000), 39–54.
3   See in particular Badiou, *Saint Paul* (1997).
4   Badiou, 'Huit Thèses sur l'Universel' (2000): 11–20; cf. Hallward, *Subject to Truth*, pp. 250–1.
5   Cf. Spinoza, *Tractatus Theologico-Politicus*, Chapter VI.
6   Slavoj Žižek, *The Ticklish Subject* (London: Verso, 1999), p. 183.
7   See for instance Badiou, *Une Soirée philosophique*, pp. 24–5.
8   Jacques Rancière, *Aux Bords du politique* (Paris: La Fabrique, 1998).
9   Lucien Goldmann, 'Le Pari est-il écrit pour le libertin?', *Recherches dialectiques* (Paris, Gallimard, 1967), pp. 169ff.
10 Ibid.
11 See the articles by Kouvélakis and Žižek in *Actuel Marx* 28 (2000).
12 Badiou, 'Nous pouvons redéployer la philosophie', 2.
13 Badiou, 'Réponses écrites d'Alain Badiou', *Philosophie, philosophie* (1992), 70.
14 Cf. Hallward, *Subject to Truth*, p. 228; *La Distance politique* 19–20 (April, 1996), 9; *La Distance politique* 17–18 (October, 1996), 13.
15 *La Distance politique* 15 (December, 1996), 11.
16 Cf. Badiou, 'Théorie axiomatique du sujet', seminar of 26 November 1997, and Badiou's letter to Hallward, 17 June 1996, in Hallward, *Subject to Truth*, pp. 41, 226.
17 Cf. 'Proposition de réforme de la Constitution', *La Distance politique* 12 (February 1995), 5–6; Hallward, *Subject to Truth*, p. 239.
18 [Bensaïd is referring to unpublished lectures given by Françoise Proust in the late 1990s, just before she died; see also Bensaïd's interview with Proust, 'Résister à l'irrésistible', in *Art, culture, politique*, ed. Jean-Marc Lachaud (Paris: PUF, 2000), pp. 149–60, editor's note].
19 Badiou, 'Réponses écrites d'Alain Badiou' (1992), 66–71.
20 Except for the following: 'The true content of Marx's conception of the end of philosophy is in fact the thesis of the end of the State, hence an ideologico-political thesis, the thesis of communism. It is not the idea of an end of philosophy that identifies the sophist. What identifies him is his position with regard to the link between language and truth. Granted, by announcing the realization of philosophy in revolution, its dissolution into a real praxis, Marx certainly sutures philosophy to politics. Ultimately, this suture brings about a sort of exhaustion of philosophy. But this suture should not be confused with the sophist's demoralizing arrogance' (Badiou, 'Réponses écrites').
21 Hallward, *Subject to Truth*, 284–91.

CHAPTER 8

1   Theodor W. Adorno, *Problems of Moral Philosophy*, trans. Rodney Livingstone (Cambridge: Polity Press, 2000).
2   Ibid., p. 165.
3   Ibid., pp. 98–9.
4   For reflections on the uneasy relation, after Kant, between normative ethical theory and a counter-tradition which suspects the notion of an autonomous ethical domain, see Raymond Geuss, 'Outside Ethics', *European Journal of Philosophy* 11:1 (April 2003): 29–53.

5   Michel Foucault, *Remarks on Marx: Conversations with Duccio Trombatori* (1981) (New York: Semiotext(e), 1991), p. 31.
6   Marjorie Garber, Beatrice Hanssen and Rebecca L. Walkowitz (eds), *The Turn to Ethics* (London: Routledge, 2000), pp. viii–ix.
7   Ibid., p. 15.
8   Ibid., p. 86.
9   For Badiou's theory of the three forms of evil, see *E* 64–75/72–87.
10 *E* 44/49. Even Raymond Geuss, who is enthusiastic about the general thesis of *Ethics*, emphasizes that Badiou has an 'explicitly dualist theory' of the human being (see his review in *European Journal of Philosophy* 9:3 [December 2001], 410). He does not, however, note the tension with Badiou's immanentist commitments elsewhere.
11 Cf. Immanuel Kant, *Religion within the Limits of Reason Alone*, trans. Theodore M. Greene and Hoyt H. Hudson (New York: Harper, 1960), book 1, pp. 15–39.
12 Ibid., p. 48.
13 Ibid., p. 49.
14 Ibid., pp. 22–33.
15 Arthur Schopenhauer, *The World as Will and Representation*, trans. E. F. J. Payne (New York: Dover, 1966), vol. I, p. 404.
16 Ibid.
17 Ibid.
18 Kant, *Religion within the Limits of Reason Alone*, p. 179.
19 Schopenhauer, *The World as Will and Representation*, vol. I, p. 411.
20 Kant, *Religion within the Limits of Reason Alone*, p. 48.
21 For an interpretation of Kant's ethics which stresses the excessiveness of the moral demand for unaided human nature, and the religious character of Kant's solution, see John E. Hare, *The Moral Gap: Kantian Ethics, Human Limits and God's Assistance* (Oxford: Clarendon Press, 1996).
22 Jürgen Habermas, *Faktizität und Geltung: Beiträge zur Diskurstheorie des Rechts und des demokratischen Rechtsstaats* (Frankfurt-am-Main: Suhrkamp, 1992), p. 149. In his work on the philosophy of law Habermas emphasizes the overload of expectations on the individual produced by modern autonomous and universalistic morality (*die Vernunftmoral*). However, his suggestion that this problem can be addressed by displacing obligations from the moral to the legal domain seems to raise as many questions as it resolves. See ibid., pp. 144–51, 565–7.
23 See 'Meditations on Metaphysics', in Theodor Adorno, *Negative Dialectics*, trans E. B. Ashton (New York: Continuum, 1973), pp. 361–408 and Theodor Adorno, *Metaphysics: Concept and Problems*, trans. Edmund Jephcott (Cambridge: Polity Press, 2000), pp. 97–145.
24 On this see Gordon Finlayson, 'Adorno on the Ethical and the Ineffable', *European Journal of Philosophy* 10:1 (April 2002): 1–25.
25 Adorno, *Problems of Moral Philosophy*, p. 169.

CHAPTER 9

1   Slavoj Žižek, *The Ticklish Subject: The Absent Centre of Political Ontology* (London: Verso, 1999), pp. 172–3.
2   I have been told that, in his courses of the late 1990s, Badiou has partially addressed this objection through his reference to 'reactionary' and 'obscure' subject positions. I can only refer however to his published material.
3   Slavoj Žižek, 'Class Struggle or Postmodernism? Yes, please', in Judith Butler, Ernesto Laclau and Slavoj Žižek, *Contingency, Hegemony, Universality: Contemporary Dialogues on the Left* (London: Verso, 2000), p. 125.
4   Ibid., pp. 124–5.

5   The fact that Žižek makes more explicit than Badiou what I have called the 'third discourse' does not mean that his theoretical stance is more consistent. He constantly oscillates between grounding his ethico-political options in a Marxist theoretical approach (even an *ad usum Delphini* Marxism, as in the passage that I have just quoted) and the exaltation of the purely formal virtues of '*vivere pericolosamente*'. And when it is a matter of opting for the latter – for being anti-system for the sake of being so – he can be quite relaxed concerning ideological constraints. He suggests, for instance, that 'the only "realistic" prospect is to ground a new political universality by opting for the *impossible*, fully assuming the place of exception, with no taboos, no a priori norms ("human rights", "democracy"), respect for which would prevent us also from "resignifying" terror, the ruthless exercise of power, the spirit of sacrifice [. . .]. If this radical choice is decried by some bleeding-heart liberals as *Linkfaschismus*, so be it!' (Žižek, 'Holding the Place', in Butler et al., *Contingency, Hegemony, Universality*, pp. 326). Slightly truculent, isn't it?

6   The term 'ontology' has a particular meaning in Badiou's theoretical approach, different in some respects from the current philosophical use. I am employing it in the latter sense. The opposition ontic/ontological comes, of course, from Heidegger.

7   My basic assumption is that the central terms of a discursive formation universalize themselves by operating as nodal points (as master signifiers in the Lacanian sense) of an equivalential chain. I have mentioned before the example of Solidarnosc, but this universalization through equivalence is always present. Just think of the demands of 'peace, bread and land' in the Russian Revolution, which condensed a plurality of other demands, or in the role of the 'market' in Eastern European discourse after 1989. My argument is that the construction of Nazi hegemony operated in exactly the same way and that, as a result, the central symbols of its discourse – those that named the void – cannot be conceived as having a purely particularistic reference. Of course, the universal function of those names weakens but does not eliminate their particular content, but that happens with all hegemonic discourses. It is not possible for the universal to speak in a direct way, without the mediation of some particularity.

8   The notion of 'absent fullness' is mine and not Badiou's. (See my essay 'Why do empty signifiers matter to politics?', *Emancipation(s)* [London, Verso 1996].) It has no exact equivalent in Badiou's system because it is based in our different ways of conceiving the process of naming.

9   This does not mean, of course, that I am reducing Žižek's approach to these questions to assertions of that type. Žižek has the virtue of his own eclecticism, so on many occasions he develops political analyses of much higher interest, and his whole approach to the politico-ideological field is complex and, in several respects, potentially fruitful. Those assertions are, however, still there, not without producing some sterilizing theoretical and political effects.

10   Hallward, 'Translator's Introduction', in Badiou, *Ethics*, pp. xxxiii–xxxv.

11   And it would not be possible either to restrict set-theoretical analysis to the situation, given that the contamination between situation and event is a more fundamental ground than their distinction.

12   I find the whole distinction between philosophy and anti-philosophy a red herring. I do not deny that there are cases in which the notion of anti-philosophy would be pertinent – such as Nietzsche – but I find the generalization of the distinction, to the point of transforming it into a *ligne de partage* crossing the whole of the Western tradition, a rather naïve and sterile exercise. To detect a Platonic gesture as a founding moment separating conceptual thought from its 'other' is simply to ignore that the Platonic dualism is itself grounded in an army of metaphors which makes the theory of forms deeply ambiguous. And, closer to home, to claim that the *Philosophical Investigations* or *La Voix et la phénomène* are anti-philosophical

works does not make any sense to me. It is one thing to deny the validity of conceptual thought; it is another to show, through a conceptual critique, that the conceptual medium is unable to ground itself without appealing to something different from itself. To reduce the latter to the former is not a defence of the concept but just conceptual ethnocentrism.

13 As we have repeatedly asserted in this essay, the overdetermination between the situational and the evental supposes that the event cannot *just* be the exceptional kind of break that Badiou has in mind. Those breaks, no doubt, take place, and it is in them that the duality between the state of the situation and what we have called 'situationness' becomes fully visible. But the important point is that, if the event is the decision that escapes determination by what is countable within a situation, any kind of social action is dominated by the situation/event distinction. It is simply wrong to think that, apart from revolutionary breaks, social life is dominated by the purely programmed logic of what is countable within a situation. (Wittgenstein's critique of the notion of applying a rule is highly relevant for this discussion.)

CHAPTER 10

1 These three figures of the order of representation, which take the names of *esplace* [a neologism standing for 'space of placements'], state and world, are elaborated, respectively, in *Théorie du sujet* (1982), *L'Etre et l'événement* (1988) and *Logiques des Mondes* (forthcoming, 2005).

2 In *Being and Event*, Badiou himself subjected his earlier theory of the subject to criticism on the basis of this distinction. He has also made it into the principal schema through which to think both the glories and the ravages of subjectivation in the twentieth century, in *Le Siècle* [*The Century*] (forthcoming, 2004).

3 Badiou's most recent work asserts that a non-representational, procedural variety of separation is necessary in order to attain the in-separate or generic truth of being, see 'L'Ecriture du générique: Samuel Beckett', in Badiou, *Conditions*, p. 335 (translated in Badiou, *On Beckett* [2003], pp. 6–7).

4 Badiou, *D'Un Désastre obscur. Sur la fin de la verité d'État* (1991).

5 See Badiou, *Abrégé de Metapolitique* (1998).

6 Badiou and Balmés, *De l'Idéologie* (1976).

7 The primacy of revolt – that is, the primacy of *practice* – is the militant *leitmotiv* of Badiou's writings in the seventies. See especially Badiou, *Théorie de la contradiction* (1975), an intense and speculative commentary upon Mao's dictum 'it is always right to revolt against the reactionaries'. In it, we read the following: 'Revolt does not wait for its reason, revolt is what is always already there, for any possible reason whatsoever. Marxism simply says: revolt is reason, revolt is subject. Marxism is the recapitulation of the wisdom of revolt' (p. 21). Ergo, 'The real is not what brings together, but what separates. What advenes is what disjoins' (pp. 61–2).

8 On Badiou's (post-Maoist) conception of antagonism, see his 'One Divides into Two', *Culture Machine* 4 (2002) [http://culturemachine.tees.ac.uk].

9 This is what Badiou castigates as 'the fiction of the political'. See *Peut-on penser la politique?* (1985), pp. 9–21. The date of this book, two years after the recomposition of Badiou's Maoist party – the UCF(ML) – as *l'Organisation politique*, under the aegis of a 'politics without a party', is a testament to the intimate link between Badiou's metapolitical reflections and his long experience of political militancy. The notion of a transitivity of the subject to the situation is explicitly attacked in Badiou, 'Philosophie et politique', *Conditions*, p. 236.

10 The essential traits of this 'production of communism', formalized as the numericity proper to political subjectivation, are to be found in 'La Politique comme procedure de verité', in *Abrégé de Metapolitique*.

11 See 'La déliaison politique', *AM* 77–87.
12 For a political balance-sheet of classism and how it may be overcome by a 'politics without party', the reader will refer to the (anonymous) analyses published in *La Distance politique*, the newsletter of *L'Organisation politique*, in particular to the article in number 11: 'La Politique et l'état' [http://www.multimania.com/orgapoli/].
13 Badiou, *The Century* (forthcoming).
14 *PP* 27. This is where Badiou locates the (terroristic) paradox of a communist state.
15 Badiou's critique of destruction is entirely immanent to his own conceptual and political trajectory, as evinced by the theoretical proposals of *Théorie du sujet*, but especially the lapidary and uncompromising pronouncements in the earlier *Théorie de la contradiction*, such as: 'There are radical novelties because there are corpses that no trumpet of Judgment will ever reawaken' (*TC* 86). Or: 'To resolve is to reject. History has worked best when its dustbins have been the better filled' (*TC* 87). Arguably, it is precisely to the extent that his earlier writings provide us with the most extreme and consequent distillate of the destructive regime of thought that Badiou's present reflections on the century constitute a remarkable tool with which to orient ourselves in the present.
16 Much of Badiou's thought on the persistence of communism can be understood in its polemical divergence from the philosophical discourse of Jean-Luc Nancy and its resort to the category of community. See Nancy's 'La Comparution', in Jean-Luc Nancy and Jean-Christophe Bailly, *La Comparution (politique à venir)* [Paris: Christian Bourgois, 1991], pp. 49–100), whose gist is elegantly encapsulated by its subtitle: *from the 'existence' of communism to the community of 'existence'*. Badiou's critique of the concept of community is to be found in 'Philosophie et politique', in *Conditions*.
17 Badiou bases himself here on the concept of 'historical modes of politics', as developed in Sylvain Lazarus, *Anthropologie du nom* (Paris: Seuil, 1992).
18 Badiou, 'Raisonnement hautement spéculatif sur le concept de démocratie', *AM* 91, 92, 97.
19 See Badiou, *Théorie de la contradiction* (pp. 66–9) on the division within the masses as a possible site of the 'principal contradiction' pertaining to a political situation.
20 'La Déliaison politique', *AM* 81.
21 'La Politique comme procedure de verité', *AM* 165.
22 For the concepts of avoidance [*évitement*] and generic part, see *L'Etre et l'événement*, in particular pp. 369–74.
23 'La Politique comme procédure de verité', *AM* 166.
24 *EE* 447. Perhaps the point of greatest distance between this philosophy of generic truth and Badiou's Maoist period revolves around the determination of political truth. Whilst the drive and the object of this earlier work also lay in the 'eternity of the equal', the separating truth itself was unequal in its address and its operation. As we read in *Théorie de la contradiction* (pp. 16–17): 'Marxist truth is the reason that revolt makes its own in order to cut down the enemy. It repudiates all *equality* before truth. In a single movement, which is knowledge [*connaissance*] in its specific division into description and directive, it judges, pronounces the sentence, and immerses itself in its execution.'

CHAPTER 11

1 Alain Badiou, 'L'Investigation transcendantale' (2002), p. 7.
2 Badiou, 'L'Investigation transcendantale' (2002), pp. 7–8.
3 V. I. Lenin, 'Dialectics and Eclecticism', in Lenin, *Collected Works*, vol. 32 (Moscow: Progress Publishers, 1960), p. 93.

4 *D* 147/100; 'Le Flux et le parti (dans les marges de l'*Anti-Œdipe*)', in Badiou and Lazarus (eds), *La Situation actuelle sur le front philosophique* (1977), pp. 31–2.
5 Badiou, 'Can Change Be Thought? A Dialogue with Bruno Bosteels' (1999), forthcoming.
6 Badiou, 'Can Change Be Thought?'
7 Lenin, *Philosophical Notebooks*, ed. Stewart Smith, trans. Clemens Dutt, in Lenin, *Collected Works*, vol. 38 (Moscow: Progress Publishers, 1961), p. 360.
8 Badiou, 'Can Change Be Thought?'
9 Badiou, *Logiques des Mondes*, chapter 4.
10 See, for example, Peter Hallward, *Badiou: A Subject to Truth* (2003), pp. 49–50 and 290–1.
11 See also the anonymous text, most likely by Sylvain Lazarus, 'Le Mode dialectique', *La Distance Politique* 3 (May 1992): 4–6.
12 Badiou, Louis Mossot and Joël Bellassen, 'Hegel en France', *Le Noyau rationnel de la dialectique hégélienne* (1978), 11–17.
13 Badiou, 'Can Change Be Thought?'
14 Lenin, *Philosophical Notebooks*, p. 123.
15 Ibid., p. 109.
16 Badiou, *La Révolution culturelle* [2002]; *La Commune de Paris* [2003].
17 *EE* 230. Whereas Badiou is tackling this problem precisely as being inherent to the point of view of the state, Peter Hallward mistakenly cites this passage as evidence for his claim that there is no constituent relation between the event and the evental site (*Subject to Truth*, p. 413 n. 53).
18 Badiou, 'L'Entretien de Bruxelles' (1990): 15. See also *MP* 72/90–91.
19 *EE* 10. In his *Absolutely Postcolonial* (Manchester: Manchester University Press, 2001), Peter Hallward provides a remarkable critique of postcolonialism that is partly inspired by his productive disagreements with Badiou. In Argentina, the journal *Acontecimiento: Revista para pensar la política* has for years discussed specific political sequences in light of Badiou's philosophy. I myself have tried to delimit certain historical situations with a special eye on Latin America, in my articles: 'Travesías del fantasma: Pequeña metapolítica del 68 en México', *Metapolítica* 12 (1999): 733–68; 'Por una falta de política: Tesis sobre la filosofía de la democracia radical', *Acontecimiento: Revista para pensar la política* 17 (1999): 63–89; and 'In the Shadow of Mao: Ricardo Piglia's "Homenaje a Roberto Arlt"', *Journal for Latin American Cultural Studies* 12(2) (2003): 229–59.

CHAPTER 12

1 Cf. Jacques Rancière, *Disagreement: Politics and Philosophy*, trans. Julie Rose (Minneapolis: University of Minnesota Press, 1999).
2 It was of course Georg Lukács who, in his *History and Class Consciousness*, fully articulated this point.
3 This is how one should locate the shift from the biological instinct to drive: instinct is just part of the physics of animal *life*, while drive (*death* drive) introduces a meta-physical dimension. In Marx, we find the homologous implicit distinction between working class and proletariat: 'working class' is the empirical social category, accessible to sociological knowledge, while 'proletariat' is the subject-agent of revolutionary Truth. Along the same lines, Lacan claims that drive is an *ethical* category.
4 Furthermore, is there not a key difference between love and other truth procedures, in that, in contrast to others which try to force the unnameable, in 'true love', one endorses-accepts the loved Other *on behalf of the very unnameable X in him/her*. In other words, 'love' designates the respect of the lover for what should remain

unnameable in the beloved – 'whereof one cannot speak, thereof one must be silent' is perhaps the fundamental prescription of love.

5   Perhaps, along these lines, one should even take the risk of proposing that psychoanalysis – the subject's confrontation with its innermost fantasmatic kernel – is no longer to be accepted as the ultimate gesture of subjective authenticity.

6   Bruno Bosteels, 'Alain Badiou's Theory of the Subject: The Recommencement of Dialectical Materialism? (Parts I and II)', *Pli: The Warwick Journal of Philosophy* 12 (2001): 200–9; continued in *Pli* 13 (2002): 173–208.

7   Bosteels, 'Alain Badiou's Theory of the Subject (Part II)': 182.

8   Bosteels, 'Alain Badiou's Theory of the Subject (Part II)': 198. Badiou's notion of subjectivization as the engagement on behalf of Truth, as fidelity to the Truth-Event, is clearly indebted to the Kierkegaardian existential commitment 'experienced as gripping our whole being. Political and religious movements can grip us in this way, as can love relationships and, for certain people, such "vocations" as science and art. When we respond to such a summons with what Kierkegaard calls infinite passion – that is, when we respond by accepting an unconditional commitment – this commitment determines what will be the significant issue for us for the rest of our life' (Hubert Dreyfus, *On the Internet*, p. 86). What Dreyfus enumerates in this resumé of Kierkegaard's position are precisely Badiou's four domains of Truth (politics, love, art, science), *plus* religion as their 'repressed' model.

9   Bosteels, 'Alain Badiou's Theory of the Subject (Part II)': 180 and 194.

10   This is Lacan's standard definition of sublimation, in his *Seminar VII: The Ethics of Psychoanalysis*.

11   Bosteels, 'Alain Badiou's Theory of the Subject (Part II)': 196–7.

12   I am referring to Badiou's contribution to a conference for the European Graduate School in Saas Fee, August 2002. See also *E* 76/85–6.

13   One should note here that the Stalinist 'totalitarianism', far from simply standing for a total forcing of the unnameable Real on behalf of the Truth, rather designates the attitude of absolutely ruthless 'pragmatism', of manipulating and sacrificing all 'principles' on behalf of maintaining power.

14   Bosteels, 'Alain Badiou's Theory of the Subject (Part II)': 179.

15   See Theodor W. Adorno, 'Verbindlichkeit des Neuen', *Musikalische Schriften* V: 832–3.

16   Bosteels, 'Badiou's Theory of the Subject (Part II)', p. 199.

17   As to this matrix, see Jacques Lacan, *Seminar XX: Encore*.

18   In philosophical terms, Lacan introduces here a distinction, absent in Badiou, between symbolic truth and knowledge in the Real: Badiou clings to the difference between objective-neutral Knowledge which concerns the order of Being, and the subjectively engaged Truth (one of the standard topoi of modern thought from Kierkegaard onwards), while Lacan renders thematic another, unheard-of, level; that of the unbearable fantasmatic kernel. Although – or, rather, precisely because – this kernel forms the very heart of subjective identity, it cannot ever be subjectivized, subjectively assumed: it can only be retroactively reconstructed in a desubjectivized knowledge. For more on this crucial distinction see Žižek, *The Plague of Fantasies*, chapter 1.

CHAPTER 13

1   Jacques Lacan, 'Logical Time and the Assertion of Anticipated Certainty: A New Sophism', trans. Bruce Fink and Marc Silver, *Newsletter of the Freudian Field* 2:2 (1988): 4–22.

2   See Lacan, 'Le Nombre treize et la forme logique de la suspicion', in *Autres Ecrits*

(Paris: Seuil, 2001), pp. 85–99, and 'La Psychiatrie anglaise et la guerre', ibid., pp. 101–20.

3   Our presentation and interpretation of Lacan's article borrows from David Blomme and Dominiek Hoens, 'Anticipation and Subject: A Commentary on an Early Text by Lacan', in *Computing Anticipatory Systems: CASYS'99 – Third International Conference*, ed. Daniel Dubois (Woodbury, NY: American Institute of Physics, 2000), pp. 117–23.

4   *TS* 270. Discussions of Badiou's critique of Lacan can also be found in Bruce Fink, 'Logical Time and the Precipitation of Subjectivity', in *Reading Seminars I and II*, ed. Richard Feldstein et al. (Albany: SUNY Press, 1996), p. 385 n. 8, and Erik Porge, 'Une Forme du sujet: la subjectivation. D'après "Le Temps logique"', *Littoral* 25 (1988), p. 50 n. 1.

5   Badiou, *Le Siècle/The Century*, p. 99 of the typescript, quoted in Peter Hallward, *Badiou: A Subject to Truth* (2003), p. 393 n. 1.

6   A similar discussion of Badiou, Lacan and Žižek on the act can be found in Ed Pluth, 'Towards a New Signifier: Freedom and Determination in Lacan's Theory of the Subject' (PhD Dissertation, Duquesne University, 2002).

7   Slavoj Žižek, *The Ticklish Subject* (London: Verso, 1999), pp. 388, 374.

8   Badiou's analyses of the relation between an act and a line of reasoning can be found in his discussions of 'forcing'. See especially *TS* 287–90 and *EE* 438–44.

9   See Immanuel Kant, *Critique of Judgment*, trans. Werner S. Pluhar (Indianapolis: Hackett, 1987), pp. 132–7.

10 *EE* 229, also quoted in Žižek, *The Ticklish Subject*, p. 135.

11 Lacan, seminar of 19 December 1962, *Le Séminaire X: l'angoisse* (unpublished, 1962–63).

CHAPTER 14

1   Cf. Peter Hallward, *Badiou: A Subject to Truth* (Minneapolis: University of Minnesota Press, 2003), pp. 243–5.

2   Immanuel Kant, *Prolegomena to Any Future Metaphysics* (New York: The Bobbs-Merrill Company, 1950), p. 21.

3   Kant, *Critique of Pure Reason* (London: Macmillan, 1929), p. 10.

4   Kant, *Critique of Pure Reason*, p. 8.

5   Cf. Badiou, 'Dieux est mort', *CT* 9–24.

6   Cf. Eric Santner, *On the Psychotheology of Everyday Life: Reflections on Freud and Rosenzweig* (Chicago: The University of Chicago Press, 2001).

7   Heinrich Heine, 'The Homecoming', LVIII. I cite Hal Draper's translation, in *The Complete Poems of Heinrich Heine: A Modern English Version* (Boston: Suhrkamp/Insel, 1982), p. 99.

8   Gérard Wajcman, *L'Objet du siècle* (Paris: Verdier, 1998), p. 166.

9   Badiou et al., 'La Scène du Deux' (1999), in Badiou et al., *De l'amour*, p. 178.

CHAPTER 15

1   'Dance would mime thought as yet undecided' (Badiou, 'La Danse comme métaphore de la pensée', *PM* 97).

2   Badiou, 'Politics and Philosophy' (1998), p. 125.

3   Cf. Alexander García Düttmann, *Between Cultures: Tensions in the Struggle for Recognition* (London: Verso, 2000), *passim*.

CHAPTER 16

1   Gilles Deleuze, 'L'Epuisé', in Samuel Beckett, *Quad* (Paris, Minuit, 1992), trans. as
    'The Exhausted' by Anthony Uhlmann, revised by Daniel Smith and Michael A.
    Greco, in Deleuze, *Essays Critical and Clinical* (Minneapolis: University of Min-
    nesota Press, 1997), pp. 152–74.
2   Jean-Claude Milner, 'Tombeau de Mallarmé' (1997), in Milner, *Constats* (Paris:
    Gallimard, 'Folio', 2002), pp. 133–220.
3   See Jean-Jacques Lecercle, *Deleuze and language* (London: Palgrave, 2002), chapter
    6.

CHAPTER 17

1   Paul de Kock (1794–1871): a largely forgotten minor novelist who specialized in
    amusing depictions of bourgeois life, translator's note.
2   Cf. Clement Greenberg, 'Towards a Newer Laocoon', in *The Collected Essays and
    Criticism* (Chicago: Chicago University Press, 1986).
3   Alain Badiou, *Ahmed philosophe* suivi de *Ahmed se fâche* (1995), pp. 212–13.
4   'Yes, dance is in fact each time a new name that the body gives to the earth' (*PM*
    111). It would be interesting to compare this *naming* of the earth with the Hei-
    deggerean conception of the poem.
5   '*Gloire du long désir, Idées/Tout en moi s'exaltait de voir/La famille des iridées/Surgir à ce
    nouveau devoir ...*' (Mallarmé, *Prose*, in Mallarmé, *Oeuvres Complètes* [Paris: Galli-
    mard 'Pléiade', 1945], p. 56).

BIBLIOGRAPHY

(A) WORKS BY ALAIN BADIOU

1. Books of philosophy, politics and criticism

Le Concept de modèle. Introduction à une épistémologie matérialiste des mathématiques (Paris: Maspero, 1969).

Le Noyau rationnel de la dialectique hégélienne (Paris: Maspero, 1978), with Louis Mossot and Joël Bellassen.

Théorie de la contradiction (Paris: Maspero, 1975).

De l'Idéologie (Paris: Maspero, 1976), with François Balmès.

Théorie du sujet (Paris: Seuil, 1982).

Peut-on penser la politique? (Paris: Seuil, 1985); *Can Politics be Thought?*, trans. Bruno Bosteels (Durham NC: Duke University Press, 2005).

L'Etre et l'événement (Paris: Seuil, 1988); *Being and Event*, trans. Oliver Feltham (London, Continuum Press, 2005). The two chapters on 'Hegel' and 'Descartes/Lacan' were translated by Marcus Coelen and Sam Gillespie, and Sigi Jöttkandt with Daniel Collins, respectively in *Umbr(a)* 1 (Buffalo: SUNY, 1996).

Manifeste pour la philosophie (Paris: Seuil, 1989); *Manifesto for Philosophy*, trans. Norman Madarasz (Albany: SUNY University Press, 1999).

Le Nombre et les nombres (Paris: Seuil, 1990).

Rhapsodie pour le théâtre (Paris: Le Spectateur français, 1990).

D'un Désastre obscur (Droit, Etat, Politique) (Paris: L'Aube, 1991); *Of an Obscure Disaster: On the End of the Truth of State*, trans. Barbara P. Fulks, *lacanian ink* 22 (Autumn 2003).

Conditions (Paris: Seuil, 1992). Two chapters ('The (Re)turn of Philosophy *Itself*' and 'Definition of Philosophy') are included in Madarasz's translation of the *Manifesto for Philosophy* (Albany: SUNY University Press, 1999). Two other chapters, 'Psychoanalysis and Philosophy' and 'What is Love?', appeared in *Umbr(a)* 1 (1996). 'Philosophy and Art' and 'Definition of Philosophy' are included in Badiou, *Infinite Thought: Truth and the Return of Philosophy*, ed. Justin Clemens and Oliver Feltham (London: Continuum, 2003).

L'Ethique: Essai sur la conscience du mal (Paris: Hatier, 1993); *Ethics: An Essay on the Understanding of Evil*, trans. Peter Hallward (London: Verso, 2001).

Beckett: L'incrévable désir (Paris: Hachette, 1995); *On Beckett*, ed. and trans. Alberto Toscano and Nina Power with Bruno Bosteels, with a foreword by Andrew Gibson (London: Clinamen Press, 2003). The translation includes, as appendices: 'Etre, existence, pensée' from *Petit manuel d'inesthétique*, and 'L'Ecriture du générique' from *Conditions*.

Gilles Deleuze: 'La clameur de l'Etre' (Paris: Hachette, 1997); *Gilles Deleuze: The Clamor of Being*, trans. Louise Burchill (Minneapolis: University of Minnesota Press, 2000).

Saint Paul et la fondation de l'universalisme (Paris: PUF, 1997); *Saint Paul: The Foundation of Universalism*, trans. Ray Brassier (Stanford: Stanford University Press, 2003).

Abrégé de métapolitique (Paris: Seuil, 1998); *Abridged Metapolitics*, trans. Jason Barker (London: Verso, 2004).

Court Traité d'ontologie transitoire (Paris: Seuil, 1998). Several chapters are included in Badiou, *Theoretical Writings*, ed. and trans. Ray Brassier and Alberto Toscano (London: Continuum, 2004).

Petit Manuel d'inesthétique (Paris: Seuil, 1998); *Handbook of Inaesthetics*, trans. by Alberto Toscano (Stanford: Stanford University Press, 2003).

Circonstances I: Kosovo, 11 septembre, Chirac/Le Pen (Paris: Editions Lignes & Manifestes/Editions Léo Scheer, 2003). Two of the three essays collected in this volume have been translated by Steven Corcoran for the online journal *Theory and Event* (web address: muse.jhu.edu/ journals/ tae/toc/index.html) as 'Philosophical Considerations of Some Recent Facts' [on September

11th], *Theory & Event* 6 (2) (2002), and 'Philosophical Considerations of the Very Singular Custom of Voting: An Analysis Based on Recent Ballots in France', *Theory and Event* 6 (3) (2002).

Infinite Thought: Truth and the Return to Philosophy, ed. Justin Clemens and Oliver Feltham (London: Continuum, 2003).

Le Siècle (Paris: Seuil, 2004). A slightly expanded version of chapter six has appeared as 'One Divides into Two', *Culture Machine* 4 (2002) [http://culturemachine.tees.ac.uk]. Chapter nine has appeared as 'Seven Variations on the Century', *Parallax* 9 (2) (2003): 72–80.

Theoretical Writings, ed. and trans. Ray Brassier and Alberto Toscano (London: Continuum, 2004).

Logiques des mondes (Paris: Seuil, forthcoming 2005).

2. Novels and plays

Almagestes [novel] (Paris: Seuil, 1964).

Portulans [novel] (Paris: Seuil, 1967).

L'Echarpe rouge [romanopéra] (Paris: Maspero, 1979).

Ahmed le subtil [theatre] (Arles: Actes Sud, 1994).

Ahmed se fâche, suivi par *Ahmed philosophe* [theatre] (Arles: Actes Sud, 1995).

Citrouilles [theatre] (Arles: Actes Sud, 1995).

Calme bloc ici-bas [novel] (Paris: P.O.L., 1997).

3. Articles, pamphlets and interviews

'Matieu', in *Derrière le miroir: 5 peintres et un sculpteur* (Paris: Maeght Editeur, 1965), pp. 24–31.

'L'Autonomie du processus historique', *Cahiers Marxistes-Léninistes* (Paris: Ecole Normale Supérieure) 12/13 (1966): 77–89.

'L'Autorisation' [short story], *Les Temps modernes* 258 (1967): 761–89.

'Le (Re)commencement du matérialisme dialectique', review of Althusser, *Pour Marx* [Paris: Maspero, 1965] and Althusser et al., *Lire le Capital* [Paris: Maspero, 1966], *Critique* 240 (May 1967): 438–67.

'La Subversion infinitésimale', *Cahiers pour l'analyse* (Paris: Ecole Normale Supérieure) 9 (1968): 118–37.

'Marque et manque: à propos du zéro', *Cahiers pour l'analyse* 10 (1969): 150–73.

Et al. *Contribution au problème de la construction d'un parti marxiste-léniniste de type nouveau* (Paris: Maspero, 1969).

Le Mouvement ouvrier révolutionnaire contre le syndicalisme [pamphlet] (Marseille: Potemkine, 1976).

La Situation actuelle sur le front de la philosophie, Cahiers Yenan No. 4 (Paris: Maspero, 1977), with Sylvain Lazarus (eds).

'Le Flux et le parti (dans les marges de *L'Anti-Œdipe*)', *La Situation actuelle sur le front de la philosophie* ... (1977), pp. 24–41.

La 'Contestation' dans le P.C.F. [pamphlet] (Marseille: Potemkine, 1978).

Jean-Paul Sartre [pamphlet] (Paris: Potemkine, 1981).

'Custos, quid noctis?', review of Lyotard, *Le Différend* [Paris: Minuit, 1983], *Critique* 450 (November 1984): 851–63.

'Poème mise à mort', suivi de 'L'ombre où s'y claire', in *Le Vivant et l'artificiel* (Sgraffite: Festival d'Avignon, 1984), pp. 19–23.

'Six propriétés de la vérité', *Ornicar?* 32 (January 1985): 39–67; continued in *Ornicar?* 33 (April 1985): 120–49.

Est-il exact que toute pensée émet un coup de dés? [pamphlet] (Paris: Conférences du Perroquet, 1986).

Et al. *Une Soirée philosophique* [pamphlet] (Paris: Potemkine/Seuil, 1988).

'Untitled Response', *Témoigner du différend. Quand phraser ne peut. Autour de Jean-François Lyotard*, (eds) Francis Guibal and Jacob Rogozînskî (Paris: Osiris, 1989) pp. 109–13.

'Dix-neuf Réponses à beaucoup plus d'objections', *Cahiers du Collège Internationale de philosophie* 8 (1989): 247–68.

Samuel Beckett: L'Ecriture du générique [pamphlet] (Paris: Editions du Perroquet, 1989).

'D'un Sujet enfin sans objet', *Cahiers Confrontations* 20 (1989): 13–22; 'On a Finally Objectless Subject', trans. Bruce Fink. *Who Comes After the Subject?*, ed. Eduardo Cadava, Peter Connor, Jean-Luc Nancy (London: Routledge, 1991), pp. 24–32.

'L'Entretien de Bruxelles', *Les Temps modernes* 526 (1990): 1–26.

'Lacan et les présocratiques' (1990), unpublished typescript.

'Pourquoi Antoine Vitez a-t-il abandonné Chaillot pour le Français', *L'Art du théâtre* 10 (1990): 143–5.

Review of Gilles Deleuze, *Le Pli: Leibniz et le baroque* [Paris: Minuit, 1988], *Annuaire philosophique 1988–1989* (Paris: Seuil, 1990) 161–84; 'Gilles Deleuze, *The Fold: Leibniz and the Baroque*', trans. Thelma Sowley. *Gilles Deleuze: The Theatre of Philosophy*, eds. Constantin Boundas and Dorothea Olkowski (New York: Columbia University Press, 1994), pp. 51–69.

'Saisissement, dessaisie, fidélité' [on Sartre], *Les Temps modernes* 531–3, vol. 1 (1990): 14–22.

'Ta Faute, ô graphie!', in *Pour la photographie III* (Paris: Germs, 1990), pp. 261–5.

'L'Etre, l'événement et la militance', interview with Nicole-Edith Thévenin, *Futur antérieur* 8 (1991): 13–23.

'Objectivité et objectalité' (1991), review of Monique David-Ménard, *La Folie dans la raison pure: Kant lecteur de Swedenborg* [Paris: Vrin, 1990], unpublished typescript (11 pages).

'L'Age des poètes', in *La Politique des poètes. Pourquoi des poètes en temps de détresse*, ed. Jacques Rancière (Paris: Albin Michel, 1992), pp. 21–38.

Casser en deux l'histoire du monde? [pamphlet on Nietzsche] (Paris: Le Perroquet, 1992).

'Les Lieux de la vérité', interview with Jacques Henri, *Art Press spécial: '20 ans: l'histoire continue'*, hors série no. 13 (1992): 113–18.

Monde contemporain et désir de philosophie [pamphlet] (Reims: Cahier de Noria, No. 1, 1992); 'The Contemporary World and the Desire for Philosophy', trans. Justin Clemens and Oliver Feltham, in *Infinite Thought: Truth and the Return of Philosophy*, ed. Clemens and Feltham (London: Continuum, 2003).

'Le Pays comme principe', *Le Monde. Bilan économique et social 1992* (Paris: Le Monde, 1992): 134–5.

'Réponses écrites d'Alain Badiou', interview with student group at the University of Paris VIII (Vincennes/Saint-Denis), *Philosophie, philosophie* 4 (1992): 66–71.

'Le Statut philosophique du poème après Heidegger', in *Penser après Heidegger*, eds. Jacques Poulain and Wolfgang Schirmacher (Paris: L'Harmattan, 1992), pp. 263–8.

'Y-a-t-il une théorie du sujet chez Georges Canguilhem?', in *Georges Canguilhem, Philosophe, historien des sciences* (Bibliothèque du Collège International de la Philosophie, Paris: Albin Michel, 1992), pp. 295–304; 'Is There a Theory of the Subject in Georges Canguilhem?', trans. Graham Burchell, *Economy and Society* 27 (2/3) (1998): 225–33.

'Nous pouvons redéployer la philosophie', interview with Rober-Pol Droit, *Le Monde*, 31 August 1993: 2.

'Philosophie et poésie au point de l'innommable', *Poésie* 64 (1993): 88–96.

'Que pense le poème?', in *L'Art est-il une connaissance?*, ed. Roger Pol Droit (Paris: Le Monde Editions, 1993), pp. 214–24.

'Qu'est-ce que Louis Althusser entend par "philosophie"?', in *Politique et philosophie dans l'oeuvre de Louis Althusser*, ed. Sylvain Lazarus (Paris: PUF, 1993), pp. 29–45.

'Sur le livre de Françoise Proust, *Le Ton de l'histoire*', *Les Temps modernes* 565/566 (1993): 238–48.

Topos, ou Logiques de l'onto-logique. Une Introduction pour philosophes, tome 1, unpublished typescript, 1993 (153 pages).

'1977, une formidable régression intellectuelle', *Le Monde 1944/1994*, Le Monde, SARC (November 1994): 78.

'Art et philosophie', in *Artistes et philosophes: éducateurs?*, ed. Christian Descamps (Paris: Centre Georges Pompidou, 1994), pp. 155–70.

'La Question de l'être aujourd'hui' (1994), unpublished lectures (partially published in *Court traité*) given at the Ecole Normale Supérieure, Paris.

'Being by Numbers', interview with Lauren Sedofsky, *Artforum* 33 (2) (Oct. 1994): 84–7, 118, 123–4.

'Silence, solipsisme, sainteté: l'antiphilosophie de Wittgenstein', *BARCA! Poésie, Politique, Psychanalyse* 3 (1994): 13–53.

'L'Impératif de la négation' (1995), review of Guy Lardreau, *La Véracité* [Paris: Verdier, 1993], unpublished typescript (14 pages).

'Platon et/ou Aristote-Leibniz. Théorie des ensembles et théorie des Topos sous l'oeil du philosophe', *L'Objectivité mathématique. Platonismes et structures formelles*, ed. Marco Panza (Paris: Masson, 1995), pp. 61–83 (partially published in *Court traité*).

'Préface: Il faut descendre dans l'amour', Henry Bauchau, *Heureux les déliants: poèmes 1950–1995* (Brussels: Labor, 1995), pp. 7–16.

'Les Gestes de la pensée [on François Châtelet]', *Les Temps modernes* 586 (1996): 196–204.

'Jean Borreil: le style d'une pensée', in *Jean Borreil: la raison de l'autre*, eds. Maurice Matieu and Patrice Vermeren (Paris: L'Harmattan, 1996), pp. 29–35.

'Logologie contre ontologie', review of Barbara Cassin, *L'Effet sophistique* [Paris: Gallimard, 1995], *Poésie* 78 (December 1996), 111–16.

Théorie axiomatique du sujet. Notes du cours 1996–1998, unpublished typescript (121 pages).

'Vérités et justice', in *Qu'est-ce que la justice? Devant l'autel de l'histoire*, ed. Jacques Poulain (Paris: Presses Universitaires de Vincennes, December 1996), pp. 275–81.

'Ce qui arrive' [on Beckett] (1997–98), unpublished typescript (4 pages).

'L'Insoumission de Jeanne', *Esprit* 238 (December 1997): 26–33.

'Lieu et déclaration', in *Paroles à la bouche du présent. Le négationnisme: histoire ou politique?*, ed. Natacha Michel (Marseille: Al Dante, 1997), pp. 177–84.

'De la Vie comme nom de l'Etre', *Rue Descartes* 20 (May 1998): 27–34.

'Le Dépli du désert', Preface to Salam al-Kindy, *Le Voyageur sans Orient: Poésie et philosophie des Arabes de l'ère préislamique* (Arles: Sindbad/Actes Sud, 1998), pp. 11–15.

'On ne passe pas' [on Badiou's own practice of writing], *Théorie, littérature, enseignement* (Revue du Departement de Lettres, Université de Paris VIII) 16 (Autumn, 1998): 17–20.

'Paul le saint', interview with Jacques Henric, *Artpress* 235 (May 1998): 53–8.

'Penser le surgissement de l'événement', interview with Emmanuel Burdeau and François Ramone, *Cahiers du Cinéma*, numéro spécial (May 1998).

'Le plus-de-Voir' [on Godard's *Histoire(s) du cinéma*], *Artpress*, hors série 1998.

'Politics and Philosophy', interview with Peter Hallward, *Angelaki*, 3 (3) (1998): 113–33.

'La Sainte-Alliance et ses serviteurs' [on Kosovo], *Le Monde*, 20 May 1999 (available online at: http://www.lemonde.fr/article/0,2320,6246,00.html).

'Théâtre et politique dans la comédie', in *Où va le théâtre?*, ed. Jean-Pierre Thibaudat (Paris: Hoëbeke, 1998), pp. 17–24.

'Considérations sur l'état actuel du cinéma, et sur les moyens de penser cet état sans avoir à conclure que le cinéma est mort ou mourant', *L'Art du cinéma* 24 (March 1999): 7–22.

'De la Langue française comme évidement' (1999), unpublished typescript (9 pages).

'Entretien avec Alain Badiou', interview with Nicola Poirier, *Le Philosophoire* 9 (1999): 14–32.

'Les Langues de Wittgenstein', *Rue Descartes* 26 (December 1999): 107–16.

'Préface', to Danièle Moatti-Gornet, *Qu'est-ce qu'une femme? Traité d'ontologie* (Paris: L'Harmattan, 1999).

'La Scène du Deux', Badiou et al., sous la direction de L'Ecole de la Cause Freudienne (with other contributions by Roger Dragonetti, Alain Grosrichard, Brigitte Jaques, Charles Méla, Jacques Roubaud), in *De l'Amour* (Paris: Flammarion, 1999), pp. 177–90; 'The Scene of Two', trans. Barbara P. Fulks, *lacanian ink* 21 (Spring 2003): 42–55.

'Art and Philosophy' [extract from *Petit manuel d'inesthétique*], trans. Jorge Jauregui, *lacanian ink* 17 (Autumn 2000): 51–67.

'L'Existence et la mort', in *Philosopher T2: Les Interrogations contemporaines, matériaux pour un enseignement*, eds Christian Delacampagne and Robert Maggiori (Paris: Fayard, 2000), pp. 293–302; trans. Alberto Toscano and Nina Power as 'Existence and Death' in *Discourse: Journal for Theoretical Studies in Media and Culture* 24.1 (Winter 2002), pp. 63–73.

'Frege' and 'On a Contemporary Usage of Frege' [extracts from *Le Nombre et les nombres*], trans. Justin Clemens and Sam Gillespie, *Umbr(a) 2000: Science and Truth* (2000): 99–113.

'Highly Speculative Reasoning on the Concept of Democracy' [extract from *Abrégé de métapolitique*], trans. Jorge Jauregui, *lacanian ink* 16 (2000): 28–43.

'Huit thèses sur l'universel', in *Universel, singulier, sujet*, ed. Jelica Sumic (Paris: Kimé, 2000), pp. 11–20.

'Les Lieux de la philosophie', *Bleue: Littératures en force* 1 (Winter, 2000): 120–5.

'Metaphysics and the Critique of Metaphysics', trans. Alberto Toscano, *Pli (Warwick Journal of Philosophy)* 10 (2000): 174–90.

'Of Life as a Name of Being, or Deleuze's Vitalist Ontology' [translation of *Court traité d'ontologie transitoire*, ch. 4], trans. Alberto Toscano, *Pli (Warwick Journal of Philosophy)* 10 (2000): 191–9.

'Psychoanalysis and Philosophy', trans. Oliver Feltham, *Analysis* 9 (Melbourne, 2000): 1–8.

'Saint Paul, fondateur du sujet universel', *Etudes Théologiques et Religieuses* 75 (March 2000): 323–3.

'Sur *La Parole muette* de Jacques Rancière', *Horlieu-(x)* 18 (2000): 88–95.

'Un, Multiple, Multiplicité(s)' [on Deleuze], *Multitudes* 1 (March 2000): 195–211.

'Une Tâche philosophique: être contemporain de Pessoa', in *Colloque de Cerisy: Pessoa*, eds Pascal Dethurens and Maria-Alzira Seixo (Paris: Christian Bougois, 2000), pp. 141–55.

'Vide, séries, clairière. Essai sur la prose de Severo Sarduy', Severo Sarduy, *Obras completas*, ed. François Wahl (2000), vol. 2: 1619–25.

L'Etre-là: mathématique du transcendental (2000), unpublished typescript (109 pages).

'Théâtre et philosophie', *Frictions* 2 (Spring, 2000): 131–41.

'Can Change Be Thought? A Dialogue With Alain Badiou' (1999), interview with Bruno Bosteels, in *Alain Badiou: Philosophy Under Conditions*, ed. Gabriel Riera (Albany: State University of New York Press, in preparation).

'Destin politique du théâtre, hier, maintenant' (2001), unpublished typescript (7 pages).

'La Dialectique romantique de Gilles Châtelet' (2001), talk given at the conference *Autour Gilles Châtelet*. Ecole Normale Supérieure, Paris, 27 June 2001, unpublished typescript (7 pages).

'Esquisse pour un premier manifeste de l'affirmationisme' (2001), unpublished typescript (19 pages).

'Le Gardiennage du matin', in *Jean-François Lyotard: l'exercise du différend*, ed. Dolorès Lyotard et al. (Paris: PUF, 2001), pp. 101–11.

'On Evil: An Interview with Alain Badiou', interview with Christoph Cox and Molly Whalen, *Cabinet* 5 (Winter 2001): 69–74 (available online at: http://cabinetmagazine.org/issues/5/alainbadiou.php).

'The Political as a Procedure of Truth', trans. Barbara P. Fulks, *lacanian ink* 19 (Autumn 2001): 70–81.

'Who is Nietzsche?', trans. Alberto Toscano, *Pli (Warwick Journal of Philosophy)* 11 (2001): 1–11.

'L'Aveu du philosophe' [lecture given at Centre Pompidou in Paris, 3 April 2002], unpublished typescript (12 pages).

'The Caesura of Nihilism' [lecture at the University of Cardiff, 25 May 2002], unpublished typescript (10 pages).

'Depuis si longtemps, depuis si peu de temps' [on Françoise Proust], *Rue Descartes* 33: *Une philosophie de la résistance: Françoise Proust* (Spring 2002): 101–4.

'The Ethic of Truths: Construction and Potency', trans. Thelma Sowley, *Pli (Warwick Journal of Philosophy)* 12 (2002): 247–55.

'L'Investigation transcendantale', in *Alain Badiou: Penser le multiple*, ed. Charles Ramond (Paris: L'Harmattan, 2002), pp. 7–18.

'Que penser? Que faire?' [on the French presidential elections of April 2002, co-written with Sylvain Lazarus and Natacha Michel], *Le Monde*, 28 April 2002; 'What is to be Thought? What is to be Done?', trans. Norman Madarasz, *Counterpunch*, 1 May 2002 (http:// counterpunch.org/ badiou0501.html).

La Révolution culturelle: La dernière révolution? (Paris: Les Conférences du Rouge-Gorge 2002) [pamphlet].

'Le Balcon du présent' *Failles* 1 (October 2003). [Page numbers not available].

'Beyond Formalisation', interview with Bruno Bosteels and Peter Hallward, *Angelaki* 8 (2) (August 2003), pp. 111–36.

La Commune de Paris: une déclaration politique sur la politique (Paris: Les Conférences du Rouge-Gorge, 2003, and forthcoming in revised form in Badiou *Logiques des mondes* [2005]).
'Dialectiques de la fable: Mythes philosophiques et cinéma.' Badiou et al., *Matrix, machine philosophique*. Paris: Ellipses, 2003.
'Foucault: continuité et discontinuité' (2003), unpublished typescript (10 pages).
'Lacan, la philosophie, la folie' (2003), unpublished typescript (5 pages).
'Mathématiques et philosophie' (2003), unpublished typescript (18 pages); 'Mathematics and Philosophy', trans. Ray Brassier and Alberto Toscano in *Theoretical Writings* (London: Continuum, 2004).
'Le Sujet supposé chrétien de Paul Ricoeur: à propos de Ricoeur, *La Mémoire, l'histoire, l'oubli* [Paris: Sevil, 2000], *Elucidations* 7 (March 2003). [Page numbers not available].

(B) WORKS ON ALAIN BADIOU

Aguilar, Tristan, 'Badiou et la non-philosophie: un parallèle', in *La Non-Philosophie des Contemporains*, ed. François Laruelle (Paris: Kimé, 1995), pp. 37–46.
Alliez, Eric, 'Que la vérité soit', in *De l'Impossibilité de la phénoménologie: sur la philosophie française contemporaine* (Paris: Vrin, 1995), pp. 81–7.
Alliez, Eric, 'Badiou/Deleuze', *Futur antérieur* 43 (1998): 49–54.
Alliez, Eric, 'Badiou. La grâce de l'universel', *Multitudes* 6 (2001): 26–34.
Barker, Jason, *Alain Badiou: A Critical Introduction* London: Pluto, 2002.
Bensaïd, Daniel, 'Alain Badiou et le miracle de l'événement', in *Résistances: Essai de taupologie générale* (Paris: Fayard, 2001), pp. 143–70.
Bosteels, Bruno, 'Por una falta de política: Tesis sobre la fílosofía de la democracia radical', *Acontecimiento: Revista para pensar la política* 17 (1999): 63–89.
Bosteels, Bruno, 'Travesías del fantasma: Pequeña metapolítica del "68 en México"', *Metapolítica: Revista Trimestral de Teoría y Ciencia de la Política* 12 (1999): 733–68.
Bosteels, Bruno, 'Alain Badiou's Theory of the Subject: Part I. The Re-Commencement of Dialectical Materialism', *Pli (Warwick Journal of Philosophy)* 12 (2001): 200–9.
Bosteels, Bruno, 'Alain Badiou's Theory of the Subject: Part II', *Pli (Warwick Journal of Philosophy)* 13 (2002): 173–208.
Bosteels, Bruno, *Badiou and the Political*. Durham NC: Duke University Press, in preparation.
Brassier, Ray, 'Stellar Void or Cosmic Animal? Badiou and Deleuze', *Pli (Warwick Journal of Philosophy)* 10 (2000): 200–17.
Burchill, Louise, 'Translator's Preface: Portraiture in Philosophy, or Shifting Perspective', in Badiou, *Deleuze: The Clamor of Being* (Minneapolis: University of Minnesota Press, 1999), pp. vii–xxiii.
Châtelet, Gilles, review of Badiou, *Le Nombre et les Nombres, Annuaire philosophique 1989–1990*. (Paris: Seuil, 1991), 117–33.
Clemens, Justin, 'Platonic Meditations: The Work of Alain Badiou', *Pli (Warwick Journal of Philosophy)* 11 (2001): 200–29.
Clucas, Stephen, 'Poem, Theorem'. *Parallax* 7 (4) (2001): 48–65.
Critchley, Simon, 'Demanding Approval: On the Ethics of Alain Badiou', *Radical Philosophy* 100 (2000): 16–27.
Eagleton, Terry, 'Subjects and Truths', review of Badiou, *Ethics, New Left Review* 9 (May 2001): 155–60.
Feltham, Oliver, *As Fire Burns: Of Ontology, Praxis and Functional Work*, unpublished PhD thesis, Deakin University, Australia, 2000.
Fink, Bruce, 'Alain Badiou', *Umbr(a)* 1 (Buffalo: SUNY, 1996): 11–12.
Geuss, Raymond, review of Badiou, *Ethics, European Journal of Philosophy* 9 (3) (December 2001).
Geuss, Raymond, 'Outside Ethics', *European Journal of Philosophy* 11 (1) (April 2003): 29–53.
Gil, José, 'Quatre méchantes notes sur un livre méchant', review of Badiou, *Deleuze, Futur antérieur* 43 (1998): 71–84.
Gillespie, Sam, 'Hegel Unsutured (An Addendum to Badiou)', *Umbr(a)* 1 (Buffalo: SUNY,

1996): 57–69.

Gillespie, Sam, 'To Place the Void: Badiou Reads Spinoza', *Angelaki* 6 (3) (December 2001).

Gillespie, Sam, 'Neighborhood of Infinity: On Badiou's *Deleuze: The Clamor of Being*', *Umbr(a)* 2001: 91–106.

Gillespie, Sam, review of Badiou, *Ethics*, *Pli (Warwick Journal of Philosophy)* 12 (2002): 256–65.

Hallward, Peter, 'Generic Sovereignty: The Philosophy of Alain Badiou', *Angelaki* 3 (3) (1998): 87–111.

Hallward, Peter, 'Ethics without Others: A Reply to Simon Critchley', *Radical Philosophy* 102 (July 2000): 27–31.

Hallward, Peter, 'Translator's Introduction' to Badiou, *Ethics: An Essay on the Understanding of Evil* (London: Verso, 2001), vii–li.

Hallward, Peter, *Badiou: A Subject to Truth* (Minneapolis: University of Minnesota Press, 2003).

Hallward, Peter, 'Introduction to Badiou', *Angelaki* 8 (2) (December 2003).

Hyldgaard, Kirsten, 'Truth and Knowledge in Heidegger, Lacan and Badiou', *Umbr(a)* 2001: 79–90.

Ichida, Yoshihiko, 'Sur quelques vides ontologiques' [on Badiou and Negri]. *Multitudes* 9 (May 2002): 49–65.

Jambet, Christian, review of Badiou, *L'Etre et l'événement*, *Annuaire philosophique 1987–1988* (Paris: Seuil, 1989), pp. 141–183.

Kouvélakis, Eustache, 'La Politique dans ses limites, ou les paradoxes d'Alain Badiou', *Actuel Marx* 28 (2000), pp. 39–54.

Lacoue-Labarthe, Philippe, untitled discussion of *L'Etre et l'événement*, *Cahiers du Collège Internationale de philosophie* 8 (1989), pp. 201–10.

Lacoue-Labarthe, Philippe, 'Poésie, philosophie, politique', in *La Politique des poètes. Pourquoi des poètes en temps de détresse*, ed. Jacques Rancière (Paris: Albin Michel, 1992), pp. 39–63.

Laerke, Mogens, 'The Voice and the Name: Spinoza in the Badioudian Critique of Deleuze', *Pli (Warwick Journal of Philosophy)* 8 (1999): 86–99.

Lecercle, Jean-Jacques, 'Cantor, Lacan, Mao, Beckett, *même combat*: The Philosophy of Alain Badiou', *Radical Philosophy* 93 (January 1999): 6–13.

Lyotard, Jean-François, untitled discussion of *L'Etre et l'événement*, *Cahiers du Collège Internationale de philosophie* 8 (1989): 227–46.

Madarasz, Norman, 'Translator's Introduction' to Badiou, *Manifesto for Philosophy* (Albany: SUNY University Press, 1999), pp. 3–23.

Ophir, Adi and Ariella Azoulay, 'The Contraction of Being: Deleuze after Badiou', *Umbr(a)* 2001: 107–20.

Pesson, René, review of Badiou, *Manifeste pour la philosophie*, *Annuaire philosophique 1988–1989* (Paris: Seuil, 1989), 243–51.

Ramond, Charles (ed.) *Alain Badiou: La pensée du multiple* (papers given at the international conference on Badiou, Bordeaux, 21–23 October 1999) (Paris: L'Harmattan, 2002).

Rancière, Jacques, untitled discussion of *L'Etre et l'événement*, *Cahiers du Collège Internationale de philosophie* 8 (1989): 211–26.

Riera, Gabriel (ed.), *Alain Badiou: Philosophy Under Conditions* (Albany: SUNY Press, in preparation).

Rothberg, Michael, review of Badiou, *Ethics*, *Criticism* 43 (4) (Autumn 2001): 478–84.

Simont, Juliette, 'Le Pur et l'impur (sur deux questions de l'histoire de la philosophie dans *L'Etre et l'événement*)', *Les Temps modernes* 526 (May 1990): 27–60.

Terray, Emmanuel, 'La Politique dans *L'Etre et l'événement*', *Les Temps modernes* 526 (May 1990): 72–8.

Toscano, Alberto, 'To Have Done with the End of Philosophy', review of Badiou *Manifesto for Philosophy* and Badiou, *Deleuze*, *Pli (Warwick Journal of Philosophy)* 9 (2000): 220–39.

Verstraeten, Pierre, 'Philosophies de l'événement: Badiou et quelques autres', *Les Temps modernes* 529–30 (August 1990): 241–94.

Villani, Arnaud, 'La Métaphysique de Deleuze' [critique of Badiou's *Deleuze*], *Futur antérieur* 43 (1998): 55–70.

Wahl, François, 'Le Soustractif', Preface to Badiou, *Conditions*, (1992), pp. 9–54.

Žižek, Slavoj, 'The Politics of Truth, or, Alain Badiou, as a Reader of St Paul', Žižek, *The Ticklish Subject* (London: Verso, 1999), pp. 127–70. (An abridged version of this essay appeared as 'Psychoanalysis in Post-Marxism: The Case of Alain Badiou', *South Atlantic Quarterly* 97 (2) (Spring 1998): 235–61.)

INDEX

Abel, Niels 86, 87
Acontecimiento 255n.19
Adorno, Theodor 106–7, 118, 158, 168
Aeschylus 172, 229
aesthetics *see* art
affirmation *see* prescription
Althusser, Louis 98, 108, 161–2, 170, 227
American situation 7, 10–11
Antigone 165
antiphilosophy 171, 191–3, 253n.12
appearing 10–12, 19–20, 174
Aristotle 4, 48, 59, 133, 219, 225, 233, 237
arithmetization 81
art 3, 210, 218–31, 234, 235
   aesthetic regime of 218–21, 223
   Badiou's modernist understanding of 217,
      222–5, 231
   see also language, modernism, poetry
atom (as onto-logical category) 19, 234–5
Augustine, Saint 89
axiomatics 79–86, 249n.57

Balibar, Etienne 166
Balzac, Honoré de 221, 227, 230
Bazin, André 229
Beckett, Samuel 208, 214
beginnings of philosophy 43–4
being: *see* multiplicity
being-there *see* appearing
Benjamin, Walter 100–101
Bergson, Henry 74–5, 90
Berkeley, George 81
Besana, Bruno 241n.39
Bhattacharyya, Anindya 238n.9
biology 233–4, 239n.22, 249n.43
Bosteels, Bruno 171–2, 174–5, 179, 238n.12,
   239n.16, 255n.19
Boundas, Constantin 71
Bourbaki, Nicolas 83
Bourdieu, Pierre 101
Brecht, Bertolt 210
Breton, Stanislas 37
Butler, Judith 108

calculus 77–82, 86, 89
   see also Deleuze, mathematics
Canguilhem, Georges 24–6, 36
Cantor, Georg 5, 15, 32, 51, 63, 82, 85, 86
   see also set theory
capitalism 37, 52–4, 91, 105
Carnap, Rudolf 208
Cauchy, Augustin 81
Cavaillès, Jean 18, 30, 105
Celan, Paul 209
Chaitin, Gregory 56–7, 245n.21
chance 55–7
Chomsky, Noam 240n.36
Christianity 22, 131, 167, 168
   see also Paul, Saint
cinema 229–31
class struggle 141, 144, 145, 175
Cohen, Paul 16, 30, 32, 63, 65–6, 82
   see also forcing, generic set theory
Commune (Paris) 11–12, 19, 162
communism 138–9, 143, 144–6, 148–9,
   254n.16
communist invariants 140
computation 55–7
conditions of philosophy 39–40, 51,
   191–201
consistency *see* multiplicity
continuity, geometric 80–2, 85–6, 91
   see also continuum hypothesis
continuum hypothesis (CH) 65–66, 245n.28
Critchley, Simon 240n.34
Cultural Revolution (Chinese) 162

D'Alembert, Jean 81
dance 202, 226–8, 229, 258n.4
Davidson, Donald 31
death 237
Debord, Guy 230
decision 32, 44
deconstruction 40, 43–4
Dedekind, Julius 82, 84
de Kock, Paul 221
DeLanda, Manuel 248n.39

Deleuze, Gilles 4, 5, 35, 67–76, 77–93, 113,
    152, 179, 208, 210–11, 215, 216, 235
    and difference 71, 75–6
    and Guattari, Félix 53
    and immanence 73–4
    and mathematics 77–93
    and multiplicity 75, 77–9, 86–90, 92
    and problematics 78–84, 89–90, 92–3
    and royal science 78, 80, 84, 89
    as thinker of the One 67–69, 72, 88–9
    and univocity 68–70, 88
    and vitalism 89–90
    and the virtual 70–2
    see also calculus
déliaison see relation, unbinding
democracy 180
Derrida, Jacques 23–5, 36, 41, 209, 242n.25
Desanti, Jean-Toussaint 241n.17
Descartes, René 91
destruction 142, 143, 254n.15
    as distinct from subtraction 138
dialectics 150–64
Dieudonné, Jean 83
dikrania 61, 63–4
disaster see evil
Dreyfus, Hubert 256n.8

Einstein, Albert 179
enthusiasm 188–90
equality 147–9
ethics 106–19, 120–37, 174
    and deliberation 135
Euripides 229
event 2, 16, 93, 97, 121–2, 131, 134, 175,
    202–7, 253n.13
evental site 8–9, 153
evil 108, 111–12, 122, 128–9
    see also Nazism
existence 10, 236
    and appearing 10–11

fanaticism 117, 188–90
Fanon, Frantz 12
Feltham, Oliver 239n.24
Ferry, Luc 170
Fichte, Johann 118
fidelity 32, 100–1, 104, 106, 122–2, 202–7
    anticipatory 204–6
finitude 237
Flaubert, Gustave 221
forcing 54, 216, 239n.22, 244n.15, 257n.8
formalization 234
Foucault, Michel 26–7, 107, 108, 242n.21
Frank, Otto 18
French Revolution 3, 95, 98, 166, 196

Freud, Sigmund 197
Furet, François 176

Galileo, Galilei 233
Galois, Evariste 86
generic see truth
generic sets 54
genes (as example of the virtual) 71, 74
geometry 79–81
Geuss, Raymond 251n.4, 251n.10
Gies, Miep 18
Gillespie, Sam 240n.34
Giorello, Giulio 81
God: death of 40, 114, 195, 200, 243n.9
    see also the One
Gödel, Kurt 55, 82
Goldmann, Lucien 99
Gouhier, Henri 21
grace: as metaphor for an event 97, 114–7,
    118, 245n.27
Gramsci, Antonio 100, 125, 131
Guattari, Félix see Deleuze

idealism 169

Habermas, Jürgen 118, 251n.22
Haitian revolution 238n.10
halting function 55, 56
Hegel, Georg 61, 106, 151, 154, 155–6, 158,
    161, 162, 167, 191, 194, 197, 223, 237
hegemony 127, 131–2, 252n.7
Heidegger, Martin 40, 41, 42–3, 45, 113,
    118, 153, 179, 210, 229, 243n.4
Heine, Heinrich 197
Hilbert, David 82, 83
historicity 35, 40, 42–3, 51–2, 98–9, 162,
    243n.8
Hobbes, Thomas 133
Hölderlin, Friedrich 209, 214
Homer 221
human rights 109
human sciences 234
Hume, David 192
Husserl, Edmund 24–5

immortality 117, 237
    see also time
inaesthetics 218, 222–4, 231
    see also art
infinitesimals 81
infinity 15, 32, 237
    see also Cantor
intuitionism 90

Jacobins, the 3

Joyce, James 175, 215
Judaism 167
Jünger, Ernst 165

Kandinsky, Wassily 175
Kant, Immanuel 6, 12, 14, 89, 106, 112,
    115–7, 119, 151, 167, 171, 173, 188–90,
    192–3
Kierkegaard, Søren 256n.8
Kojève, Alexandre 156
Kouvélakis, Stathis 101

Lacan, Jacques 3, 12, 17, 167, 171–2, 175–7,
    182–90, 199–200, 256n.3, 256n.18
    as antiphilosopher 171
    and the four discourses 176–7
    see also real, Žižek
Laclau, Ernesto 166, 180
Lacoue-Labarthe, Philippe 45
language 14, 208–9, 211–16
Lautman, Albert 18, 105
Lautréamont 79
Lazarus, Sylvain 155
Lefort, Claude 180
Leibniz, Gottfried 4, 60, 81
Lenin, Vladimir 95, 151, 152, 161, 168, 170,
    180–1, 190, 238n.11
Levinas, Emmanuel 41, 107, 108, 111, 113–14
Lin Piao 237
linguistics 136
logic 10
love 170–1, 198, 201, 234, 256n.4
Lukács, Georg 255n.2
Lyotard, Jean-François 5, 42, 209

Macherey, Pierre 18
Maddy, Penelope 82
Malevitch, Kazimir 178
Mallarmé, Stéphane 18, 209, 211–14, 222,
    225–30
Mandelstam, Osip Emilyevich 96
Mao Zedong 50, 131, 253n.7
Maoism 101–2, 103–4, 154, 162
    and post-Maoism 160
Mars 233
Martineau, Emmanuel 21
Marx, Karl 8, 9, 52, 104–5, 120, 164, 170,
    180, 191, 197, 250n.20, 256n.3
Marxism 140–2, 143, 154, 156, 175, 253n.7,
    254n.24
mass movement 147–8
materialism 50–1, 169
mathematics 3–4, 77–93, 233–5, 238n.6
    see also set theory, multiplicity, ontology
matter 234–5, 243n.3

meditation 61–2
Merleau-Ponty, Maurice 17, 25
Mesnard, Jean 22
meta-mathematics 29–35
metaphysics, exhaustion of 42–3, 44–5, 47
metapolitics 139
militancy 35, 37
Milner, Jean-Claude 212
Milosz, Czeslaw 213
mimesis 219, 200
modernism 221–2
    see also art
Mouffe, Chantal 166
multiplicity 3–4, 121, 195–6, 200
    consistent 5
    inconsistent 5–6, 8, 12–13, 62
    see also Deleuze

Nancy, Jean-Luc 254n.16
nature 46
Nazism 111, 122–3, 127–9
Nietzsche, Friedrich 73, 115, 168, 197, 229,
    237
nihilism 50, 52
Novalis 227
novel, the 215–6
novelty 2–3, 152

One, the 3–4, 15, 194–6
    see also Deleuze, God
ontology 41, 59–62, 77–93, 136–7, 243n.6
    see also mathematics, set theory
opera 230

Panofsky, Erwin 222
Parmenides 50, 209–10
party, the 99
    see also politics
Pascal, Blaise 21–23, 27, 28, 34, 97, 98–9,
    100, 205, 206
Paul, Saint 3, 37, 38, 110, 125, 242n.29
Péguy, Charles 97
Pessoa, Fernando 165, 209, 213, 214
Picasso, Pablo 175
Plato 2, 5, 33–4, 133, 208–9, 210, 219, 237
Platonism 33, 34, 35–6, 46, 69
    and art 222–5, 231
poetry 209–16
politics 100–05, 138–49, 162, 166, 234,
    244n.14
    without party 99–100, 145–6
postmodernism 96, 110, 217
presentation 9, 121, 159, 233
    see also representation
pre-Socratics, the 4

problematics *see* Deleuze
Proclus 79
production 140–1, 143–4, 149
proletariat 8, 140–1
Proudhon, Pierre Joseph 105
Proust, Marcel 221, 227
Proust, Françoise 104, 240n.29

Rancière, Jacques 98, 165–6
randomness *see* chance
real, the 138, 145–6, 148, 167–8, 171–2, 175, 177–81, 184, 187, 214, 253n.7
    as crack within representation 199–201
    passion for (in the twentieth century) 157–8, 165, 180–1
    see also Lacan
relation, Badiou's critique of 12–20
    see also unbinding
religion 98, 102, 114–7
representation 9, 15, 18, 121, 141, 143, 159, 163–4, 195, 197–201, 232, 235–6, 253n.1
    and art 219
    see also presentation, state
revolt, primacy of 253n.7
Riemann, Georg 85, 86, 248n.37
Rimbaud, Arthur 105, 214, 221, 230
Robespierre, Maximilien 95
Robinson, Abraham 85, 248n.28
romanticism 220, 223–4
Rousseau, Jean-Jacques 3, 37, 100
Russell's paradox 136

sans papiers [undocumented workers] 126
Santner, Eric 197
Sartre, Jean-Paul 2, 4, 6, 12, 14, 17, 35, 102, 153, 158, 161–2, 215
Schelling, Friedrich 229
Schoenberg, Arnold 175, 206
Schopenhauer, Arthur 116–7
science 233–34
separation 138, 224, 228–9
    see also subtraction
September 11 (2001) 7
Serres, Michel 5, 241n.17
set theory 51, 61, 135–6, 156
    see also mathematics, multiplicity, Deleuze
Shalamov, Varlam 176
Shiying, Zhang 158
Solidarnosc 126–7, 137
sophistry 48, 96–7, 104–5, 193, 208, 209
Sophocles 172
speculative leftism 16, 163
Spinoza, Baruch 61, 69, 71, 91, 235
Stalinism 103–4

state, the 9, 121, 166, 232, 244n.14
    see also representation
Stiegler, Bernard 17
subject, the 3, 98–9, 141, 182–90
    see also truth
subtraction 134, 147–8, 180, 223–5, 243n.4
    and ontology 4–5, 51
    see also destruction
Sue, Eugène 197
suture 94–5

Tarski, Alfred 30–1, 33
Taylorism 83
technics 46, 48–9
technology 17
theatre 215–6, 229–30
Thermidor 104
time 74–6, 184
    of a truth 11, 16, 94, 240n.27
transcendental regime [*le transcendantal*] 19–20, 233, 235
truth 2–3, 9–10, 54, 95–6, 102, 110, 192, 234–5, 256n.8
    history of 22–9
Turing, Alan 55
twentieth century, Badiou's conception of 157–8
Two, the 142, 145, 160, 200
    and love 200–201

unbinding 143, 144, 146–7, 157
universality 36, 38
    see also truth
univocity 35–6
unnameable, the 57, 173

Vico, Giovanni 221
void, the 4, 8–9, 13, 51, 53–4, 121, 122, 124, 159, 171
    edge of 8–9, 124–5, 130
    filling in of 125–7, 130, 133, 135
    and representation of 10
    see also evental site, inconsistency
Vuillemin, Jules 241n.17

Wajcman, Gérard 198
Weierstrass, Karl 81–2, 84, 85, 86, 247n.15, 247n.22

Zermelo-Fraenkel (ZF) axioms of set theory 60, 82
Žižek, Slavoj 17, 98, 100, 102, 120, 123–4, 127, 129, 133, 151, 160, 164, 187, 252n.5, 252n.9